Capitalists and Conquerors

More praise for
CAPITALISTS AND CONQUERORS

"McLaren has crafted a book that follows in the footsteps of Paulo Freire and other leading pedagogical thinkers. This is a book that not only educators need to engage, but students, teachers, intellectuals and activists from all walks of life."

—**Daniel Kelly**, Veterans for Peace and director of development at the Paulo Freire
Democratic Project, Chapman University School of Education

"*Capitalists and Conquerors* is McLaren's most incisive book yet. . . . [it] will quickly become a contemporary classic, a must read for every student, teacher and citizen of consciousness."

—**Sandy Grande**, Connecticut College and author of *Red Pedagogy:*
Native American Social and Political Thought

"Anyone committed to social justice must grab a copy of this book written by one of the world's leading critical educationists."

—**Peter Mayo**, University of Malta

"Peter McLaren demonstrates in revolutionary fashion how to put material issues back on the agenda of critical pedagogy and to understand and overcome the capitalist forces eroding the very foundations of life. A must read!"

—**Juha Suoranta**, University of Joensuu, Finland

"I never cease to be amazed by McLaren's ability to bravely forge . . . beyond the accepted borders of mainstream academic discourse. . . . Through his no-holds-barred analyses of capital and its aftermath . . . he continues to distinguish himself as North America's leading Marxist educator."

—**Marc Pruyn**, New Mexico State University and coeditor
(with Luis Huerta-Charles) of the forthcoming *Teaching Peter McLaren: Paths of Dissent*

"This book is a must-read for educators and activists willing to make a difference in the lives of learners, community, and the democratic sphere."

—**Lourdes Diaz Soto**, Pennsylvania State University

"There is wide agreement among all shades of political opinion that we are witnessing a new age of imperialism. Opposition is widespread, but fragmented. All the more reason why Peter McLaren's articulate and powerful Marxist alternative of social justice and true equality be heard."

—**Mike Cole**, University of Brighton, UK and author of
Marxism, Postmodernism and Education: Pasts, Presents and Futures

"McLaren's passionate poetry and principle, intellectual power, and experience pull neoliberal global imperial capital apart, developing and implanting critical consciousness and praxis against barbarism in the service of equality, humanity and the peoples of the world. . . . This really is advancing over the barricades and not just building them."

—**Dave Hill**, University College Northampton, UK

Capitalists and Conquerors

A Critical Pedagogy against Empire

Peter McLaren

ROWMAN & LITTLEFIELD PUBLISHERS, INC.
Lanham • Boulder • New York • Toronto • Oxford

ROWMAN & LITTLEFIELD PUBLISHERS, INC.

Published in the United States of America
by Rowman & Littlefield Publishers, Inc.
A wholly owned subsidiary of The Rowman & Littlefield Publishing Group, Inc.
4501 Forbes Boulevard, Suite 200, Lanham, MD 20706
www.rowmanlittlefield.com

P.O. Box 317, Oxford OX2 9RU, UK

British Library Cataloguing in Publication Information Available

Library of Congress Cataloging-in-Publication Data
McLaren, Peter, 1948–
    Capitalists and conquerors : a critical pedagogy against empire / Peter McLaren.
        p. cm.
Includes bibliographical references and index.
    ISBN 0-7425-4192-4 (cloth: alk. paper) — ISBN 0-7425-4193-2 (pbk.: alk. paper)
    1. Critical pedagogy. 2. Education and globalization. 3. Educational sociology. I. Title.
LC196.M28 2005
370.11'5—dc22

                                                                                        2004026498

Printed in the United States of America

⊗™ The paper used in this publication meets the minimum requirements of American
National Standard for Information Sciences—Permanence of Paper for Printed Library
Materials, ANSI/NISO Z39.48-1992.

This book is dedicated to Jennifer McLaren, a woman for whom I can only hope one day to be worthy.

Contents

Foreword

Carl Boggs

In this far-reaching and provocative collection of essays, Peter McLaren has managed the rare feat of incorporating some of the most compelling issues of our historical period—globalization, corporate domination, Empire, ecological crisis, democratic politics—into a richly dialectical framework of critical pedagogy. The result is a powerful synthesis addressing those broad material and institutional forces that shape our world, configuring its multiple dimensions of hierarchy and control, within a visionary sensibility grounded in radical social movements and oppositional politics. Such a dialectic, of course, owes much to the legacy of Karl Marx and twentieth-century writers like Antonio Gramsci, as well as the path-breaking work of Paulo Freire, but McLaren builds upon and reappropriates these earlier paradigms in weaving together a set of transformative discourses that lend radicalized popular consciousness articulation through the main spheres of human existence: politics, culture, workplace, community, and of course education. If McLaren focuses special attention on schooling as a crucial site of knowledge production and politicization, he never fails to locate it within the parameters of these other spheres. Critical pedagogy, when framed against the partial, fragmentary, accommodating, largely depoliticizing intellectual trends found in postmodernism, cultural studies, mainstream positivism, even the bulk of academic Marxism, lays the foundation of the sort of radical imagination and political action we will need for the future. At the same time, critical pedagogy as such turns out to be simply one step along a protracted transformative journey that must engage the omnipresent realities of globalization, Empire, and mounting ecological devastation, motifs that McLaren now brings into his work to provide the basis of a *radical* critical pedagogy.

No in-depth, critical understanding of education is possible today outside the historical recognition of capitalist power, outside the incessant and brutal commodification of the world that Marx and Engels so brilliantly foresaw in *The Communist Manifesto* more than 150 years ago. The seemingly fatalistic pull of capital accumulation enters into and reshapes every aspect of human life, reconstituting and breaking down anything standing in the way of the drive toward expanded markets and profits. As McLaren observes, this thrust of modern, state-engineered, hypertechnological capital—marked by the spread of commodity production into every corner of the globe—has become *more* extensive today than at any time in the past, contrary to all those self-serving, hegemonic academic discourses proclaiming the obsolescence of Marx's theories. By reclaiming (while also restating and *extending*) Marx's penetrating critique for the contemporary era, we are theoretically better armed to grasp the transformed nature of class and power relations today, reflected in the commodification of daily life, massive growth of corporate power, the internationalized and thus more explosive cauldron of class warfare, and the entrenched ideological obstacles to radical change. At the same time, these conceptual signposts take on new meaning for critical pedagogy to the degree they enable us to explore conditions making possible the growth of unprecedented economic globalization, U.S. imperial domination, the spread of militarism, and deepening ecological crisis. As McLaren shows, while the famous labor–capital dialectic constitutes the starting point for both radical theory and oppositional politics, it must be extended onto these new terrains where, as we have recently seen, some of the most hopeful popular movements of the current period have burst onto the political landscape.

McLaren argues persuasively that the power structure—integrated through a vast, labyrinthine system of capitalist production, state governance, and multiple forms of social domination—must be denied its "natural" definitions of hegemony that ensure perpetual reproduction of this status quo. The entire neoliberal system is held together by what appear to be commonsensical myths and deceits, superstitions and beliefs that will have to be questioned, probed, challenged, ultimately overturned—part of a Gramscian counter-hegemonic assault—if that system is to be effectively transformed. While the educational sphere hardly stands alone as a major locus of ideological contestation, it being much too intertwined with the other spheres, it does, however, remain at the core of this process, all the more so given the increasing centrality of knowledge production, mental labor, technology, and communications to modern-day capitalism. If the prevailing educational system reinforces among students and teachers alike a view of commodification and hierarchy as something "natural," that is given, fixed, and irreversible, then logic dictates that subversive assaults on that system are needed to counter its great hegemonic force. Building upon the classic contributions of Marx, Gramsci, and Freire, we arrive at a position where critical pedagogy can be further elaborated and revitalized.

Globalization unfolds not as some abstract, independent, natural developmental process but rather as a ruthless, corporate-driven extension of commodity production across the planetary landscape, solidifying its hold over local institutions, labor, culture, even daily life. The neoliberal economy, relying heavily on its well-known assemblage of international organizations, powerful states, the military, and various manifestations of technological power, has redefined the very contours of class struggle and popular movements at the start of the twenty-first century. Its harsh regimen throws up roadblocks in the way of antisystem struggles, simultaneously generating new social contradictions and heightened levels of global crisis. As McLaren points out, globalization can be understood as the "grand finale of Western modernity," a chaotic, destructive, seemingly endless playing out of Enlightenment rationality. It knows of no boundaries or limits to its grand designs, to its gathering of wealth, privilege, and power. Where capital and class relations come to so thoroughly reshape every dimension of human activity, where the commodity penetrates into the deepest workings of the individual psyche, then the hegemonic project winds up more comprehensive and total, yet more problematic in its reach and efficacy. Here education, always a crucial zone of ideological and cultural combat, ends up all the more ensconced within the globalized network of corporate, government, and military power.

This epic development coincides with the ongoing expansion of U.S. imperial and military power, its purpose to help enforce the capitalist world order, most notably where hegemonic functions are weak or have broken down. It becomes even more inescapable as corporate globalization gives rise to its own bundle of material and ideological contradictions—notably intensifying social divisions rooted in the class oppression, poverty, and anarchy endemic to this world system. Where pedagogical theorists often restrict their scope of attention to identifiable local or national institutions, McLaren goes on to adroitly engage the problematic of Empire, all the more imperative since the events of 9/11, the war on terrorism, and the harsh militaristic turn of U.S. foreign policy under the Bush-II. McLaren focuses on the deep connection existing not only between globalization and Empire, both linked to the U.S. drive toward world supremacy, but also between each of these overpowering forces and the daily challenges facing ordinary people at their workplaces, in their communities, and in their schools and institutions of higher learning. He explores the organic linkage between the long tradition of U.S. worldwide military intervention, most recently in the Middle East, and the rise of terrorism (and other modes of resistance) as a form of blowback against Empire.

This deadly cycle of militarism and terrorism is part of a dialectical relationship likely to persist until the forces and interests behind corporate globalization and U.S. Empire are forced to abandon their power. As the cycle builds ever menacingly, it inevitably undermines democratic governance and closes off the public sphere, possibly accompanied by novel (and some not so novel) forms of authoritarianism that have been the hallmark of historical fascism. In this setting, the prospects for American politics, even short of fascism, are dystopic and frightening.

If unbridled capital accumulation gives rise to such a nightmarish world, it brings added misery with the spread of ecological devastation, which by definition sadly recognizes no territorial or cultural boundaries—that is, it follows the logic of global expansion without limits. Devoid of any meaningful social ethics or planning mechanisms, capitalism destroys the planetary ecological balance, having already produced widespread toxic contamination of the water, air, soil, and food along with global warming, resource depletion, threats to agriculture, and urban deterioration—all felt more severely *outside* the borders of those industrial powers mostly culpable for the devastation. As capital ravages nature, it does so in the absence of any effective countervailing governing or social forces that might keep such cataclysmic processes in check. The global ecological crisis represents yet another face of corporate colonization, working to destroy nature and human communities with equal force. Where even critical pedagogy discourses have for so long overlooked this crushing phenomenon, subordinating it to the presumably deeper concerns of work, politics, community, and education, the time has come to bring ecological or "green" sensibilities directly into the picture if only because it so profoundly impacts those concerns, and McLaren has authored a book here that sets out to do precisely that.

What McLaren has achieved in this volume, working at times with different collaborators, is to revise, broaden, and deepen what we understand as critical pedagogy, radicalizing both its discourse and practice simultaneously. From lived experience to globalization, from daily life to Empire, from schooling to ecological crisis, what we have in this unique body of writings is the kind of "philosophy of praxis" Gramsci championed as a revolutionary Marxist several decades ago, now reconfigured to meet the challenges of a new historical period. This mode of critical pedagogy suggests more than anything a democratic reclaiming of public life, a relentless debunking of hegemonic myths, a new language of radical opposition—in toto, a discursive paradigm that engages creatively and progressively the epic contributions of Marx, Gramsci, and Freire.

Capitalists and Conquerors
An Introduction

Peter McLaren

When I was a child growing up in Canada in the 1950s, I shared a fear similar to that of some of my neighborhood friends: that one day all the mannequins in the downtown department stores (the now defunct Eatons and Simpsons) would come to life and take over the world. It seems, a half century later, that my fear was duly justified. The department store mannequins have indeed taken over the world. They captured the Bush Jr. White House in that notorious stolen presidential election that my UCLA colleague, Doug Kellner, refers to as "grand theft 2000." Having convinced a large segment of the American population that they are the only ones capable of looking after the security and well-being of U.S. citizens, the Bush Jr. *junta* took advantage of a tragic terrorist attack on the country to create a climate of fear that would rival even the skills of Sauron—a culture of intimidation and hostility that continues to serve as a smokescreen for its empire building.

The world has become President Bush's private whirligig, spinning across his global playground. Few world leaders refuse to play along, because the stakes are too high. But they are even higher when the game is allowed to continue uncontested by any rival superpower that can hold the rapacious quest for U.S. world domination in check. It is not the willing players who will bring the game to a halt. Neither is it the intercession or political inertia of history. Rather, it is the poor and the dispossessed who are suffering the most as a result of it.

The force that keeps the whirligig spinning is not democracy unchained, or the role that God has ordained the United States to play on the world stage, or the desire of a free people to bring freedom and democracy to those suffering under the jackboots of dictatorship. It is the zealotry of a fanatic and

1

his advisors spinning the Big Lie: that U.S. policy is ordained by the Creator as inherently just and must not be questioned, that its leadership must never be placed in doubt, or that its global mission must never be interrupted by counter evidence during a time of war because our Homeland is in immanent danger of being wounded by evil-doers who hate our freedom and democracy. The Bush administration takes this stand even as its forces are committing war crimes across Al Anbar province. Jonathan Schell (2004) describes the attack on Fallujah:

> When the attack came, the first target was Falluja General Hospital. The *New York Times* explained why: "The offensive also shut down what officers said was a propaganda weapon for the militants: Falluja General Hospital, with its stream of reports of civilian casualties." If there were no hospital, there would be no visible casualties; if there were no visible casualties, there would be no international outrage, and all would be well. What of those civilians who remained? No men of military age were permitted to leave during the attack. Remaining civilians were trapped in their apartments with no electricity or water. No one knows how many of them have been killed, and no official group has any plans to find out. The city itself is a ruin.

Dick Cheney, our perma-sneer vice-president, whom William Rivers Pitt (2004) calls "every inch the snarling, hunch-shouldered golem that has made him one of the least popular politicians in recent memory," is clearly invested in the philosophy of the Big Lie and is the frontal lobe of Bush's brain, leaving plenty of Bush's brainpan to be occupied by Bush's über-tactician, Karl Rove, and, of course, God. He has taken the art of malversation to new and commanding heights.

For me, one of the most alarming aspects of life in the United States after the terrorist attacks of September 11, 2001—what I have referred to as a "saber slash across the cheekbones of world history"—has been the religious punditry that characterizes Bush's claim to be a special envoy of God, providing him in the eyes of many U.S. citizens with the moral authority to turn the carnage inflicted by the world's most fearsome military machine into a mass graveyard for evil-doers and those who have been deemed enemies of civilization. For many, it has also put God's stamp of approval on capitalism as a way of life in a way much more ideologically formidable than being a winning contestant on *Survivor*. For the true believers, God apparently regulates the world through the deregulation of the economy, where human beings can rise out the ashes of poverty and into the wellspring of the American middle-class dream, if only they would commit themselves to the trickle-down inevitability of capitalist self-interest and trust the global robber barons to make life better for everyone. After all, trusting in God is one way to become rich, as the evangelical mega-churches so vociferously proclaim in their "prosperity preaching" throughout the country.

In effect, what we have in the Bush administration is what Ron Suskind (2004) calls a "faith-based presidency." Such a presidency is not dependent upon a critical analysis of empirical reality, or even uncritical analysis, but rather the president's divinely guided intuition, gut feelings, and praying points. Many of the president's base of supporters believe, in fact, that as a result of Bush's personal religious faith, God is now present in the White House. As Suskind (2004) writes:

> This is one key feature of the faith-based presidency: open dialogue, based on facts, is not seen as something of inherent value. It may, in fact, create doubt, which undercuts faith. It could result in a loss of confidence in the decision-maker and, just as important, by the decision-maker. Nothing could be more vital, whether staying on message with the voters or the terrorists or a California congressman in a meeting about one of the world's most nagging problems. As Bush himself has said any number of times on the campaign trail, "By remaining resolute and firm and strong, this world will be peaceful."

For the approximately 42 percent of U.S. citizens who identify themselves as evangelical or born-again Christians, the idea that facts or reasoned judgment should not get in the way of faith is perhaps not that big an issue. But for those of us who would like to see foreign and domestic policy run by carefully considered deliberation based on sound intelligence and critical analysis, a faith-based presidency presents a crisis of inestimable proportions. You can't run the world on the supreme confidence that your views are right because they are guided by God. You can't legitimate being reckless actors on the side of history because God will eventually sort out any mistakes in favor of the United States. Confidence without substance is like art without creativity. Suskind (2004) concludes:

> George W. Bush, clearly, is one of history's great confidence men. That is not meant in the huckster's sense, though many critics claim that on the war in Iraq, the economy and a few other matters he has engaged in some manner of bait-and-switch. No, I mean it in the sense that he's a believer in the power of confidence. At a time when constituents are uneasy and enemies are probing for weaknesses, he clearly feels that unflinching confidence has an almost mystical power. It can all but create reality.

Many U.S. citizens may wish to reevaluate the meaning of democracy when in its name torture and war crimes are treated as little more than an embarrassing solecism. When the Defense Department's chief counsel, Alberto "Mr. Torture" Gonzales, assures the president that inflicting mental and physical pain could be made legal, and that Bush and his torturers would remain immune from any charges related to the treatment of "illegal combatants," and when the president is tacitly complicitous in redefining torture and refuses to disclose any of the twenty-four supposedly humane interrogation methods for foreign prisoners, we have good cause to consider what it means to be an envoy of God, a Joan of Arc in Texas chaps occupying the Oval Office. Or are we dealing here with just your rank-and-file imperialist claiming the sovereign right of nullification, or perhaps even the Divine Right of Kings? When the best minds that Bush can muster in his circle of advisors and among the military elite are reading *The Arab Mind* by Raphael Patai (2002) to understand Iraqis and giving credence to the insights generated within its pages (such as "Arabs only understand force," and that the "biggest weakness of Arabs is shame and humiliation"), and when Jay Bybee, the author of an infamous Justice Department memo justifying the use of torture as a method of interrogation in the war on terror, is made a federal appeals judge, then perhaps we can better understand the horror that has come to be known as Abu Ghraib.

Although Bush rhapsodizes about our "freedom and democracy" at home, the truth is that freedom and democracy have effectively been put on hold, with our commander-in-chief demanding: "Secure the hatch!" Arundhati Roy (2004) asserts:

> And what of the U.S. elections? Do U.S. voters have a real choice? . . . Those positions of real power—the bankers, the CEOs—are not vulnerable to the vote (. . . and in any case, they fund both sides). . . . The U.S. political system has been carefully crafted to ensure that no one who questions the natural goodness of the military-industrial-corporate power structure will be allowed through the portals of power.

Perhaps Gore Vidal (2004) said it best: "We have only one political party in the United States, the Property Party, with two right wings, Republican and Democrat" (p. 24).

The Office of Homeland Security is dedicated to ensuring domestic safety; yet, at the same time, it is designed to promote what conservative scholar James M. Rhodes has called (in the context of his discussion of the Hitler movement) "ontological hysteria," summarized by Michael Grosso (1995) as follows: "Ontological hysteria consists of a prolonged fear of imminent annihilation, panic over the insecurity of existence. People experience it in disastrous, disorienting times" (p. 197). A key tactic of the Bush administration is to take advantage of this ontological terrorism, to keep the hoi polloi disoriented and in a sustained state of dependency on Bush the Crusader to protect them. Whenever the public seems ready to let down its guard (and perhaps even think about questions about democracy, jobs, equality, freedom), we receive an announcement from Homeland Security that a terrorist attack is expected soon, perhaps in a matter of days. Roy (2004) strikingly proclaims:

> Ordinary Americans have been manipulated into imagining they are a people under siege whose sole refuge and protector is their government. If it isn't the Communists, it's al-Qaeda. If it isn't Cuba. it's Nicaragua. As a result, this, the most powerful nation in the world—with its unmatchable arsenal of weapons, its history of having waged and sponsored endless wars, and the only nation in history to have actually used nuclear bombs—is peopled by a terrified citizenry, jumping at shadows. A people bonded to the state not by social services, or public health care, or employment guarantees, but by fear. This synthetically manufactured fear is used to gain public sanction for further acts of aggression. And so it goes, building into a spiral of self-fulfilling hysteria, now formally calibrated by the U.S government's Amazing Technicolored Terror Alerts: fuchsia, turquoise, salmon pink.

When Garrison Keillor (2004) up in Lake Wobegon country writes that the "Party of Lincoln and Liberty was transmogrified into the party of hairy-backed swamp developers and corporate shills, faith-based economists, fundamentalist bullies with Bibles, Christians of convenience, freelance racists, misanthropic frat boys, shrieking midgets of AM radio, tax cheats, nihilists in golf pants, brownshirts in pinstripes, sweatshop tycoons, hacks, fakirs, aggressive dorks, Lamborghini libertarians, people who believe Neil Armstrong's moonwalk was filmed in Roswell, New Mexico, little honkers out to diminish the rest of us, Newt's evil spawn and their Etch-A-Sketch president, a dull and rigid man suspicious of the free flow of information and of secular institutions, whose philosophy is a jumble of badly sutured body parts trying to walk," we can admire the skill of his satire but also shudder at how close it hits home.

While free-market democracies are spreading globally like fungus spores in a tornado, those whose labor-power is now deemed worthless have the choice of selling their organs, working the plantations or mines, or going into prostitution. The United States is free to export its pollution to Latin America, where *maquiladoras* factories dot the free-trade zones. In Africa, thriving businesses sell "dead white men's clothing" in places such as the Congo, Nigeria, Lagos, Liberia, Uganda, Kenya, Tanzania, and Malawi and Togo where global capitalism has turned Africa into the world's recycling bin that includes not only secondhand clothes, but also expired medicines, antiquated computers, polluting refrigerators and air conditioners, old mattresses, and used vehicles imported from Japan (Maharaj 2004).

Tony Wilden published the following quotation in his famous 1980 book, *The Imaginary Canadian*, a statement that reverberates with as much relevance and intensity today as it did a quarter of a century ago.

Capitalism has sown the whirlwind; the peoples of the world are forces to reap it. Capitalism is closer to being totally out of control than it has ever been before. It is a system that can never be satisfied, no matter what we do. The colonisation of the wretched of the earth continues to increase. Feudal, slave, and other kinds of fascist relations—in the family, in the factory and the field, in the corporation, in the schools—was ever more oppressive. At the same time, capitalism's suicidal attempt to colonise nature proceeds as yet unchecked. There is no longer any doubt that the short-range survival values of capitalism are in direct, and violent conflict with the long-range survival—as human beings—of everyone on earth. . . . In order for the production of exchange values to keep growing, it becomes necessary to invent practically useless use values—and to create and recreate an environment of consumers who think they need them. Capitalism ignores constraints on such growth invented by non-capitalist societies in their quest for long-range survival, the ultimate use value. Unfortunately, these other societies did not know how to survive capitalism—and we don't know either, as yet. (1980, p. 223)

At a time of an unprecedented globalization of capital, the increasingly privatized public sphere gives form and substance to the avidity of the ruling elite as reemerging rivalries between national bourgeoisie and cross-national class formations hold the working classes hostage to one overarching goal: competitive return on investment capital. The pettifogging advocates of capital armed with one-dimensional banality continually traduce the principles of participatory democracy and present us with what I have called over the years a "democracy of empty forms"—a formal democracy. It is this hollow democracy—defended by the shameful ferreters working for the corporate media—against which critical pedagogy fights an uphill battle, calibrating its project of social transformation.

What is even more disconcerting is that this hollow democracy has, since September 11, 2001, been quickly filled with both a poisonous broth—to keep the public in a paranoid state so that they jump at their reflections in the spit-polished boots of Homeland Security's shock troops—and bromide—to put their faculties of critical reasoning to sleep. Bush's naïve and declaratory diagnosis of the terrorist threat—they hate our freedom—is imbibed by the Bible Belt masses like an army of Charles Bukowskis trolling the pubs of Tijuana during happy hour. That such box-trained banality is cadging the political loyalties of an equally naïve electorate will not be surprising but should be alarming.

Meanwhile, at home, a general intensification of labor proceeds apace: a relentless overextension of the working day, cutbacks in resources and social programs, tax breaks for the very rich, egregious violations of laws by corporate executives, and a lack of waged work. All of this is taking place under the banner of the preferred euphemism for imperialism: fighting terrorism and bringing about free-market democracy. It's hard to posit a socialist alternative to such global misery without feeling like Sisyphus with his block of stone toiling in the realm of the dead, or like Tantalus stranded in America, locked in a strip mall diner and each time he reaches for a burger and fries, his Formica table top arches out of reach.

The melding of Christian and fascist iconography that characterized the recent Republican National Convention in New York City—where Bush's presence seemed suffused with a faux-divine emanation—was unmistakably eerie and reflected a language that was both theocratic and populist. With the flagging economy, the bloody war in and pillage of Iraq, and the specter of U.S. concentration camps at Guantánamo Bay and Diego Garcia (where the invented category of "illegal combatants" places these detainees outside any legal frame, without indictment, without access to lawyers, without family visits, without rights, and literally in a space outside the legal territory of the United States where the Geneva Conventions do not apply—see Lobe 2004) carefully tucked away behind slick propaganda about freedom and democracy, the speeches and comments from the speakers were chillingly effective:

> So it went: blood and fire and God and country and "Amazing Grace." It was a proper war party at the Garden, charged with the language of Christian martyrology, and Bush could not have been more at home on closing night, when he strode out on a catwalk that had been built to lead him to a special altar in the round, which placed him in the middle of the floor, amid the masses, "a man of the people." (Gourevitch 2004)

The lurid hypocrisy of the Republicans was in full view, but no doubt the imagination of the party faithful was too out of focus for them to see it clearly, if at all. Here was a performance that went directly against the grain of what the Republicans have decried for decades: identity politics wrapped in the ideology of victimology. Gourevitch (2004) notes:

> During the culture wars of the early nineties, Republicans deplored the bullying political correctness that came from the intertwining of victimology and identity politics, and yet in the construct of recent history promoted by the White House, and by speaker after speaker and video after video at Madison Square Garden, America's great wound was featured as a sort of national treasure—the ultimate and all-justifying source of legitimacy of the Bush Presidency. So the constant invocations of mass death and devastation were proffered to the conventioneers and their television audience not only as a bad thing but also, perversely, as something to cherish, even to celebrate, as a source of unity and purpose. Giuliani, in

whose life story September 11th is a very good very bad day, set the tone on opening night by recycling the bullying, jingoist credo that Bush originally extracted from Ground Zero: "Either you are with us or you are with the terrorists."

Bush's messianic cry, "America is called to lead the cause of freedom in a new century. . . . The freedom of many and the future security of our nation now depends on us" was met with vigorous cheering at the recent Republican National Convention. The American military, the "treaders down of cities," have become the enforcers of a naked imperialism under Bush the lesser. As the country remains divided over whether the United States should engage in hard or soft imperialist adventures, critical educators have their work clearly cut out for them. Of course, in the Manichean divide created by the Bush administration, the "we" are held together by the spiritual ectoplasm of universal progress and a commitment to shared Christian values whereas the "them" is an aberrant blip in the frictionless and flat-lined future guaranteed by the character and moral steadfastness of our great leaders chosen by a blonde Jesus in a dazzling white robe surrounded by a host of graduates from Bob Jones University.

While some of us might chuckle at Bush's faux-barnyard wisdom, laconically served up to the cameras outside his fake movie set ranch in Crawford, Texas, it's not God who is pulling all the strings that make this yokel dance. While God might be hunkered down in Bush's armor-plated cortex issuing direct orders on how to destroy evil-doers, far less powerful voices, like those of ten million protestors around the world who demonstrated against the U.S. war in Iraq (setting an all-time record for simultaneous protest), might also have an equal—though less vatic—claim to be following God's will. That's not to say that God doesn't exist. It's just that Bush Jr. doesn't have a direct line of communication to the Almighty. It's entirely possible that, from time to time, God likes to indulge in some Texas line dancing or to take in a Longhorns game, but it's also just as likely that God occasionally sits in on the meetings of Bush's war cabinet and doesn't like what she sees. And I am not as certain as Bush is that God is an American. I am not trying to argue that Bush isn't a shrewd politician—with Karl Rove at his side, he most certainly is. It's more the case that he is singularly incomplete without his handlers, including those he has manufactured for himself, like God.

The construction of a new vision of human sociality has never been more urgent in a world of where the United States seeks unchallenged supremacy over all other nation-states by controlling the regulatory regimes of supranational institutions such as the World Bank and the International Monetary Fund.

But a new vision of human sociality is precisely what is not on offer by progressive educators, often despite sedulous research underlain by an unbidden impulse to make sense of what has gone wrong with schools and universities and the society in which they function. Woefully absent in their work is an alternative social vision of what the world should and could look like outside the value form of capital. For Marxist educators, the struggle ahead will be a particularly difficult one. Mike Cole (in press) writes: "For Marxists, an understanding of the metanarrative of imperialism, past and present . . . takes us to the crux of the trajectory of capitalism from its inception right up to the twenty-first century. . . . Education . . . could contribute to a critical awareness of New Imperialism's manifestations, and, from a Marxist perspective, the need for its demise, and replacement with a new world order."

Enter critical pedagogy.

Critical pedagogy is secured by the most fecund of revolutionary talismans: critique. It is focused not only on the practice of critique but also on the critique of establismentarian pedagogical practice. Unfortunately, too many progressive educators still in the thrall of postmodern social theory mistake discursive empowerment for social and economic transformation. Their "coming to voice" and the politics of self-affirmation and self-identity that they so tenaciously advocate fails in the main to challenge the gross "materiality" of exploitation. The decompression chamber in which their pedagogy currently rests must be opened up to a rematerialized critique. This is one of the many issues and challenges that *Capitalists and Conquerors* attempts to address.

In creating necessary conditions for revolutionary social change, the critical pedagogy advanced throughout this volume recognizes the limits of traditional "pragmatist" reformist practice by prioritizing the need to question the deeper problems, particularly the violent contradictions (e.g., the gap between racism and the American dream, between capital and labor), under which students—and the general population—are forced to live. Critical revolutionary pedagogy begins with the following questions: Do we know whose hands ground the capitalist lenses through which we comprehend the world and do we know from whence came the bloodstains on the lens grinder's workbench? Whether we know the answers to such questions, they must be followed by a further question: How and why is this so? If we know the answers, what are they? If we don't know, why is this so? If there are better questions to be asked, what are they?

Critical revolutionary pedagogy serves the important purpose of generating new ways of thinking about the state and its relationship to the production of and possibilities for human agency both now and in the crucial years ahead of us. Humans are conditioned by structures and social relations just as they create and transform those structures and relations. But what has been forgotten or at least neglected at great peril—and this is perhaps the central theme of *Capitalists and Conquerors*—is the overdetermining effects of capital as a social relation.

Against tremendous odds, the challenge of educators over the last several decades has been to humanize the classroom environment and to create pedagogical spaces for linking education to the praxiological dimensions of social justice initiatives and to that end we are indebted to critical pedagogy. Given the urgent times we live in, we need to ratchet up the struggle ahead. This has been the singular challenge of *Capitalists and Conquerors*. For this reason, I have attempted to expand the pedagogical encounter to consider its own insinuation into globalized social relations of exploitation and to live up to its revolutionary potential of becoming a transnational, gender-balanced, multiracial, anti-imperialist struggle. Everything in human history passes through the realm of subjectivity and it is through this dance of the dialectic that we create history. The democracy in which we live is indeed at a tragic crossroads, as is capitalism itself, and we must fiercely continue to question the present historical course that has wedded the two together.

In our book *Teaching against Global Capitalism and the New Imperialism*, Ramin Farahmandpur and I set out for consideration a series of questions as a challenge to the doyens of the global plantocracy: How can we liberate the use value of human beings from their subordination to exchange value? How can we convert what is least functional about ourselves as far as the abstract utilitarian logic of capitalist society is concerned—our self-realizing, sensuous, species-being—into our major instrument of self-definition? How can we make what we represent to capital—replaceable commodities—subordinate to who we have also become as critical social agents of history? How can we make critical self-reflexivity a demarcating principle of who we are and critical global citizenship the substance of what we want to become? How can we make the cultivation of a politics of hope and possibility a radical end in itself? How can we de-commodify our subjectivities? How can we materialize our self-activity as a revolutionary force and struggle for the self-determination of free and equal citizens in a just system of appropriation and distribution of social wealth? How can we make and remake our own nature within historically specific conventions of capitalist society such that we can make this self-activity a revolutionary force to dismantle capitalism itself and create the conditions for the development of our full human potential? How can we confront our "producers" (i.e., social relations of production, the corporate media, cultural formations and institutional structures) as an independent power?

Capitalists and Conquerors has been written both to provide at least partial answers to these questions and to formulate new ones. For instance, I would ask why the following assertion by Gore Vidal (2004) is so pertinent to our current times: "We hate this system that we are trapped in, but we don't know what our cage looks like because we have never seen it from the outside" (p. 29). Throughout this book further questions such as these are posed.

Raising such questions is a useful beginning in developing a coherent philosophy of praxis. I have tried to raise these, and more, throughout this book. Planning strategies of action—local and transnational in scope—is another, and perhaps the most crucial, dimension of revolutionary social transformation that is a necessary aspect of revolutionary critical pedagogy. This book has attempted to provide a framework in which such practices might be discussed.

Capitalists and Conquerors is one particular foray into the politics of critical pedagogy. I am not claiming that it is the only path. But I do believe it is a necessary one. Clearly, it is critical of the way that this emergent field has already shown signs of political domestication. In my criticisms I have tried to make a case for including Marxist analysis—namely historical materialism—in critical educational studies, not an easy task, especially during the organic crisis of capitalism we are facing at this current historical juncture, not to mention the steady movement toward fascism we have been experiencing in the United States.

George Bush—who represents to progressives what Nicolae Carpathia (the Anti-Christ character in the "Left Behind" book series by Tim F. LaHaye and Jerry B. Jenkins) represents to evangelical Christians—has won a second term. And he has claimed a mandate. A few cries of fraud are being sounded in the icy wilderness of defeat such as those of Thom Hartmann:

> Why have we let corporations into our polling places, locations so sacred to democracy that in many states even international election monitors and reporters are banned? Why are we allowing corporations to exclusively handle our vote, in a secret and totally invisible way? Particularly a private corporation founded, in one case, by a family that believes the Bible should replace the Constitution; in another case run by one of Ohio's top Republicans; and in another case partly owned by Saudi investors? Of all the violations of the commons—all of the crimes against We The People and against democracy in our great and historic republic—this is the greatest. Our vote is too important to outsource to private corporations. (2004)

Most people, however, remain in a state of numbing resignation. Whereas the majority in the international community were willing to forgive the American people for the "selection" of George Bush by the Supreme Court the first time around in 2000, the fact that he was elected by the majority of American voters in 2004 will further polarize the rest of the world against us.

Why so many workers and poor people voted against their economic and social interests, felt connected to Bush's campaign theme of "moral values" which amounted to bigotry against gays, immigrants, Arabs, abortion advocates, and what was perceived as a Hollywood secularism in general), and actively engaged in a primitive patriotism and crude nationalism is an issue that needs to be taken seriously by the left. People who have been commodified by capital, denied union protection, brutalized and terrorized by their bosses, and raised against a background of Christian fundamentalist television and talk radio often rebel against their alienation by an equally alienating act of completely disavowing counterintuitive explanations and misplacing blame while conflating the instruments of their oppression into a sacred fetish of obedience: God (who speaks through their leader, a paladin of moral values), country (the homeland), and freedom (free to discriminate against others, to get rich at the expense of others). All three signifiers are linked together through a spectacle of demonizing antiwar and antiglobalization protesters and pro-choice liberals, and sometimes even equating them with the foreign evil- doers they are already slaughtering in Afghanistan and Iraq. In this way, the Bush administration is able to appeal both to the capitalist elite and to the average working stiff. As Hansen and Kolhatkar (2004) point out: "By cornering the market on strength and religion and good versus evil, they've managed to be both the party of the elites and the party of the little guy, seducing one side with tax breaks and the other with the idolization of the traditional family, and both with the good fight against evil."

Already Christian leaders are proclaiming the election of Bush as "divine intervention" and religious politics has now fully become a major weapon of the Christian Right to attack Roe versus Wade. School officials in Grantsburg, Wisconsin, have revised the science curriculum to allow the teaching of creationism. And there will be plenty more to come. It is disconcerting, to say the least, that those "gun-owning churchgoers" who helped put Bush in office for a second term and who profess to care so much about the unborn, betray such contempt for the aborning and the already born, not only people of color within their own borders but also hundreds of thousands of innocent victims of U.S. bombing runs in Iraq. There will be future victims of those already born, those who, in some other oil-rich country, will one day find themselves captured in the night-seeing goggles of Neanderthal Nation's imperial militia and in the crosshairs of an M40A3.

No doubt some answers are to be found in the history of religious war and fascism. The increasingly central role played by "moral values" among the U.S. electorate will unquestionably witness a research industry of its own in the years to come. In the meantime, progressives continue to shake their heads in disbelief. And while there would seem to be no condign imprecations vile enough to throw at Kerry and his incompetent campaign that would satisfy the rage of the millions of voters who rallied against Bush, there is much work to be done when we take sober stock of the seriousness of the challenge ahead. Backed by corrupt solons, populist fantasists, well-heeled Straussians, and Christian Zionists who interpret world events in light of Biblical prophecies as fiercely as tycoons see the world through the eyes of their stock brokers, Bush and his ilk could push U.S. democracy into a free-fall: foreign investors might start unloading the dollar and U.S. Treasury securities sending the economy into a tailspin, draconian security measures will possibly accelerate an exodus of intellectuals to Canada, the National Rifle Association will win more protection for gun manufacturers in criminal lawsuits, the Supreme Court will start looking more like a Taliban tribunal, the city of Fallujah will be razed with the same war crime frenzy and fury as was directed at the city of Hue after the Tet Offensive of 1968, the number of foreign graduate students in U.S. universities will demonstrably decline as student visas become more difficult to obtain, education will become more market-oriented and ideologically driven (already in places like Texas publishers such as Holt, Rinehart, and Winston have been pushed to include a definition of marriage as a "lifelong union between a husband and a wife" in middle school textbooks, and Glencoe/McGraw-Hill has agreed to substitute the term "husband and wife" for marriage "partners"), and the sons and daughters of the 100,000 Iraqi civilians thus far killed or mutilated by the U.S. military death machine will dedicate themselves to the art of revenge, holy war style.

Before the second campaign of the holy war in the city of Fallujah, Jesus watched over Christian troops loyal to the Lamb of God, who, dressed as gladiators, staged a chariot race reminiscent of the film, Ben-Hur, with confiscated Iraqi horses. After the race, they prepared themselves to kill barbarians, invoking the Holiest of Holies and transforming themselves into the sword arm of revenge. A report by Agence France-Presse vividly captures the scene:

> Men with buzzcuts and clad in their camouflage waved their hands in the air, M-16 assault rifles beside them, and chanted heavy metal-flavoured lyrics in praise of Christ late on Friday in a yellow-brick chapel. They counted among thousands of troops surrounding the city of Fallujah, seeking solace as they awaited Iraqi Prime Minister Iyad Allawi's decision on whether or not to invade Fallujah. "You are the sovereign. Your name is holy. You are the pure spotless lamb," a female voice cried out on the loudspeakers as the marines clapped their hands and closed their eyes, reflecting on what lay ahead for them. . . . "Thus David prevailed over the Philistines," [one] marine said, reading from scripture, and the marines shouted back, "Hoorah, King David," using their signature grunt of approval. The marines drew parallels from the verse with their present situation, where they perceive themselves as warriors fighting barbaric men opposed to all that is good in the world. "Victory belongs to

the Lord," another young marine read. Their chaplain, named Horne, told the worshippers they were stationed outside Fallujah to bring the Iraqis "freedom from oppression, rape, torture and murder. . . . We ask you God to bless us in that effort." The marines then lined up and their chaplain blessed them with holy oil to protect them. "God's people would be anointed with oil," the chaplain said, as he lightly dabbed oil on the marines' foreheads. The crowd then followed him outside their small auditorium for a baptism of about a half-dozen marines who had just found Christ.

Such a description brings to mind a passage from Wilhelm Reich's *A Mass Psychology of Fascism*:

> Fascism is the supreme expression of religious mysticism. As such, it comes into being in a peculiar social form. Fascism countenances that religiosity that stems from sexual perversion, and it transforms the masochistic character of the old patriarchal religion of suffering into a sadistic religion. In short, it transposes religion from the "other-worldliness" of the philosophy of suffering to the "this worldliness" of sadistic murder. (1970, xv)

Back in the White House, a beaming George Bush huddles with Karl Rove. Victory celebrations might include a viewing of Mel Gibson's *The Passion of Christ*. Grand plans will soon be hatched at Camp David. Students around the country will take their seats in crowded classrooms and ponder their future with the comforting knowledge that evil-doers are being slaughtered in Jesus's name throughout the world so that the American dream can be kept alive for them.

In the words of Harold Myerson,

> Inmates run the asylum. The men who failed to plan for the war that they began keep on mismanaging it. The men with the worst economic record since Herbert Hoover still set economic policy. The men who enraged the rest of the planet still strut their stuff. Tuesday was a long night's journey into hell. And it's only going to get worse. (2004, p. 61)

This book is intended to focus the reader's imagination so that when you look closely at Bush Jr.'s trademark smirk and the bloodshot eyes of Rumsfeld, Rove, Rice, and Wolfowitz, you'll find Leo Strauss, J. Edgar Hoover, Joe McCarthy, Roy Cohn, and William McKinley staring back at you behind their masks. It is also an attempt to stare back at them.

And to make their bloody journey of ideological and material conquest more difficult. The rest will depend upon the power of our critique, our efforts at disobedience and dissent and our steadfast determination oxygenated by a revolutionary optimism of the will.

REFERENCES

Agence France-Presse. 2004. "Holy War: Evangelical Marines Prepare to Battle Barbarians." *Common Dreams News Center*, November 7, at www.commondreams.org/headlines04/1107-02.htm.

Cole, Mike. 2004. "'Rule Britannia' and the New American Empire: A Marxist Analysis of the Teaching of Imperialism, Actual and Potential, in the British School Curriculum." *Policy Futures in Education* 2(3).

Gourevitch, Philip. 2004. "Bushspeak: The President's Vernacular Style." *The New Yorker*. September 13, 2004. At www.newyorker.com/fact/content/?040913fa_fact1.

Grosso, Michael. 1995. *The Millennium Myth: Love and Death at the End of Time*. Wheaton, Ill.: Quest Books.

Hansen, Suzy, and Sheelah Kolhatkar. 2004. "It's Super Bush!" *The New York Observer*, November 15, at www.nyobserver.com/pages/story.asp?ID=9835.

Hartmann, Thom. 2004. "The Ultimate Felon Against Democracy." *Common Dreams News Center*. November 4, at www.commondreams.org/views04/1104-38.htm.

Keillor, Garrison. 2004. "We're Not in Lake Wobegon Anymore." *In These Times*, September 20, 31.

Kellner, Doug. 2001. *Grand Theft 2000: Media Spectacle and a Stolen Election*. Lanham, Md.: Rowman & Littlefield Publishers.

LaHaye, Tim, and Jenkins, Jerry. 1996. *Left Behind: A Novel of the Earth's Last Days*. Carol Stream, Ill.: Tyndale House.

Lobe, Jim. 2004. "Seeking Method in the Madness of Abu Ghraib: An Interview with Belgian Philosopher Lieven De Cauter." *Common Dreams News Center.* At www.commondreams.org/headlines04/0910-06.htm.

Maharaj, Davan. 2004. "For Sale—Cheap: 'Dead White Men's Clothing.'" *Los Angeles Times*. Wednesday, July 14, at www.latimes.com/news/specials/world/la-fg-clothes14jul14,1,5275395.story?coll=la-home-headlines (accessed July 14, 2004).

McLaren, Peter, and Ramin Farahmandpur. 2004. *Teaching against Globalization and the New Imperialism*. Lanham, Md.: Rowman & Littlefield Publishers.

Meyerson, Harold. 2004. "Long Night's Journey into Hell." *LA Weekly,* November 5-11, 61.

Patai, Raphael. 2002. *The Arab Mind*. Long Island City, N.Y.: Hatherleigh Press.

Pitt, William Rivers. 2004. "Cheney's Avalanche of Lies." *Truthout*. October 6, at www.truthout.org/docs_04/100704Z.shtml.

Reich, Wilhelm. 1970. *The Mass Psychology of Fascism*. New York: Farrar, Straus and Giroux.

Roy, Arundhati. 2004. "Tide? Or Ivory Snow? Public Power in the Age of Empire." At www.democracynow.org/static/Arundhati_Trans.shtml.

Schell, Jonathan. 2004. "What Happened to Hearts?" *Truthout*. December 6, at www.truthout.org/docs_04/111904Z.shtml.

Steinberg, Jonathan. 2004. "A Mighty Fortress is His God." *The Miami Herald*. July 18, at www.miami.com/mld/miamiherald/news/9172536.htm?1c (accessed July 18, 2004).

Suskind, Ron. 2004. "Without a Doubt." *New York Times Magazine.* October 17, at www.nytimes.com/2004/10/17/magazine/17BUSH.html?oref=login.
Vidal, Gore. 2004. "State of the Union, 2004." *The Nation,* 279(7, September), 23–29.
Wilden, Anthony. 1980. *The Imaginary Canadian: An Examination for Discovery.* Vancouver, Canada: Pulp Press.

I

THE FUTURE OF CRITICAL PEDAGOGY

1

Critical Pedagogy in the Age of Neoliberal Globalization

Peter McLaren

Political propaganda, the art of anchoring the things of the state in the broad masses so that the whole nation will feel a part of them, cannot therefore remain merely a means to the goal of winning power. It must become a means of building and keeping power.

—Joseph Goebbels, 1934

THE CRISIS OF THE EDUCATIONAL LEFT IN THE UNITED STATES

Part of the problem faced by the educational left today is that even among the most progressive educators there appears to exist an ominous resignation produced by the seeming inevitability of capital, even as financial institutions expand capacity in inverse proportion to a decline in living standards and job security. It has become an article of faith in the critical educational tradition that there is no viable alternative to capitalism. When class relations are discussed, they are not talked about in the Marxist sense of foregrounding the labor–capital dialectic, surplus value extraction, or the structure of property ownership, but instead refer to consumption, lifestyle politics, theories of social stratification in terms of access to consumption, or job, income, and cultural prestige. The swan song for Marxist analysis apparently occurred during the intellectual collapse of Marxism in the 1980s after the Berlin Wall came crashing down and along with it a bipolar imperialist world. Capitalism was loudly proclaimed to be the victor over socialism. Despite mounting signs of desperation and indigence, the globalization of capital was to be the savior of the world's poor and powerless. But as it is now known, its function, far from supplicatory or transitive, has been deadly alienating. Gobbling up the global

19

lifeworld in the quest for an endless accumulation of surplus value, capital has produced some world-historical excretory excesses, turning the world into a global toilet of toxic waste while adding legions to Marx's reserve army of labor. The cutbacks in government expenditure on health, education, and housing investment; the creation of shantytowns in urban industrial areas; the concentration of women in low-wage subcontracted work; the depletion of natural resources; the rampant deunionization; the growth of labor discipline; the expansion of temporary and part-time labor; the pushing down of wages; and the steady decline of decent working conditions have proceeded apace but the rule of capital is not challenged, only its current "condition."

In Russia today, the *prikhvatizatisiya* (grabitization) that has been bequeathed to the masses by a kleptocratic capitalism that dragged itself out of the carrion house of economic shock therapy has led to "blitzkrieg liquidations," the destruction of industry, the disappearance of health benefits and housing, the slashing of salaries, and the transfer of wealth to a dozen or so private owners who now commandeer one public property. As poverty shifts from 2 percent to 50 percent, Western free-market fundamentalists keep reminding the Russians how awful it must have been to live under communism. Western countries that had established their economic fiefdoms by protecting key industries and subsidizing some domestic producers continue to preach the gospel of free trade and deregulation to other countries. Even when the messianic monopoly fantasies of Enron, WorldCom, and Global Crossings' CEOs end in bankruptcy disasters that shake the very pillars of the marketplace, the belief in the sanctity of the market remains undisturbed. Capital stealthily hides behind Nietzsche's veil, maintaining its secret of reversibility—that its economic assistance to the Third World reproduces underdevelopment and ensures the continuity of dependency.

The belief that there is no alternative to capitalism had pullulated across the global political landscape before the fall of the Soviet Union and the Eastern Bloc, attaching itself like a fungus to regional and national dreams alike. The winds of the Cold War had spread its spores to the farthest reaches of the globe. After lying dormant for over a decade, these spores have been reactivated and have seemingly destroyed our capacity to dream otherwise. Today most nations celebrate capital as the key to the survival of democracy. Watered by the tears of the poor and cultivated by working-class labor, the dreams that sprout from the unmolested soil of capital are those engineered by the ruling class. Plowed and harrowed by international cartels of transnational corporations, free-marketeers, and global carpetbaggers poised to take advantage of Third World nations in serious financial debt to the West, the seeds of capitalism have yielded a recordbreaking harvest. The capitalist dream factories are not only corporate board rooms and production studios of media networks that together work to keep the capitalist dream alive, but a spirit of mass resignation that disables the majority of the population from realizing that capitalism and exploitation are functional equivalents, that globalization of capital is just another name for what Lenin (1951) termed imperialism. U.S. imperialism—what Tariq Ali (2002, p. 281) calls "the mother of all fundamentalisms"—has decamped from its Keynesian position of pseudoliberalism to fully embrace a fanatical neoliberalism. One might recall that the grand mullah of neoliberalism, Von Hayek, an avatar to both Thatcher and Reagan:

> favored military actions to defend U.S. interests abroad. On the domestic front he favored the invisible magic of a manipulated market. No state intervention against the interests of capital was to be tolerated. But the state was vital to undertake military operations in the sphere of international relations. (Ali 2002, p. 286)

Further, Von Hayek's neoliberal followers:

> were staunch defenders of the Vietnam war. They supported the U.S.-backed military coup in Chile. In 1979, Hayek favored bombing Tehran. In 1982, during the Malvinas conflict, he wanted raids on the Argentinian capital. This was the creed of neoliberal hegemony most favoured by its founder. (Ali 2002, p. 286)

The fact that neoliberalism—the midwife to the return of a fanatical belief in nonstate intervention into capital movements that was spawned by nineteenth-century libertarianism—has resoundingly defeated the bureaucratic state capitalism of the former Soviet "evil empire," and has created a seismic shift in the geopolitical landscape. Michael Parenti grimly comments that the overthrow of the Soviet Union has abetted a reactionary "rollback" of democratic gains, public services, and common living standards around the world as the United States continues to oppose economic nationalism and autonomous development in Asia, Africa, and Latin America, primarily though debt payments and structural adjustment programs imposed by the World Bank and the International Monetary Fund. Particularly hard hit have been the so-called Third World countries. The Soviet Union's collapse has opened the political floodgates of U.S. imperialism, permitting the United States to pursue virtually uncontested an agenda of "arrogance and brutality." The United States is no longer faced with a competing superpower that imposed constraints on the dream of U.S. global dominance. Parenti offers this disillusioned comment:

> The record of U.S. international violence just in the last decade is greater than anything that any socialist nation has ever perpetrated in its entire history. U.S. forces or proxy mercenary forces wreaked massive destruction upon Iraq, Mozambique, Angola, Nicaragua, El Salvador, Guatemala, East Timor, Libya,

and other countries. In the span of a few months, President Clinton bombed four countries: Sudan, Afghanistan, Iraq repeatedly, and Yugoslavia massively. At the same time, the U.S. national security state was involved in proxy wars in Angola, Mexico (Chiapas), Colombia, East Timor, and various other places. And U.S. forces occupied Macedonia, Bosnia, Kosovo, and Afghanistan, and were deployed across the globe at some 300 major overseas bases—all in the name of peace, democracy, national security, counterterrorism, and humanitarianism. (2002, p. 44)

Today's international political economy is the toast of the global ruling class, and the bourgeoisie see it as their biggest opportunity in decades to join their ranks. Free-marketeers have been given the New World Order's *imprimatur* to loot and exploit the planet's resources and to invest in global markets without restriction. The menacing concomitant of capital's destructive juggernaut is the obliteration of any hope for civilization, let alone democracy. While liberals are plumping for fairer distribution of economic resources, the working classes are taught to feel grateful for the *maquiladoras* that are now sprouting up in countries designated to provide the cheap labor and dumping grounds for pollution for the Western democracies. They are taught that socialism and communism are congenitally evil and can only lead to a totalitarian dictatorship. In short, capitalism and the legitimacy of private monopoly ownership has been naturalized as common sense.

It is no longer just the capitalists who believe that they are the salvation for the world's poor, but the workers themselves have become conditioned to believe that without their exploiters, they would no longer exist. The entrails of the eviscerated poor now serve as divining mechanisms for the soothsayers of the investment corporations. Even many trade unions have been little more than adjuncts of the state, reimposing the discipline of capital's law of value. Those who wish to avoid both Communist-type centralized planning and the disequilibrium and instability of laissez-faire capitalism have turned to a type of market socialism through labor-managed firms, but doing little to challenge the deep grammar of capital itself.

Everywhere we look, social relations of oppression and contempt for human dignity abound. It is not that workers are being press-ganged to serve in the social factory; it is more that they are being made to feel grateful for having some source of income, as meager as that may be. As the demagogues of capitalist neoliberal globalization spin their web of lies about the benefits of "global trade" behind erected "security" walls, protesters are gassed, beaten, and killed. As the media boast about the net worth of corporate moguls and celebrate the excesses of the rich and famous, approximately 2.8 billion people—almost half of the world's people—struggle in desperation to live on less than two dollars (U.S.) a day (McQuaig 2001, p. 27).

The "free-market revolution," driven by continuous capitalist accumulation of a winner-take-all variety, has left the social infrastructure of the United States in tatters (not to mention other parts of the globe). Through policies of increasing its military-industrial-financial interests, it continues to purse its quivering bourgeois lips, bare its imperialist fangs, and suck the lifeblood from the open veins of South America and other regions of the globe. The sudden collapse of the Soviet Union in the 1990s and the shift to capitalism in Eastern Europe has brought nearly five billion people into the world market. The globalization of capitalism and its political bedfellow, neoliberalism, work together to democratize suffering, obliterate hope, and assassinate justice. The logic of privatization and free trade—where social labor is the means and measure of value and surplus social labor lies at the heart of profit—now odiously shapes archetypes of citizenship, manages our perceptions of what should constitute the "good society," and creates ideological formations that produce necessary functions for capital in relation to labor. Schools have been effectively transformed into holding pens where students exercise their everyday consciousness, assert their private interests, articulate their practical intentions, and dream their secret lives within given capitalist social relations and objective forms of thought that emerge from categories of bourgeois social economy, which themselves are bound up with the structural characteristics of stages of social development.

The ideological formations intergenerationally reproduced within schools betray a pragmatic efficacy and validity of apologetic purpose as well as the fetishistic character of everyday thinking. Such formations help to orient students into an unreflexive acceptance of the capitalist social world. Of course, the accession into the social order has always been incomplete, always in process, in that there has always been a space between self-formation and its dismemberment. Critical pedagogy seizes upon this space as its major terrain of struggle.

As schools become increasingly financed more by corporations that function as service industries for transnational capitalism, and as bourgeois think-tank profiteerism and educational professionalism continue to guide educational policy and practice, the U.S. population faces a challenging educational reality. Liberals are calling for the need for capital controls, controls in foreign exchange, the stimulation of growth and wages, labor rights enforcement for nations borrowing from the United States, and the removal of financial aid from banking and capital until they concede to the centrality of the wage problem and insist on labor rights. However, very few are calling for the abolition of capital itself.

The commercialization of higher education, the bureaucratic cultivation of intellectual capital—what Marx referred to in the *Grundrisse* as the "general intellect" or "social brain"—and its tethering to the machinery of capital, the rise of industrial business partnerships, and the movement of research into the commercial arena of profit and in the service of trade organizations and academic-corporate consortia have garnered institutions of higher learning profound suspicion by those who view education as a vehicle for emancipation. In the hands of the technozealots, teachers are being reproletarianized and labor is being disciplined, displaced, and deskilled. Teacher autonomy, independence, and control over work are being severely reduced, while workplace knowledge and control is given over more and more to the hands of the administration.

The educational left is finding itself without a revolutionary agenda for challenging in the classrooms of the nation the effects and consequences of the new capitalism. This situation is only exacerbated by the educational left's failure to challenge the two-party system that is organically linked to the exploitation of human labor and the well-being of corporate profits. Consequently, we are witnessing the progressive and unchecked merging of pedagogy to the productive processes within advanced capitalism. Education has been reduced to a subsector of the economy, designed to create cybercitizens within a teledemocracy of fast-moving images, representations, and lifestyle choices powered by the seemingly frictionlessness of finance capital. Capitalism has been naturalized as commonsense reality—even as a part of nature itself—while the term "social class" has been replaced by the less antagonistic term, "socioeconomic status." It is impossible to examine educational reform in the United States without taking into account continuing forces of globalization and the progressive diversion of capital into financial and speculative channels—what some have called "casino capitalism on a world scale."

CRITICAL EDUCATION AGAINST NEOLIBERALISM

William Robinson (1996, 2001, 2004) has made a convincing argument for the appearance of a transnationalist capitalist class. By employing a renewed historical materialist conception of the state in this current epoch of neoliberal globalization, Robinson is able to de-reify the state/nation-state in order to identify the social classes operating within formal state institutions and to analyze the constellation of social forces in cooperation and in conflict as they develop historically. Robinson argues for a conception of globalization that transcends the nation-state system. He has effectively reconceptualized the dominant Weberian conception of the state through a Marxist problematic as the institutionalization of class relations around a particular configuration of social production in which the economic and the political are conceived as

oments of the same totality. Here, the relation between the economy
is an internal one. There is nothing in this view that necessarily ties
o territory or to nation-states. While it is true that, seen in aggregate
ate terms, there are still very poor countries and very rich ones, it is
that poverty and marginalization are increasing in so-called First
ountries, while the Third World has an expanding new strata of con-
The labor aristocracy is expanding to other countries such that core
iphery no longer denote geography as much as social location. The
l circumstances that gave rise to the nation-state, are, Robinson ar-
eing superceded by globalization such that the state—conceived in
st terms as a congealment of a particular and historically determined
llation of class forces and relations (i.e., a historically specific social re-
inserted into larger social structures)—can no longer simply be con-
d solely in nation-state–centric terms.

binson's argument—that a transnational state apparatus is emerging un-
globalization from within the system of nation-states—rests on the notion
the production process itself has become increasingly transnationalized
as national circuits of accumulation become functionally integrated into
global circuits. Neoliberal globalization is unifying the world into a single
mode of production and bringing about the organic integration of different
countries and regions into a single global economy through the logic of capital accumulation on a world scale. Nonmarket structures are disappearing as
they are fast becoming penetrated and commodified by capitalist relations.
Global class formation has involved the accelerated division of the world into
a global bourgeoisie and a global proletariat. The transnationalized fractions
of dominant groups have become the hegemonic fraction globally.

Social groups and classes are central historical actors rather than "states," as
power is produced within the transnational capitalist class by transnationally
oriented state-managers and a cadre of supranational institutions such as the
World Bank, the World Trade Organization, the Trilateral Commission, and the
World Economic Forum. Of course, there is still a struggle between descen-
dant national fractions of dominant groups and ascendant transnational fractions. The class practices of a new global ruling class are becoming condensed
in an emergent transnational state in which members of the transnational capitalist class have an objective existence above any local territories and polities.
The purpose of the transnational ruling class is the valorization and accumulation of capital and the defense and advance of the emergent hegemony of a
global bourgeoisie and a new global capitalist-historical bloc. This historical
bloc is composed of the transnational corporations and financial institutions,
the elites that manage the supranational economic planning agencies, major
forces in the dominant political parties, media conglomerates, and technocratic

elites. This does not mean that competition and conflict have come to an end
or that there exists a real unity within the emergent transnational capitalist
class. Competition among rivals is still fierce and the United States is playing
a leadership role on behalf of the transnational elite, defending the interests of
the emergent global capitalist-historical bloc.

Of course, there are scholars who would argue—incorrectly in our view—
that Robinson is making a case for the growing unimportance and irrelevance
of the nation-state in global politics. This would be to misunderstand what
Robinson is trying to say. Clearly, in Robinson's work the nation-state plays
a central role, but one that is being reconfigured by current forces and relations of globalized capital. Feldman and Lotz (2004) are worth quoting on
this issue *in extenso*:

> Recent globalization of production and commerce, by contrast, has been struc-
> turally dependent upon the role of transnational corporations, which are no
> longer based upon a particular nation-state. This does not mean that the role of
> the nation-state has become superfluous, or that inter-imperialist rivalries have
> been transcended. But it does indicate that economic development is no longer
> based upon rival trading and political empires that aim at the protection of the
> interests of monopoly capital. Instead, because the growth of global corpora-
> tions, capital has become a more integrated economic system. This is expressed
> by the development of international financial institutions, such as the World
> Bank and the International Monetary Fund and the creation of the World Trade
> Organization. . . . The development of global capital represents a new phase in
> the imperialist stage of capitalism. For what is occurring is the intensification
> of the exploitation of the labor of those subordinated and dominated countries
> within the world economy. In this sense, imperialism remains an expression of
> a relation of exploitation and oppression of oppressed nations, despite the im-
> portant gain of political independence in the period of colonial liberation. But
> the content of this imperialism is no longer primarily based upon antagonistic
> and rival national monopoly capitals, but the forces of the TNCs. These new
> conditions are generally upheld by the nation-state.

Arundhati Roy (2004) strikingly captures the dynamic between the state
and capital in the following remarks:

> On the global stage, beyond the jurisdiction of sovereign governments, interna-
> tional instruments of trade and finance oversee a complex system of multilateral
> laws and agreements that have entrenched a system of appropriation that puts
> colonialism to shame. This system allows the unrestricted entry and exit of mas-
> sive amounts of speculative capital—hot money—into and out of third world
> countries, which then effectively dictates their economic policy. Using the threat
> of capital flight as a lever, international capital insinuates itself deeper and
> deeper into these economies. Giant transnational corporations are taking control

of their essential infrastructure and natural resources, their minerals, their water, their electricity. The World Trade Organization, the World Bank, the International Monetary Fund, and other financial institutions like the Asian Development Bank, virtually write economic policy and parliamentary legislation. With a deadly combination of arrogance and ruthlessness, they take their sledgehammers to fragile, interdependent, historically complex societies, and devastate them. All this goes under the fluttering banner of "reform."

As a consequence of this reform, in Africa, Asia, and Latin America, thousands of small enterprises and industries have closed down, millions of workers and farmers have lost their jobs and land. The *Spectator* newspaper in London assures us that "[w]e live in the happiest, healthiest and most peaceful era in human history." Billions wonder: who's "we"? Where does he live? What's his Christian name?

This dynamic works along the singular trajectory of capitalist logic. Just as public capital is used to finance private investment risk, the profits of which are not returned to the public but line the pockets of the private investors, so too the nation-state cannot challenge the power of corporate finance, but is compelled to defend it. Roy (2004) puts it this way:

> The thing to understand is that modern democracy is safely premised on an almost religious acceptance of the nation-state. But corporate globalization is not. Liquid capital is not. So, even though capital needs the coercive powers of the nation-state to put down revolts in the servants' quarters, this set up ensures that no individual nation can oppose corporate globalization on its own.

Marxists have long recognized the dangers of the rule of capital and the exponentiality of its expansion into all spheres of the lifeworld. Today, capital is in command of the world order as never before, as new commodity circuits and the increased speed of capital circulation work to extend and globally secure capital's reign of terror. The site where the concrete determinations of industrialization, corporations, markets, greed, patriarchy, and technology all come together—the center where exploitation and domination are fundamentally articulated—is occupied by capital. The insinuation of the coherence and logic of capital into everyday life—and the elevation of the market to sacerdotal status, as the paragon of all social relationships—is something that has successfully occurred and the economic restructuring that we are witnessing today offers both new fears concerning capital's inevitability and some new possibilities for organizing against it. Critical pedagogy is, I maintain, a necessary (but not sufficient) possibility.

Particularly during the Reagan years, hegemonic practices and regulatory forces that had undergirded postwar capitalism were dramatically destabilized. And it is an ongoing process. The halcyon days before the arrival of the New Leviathan of globalization—when liberal Keynesian policy-making established at least a provisional social safety net—have been replaced by pan-national structures of production and distribution and communication technologies that enable a "warp speed capitalism" of instant worldwide financial transactions. According to Scott Davies and Neil Guppy (1997), one of the central tenets of the neoliberal argument is that schools must bring their policies and practices in line with the importance of knowledge as a form of production. According to the neoliberal educationalists, schools are largely to blame for economic decline, and educational reform must therefore be responsive to the postindustrial labor market and restructured global economy.

Business has been given a green light to restructure schooling for their own purposes, as the image of *homo economicus* drives educational policy and practice and as corporations and transnational business conglomerates and their political bedfellows become the leading rationalizing forces of educational reform. Davies and Guppy (1997) argue that globalization has also led schools to stress closer links between school and the workplace in order to develop skills training and "lifelong learning." In a knowledge-intensive economy, schools can no longer provide the skills for a lifetime career. This means that schools are called upon by the market-oriented educational thinkers to focus more on adult learners through enterprise-based training. And further, schools are called upon to teach new types of skills and knowledge.

It is growing more common to hear the refrain: "education is increasingly too important to be left to the educators," as governments make strong efforts at intervention to ensure schools play their part in rectifying economic stagnation and ensuring global competitiveness. And standardized tests are touted as the means to ensure that the educational system is aligned well with the global economy. There is also a movement to develop international standardized tests, creating pressures toward educational convergence and standardization among nations. Such an effort, note Davies and Guppy (1997), provides a form of surveillance that allows nation-states to justify their extended influence and also serves to homogenize education across regions and nations. School choice initiatives have emerged in an increasing number of nations in North America and Europe, sapping the strength of the public school system and helping to spearhead educational privatization.

Because capital has itself invaded almost every sphere of life in the United States, the focus of the educational left has been distracted for the most part from the great class struggles that have punctuated this century. The leftist agenda now rests almost entirely on an understanding of asymmetrical gender and ethnic relations. While this focus surely is important, class struggle is now perilously viewed as an outdated issue. When social class is discussed, it is usually viewed as relational, not as oppositional. In the context of discussions of "social status" rather than "class struggle," technoelite curriculum innovation has secured a privileged position that is functionally advantageous to the socially reproductive logic of entrepreneurial capitalism, private ownership, and the personal appropriation of social production. This neoliberal dictatorship of the comprador elite has resecured a monopoly on resources held by the transnational ruling class and their allies in the culture industry. The very meaning of freedom has come to refer to the freedom to structure the distribution of wealth and to exploit workers more easily across national boundaries by driving down wages to their lowest common denominator and by eviscerating social programs designed to assist laboring humanity. Territories that were once linked to national interests have given way to networks inscribed within world markets largely independent of any national political constraints. History, the economy, and politics no longer are bound together in a secure fashion but operate in the perfervid imaginations of our cultural studies scholars as if they constituted independent spheres. Yet behind this chimera of separation is the transnationalization of the means of production.

What should today's global educators make of the structural power embodied within new forms of today's transnational capital, especially in terms of the shift in the relation between nation-states and formerly nation-based classes, the scope of economic restructuring and its ability to erode the power of organized labor, and the extent to which global mass migrations pit groups in fierce competition over very scarce resources. Robinson and Harris (2000) note that the transnational elite has now been able to put democracy in the place of dictatorship (what can be called the neoliberal state) in order to perform at the level of the nation-state the following functions: adopting fiscal and monetary policies that guarantee macroeconomic stability; providing the necessary infrastructure for global capitalist circuitry and flows; and securing financial control for the transnational comprador elite as the nation-state moves more solidly in the camp of neoliberalism, while maintaining the illusion of "national interests" and concerns with "foreign competition." In fact, the concept of "national interests" and the term "democracy" themselves function as an ideological ruse to enable authoritarian regimes to move with a relative lack of contestation toward a transformation into elite polyarchies. So many of the literary practices in today's schools are functionally linked to this new global economy—such as "cooperative learning" and developing "communities of good citizens"—and promote a convenient alliance between the new fast capitalism and conventional cognitive science. While these new classroom measures are helping to design and analyze symbols, they are also being co-opted by and facilitating the new capitalism.

FAREWELL TO ALL THAT

These days it is far from fashionable to be a radical educator. The political gambit of progressive educators in this time of empire appears as silence in the face of chaos, with the hope that the worst will soon pass. There are not many direct heirs to the Marxist tradition among leftist educational scholars in the United States. To identify your politics as Marxist—especially in the slip-stream of the recent terrorist attacks of September 11 and the bombastic odes to the military machine and the United States' unilateral quest to create a New World Order that are now suffusing U.S. politics—is to invite derision and ridicule from many quarters, including many on the Left. It is to open one's work to all species of dyspeptic criticism, from crude hectoring to sophisti-cated Philippics. Charges range from being a naïve leftist to being stuck in a time warp, to being hooked on an antediluvian patriarch, to giving in to cheap sentimentality or romantic utopianism. Marxists are accused with assuming an untenable political position that enables them to wear the mantle of the revo-lutionary without having to get their hands dirty in the day-to-day struggles of rank-and-file teachers who occupy the front lines in the schools of our major urban centers. Marxist analysis is also frequently derided as elitist in its sup-posed impenetrable esotericism, and if you happen to teach at a university your work can easily be dismissed as dysphoric ivory tower activism—even by other education scholars who also work in universities. Critics often make as-sumptions that you are guilty of being terminally removed from the lives of teachers and students until proven otherwise. Some of the criticism is produc-tive and warranted but much of it is a desperate attempt to dismiss serious challenges to capitalism—to displace work that attempts to puncture the aura of inevitability surrounding global capitalism. While some criticism is sub-stantive—including a welcomed critique of the enciphered language of some academics and a challenge to radical educators to come up with concrete pedagogical possibilities—much of it is small-minded and petty. The benefi-ciaries of the current disunity among the educational left are the business-education partnerships and the privatization of schooling initiatives that are currently following in the wake of larger neoliberal strategies.

Marxist educationalists maintain that neoliberal ideology as it applies to schooling is often given ballast by poststructuralist-postmodernist/ deconstructive approaches to educational reform because many of these ap-proaches refuse to challenge the rule of capital and the social relations of pro-duction as the basis of the capitalist state. Neoliberalism ("capitalism with the gloves off," or "socialism for the rich") refers to a corporate domination of society that supports state enforcement of the unregulated market, engages in the oppression of nonmarket forces and antimarket policies, guts free public services, eliminates social subsidies, offers limitless concessions to transnational corporations, enthrones a neomercantilist public policy agenda, establishes the market as the patron of educational reform, and permits private interests to control most of social life in the pursuit of profits for the few (i.e., through lowering taxes on the wealthy, scrapping environmental regulations, and dismantling public education and social welfare programs). It is undeniably one of the most dangerous politics that we face today.

Neoliberal free-market economics—the purpose of which is to avoid stasis and keep businesses in healthy flux—functions as a type of binding arbitration, legitimizing a host of questionable practices and outcomes: deregulation, unrestricted access to consumer markets, downsizing, outsourcing, flexible arrangements of labor, intensification of competition among transnational corporations, increasing centralization of economic and political power, and finally, widening class polarization. As Dave Hill and Mike Cole (2001) have noted, neoliberalism advocates a number of pro-capitalist positions: that the state privatize ownership of the means of production, including private-sector involvement in welfare and social, educational, and other state services (such as the prison industry); sell labor-power for the purposes of creating a "flexible" and poorly regulated labor market; advance a corporate managerialist model for state services; allow the needs of the economy to dictate the principal aims of school education; suppress the teaching of oppositional and critical thought that would challenge the rule of capital; support a curriculum and pedagogy that produces compliant, pro-capitalist workers; and make sure that schooling and education ensure the ideological and economic reproduction that benefits the ruling class.

Of course, the business agenda for schools can be seen in growing public-private partnerships, the burgeoning business sponsorships for schools, and business "mentoring" and corporatization of the curriculum (McLaren and Farahmandpur 2001a, 2001b) and calls for national standards, regular national tests, voucher systems, accountability schemes, financial incentives for high-performance schools, and "quality control" of teaching. Schools are encouraged to provide better "value for money" and must seek to learn from the entrepreneurial world of business or risk going into receivership. In short, neoliberal educational policy operates from the premise that education is primarily a subsector of the economy.

In this interregnum, in particular, where the entire social universe of capital is locked up in the commodity form, where capital's internal contradictions have created a global division of labor that appears astonishingly insurmountable, and where the ecological stakes for human survival have shifted in such seismic proportions, creating a vortex in which reactionary terrorism has unleashed its unholy cry, we lament the paucity of critical-pedagogical approaches to interrogating the vagaries of everyday life within capital's social universe.

In retrospect, progressive educators are often wont to ask: Were the 1960s the last opportunity for popular revolutionary insurgency on a grand scale to be successful? Did the political disarray of prodigious dimensions that followed in the wake of the rebuff of the post-1968 leftist intelligentsia by the European proletariat condemn the revolutionary project and the "productionist" meta-narrative of Marx to the dustbin of history? Have the postmodernist emendations of Marxist categories and the rejection—for the most part—of the Marxist project by the European and North American intelligentsia signaled the abandonment of hope in revolutionary social change? Can the schools of today build a new social order?

A nagging question has sprung to the surface of the debate over schooling and the new capitalist order: Can a renewed and revivified critical pedagogy distinctly wrought by a historical materialist approach to educational reform serve as a point of departure for a politics of resistance and counterhegemonic struggle in the twenty-first century? And if we attempt to uncoil this question and take seriously its full implications, what can we learn from the legacy and struggle of revolutionary social movements? The fact that Marxist analysis has been discredited within the educational precincts of capitalist America does not defray the substance of these questions. On the surface, there are certain reasons to be optimistic. Critical pedagogy has, after all, joined antiracist and feminist struggles in order to articulate a democratic social order built around the imperatives of diversity, tolerance, and equal access to material resources. But surely such a role, while commendable as far as it goes, has seen critical pedagogy severely compromise an earlier, more radical commitment to anti-imperialist struggle that we often associate with the antiwar movement of the 1960s and earlier revolutionary movements in Latin America.

What does the historical materialist approach often associated with an earlier generation of social critics offer educators who work in critical education? I raise this question at a time in which it is painfully evident that critical pedagogy and its political partner and rough congener, multicultural education, no longer serve as an adequate social or pedagogical platform from which to mount a vigorous challenge to the current social division of labor and its effects on the socially reproductive function of schooling in late capitalist society. In fact, critical pedagogy no longer enjoys its status as a herald for democracy, as a clarion call for revolutionary praxis, as a language of critique and possibility in the service of a radical democratic imaginary, which was its promise in the late 1970s and early 1980s. Part of this has to do with the lack of class analysis evinced in its work, but it also is related to the general retreat of the educational left in the United States over the last several decades.

POSTMODERNIST THEORY AND THE DISAPPEARANCE OF CLASS

It is impossible to disclose all the operative principles of critical pedagogy. Suffice it here to underscore several of its salient features. Critical pedagogy's basic project over the last several decades has been to adumbrate the problems and opportunities of political struggle through educational means. It is incoherent to conceptualize critical pedagogy, as do many of its current exponents, without its enmeshment within anticapitalist struggle. Once considered by the faint-hearted guardians of the American dream as a term of opprobrium for its powerful challenge to the bedrock assumptions characterizing the so-called U.S. 'meritocracy', critical pedagogy has become so completely psychologized, so liberally humanized, so technologized, and so conceptually postmodernized that its current relationship to broader liberation struggles seems severely attenuated if not fatally terminated. While its urgency was once unignorable, and its hard-bitten message had the pressure of absolute *fiat* behind it, critical pedagogy seemingly has collapsed into an ethical licentiousness and a complacent relativism that has displaced the struggle against capitalist exploitation with its emphasis on the multiplicity of interpersonal forms of oppression.

The conceptual net known as critical pedagogy has been cast so wide and at times so cavalierly that it has come to be associated with anything dragged up out of the troubled and infested waters of educational practice, from classroom furniture organized in a "dialogue friendly" circle to "feel-good" curricula designed to increase students' self-image. It's multicultural education equivalent can be linked to a politics of diversity that includes "respecting difference" through the celebration of "ethnic" holidays and themes such as "black history month" and "Cinco de Mayo." I am scarcely the first to observe that critical pedagogy has been badly undercut by practitioners who would mischaracterize its fundamental project. In fact, if the term "critical pedagogy" is refracted onto the stage of current educational debates, we have to judge it as having been largely domesticated in a manner that many of its early exponents, such as Brazil's Paulo Freire, so strongly feared.

Arguably the vast majority of educationalists who are committed to critical pedagogy and multicultural education propagate versions of it that identify with own their bourgeois class interests. One doesn't have to question the integrity or competence of these educators or dismiss their work as disingenuous—for the most part it is not—to conclude that their articulations of critical pedagogy and multicultural education have been accommodated to mainstream versions of liberal humanism and progressivism. While early exponents of critical pedagogy were denounced for their polemical excesses and radical political trajectories, a new generation of critical educators has since that time emerged who have largely adopted what could be described as a pluralist approach to social antagonisms. These educators' work celebrates the "end of history," and the critique of global capitalism is rarely, if ever, brought into the debate. These pedagogues primarily see capital as sometimes maleficent, sometimes beneficent, as something that, like a wild stallion, can eventually be tamed and made to serve humanity. Marxism is seen from this perspective as a failed experiment and the teaching of Marx is viewed as something that should be put to rest since the persistence of capital appears to have rendered the old bearded devil obsolete. Apparently no one noticed—or cared to notice—that Marx had outwitted its Cyclopian capitalist foe by clinging to the underbelly of lost revolutionary dreams that have been herded out of the caves of the Eastern Bloc. After biding time for the last decade—a period that witnessed a particularly virulent example of capital's slash-and-burn policy—his ghost is reappearing in reinvigorated form in the West (at least among some members of the academic left) where Marx is now seen to have anticipated much about the manner in which the current world-historical crisis of capitalism would manifest itself.

Authoritative as the term may sound, "critical pedagogy" has been extraordinarily misunderstood and misrepresented. To penetrate the glimmering veil of rhetoric surrounding it would require a chapter of its own. Suffice it to say that it is an approach to curriculum production, educational policy making, and teaching practices that challenges the received "hard sciences" conception of knowledge as "neutral" or "objective" and that is directed toward understanding the political nature of education in all of its manifestations in everyday life as these are played out in the agonistic terrain of conflicting and competing discourses, oppositional and hegemonic cultural formations, and social relations linked to the larger capitalist social totality. The critical pedagogy we are envisioning here operates from the premise that capital in its current organizational structure provides the context for working-class struggle. Specifically in the context of school life, capital produces new human productive and intellectual capacities in alienated form.

In its U.S. variants, the genesis of critical pedagogy can be traced to the work of Paulo Freire in Brazil and John Dewey and the social reconstructionists writing in the postdepression years. Its leading exponents have cross-fertilized critical pedagogy with just about every transdisciplinary tradition imaginable, including theoretical forays into the Frankfurt School of critical theory and the work of Richard Rorty, Jacques Lacan, Jacques Derrida, and Michel Foucault. Here the focus has mainly been on a critique of instrumental reason and the nature of governmentality in educational sites. An emphasis has been placed on the nonconceptual in which thinking is constructed as a performance of ethics, or as a post-truth pragmatics, or as an open-ended, nondeterminate process that resists totalizing tropological systems (hence the frequent condemnation of Marxism as an oppressive totalizing meta-narrative). Critical pedagogy's reach now extends to multicultural education, bilingual education, and fields associated with language-learning and literacy (including media literacy). My concern over the last decade has been to introduce Marxist scholarship into the field of critical pedagogy, since it has been taken over by postmodernists who have been attempting to suture together in recent decades the ontological tear in the universe of ideas that was first created when history was split in two by the dialectical wave of Marx's pen in the *Communist Manifesto* and the subsequent development of the communist movement in the mid-1800s. My own Marxism is informed by the philosophy of Marxist-Humanism, which posits, after Hegel, that forward movement emerges from the negation of obstacles. It is the negation of "what is" and a critique of the given that spurs development and creates the path to liberation. Absolute negativity occurs when negativity becomes self-directed and self-related to become the seedbed of the positive. According to *News & Letters* (2002), a Marxist-Humanist publication,

> The key is the difference between the first and second negation—the two moments of the dialectic. The first negation is the negation of the given; it takes what appears positive, the immediate, and imbues it with negativity. The second negation, "the negation of the negation," turns the power of negativity upon the act of negation; it takes what appears negative and shows that it is the source of the truly positive.

It is not my purpose here to develop an exegesis of Marxist-Humanism (one of dozens of identifiable schools of Marxist thought) but merely to draw attention to the ways in which the Marxist tradition has been woefully absent from critical pedagogy as it is engaged in the U.S. academy (i.e., in Colleges of Education or University Departments of Education)—an absence that has brought with it irreparable damage to the tradition of critical education. Unscrolling the present state of critical pedagogy and examining its depotentiated contents, processes, and formations puts progressive educators on notice in that few contemporary critical educators are either willing or able to ground their pedagogical imperatives in the concept of labor in general, and in Marx's labor theory of value in particular. This is certainly more the case in North American educational settings than it is in the United Kingdom, the latter context having had a much more serious and salutary engagement with the Marxist tradition in the social sciences and in one of its professional offshoots: adult education.

In the United States, critical pedagogy has collapsed into left liberal attempts by progressive educators to remediate the educational enterprise. This has resulted in a long list of reform initiatives that include creating "communities of learners" in classrooms; bridging the gap between student culture and the culture of the school; engaging in cross-cultural understandings; integrating multicultural content and teaching across the curriculum; developing techniques for reducing racial prejudice and conflict-resolution strategies; challenging Eurocentric teaching and learning as well as the "ideological formations" of European immigration history by which many white teachers judge African American, Latino/Latina, and Asian students; challenging the meritocratic foundation of public policy that purportedly is politically neutral and racially color-blind; creating teacher-generated narratives as a way of analyzing teaching from a "transformative" perspective; improving academic achievement in culturally diverse schools; affirming and utilizing multiple perspectives and ways of teaching and learning; and de-reifying the curriculum and exposing "meta-narratives of exclusion." Most of these pedagogical initiatives are acting upon the recommendations of the National Commission on Teaching and America's Future—a commission bent upon challenging social class and ethnicity as primary determinants of student success. And for all the sincere attempts to create a social justice agenda by attacking asymmetries of power and privilege and dominant power arrangements in U.S. society, progressive teachers have, unwittingly, operated under the assumption that these changes can be accomplished within the existing social universe of capital. Critical pedagogy has been taken out of the business of class analysis and focused instead on a postmodernist concern with a politics of difference and inclusion that effectively substitutes truth for singular, subjective judgment and silences historical materialism as the unfolding of class struggle (Ebert 2002).

The aforementioned is unavoidably a sweeping synthesis of the limitations of critical pedagogy in the North American context. The main bone of contention that I have with the direction of increasingly postmodernized critical pedagogy over the last several decades is its studied attempt to leave the issue of sexism and racism—that is, the politics of difference—unconnected to class struggle. Of course, this conveniently draws attention away from the crucially important ways in which women and people of color provide capitalism with its superexploited labor pools—a phenomenon that is on the upswing all over the world. E. San Juan Jr. (2002) sees the continuing racialization of American national identity occurring in novel ways as long as citizenship is based on individual rights that are needed to legitimate private property and to further capital accumulation. Capitalism *is* an overarching totality that is, unfortunately, becoming increasingly invisible in postmodernist narratives that eschew and reject such categories *tout court*. Postmodernist educators tend to ignore that capitalism is a ruthless "totalizing process which shapes our lives in every conceivable aspect" and that "even leaving aside the direct power wielded by capitalist wealth in the economy and in the political state" capitalism also subjects all "social life to the abstract requirements of the market, through the commodification of life in all its aspects." This makes a "mockery" out of all aspirations to "autonomy, freedom of choice, and democratic self-government" (Wood 1995, pp. 262–263).

In this fundamental regard, the voguish academic brigandism of educational postmodernists that gives primacy to incommensurability as the touchstone of analysis and explanation has diverted critical analysis from the global sweep of advanced capitalism and the imperialist exploitation of the world's laboring class. Their pedagogically distilled animosity toward Marxism is no secret. This is not the time to evaluate the jousts between Marxists and postmodernists for the spoils of the critical edition (see Cole, Hill, McLaren, and Rikowski 2001). Suffice it to say that in the years that "difference politics" have taken hold of the Left, the rich are getting richer and the poor even poorer in every part of the globe.

OBSTACLES TO A MARXIST EDUCATION

Accompanied by what some have described as the "particular universalism" of Marxist analysis as opposed to the "universal particularism" of the postmodernists, critical educators collectively assert—all with their own unique focus and distinct disciplinary trajectory—that the term "social justice" all too frequently operates as a cover for legitimizing capitalism or for tacitly admitting to or resigning oneself to its brute intractability. Consequently, it is essential to develop a counterpoint to the way in which social justice is used in progressive education by inviting students to examine critically the epistemological and axiological dimensions of social democracy so that they might begin to reclaim public life from its embeddedness in the corporate-academic-complex (McLaren and Houston, in press).

Amidst the Bush regime's star-spangled war on hope and freedom, the post-Marxists and anti-Marxist educationalists have intensified their assault on attempts to rethink critical pedagogy from an anticapitalist perspective. J. Martin Rochester's (2003) "Critical Demogogues: The Writings of Henry Giroux and Peter McLaren," published in the Hoover Institute's flagship education journal *Education Next*, represents a neoconservative assault on critical pedagogy for contributing to the development of a left-wing anti-intellectualism by means of emphasizing ideology over inquiry. For Rochester, critical pedagogy is nothing less than a "chiliastic movement." Instead of participating in pernicious forms of ideological indoctrination, the role that Rochester has set for pedagogy should be, "to reaffirm education as that which promotes, in the words of an 1830 Yale University report, 'the discipline and furniture of the mind.'" Rochester contends that it is impossible to teach a social justice agenda and at the same time foster "a solid foundation of knowledge and understanding, a love of learning, and the tools for pursuing that learning." The latter, not the former, should be the first principle of education. The debates over values and truths should, Rochester argues, "be guided by a disposition toward objectivity, the spirit of free inquiry, and academic integrity rather than by chiliastic movements." According to this languid logic, not even history-shaking movements such as a national literacy movement can ever be guided by anything but craven self-interest and therefore revolution always makes for bad pedagogy. What doesn't get explored by Rochester is exactly what is meant by the term "ideology." As criticalists surely know, ideology achieves its purpose when it is able to erase evidence of its presence, and often we are aware of its presence only retroactively, when it has exhausted its welcome and is replaced with another offspring. A plenipotentiary of the conservative restoration, Rochester lives in a perfumed world where pedagogy is taught from the Mount Olympus of objectivity, a perspective that itself is shrouded in a debilitating epistemological positivism.

For rabid anti-Marxists like C. A. "Chet" Bowers (in press, 2003b, 2003a, 2001), master narratives, universalism, and objectivity—disparaged as European Enlightenment ideals—must be rejected for their Eurocentrism associated with European economic, social, and political dominance. Bowers is part of a group of enduringly deep-seated antagonists of critical pedagogy, the writings of which he lumps together as a convenient way of minimizing the often considerable differences (differences that include basic assumptions about the role of capital) that mark the various strands of critical pedagogy. Bowers's simultaneous tongue-lashing of Marxist universalism and tongue-polishing of postmodern "difference" resembles that of postmodern pundit and critical pedagogy opponent Patti Lather (1991, 1998).

All that is bad about critical pedagogy can, in Bowers's view, be laid at the feet of its peccant father, Paulo Freire, whose work amounts in Bowers's view to little more than a cultural imperialist assault from the south. What gives Bowers the megrims and compels him to bloviate in his trademark fashion of substituting substantive critique with flummery is critical pedagogy's supposed attack on all things traditional. And what makes Bowers's work a form of reactionary anti-imperialism is not his focus on conserving natural systems (we agree that it is necessary to recognize what needs to be conserved and to discriminate between forms of conservatism that promote justice and those that perpetuate injustice) but his failure to offer more than a hidebound denunciation of critical pedagogy as an ethnocentric critique that fails to comprehend the cultural roots of ecological crisis (citing, all the while, his own work as the antidote), that colonizes the commons with universalistic "god words" and "cliches," that works against the self-sufficiency of Indigenous groups (and retards their revitalization in the process), and that asserts that any and all traditions must be overthrown by means of critical thinking. Not only has Bowers recycled the same pervicacious critique of critical pedagogy for decades (which would be understandable if critical pedagogy had remained frozen in time), in misprizing its Marxist dimensions (which are not as readily embraced by all critical pedagogues), he has misunderstood the dialectical theory and humanism that undergirds its most radical formulations—a dialectical humanism that speaks both to innovation and to conservation. Ensorcelled by the mistaken assumptions he has harbored for so long about Marxism, Bowers prolongs his own ignorance and that of his gullible readers about the fundamentals of Marx's work. Skimming the surface of critical pedagogy like a hovercraft navigating a swamp, his work (in press) either overgeneralizes or cites ideas out of context. His detached regard for philosophical understanding is perhaps best seen in his erroneous view that Marx accepts "that change is linear and inherently progressive in nature" leading to some future industrial Cockaigne. Further, Bowers stubbornly rejects the notion (if indeed it registers in his thinking at all) that dialectical reasoning involves a two-way movement from practice and from theory that breaks through the false universalism of bourgeois liberalism that he so distains as "politically correct." Consequently, his oleaginous punditry, marked as much by an aura of self-importance as by an antimodern and counter-Enlightenment antifoundationalism, balefully discovers commonality with reactionary incarnations of postmodernism. His antiliberal agon hides itself under a veneer of progressive conservatism but which echoes the remark made by the philosopher Carl Schmitt: "whoever invokes humanity lies" (cited in Skolnik 2004, p. 5). Yet in Bowers's very denunciation of Marxist "interpretive schema," "formulaic thinking," "cultural assumptions," "lexicon," and "the 'transformative' dynamics of the industrial culture," he recuperates his own abstract valorization of difference, effectively making the relative *absolute*, and the absolute *relative*. It is difficult to read Bowers's blustering, fuel-injected tirades without feeling that acrimony intensifies his own delectation.

Postmodernists often associate universalism with European imperialism and colonialism that marked the Spanish, Portuguese, and British conquest of the Americas and consider their universal values to exercise forms of violence against Indigenous voices and traditional practices. However, Willie Thompson reminds us that atrocities committed by these imperialists were not justified by a reliance on specific universal discourses similar to the Enlightenment ideas. In fact, Enlightenment thinkers frequently stressed the significance of other cultures' moral and ethical commitments by comparing and contrasting them to their own European origins. According to Thompson (1997),

> The Spanish conquistadors did not require the Enlightenment to commit geno-
> cide upon the populations of the Caribbean, Mexico and Peru and subject the
> remnant to slavery, nor Genghis Khan to do similar things in Central Asia dur-
> ing the earlier period. These acts were committed by cultures with no preten-
> sions to universalism (unless Christianity is to be regarded as such, in which
> case the root of all evil has to be sought a lot further back). (p. 219)

Without universal criteria for evaluating the validity of truth claims, the post-Marxist, antifoundationalists paint themselves into a political corner when confronted by depredations associated with capitalist social relations. Not every truth claim is equally valid, since truth claims conceal asymmetrical social and economic relations. Teresa Ebert (1996) is worth quoting on this issue:

> The question of knowing the "truth" is neither a question of describing some
> "true" metaphysical or ontological "essence" nor a matter of negotiating in-
> commensurable language games, as Lyotard suggests. Rather it is a question of
> dialectical understanding of the dynamic relations between superstructure and
> base: between ideology—(mis)representations, signifying practices, discourses,
> frames of intelligibility, objectives—and the workings of the forces of produc-
> tion and the historical relations of production. Crucial to such a dialectical
> knowledge is ideology critique—a practice for developing class consciousness.
> (p. 47)

By contrast, the post-Marxist emphasis on monadic local efforts at im-
proving resource allocation and warning the public against excessive consumptive practices is not enough to challenge imperial capital's superexploitation of labor (see Ebert 2001). The challenge, it seems to us, must occur on the terrain of the nation-state, which has grown more dependent upon capital than ever before. According to Aijaz Ahmad (1998/1999),

> The currently fashionable postmodern discourse has its own answer: it leaves
> the market fully intact while debunking the nation-state and seeking to dissolve
> it even further into little communities and competitive narcissisms, which some-
> times gets called "multiculturalism." In other words, postmodernism seeks an
> even deeper universalization of the market, while seeking to decompose "social
> humanity" even further, to the point where only the monadic individual remains,
> with no dream but that of, in Jean-François Lyotard's words, "the enjoyment of
> goods and services." Or, to put it somewhat differently: the postmodern utopia
> takes the form of a complementary relationship between universalization of the

market and individualization of commodity fetishisms. This, of course, has been a dream of capitalism since its very inception. (pp. 21–22)

An antifoundationalist cynicism surrounding the telos of human progress often leads post-Marxists such as Bowers to condemn Marxism for its teleological emphasis on historical inevitability. However, the Marxist humanist emphasis on teleology is decidedly nonteleological; it arches toward an eradication of social injustice, poverty, racism, and sexism while recognizing that history is mutable and contingent. Not everything about history was progressive in Marx's estimation. The engine of historical materialism that drove Marx's critique of political economy held that historical progress is never secured or guaranteed but rather moves in and between contradictory and conflicting social spaces and zones of engagement. What concerned Marx was how historical contingencies and social circumstances impacted the way in which human beings engaged the present. Peter Hudis (2004) describes Marx's concept of progress as "development"—that is, as an "immanent unfoldment of the reaching beyond the immediate found in given social formations, which can move in one direction or another, all depending on the interaction between subjective revolt, material conditions, and conceptual understanding" (personal communication).

Alex Callinicos (1989) situates Marx's concept of development where it should be situated: within the overall concept of historical materialism. His following remarks are apposite:

[H]istorical materialism is a non-teleological theory of social evolution: not only does it deny that capitalism is the final stage of historical development, but communism, the classless society which Marx believed would be the outcome of socialist revolution, is not the inevitable consequences of the contradictions of capitalism, since an alternative exists, what Marx called "the mutual ruination of the contending classes." (p. 36)

The question of universalism is directly posed by Samir Amin (1996): "How are we to create conditions that allow the genuine advance of universalist values beyond their formulations by historical capitalism?" (p. 8). The answer is not to be found in local or regional communal struggles alone. For instance, Boris Kagarlitsky (2000) advocates a "hierarchy of strategic priorities" that is committed to "a real equality of people in the movement" (p. 71). He articulates the struggle as encompassing a multiplicity of social movements, all centered around the defeat of capitalism:

We must realize our ecological project; we must affirm women's rights and minorities' rights through and in the process of anticapitalist struggle, not as a substitution or alternative to it. Finally, this does not mean that other movements,

not addressing the central issues of the system, must necessarily be seen as enemies or rivals of socialists. These movements are just as legitimate. Everyone
has the same rights. It means simply that no one must expect the socialist left to
drop its own culture, tradition and, last but not least, its identity for the sake of
"democratic equivalence." (pp. 71–72)

Universal rights are central to the development of a democratic socialist society and should not be jettisoned outright as anti-Marxists such as Bowers
would often have us do. Ahmad (1997) captures the dimensions of this position when he writes:

Contrary to prevailing fashions, I am a shameless advocate of the idea of universality. This is so despite the fact that colonialism has been intrinsic to the
kind of universality that we have had so far and that the only universal civilization that exists today is the capitalist civilization. I think that human beings are
perfectly capable of waking up to the barbarities of this civilization and making
a far better universality—for which my word continues to be "socialism," but
you are welcome to use some other word so long as you mean the same thing.
(p. 57)

We abominate a post-Marxist rejection of universalism, calling instead for
what Kagarlitsky (2000, p. 75) refers to as an "open universalism" based on
a dialogue of cultures. As McLaren and Farahmandpur (in press) have noted,
"universals are not static; they are rooted (routed) in movement. They are
nomadically grounded in living, breathing subjects of history who toil and
who labor under conditions not of their own making." Clearly the limitations
of the Enlightenment project of universalism need to be recognized and prob-
lematized. We are not defending Eurocentrism here, far from it, as it is clear
that Eurocentrism has provided much of Western history with a flimsy veneer
for genocidal acts. The restricted and often dangerously destructive Western
bourgeois character of Enlightenment universalism is a worthy and necessary
object of critique, but to attack the idea of universalism itself is not only fool-
ish but also politically dangerous.

Bruce Robbins (1999) correctly asserts that all universal standards are in
some sense provisional. In other words, they deal with "provisional agreements arrived at by particular agents" (p. 74). He further maintains that universal standards "are provided in a situation of unequal power, and they are
applied in a situation of unequal power" (p. 74). There is no such thing as a
clean universalism that is not tainted by power and interest of some sort. Robbins concludes, "All universalisms are dirty. And it is only dirty universalism
that will help us against the powers and agents of still dirtier ones" (p. 75).
While we resist efforts to police the expression of non-European viewpoints,

we find the politics of postmodern pluralism—that is, providing voice to those marginalized social groups who have been denied political participation—to be only a partial solution that itself needs to become an object of critique. The belief that an increased diversity of marginalized voices will automatically ensure that marginalized social groups will gain social, political, and economic demands and interests is politically naïve. We argue that the struggle for diversity must be accompanied by a transnational revolutionary socialist politics. Kenan Malik (1996) asserts convincingly that postmodernism's refutation of universalism is, for the most part, similar to the crude nineteenth-century racial theories that rejected universal categories and instead emphasized relativism. Malik further adds that "in its hostility to universalism and in its embrace of the particular and the relative, poststructuralism embodies the same romantic notions of human difference as are contained in racial theory" (p. 4). Malik asserts, "While difference can arise from equality, equality can never arise from difference" (p. 4).

Marxist-humanist scholar Peter Hudis has written brilliantly about the cultural and political roots of Marx's alleged Eurocentrism. While there is no question that Hegel was unforgivably Eurocentric (as especially seen from his comments on Africa and China), we follow Hudis (in press) in rejecting the view that Hegelian dialectical reason—which Marx held to be "the source of all dialectic"—is as culture bound and antagonistic to the internal development of non-European societies as many post-Marxists maintain. Of course the work of Hegel and Marx emerged from a specific European context that shaped the variegated aspects of their work. The question that needs to be asked is posed by Hudis (in press) as follows: "whether the *central concepts* that defined Hegel or Marx's thought are *fundamentally* opposed to the internal dynamic and development of non-European societies." Hudis argues that studying the philosophic traditions that have unfolded in the non-Western world will support the view that the dialectical mode of thinking that was universalized by Hegel into a philosophic system has roots *within* non-European societies, including in the Middle East. According to Hudis (in press), the bulk of Marx's writings on non-Western societies do not support the view that Marx held to a unilinear concept of historical progress that emanated from Europe. The tendency to single out selected writings—such as his 1853 writings on India—while ignoring the full range of his work on such subjects persists to this day. Hudis (in press) postulates that the Islamic Abu Ya'qub al-Sijistani, a member of the Ismaili underground mission—the *da'wa*, as it is known in Arabic—that operated in the Iranian province of Khurasan and Sijistan during the tenth century, was the first to use the term "negation of the negation" in extant philosophic literature. Later developed by Hegel, albeit in a radically different context, the concept of the negation of the negation served "as the core of his effort to transcend the antimonies of post-Kantian philosophy" (Hudis in press). Marx also made use of the concept of "the negation of the negation" in his *Economic and Philosophic Manuscripts of 1844* and highlighted the concept in his greatest theoretical work, *Capital*, in discussing "the expropriation of the expropriators" (cited in Hudis, in press). The fact that al-Sijistani dealt with a very different set of problems than did either Hegel or Marx, and that he took the concept of the "negation of the negation" in a decidedly different direction than Hegel himself, should not distract us from recognizing that:

> long before Hegel made "the negation of the negation" a central part of his thought, a major thinker in the Muslim world wrote that there "must be a complete negation . . . in which two negations, negation and a negation of the negation oppose each other." In light of this, the notion that dialectical, negative reason is a "western" fabrication that stands opposed to the development of non-European societies needs to be seriously rethought. (Hudis, in press)

By exploring a few aspects of Marx's "Notebooks on Kovalevsky," which he wrote in the fall of 1879 (keeping in mind that the bulk of Marx's Notebooks was published in 1975 as an appendix to Lawrence Krader's *The Asiatic Mode of Production*; the full text, which is over 100 pages long, was published in German in 1977 by Hans-Peter Harstick as *Karl Marx über Formen vorkapitalistischer Produktion: Vergleichende Studien zur Geschichte des Grundeigentums 1879-80*), Hudis draws attention to Marx's intensive study of non-Western societies in the 1870s, a study that was animated by the question of "how developments in the non-European world could feed into the development of a global revolution against capital." According to Hudis, Marx's writings on Russia in the 1870s and 1880s, his studies of India, Indonesia, and the Muslim world from this period remain little known or discussed. In his 1879 "Notebooks," Marx's comments on Kovalevsky's *The Communal Possession of the Land* is of signal importance. Hudis (in press) reports the following:

> Marx agreed with Kovalevsky's view of the regressive impact of imperialism upon these societies, in contrast to some of his views expressed in his writings on India in the early 1850s. For example, in reference to Kovalevsky's discussion of the means used by the French to rob the Algerians of their land, Marx added: "The means sometimes change, the aim is ever the same: destruction of the indigenous collective property (and its transformation) into an object of free purchase and sale, and by this means the final passage made easier into the hands of the French colonists. Kovalevsky's description of the French effort to destroy the clan-community landholding patters in Algeria evoked from Marx the comment: "The Shameless!"

Hudis further points out that Marx agreed with Kovalevsky's positive view of a communal possession of the land as a possible foundation for a "higher stage of social development." Marx harmonized with Kovalevsky's view that "the British and French imperialists propagated the idea that the monarch was *the* landowner in order to proclaim themselves the rightful inheritor of the communal lands upon subjugating the native rulers" (Hudis, in press). Hudis concludes that, "what Marx most appreciated about Kovalevsky was his refusal to accept at face value the categories used by Europeans to explain non-European societies." Hudis notes that "Marx also attacked the European effort to either impose their laws on Algerian society or to accept 'indigenous' ones on the basis of whether it suited imperialistic self-interest." But at the same time, and this is important, Marx did not refrain from identifying "the presence of internal contradictions *within* indigenous communal formations" (Hudis, in press). Hudis (in press) explains:

> While Marx, as we have seen, rejected the notion that such formations were "backward" in comparison with European private ownership, he did not view indigenous communal formations uncritically. He repeatedly called attention to such factors as castes, chiefs, and inequities of wealth and rank *within* the community. This is seen in his underlining of Kovalevsky's passing comment that some members of the community acquired fertile lands while others did not, leading to increased social stratification.

Therefore, by the 1870s (and most likely as early as the mid-1850s) Marx "viewed the imperialist destruction of precapitalist social formations as being *regressive*" (Hudis in press). In fact, he viewed such native communal formations a possible basis for creating a socialist society without going through capitalistic industrialization. Clearly, the underdeveloped nation was not fated to undergo the ravages of capitalism in order for conditions of human freedom to be established. However, at the same time Marx refused to uncritically glorify indigenous communal forms and their precapitalist relations and remained critical of the dualism that characterized many of them. The communal relations of the isolated peasant village could contain the seed of socialism since they escaped the destructive relations of modern capitalist development but were by no means a guarantee of a future socialism. Hudis (in press) writes:

> On the one hand, they provided a basis for collective interaction and reciprocity that could become a foundation for a future socialist society. Yet on the other hand the indigenous communal formations were also afflicted with an array of social inequities and incipient hierarchies—especially when it came to relations between men and women. Marx paid careful consideration to these

internal contradictions in his *Ethnological Notebooks* especially. Unlike Engels, who tended to uncritically glorify the indigenous communal forms in "primitive" society in his *Origin of the Family, Private Property, and the State*, Marx pointed to the incipient formation of class, caste, and hierarchical social relations within them. Though he singled out the superiority of Iroquois society compared to much of contemporary European societies in his *Ethnological Notebooks*, he did not assume that the presence of communal ownership of land automatically provided women with sexual equality. In several places in his *Ethnological Notebooks* he pointed out limitations to the freedom of women, since even though they had access to political decisions their votes were often only *consultative*.

While Marx's statements on India in 1853 do indeed give the impression of a Eurocentric bias, it is certainly not because his so-called obsession with a traditional Western notion of progress made him indifferent to the suffering of Indians from British imperialism. Pranav Jani (2002) notes that:

> The charge of Eurocentrism, overemphasizing the impact of the AMP [Asiatic Mode of Production] paradigm, misses Marx's real focus, the development of capitalism and the possibility of its overthrow, minimizes the anticolonial dimension of his politics, and does not allow for the fact that the AMP as a paradigm has been rejected by Marxists as the "real history" of colonialism has become apparent. Later writings by Marx and other Marxists contradict the center/periphery model that is the first premise of a Eurocentric argument. (p. 94)

Marx did not view India as an example of undifferentiated Oriental despotism but rather linked the very idea of Oriental despotism to the ideology of European imperialism (Hudis 1983). Hudis offers a summary worth quoting in full:

> Marx had a concept of progress insofar as he viewed tendencies of future social development immanently contained in the present which, given the right set of circumstances, "burst forth" from their integument (it's a notion of immanent development that he absorbed from his studies of Aristotle as well as Hegel, quite early on, in the early 1840s). That Aristotlean-Hegelian notion of "progress" does *not*, however, imply a mechanistic or unilinear concept of progress as such. Marx was always interested in historical periods of transition, as that is when the embryonic forms of the future show themselves in specific social formations and provide *indications*—not out of telological necessity, but as indications of a future course of development. When Marx looked at India in the early 1850s, the negative aspects of what he called "the asiatic mode of production" predominated; and so, as a result, the *impulse* that would set into motion the explosion of its own internal contradictions was seen as coming from

outside, from the impact of imperialism. I don't think that's because Marx *ever* viewed the third world or communal social formations as "backward": I can just imagine him as a young man walking the streets of Trier and noticing this and that residue of earlier communal forms with admiration. Rather, Marx tended to emphasize the negative aspects of the AMOP in the early 1850s because there wasn't yet a revolutionary movement in view in India with which to discern an internal way out of its contradictions. Western imperialism was therefore seen as a disruptive force that would "shake" the "East" out of its "slumber" and awaken its own immanent possibilities for social progression. It comes out *sounding* Eurocentric, because, after all, the stress is placed on the acts of the Europeans as the "prime mover"; and since the Europeans had by then absorbed the prejudice that historic initiative begins and ends with them, Marx's comments easily get read as being in the traditional line of western rationalist thought. (personal communication)

The whole concept of the Asiatic Mode of Production was a means of enabling Marx to "probe into the internal social relations of Asian nations, through the explication of those elements which pointed towards a transformation of that despotic form of production into new relations of human freedom" (Hudis 1983, pp. 14–15). It is important to understand how Marx's aversion to "naturalism" and his particular characterization and defense of "civilization" shaped what liberation theologian Jose Miranda (1980) calls his "intransigent occidentalism." Marx admittedly held to the notion that "barbarians" must enter "civilization," but before one renders judgment on this viewpoint it is important to understand what Marx actually meant by the term "barbarians" and what he meant by "civilization." In his classic work *Marx against the Marxists* (1980), Miranda explains the rationale behind Marx's use of these terms to those who might be scandalized by their seemingly racist and Eurocentric characteristics. Primitive communism and the absence of private property were not as important to Marx as becoming civilized or being uprooted "from the idiocy of natural circumstances" (Miranda 1980, p. 247). Capitalist development, in Marx's view, helped to break down the isolation of certain areas of the world. A fundamental aspect of Marx's thesis was that "the true bearer of western civilization is the socialist revolution" (Miranda 1980, p. 250). Marx believed that Western civilization would absolutely perish without communism. Marx was concerned, first and foremost, with challenging the dehumanizing conditions that force individuals to enter into relations independent of their will. The fight against barbarism was, for Marx, the fight against the ruling classes who, as "accomplices of the barbarian powers" wished "to snatch the banner of western civilization away" (Miranda 1980, pp. 250, 251). Marx believed that "capitalism produces the material means to eliminate not only its own form of human exploitation but also all the forms of exploitation that have existed in history" (Miranda 1980, p. 273). Barbarians were not limited to non-European peasants. There was no racism involved here. According to Miranda, Marx labeled both Europeans and non-European Indigenous groups barbarians if they displayed "the conduct of ruffians and swindlers, the assertion of the right of the strongest" (Miranda 1980, p. 253). Marx's concept of civilization represents, in Miranda's view, essentially the conditions for a moral life, a place where human beings are "capable of making decisions for themselves" (p. 254). Clearly, Marx felt that peasant life was an "endlessly repeated and loathsome cycle" (Miranda 1980, p. 255) where the conditions were not nearly ripe enough for individuals to become a self-reflective subjects of history. Yet Miranda emphasizes Marx's belief that *all people* are capable of developing themselves and reaching full civilization and communism. And here the term civilization is meant to refer to "the higher interest of human self-realization" (Mészáros 1986, p. 206). This struggle can only lead to victory if it is carried out by representatives of a universal class who are not capable of nor inclined to act according to exploitative or sectional interests. Mészáros (1986) writes that:

> Marx is . . . not concerned with establishing a social order simply on the basis of the *de facto* effective power of the majority to subdue the sectional interest of the formerly ruling minority, but with the superiority *de jure* of socialism over capitalism, defined as the ability to release the energies of self-realization in all individuals, as against capitalism which must deny to them the possibility of self-realization in the interest of the unhampered "self-expansion of capital," no matter how destructive its consequences. (p. 208)

THE RUSE OF REDUCTIONISM

We must refrain from falling into the trap of approaching Marx's concept of the "economic structure of society" from a technological-reductionist interpretation that we see in the puerile understanding of Marx by Bowers and others. The work of Istvan Mészáros (1986, 1995, 1999, 2003) is helpful here. According to Mészáros, the widespread idea that Marxism is a crude economic reductionism according to which the functioning of the superstructure is directly and mechanically determined by the economic structures of society represents a truncated interpretation of Marx. And with respect to the unfolding of history, Mészáros (1986) is correct when he states that a Marxist conception of progress does not view history as some kind of "hidden destiny" that is "foreshadowed from time immemorial" but rather "the *objective telos* of the unfolding historical process that itself produces such possibilities of human self-emancipation from the tyranny of the material base which are by no means anticipated from the outset" (p. 181). He offers a further clarification:

> Nor is it [history] simply a self-propelling material determination that produces the positive result of the "suspension of the basis itself." On the contrary, at a crucial point in the course of the historical development a *conscious break* must be made in order to alter radically the destructive course of the ongoing process. (p. 181)

Mészáros (1986) also notes that:

> capital's universalizing tendency can *never* come to real fruition within its own framework, since capital must declare the barriers which it cannot transcend— namely its own structural limitations—to be the "sacred limit" of all production. At the same time, what indeed should be recognized and respected as a vitally important objective determination—nature in all its complexity as "men's real body"—is totally disregarded in the systematic subjugation, degradation and ultimate destruction of nature. (p. 183)

Clearly human emancipation is not guaranteed by history, by some "spontaneous unfolding of material inevitability" (Mészáros 1986, p. 185). Any radically new mode of social intercourse and mode of production can only bring about "free, unobstructed, progressive and universal" development of social life if it is accomplished outside of the current law of value. Mészáros warns: "Without a *conscious* break from the *tyranny of the material base* necessitated by this transfer, the 'universalizing tendency' we can witness in the ever-more-chaotic interlocking of the global intercourse can only assert its destructive potentialities, given the impossibility of a viable overall control on the basis of capital's own 'presuppositions'" (p. 184).

CRITICAL PEDAGOGY RELOADED: CONTEMPORARY CHALLENGES

Critical pedagogy has had a tumultuous relationship with the dominant education community both in North America (McLaren 1997) and the United Kingdom (Allman 1999, 2001a) for the past twenty-five years. Clearly, on both sides of the Atlantic, the educational community has been aprioristically antagonistic to Marxist critique, effectively undercutting the development of Marxist criticism in education. Many of the current attempts to muster a progressive educational agenda among education scholars is suffused with an anticommunist bias. Only occasionally is the excessive rejectionism of Marxism by postmodern educationalists accompanied by analysis; rarely is it ever accomplished beyond the level of fiat. To borrow a commentary that Barbara Foley (1998) directs at the post-Marxism of Laclau and Mouffe, "it conflates politics with epistemology in an irrevocably linked chain of signifiers: the authoritarian party equals class reductionism equals logocentricity; totality equals totalitarianism."

I do not wish to rehearse this decidedly potted history here in any great detail, and as such will forgo a prolegomenon about critical pedagogy, since a polycondensation of its attributes will serve little purpose other than adding cumbersomely to its growing theoretical weight or rehashing what I assume most progressive educators already know or about which they at least have some working idea. Suffice it to say that in the mid-1970s to mid-1980s the role of critical pedagogy was much more contestatory than in the decade of the 1990s with respect to dominant social and economic arrangements. Critical pedagogy has always had an underground rapport with the working class, a rapport that virtually disappeared post-1989. In contrast to its current incarnation, the veins of critical pedagogy were not in need of defrosting in the early 1980s but were pumped up with Marxist-inspired work coming from the Birmingham School of Contemporary Cultural Studies, as well as a reengagement with the work of Dewey, Freire, and the Frankfurt School. During that time, critique flowed generally unimpeded and was directed not just at isolated relations of domination but at the totality of social relations. That it was often conflated with liberation theology in Latin America and with anti-imperialist struggle worldwide accounts for its failure to be preconized in the cultural chambers of the ruling elite. My major point here is that the debates over educational reform are far richer today when seen through the palimpsest of Marxist critique. Marxist critique serves as a counterpoint to the subversive acts of the proto-Foucauldians and Derrideans, who, garbed in the theoretical attire of Ninja academics, relish in foot-sweeping the metaphysics propping up the "totalitarian certainties" of the Marxist problematic, dismembering "totalities" by inworming them and opening them up to multiple destinies other than those circumscribed by Marx.

The point is not that the gallery-hoping titans and fierce deconstructors from the postmodern salons have not made some important contributions to a fin de siècle politics, or that they have not exerted some influence (albeit proleptically) in the arena of radical politics, but that, in the main, their efforts have helped to protect the bulwark of ruling-class power by limiting the options of educational policy in order to perpetuate the hegemony of ruling-class academics. Their herniated ideas have made for good theater, but their words have often turned to ashes before leaving their mouths. They have not left educators much with which to advance a political line of march within a theoretical framework capable of developing an international strategy to oppose imperialism.

Our own practices—what Paula Allman (2001a) has christened "revolutionary critical pedagogy"—ups the radical ante for progressive education that, for the most part over the last decade, has been left rudderless amidst an undertow of domesticating currents. It ups this ante by pivoting around the work of Karl Marx, Paulo Freire, and Antonio Gramsci and in doing so brings some desperately needed theoretical ballast to the teetering critical educational tradition. Such theoretical infrastructure is necessary, we argue, for the construction of concrete pedagogical spaces—in schools, university seminar rooms, cultural centers, unions, social movements, popular forums for political activism, and so on—for the fostering and fomenting of revolutionary praxis.

While it certainly remains the case that too many teachers take refuge in a sanctuary of assertions devoid of critical reflection, it would be wrong to admonish the educational activism of today as a form of pedagogical potvaliancy. Courageous attempts are being made in the struggle for educational reform on both sides of the Atlantic. In this case, we need to be reminded that the lack of success of the educational left is not so much the result of the conflicted sensibilities of critical educators as it is a testament to the preening success of Western Cold War efforts in indigenizing the cultural logic of capitalism, the fall of the Eastern Bloc nonprofit police states, and the degradation and disappearance of Marxist meta-narratives in the national-popular agendas of decolonizing countries. It can also be traced to the effects of the labor movement tradition that keeps labor-left educators struggling inside the labor–capital antagonism by supporting labor over capital, rather than attempting to transcend this divide entirely through efforts to implode the social universe of capital out of which the labor–capital antagonism is constituted.

Clearly, critical pedagogy is checkered with tensions and conflicts and mired in contradictions and should in no way be seen as a unified discipline. My purpose in this chapter is not to develop a comprehensive perspective on or programmatic architectonic of critical pedagogy, something that has already been accomplished in the works of Paula Allman and others. My more modest purpose therefore is to uncoil some of the conceptual tensions that exist in linking up the concept of critical pedagogy to that of class struggle. In doing so, I wish to rehearse a number of provisional points: (1) a sense of what constitutes critical agency and revolutionary praxis, and (2) a nuanced notion of what liberation means at this particular historical juncture.

My approach to understanding the relationship between capitalism and schooling and the struggle for socialism is premised upon Marx's value theory of labor as developed by British Marxist educationalists Glenn Rikowski, Dave Hill, and Mike Cole. In developing further the concept of revolutionary critical pedagogy and its specific relationship to class struggle, it is necessary to repeat, with a slightly different emphasis, some of the positions we have discussed earlier on in the chapter. We follow the premise that value is the substance of capital. Value is not a thing. It is the dominant form that capitalism as a determinate social relation takes.

Following Marx, Rikowski notes that labor-power—our capacity to labor—takes the form of "human capital" in capitalist society. It has reality only within the individual agent. Thus, labor-power is a distinctly *human force*. The worker is the active subject of production. He or she is necessary for the creation of surplus value. He or she provides through living labor the skills, innovation, and cooperation upon which capital relies to enhance surplus value and to ensure its reproduction. Thus, by its very nature, labor-power cannot exist apart from the laborer.

Labor power is what Rikowski (2000a, 2001a, 2002) describes as the primordial form of social energy within capital's social universe. Labor-power is a special kind of commodity whose use value possesses the possibility of being transformed into a source of value. It constitutes value in a unique manner as the special living commodity that possesses the capacity to generate more value—that is, surplus value—than is required to maintain its social existence as labor-power. In other words, surplus value is possible because labor-power expends more labor-time than is necessary for its maintenance. It rests upon the socially necessary labor-time required to produce any use value under conditions normal for a given society. This presupposes labor-power as the socially average. The value of labor-power is represented by the wage. The key point here is that while the labor-power that the worker expends beyond the labor necessary for his or her maintenance creates no value for him or her, it does create value for the capitalist: *surplus value*. Education and training are what Rikowski refers to as processes of labor-power production. They are, in Rikowski's view, a subspecies of relative surplus-value production (the raising of worker productivity so that necessary labor is reduced) that leads to a relative increase in surplus labor-time and hence surplus value. Human capital development is necessary for capitalist societies to reproduce themselves and to create more surplus value. The core of capitalism can thus be undressed by exploring the contradictory nature of the use value and exchange value of labor-power.

Insofar as schooling is premised upon generating the living commodity of labor-power, upon which the entire social universe of capital depends, it can become a foundation for human resistance. In other words, labor-power can be incorporated only so far. Workers, as the sources of labor-power, can engage in acts of refusing alienating work and delinking labor from capital's value form. As Nick Dyer-Witheford (1999) argues: "Capital, a relation of general commodification predicated on the wage relation, needs labor. But labor does not need capital. Labor can dispense with the wage, and with capitalism, and find different ways to organize its own creative energies: it is potentially *autonomous*" (p. 68, italics original).

In the face of such a contemporary intensification of global capitalist relations and permanent structural crisis (rather than a shift in the nature of capital itself), we need to develop a critical pedagogy capable of engaging everyday life as lived in its midst. We need, in other words, to face capital down. This means acknowledging global capital's structurally determined inability to share power with the oppressed; its implication in racist, sexist, and homophobic relations; its functional relationship to xenophobic nationalism; and its tendency toward empire. It means acknowledging the educational left's dependency upon the very object of its negation: capital. It means struggling to develop a lateral, polycentric concept of anticapitalist alliances in diversity to slow down capitalism's metabolic movement—with the eventual aim of shutting it down completely. It means looking for an educational philosophy that is designed to resist the "capitalization" of subjectivity, a pedagogy that we have called revolutionary critical pedagogy.

Marxist humanists believe that the best way to transcend the brutal and barbaric limits to human liberation set by capital is through practical movements centred around class struggle. But today the clarion cry of class struggle is spurned by the bourgeois left as politically fanciful and reads to many as an advertisement for a B-movie. The liberal left is less interested in class struggle than in making capitalism more "compassionate" to the needs of the poor. This only leads to the renaturalization of scarcity. What this approach exquisitely obfuscates is the way in which new capitalist efforts to divide and conquer the working class and to recompose class relations have employed xenophobic nationalism, racism, sexism, ableism, speciesism, and homophobia. The key here is not for critical pedagogues to privilege class oppression over other forms of oppression but to see how capitalist relations of exploitation provide the ground from which other forms of oppression are produced and how postmodern educational theory often serves as a means of distracting attention from capital's global project of accumulation.

Unhesitatingly embraced by most liberal educationalists is, of course, a concern to bring about social justice. This is certainly to be applauded. However, too often such a struggle is antiseptically cleaved from the project of transforming capitalist social relations. When somebody tries to make the case for class struggle among liberals who fervently believe that capitalism is preferable to socialism or—god forbid—communism, people react as if a bad odor has just entered the room. I am not arguing that people should not have concerns about socialism or communism. After all, much horror has occurred under regimes that called themselves communist. We are arguing that capitalism is not inevitable and that the struggle for socialism is not finished. Perhaps today this struggle is more urgent than at any other time in human history. Socialism is no longer a homogeneous struggle but, as Dunayevskaya (2002) elaborates, must involve coalition building and international working-class collaboration in the struggle against global capitalism. Such a politics is one of difference and inclusion, but a politics whose center of gravity is the struggle for socialist alternatives to capital.

Insofar as education and training socially produce labor-power, this process can be resisted. As Dyer-Witheford (1999) notes: "In academia, as elsewhere, labor-power is never completely controllable. To the degree that capital uses the university to harness general intellect, insisting its work force engage in lifelong learning as the price of employability, it runs the risk that people will teach and learn something other than what it intends" (p. 236). Critical educators push this "something other" to the extreme in their pedagogical praxis centered around a social justice, anticapitalist agenda. In our struggle to defeat capital and ensure that the exploitation of labor ceases to be the legal formalization of our reptilian brain, we must cultivate a critical optimism surrounding the possibilities of collective struggle for a socialist future. We must reject the absolute as a predicate of emancipation and discover in the kernel of our generic humanity a promise of freedom that can be set into concrete motion. In doing so, we must set our critical pedagogies against the versions of postmodern theory that conciliate an inward revolution of cultivating "authentic experience" without a public counterpart. Students and education workers can ask Glenn Rikowski's question: What is the maximum damage we can do to the rule of capital, to the dominance of capital's value form? Ultimately, the question we have to ask is: Do we, as radical educators, help capital find its way out of crisis, or do we help students and teachers find their way out of capital? The success of the former challenge will only buy further time for the capitalists to adapt both its victims and its critics, the success of the latter will determine the future of civilization, or whether or not we will have one.

For those of us fashioning a distinctive socialist philosophy of praxis within a North American context, it is clear that a transition to socialism will not be an easy struggle, given the global entrenchment of these aforementioned challenges. The overall task ahead is what Petras and Veltmeyer (2001) refer to, after Marx and Engels, as the creation of a dictatorship of the proletariat, not a dictatorship over the proletariat. It consists of managing the inherent contradiction between the internal socialist relations and the external participation in the capitalist marketplace. Meeting this challenge will require, among other things, a long list of initiatives such as those put forward by Petras and Veltmeyer. These follow from an effort to move from a globalized imperial export strategy to an integrated domestic economy that entails reorienting the economy away from the reproduction of financial elites and replacing privatization with a socialization of the means of production. These initiatives include but are not limited to the following: increasing local capacity to advance the forces of production and democratizing its relations; increasing the internal capacity to deepen the domestic market and serve popular needs; subordinating external and internal market relations (economic exchanges) to a democratic regime (as in an assembly-style democracy); moving away from an "enclave" type of export strategy that serves the interests of overseas and domestic investor elites; building linkages between the domestic economy sectors; adapting the economy to local needs and developing autonomous, innovative capacities; creating democratic control over economic processes; forging socioeconomic linkages between domestic needs and the reorganization of the productive system; dismantling the current export strategy where the labor force is perceived as a cost rather than as consumers; shifting from hyperspecialization in single commodities and limited industrial production to diversified production; establishing a better balance between local consumption and export production; creating a domestic market based on equalized property, income, education, and health; refusing to allow external economic exchanges to substitute for local production and local centers of technical knowledge creation; the redistribution of land and the transfer of property ownership to facilitate food production for mass consumption at affordable prices; replacing luxury-producing and -importing enterprises with quality goods for mass domestic consumption; avoiding the disarticulation of the rural economy and thus avoiding the bankrupting of provincial industries; creating a livable income for rural producers; and expanding agro-industrial complexes but on a decentralized plan where direct producers make the basic decisions on exchanges between regions, sectors, and classes.

It is important that the state and the nation become the central units for reconstructing a new internationalist socialist order. Petras and Veltmeyer suggest that socialists use neoliberal shock therapy in reverse by reducing profits, freezing bank accounts and financial holdings, suspending overseas payments, and creating a moratorium on debt payments in order to prevent hyperinflation and capital flight. In opening the economy for domestic production, credit and investment could be offered for expanding production and exchanges at the national, regional, and local levels. Petras and Veltmeyer (2001) also suggest implementing a "structural adjustment program from below"—redistributing land, income, and credits; breaking up private monopolies; reforming the tax system; protecting emerging industries; opening the trade of commodities that don't compete with local producers; eliminating speculative activity by means of financial controls; redirecting investments toward human capital formation and employment; decentralizing the administration of state allocations and redistributing them to local recipients in civil society to local recipients able to vote on their own priorities; generating public works and interregional production; imposing a tight monetary policy (monetarism from below) by refusing state bailouts of corrupt companies; eliminating cheap credit to exporters and tax abatements for multinational corporations in "free" trade zones; and creating local and regional assemblies to debate and resolve budget allocations (much along the lines of the participatory budget created by Brazil's Workers Party). Kovel (2002) argues that the transition to socialism will require the creation of a "usufructuary of the earth." Essentially this means restoring ecosystemic integrity across all of human participation—the family, the community, the nation, the international community. Kovel argues that use value must no longer be subordinated to exchange value but both must be harmonized with "intrinsic value." The means of production (and it must be an ecocentric mode of production) must be made accessible to all as assets are transferred to the direct producers (i.e., worker ownership and control). Clearly, eliminating the accumulation of surplus value as the motor of "civilization" and challenging the rule of capital by directing money toward the free enhancement of use values goes against the grain of the transnational ruling class.

The struggle among what Marx called our "vital powers," our dispositions, our inner selves and our objective outside, our human capacities and competencies and the social formations within which they are produced, *ensures* the production of a form of human agency that reflects the contradictions within capitalist social life. Yet these contradictions also provide openness regarding social being. They point toward the possibility of collectively resolving contradictions of "everyday life" through revolutionary/transformative praxis (Allman 1999). Critical subjectivity operates out of practical, sensuous engagement within social formations that enable rather than constrain human capacities.

In his "Fragment on Machines" in the *Grundrisse* ([1857], 1993), Marx argues that the production of wealth will not always be the result of the direct expenditure of labor-power in production but the result of a general "social knowledge" or "social intellect" or the "general powers of the human head." Marx believed that the development of the general intellect that accompanies the increasing importance of fixed capital (machine technology, etc.) will lead to capital undermining itself in the sense that technological advances reduce the requirements of direct labor in production and as a result the need for people to sell their labor-power (the basis of capital's social order) is diminished. That is, the increased importance of fixed capital and the accompanying process of deindustrialization has expelled living labor from the production process. In addition, as science is directly appropriated into the production process, information thus becomes a source of labor in its own right. However, instead of the development of the general intellect leading to the transition toward socialism, capital, instead, is reorganizing itself (and in the process reproducing the social intellect) in order to increase its global domination (Dyer-Witheford 1999). As Dyer-Witheford (1991) notes, the push to socialize the "social brain" of workers in the days of the Taylorist economy (i.e., educating for certain forms of intersubjectivity among workers developed for the accumulation of industrial capital) has been superseded by a new makeover of the general intellect driven by the needs of post-Taylorist or post-Fordist capital (what some have called the information economy). Attempts at involving workers more in the production process, and capturing the souls of the workers through the establishment of worker-teams of participatory management and "total quality management" have reflected novel attempts to dragoon worker subjectivity into the service of capital accumulation by intensifying automation, speeding up work, and increasing layoffs.

Automation has created surplus labor-time and workers are struggling to prevent this labor-time from being harnessed to the advantage and the advance of capital. Capital continues to segment post-Fordist labor-power by containing the information revolution in vertically integrated empires of capital, forcing the general intellect of workers into the world of commodity production. Yet at the same time, attempts to domesticate emancipatory forms of mass intellectuality among workers have at times backfired and have resulted in the potential development for an oppositional general intellect led by global bands of grassroots organizers and workers who are making alliances with wider communities.

While the European and North American "intellectual proletariats" engaged in technoscientific labor pose one type of challenge to capital through their "immaterial labor," the real toilers who engage in "material labor" struggle under different conditions throughout Latin America and the so-called Third World. Yet even in developing economies, there have occurred successful revolts of the world's global subjects, such as in the case of the Zapatistas in Mexico (Dyer-Witheford 1999). Critical educators must play a role in preventing the domestication of the general intellect, and directly challenge capital in its role of reifying and commodifying the production of emancipatory knowledge, of a critical social brain. But will our attempts be as domesticating as those of capital, only in a different register, and under the banner of social justice? This is perhaps the greatest future challenge of critical pedagogy.

My work in critical pedagogy—which I prefer to call (after Allman 2001a) revolutionary critical pedagogy—constitutes in one sense the performative register for class struggle. While it sets as its goal the decolonization of subjectivity, it also targets the material basis of capitalist social relations. Critical educators seek to realize in their classrooms social values and to believe in their possibilities—consequently I argue that they need to go outside of the protected precincts of their classrooms and analyze and explore the workings of capital there. Revolutionary critical pedagogy sets as its goal the reclamation of public life under the relentless assault of the corporatization, privatization, and businessification of the lifeworld (which includes the corporate-academic complex). It seeks to make the division of labor coincident with the free vocation of each individual and the association of free producers. At first blush this may seem a paradisiac notion in that it posits a radically eschatological and incomparably "other" endpoint for society as we know it. Yet this is not a blueprint but a contingent utopian vision that offers direction not only in unpicking the apparatus of bourgeois illusion but also in diversifying the theoretical itinerary of the critical educator so that new questions can be generated along with new perspectives in which to raise them. Here the emphasis is not only on denouncing the manifest injustices of neoliberal capitalism and serving as a counterforce to neoliberal ideological hegemony, but also on establishing the conditions for new social arrangements that transcend the false opposition between the market and the state.

In capturing the "commanding heights" of left educational criticism, postmodernist educators have focused their analysis on the subject as consumer in contrast to the Marxian emphasis of the subject as producer and in doing so have emphasized the importance of a textual subversion of fixed identity and a decentering of subjectivity. Too often this work collapses politics into poetics. Insofar as postmodern educationalists do not address the labor–capital dialectic or the social relations of production, postmodern educational criticism and neoliberalism can be considered to be two species of the same genus: capitalist schooling. They can be considered as two forms of one and the same social type. Both postmodern critique and neoliberalism serve as a justification for the value form of labor within capitalist society. Here postmodernists and neoliberals adopt the role of the sorcerer's apprentice who has been summoned to serve his master: capital.

In contrast, revolutionary critical pedagogy emphasizes the material dimensions of its own constitutive possibility and recognizes knowledge as implicated within the social relations of production (i.e., the relations between labor and capital). I am using the term materialism here not in its postmodernist sense as a resistance to conceptuality, a refusal of the closure of meaning, or whatever "excess" cannot be subsumed within the symbol or cannot be absorbed by tropes; rather, materialism is being used in the context of material social relations, a structure of class conflict, and an effect of the social division of labor (Ebert 2002). Historical changes in the forces of production have reached the point where the fundamental needs of people can be met—

but the existing social relations of production prevent this because the logic of access to "need" is "profit" based on the value of people's labor for capital. Consequently, revolutionary critical pedagogy argues that without a class analysis, critical pedagogy is impeded from effecting praxiological changes (changes in social relations). Revolutionary critical pedagogy begins with a three-pronged approach: First, students engage in a pedagogy of demystification centering around a semiotics of recognition, where dominant sign systems are recognized and denaturalized, where common sense is historicized, and where signification is understood as a political practice that refracts rather than reflects reality, where cultural formations are understood in relation to the larger social factory of the school and the global universe of capital. This is followed by a pedagogy of opposition, where students engage in analyzing various political systems, ideologies, and histories, and eventually students begin to develop their own political positions. Inspired by a sense of ever-imminent hope, students take up a pedagogy of revolution, where deliberative practices for transforming the social universe of capital are developed and put into practice. Revolutionary critical pedagogy supports a totalizing reflection upon the historical-practical constitution of the world, our ideological formation within it, and the reproduction of everyday life practices. It is a pedagogy with an emancipatory intent.

Within the expansive scope of revolutionary critical pedagogy, the concept of labor is axiomatic for theorizing the school/society relationship and thus for developing radical pedagogical imperatives, strategies, and practices for overcoming the constitutive contradictions that such a coupling generates. The larger goal revolutionary critical pedagogy stipulates for radical educationalists involves direct participation with the masses in the discovery and charting of a socialist reconstruction and alternative to capitalism. However, without a critical lexicon and interpretative framework that can unpack the labor/capital relationship in all of its capillary detail, critical pedagogy is doomed to remain trapped in domesticated currents and vulgarized formations. The process whereby labor-power is transformed into human capital and concrete living labor is subsumed by abstract labor is one that eludes the interpretative capacity of rational communicative action and requires a dialectical understanding that only historical materialist critique can best provide. Historical materialism provides critical pedagogy with a theory of the material basis of social life rooted in historical social relations and assumes paramount importance in uncovering the structure of class conflict as well as unravelling the effects produced by the social division of labor. Today, labor-power is capitalized and commodified and education plays a tragic role in these processes. According to Rikowski (2001c), education "links the chains that bind our souls to capital. It is one of the ropes comprising the ring for combat between labor and capital, a clash that powers contemporary history: 'the class struggle'" (p. 2). Schools therefore act as vital supports for, and developers of, the class relation, "the violent capital-labor relation that is at the core of capitalist society and development" (2001c, p. 19).

If every new society carries its own negation within itself, then it makes sense for critical educators to develop a language of analysis that can help to identify the habits, ideas, and notions that help to shape and condition—either in a forward- or backward-looking way—the material and discursive forces of production. These habits, ideas, and notions—which stir as contradictions in the womb of subjectivity—are never static but always are in motion as possibilities given birth by history, that is, by class struggle. We need to develop a critical pedagogy, therefore, that can help students reconstruct the objective and subjective contexts of class struggle by examining the capitalist mode of production as a totality in relation to the aggregate of social relations that make the human—an examination that is centered upon Marx's labor theory of value. This mandates teaching students to think dialectically, to think in terms of "internal relations," such as creating an internal relation between diversity and unity, and between our individuality and our collectivity (Allman 2001a). The idea here is not simply to play mediatively with ideas but to interrogate the social grammar of capitalist society inhibiting its refractory relations while struggling for a political recomposition of social subjects that want a different world; indeed, who seek a socialist alternative.

Consider, if you will, the current social bloc, a Euro-implanted Anglosphere, which congeals around the moral-intellectual leadership of the Bush gang and its corporate sycophants. Here, the integrative liberal version of citizenship and its corollary antagonism, multiculturalism—with its "hybrid coexistence of diverse cultural life worlds" (San Juan 2004)—authorizes the criteria of patriotism and sanctions violence against the Other. The mainstream model of multiculturalism that denounces racism as an organizing principle of the social order while facilitating its reproduction at a distance, serves as a synecdoche for a deeper structural antagonism rooted in the capitalist law of value. As E. San Juan (2004) argues, the celebration of difference within an imagined national community hides structural inequalities, occludes "the material conditions of racist practices and institutions," and legitimizes pluralist stratification and asymmetrical relations of power and privilege. By failing to recognize the necessity of altering the market and commodity exchange and negating the contradiction between labor and capital, the mainstream multiculturalism of the liberal academy unwittingly reinforces "the existing framework of the racial polity" (San Juan 2004) and transforms itself into a "disavowed, inverted, self-referential form of racism, a 'racism with a distance'—it respects the Other's identity, conceiving the

Other as a self-enclosed 'authentic' community towards which he, the multiculturalist, maintains a distance rendered possible by his privileged universal position" (San Juan 2004). However, this privileged universal position is not only self-arrogating, it conceals the suture point, the norm, against which difference is measured and evaluated. It shrouds, in other words, the ethnocentric paradigm of commodity relations premised on the capitalist law of value (and accompanying white supremacy) against which difference is foregrounded. Along the way, the public sphere is self-fragmented into a shopping mall that sells racialized national character along with Krispy Kremes while it "peacefully manages the crisis of race" (San Juan 2004), making multiculturalism "the ideal form of ideology" (San Juan 2004) of capitalism. Thus, according to San Juan (2004), "the problem of multiculturalism . . . which imposes itself today is the form of appearance of its opposite: it bears witness to the unprecedented homogenization of the contemporary world."

The myriad obstacles facing the progressive educational tradition in the United States—such as whether critical pedagogy can be revivified in this current historical juncture of neoliberal globalization—can be overcome—albeit haltingly rather than resoundingly. The recent advance of contemporary Marxist educational scholarship (Rikowski 2001a, 2002; Hill 2001; Cole 1998; Hill and Cole 2001; Hill, McLaren, Cole, and Rikowski 2002; McLaren and Farahmandpur, 2000), critical theory (Giroux 1981, 1983; Kincheloe 1998), and a rematerialized critical pedagogy (McLaren 2000; McLaren and Farahmandpur 2001a, 2001b; Fischman and McLaren 2000)—although the offerings are still only modest glimmerings—in my view is sufficient enough to begin fashioning a necessary counterweight not only to neoliberal free-market imperatives but also to post-Marxist solutions that most often advocate the creation of social movements grounded in identity politics or, as evident in recent anti-Marxist pedagogical polemics, a pedagogy of political inertia grounded in the thrall of detachment and uncertainty (Lather 2001).

THE POLITICS OF ORGANIZATION

This brings us to the question of organization. Max Elbaum (2002) notes that organizations are crucial in the struggle for social justice. He writes that "[w]ithout collective forms it is impossible to train cadre, debate theory and strategy, spread information and analysis, or engage fully with the urgent struggles of the day. Only through organisations can revolutionaries maximize their contribution to ongoing battles and position themselves to maximally influence events when new mass upheavals and opportunities arise" (2002, p. 335). Yet at the same time, Elbaum warns that we must avoid what he calls "sectarian dead-ends" in our struggle for social justice. Reflecting on his experiences with the New Communist Movement of the 1970s, he explains that when a movement becomes a "self-contained world" that insists upon group solidarity and discipline, this can often lead to the suppression of internal democracy. The rigid top-down party model is obviously a problem for Elbaum. On the one hand social activists need to engage with and be accountable to a large, active, anticapitalist social base; on the other hand, there are pressures to put one's revolutionary politics aside in order to make an immediate impact on public policy. There is the impulse to "retreat into a small but secure niche on the margins of politics and/or confine oneself to revolutionary propaganda" (2002, p. 334). Elbaum cites Marx's dictum that periods of socialist sectarianism obtain when "the time is not yet ripe for an independent historical movement" (p. 334). Problems inevitably arise when "purer-than-thou fidelity to old orthodoxies" (p. 334) are employed to maintain membership morale necessary for group cohesion and to compete with other groups. He reports that the healthiest periods of social movements appear to be when tight-knit cadre groups and other forms are able to coexist and interact while at the same time considering themselves part of a common political trend. He writes that "diversity of organizational forms (publishing collectives, research centers, cultural collectives, and broad organizing networks, in addition to local and national cadre formations) along with a dynamic interaction between them supplied (at least to a degree) some of the pressures for democracy and realism that in other situations flowed from a socialist-oriented working-class" (2002, p. 335).

It is important to avoid a uniform approach in all sectors, especially when disparities in consciousness and activity are manifold. Elbaum notes that Leninist centralized leadership worked in the short run but "lacked any substantial social base and were almost by definition hostile to all others on the left; they could never break out of the limits of a sect" (2002, p. 335). The size of membership has a profound qualitative impact on strategies employed and organizational models adopted. Elbaum warns that attempts to build a small revolutionary party (a party in embryo) "blinded movement activists to Lenin's view that a revolutionary party must not only be an 'advanced' detachment but must also actually represent and be rooted in a substantial, socialist-leaning wing of the working class" (2002, p. 335). Realistic and complex paths will need to be taken that will clearly be dependent on the state of the working-class movement itself.

It is axiomatic for the ongoing development of critical pedagogy that it be based upon an alternative vision of human sociality, one that operates outside the social universe of capital, a vision that goes beyond the market, but also one that goes beyond the state. It must reject the false opposition between the market and the state. Massimo De Angelis (2002) writes that "the historical challenge before us is that the question of alternatives . . . not be separated from the organizational forms that this movement gives itself" (p. 5). Given that we are faced globally with the emergent transnational capitalist class and the incursion of capital into the far reaches of the planet, critical educators need a philosophy of organization that sufficiently addresses the dilemma and the challenge of the global proletariat. In discussing alternative manifestations of antiglobalization struggles, De Angelis itemizes some promising characteristics as follows: the production of various countersummits; Zapatista Encuentros; social practices that produce use values beyond economic calculation and the competitive relation with the Other and inspired by practices of social and mutual solidarity; horizontally linked clusters outside vertical networks in which the market is protected and enforced; social cooperation through grassroots democracy, consensus, dialogue, and the recognition of the other; authority and social cooperation developed in fluid relations and self-constituted through interaction; and a new engagement with the other that transcends locality, job, social condition, gender, age, race, culture, sexual orientation, language, religion, and beliefs. All of these characteristics are to be secondary to the constitution of communal relations. He writes:

> The global scene for us is the discovery of the "other," while the local scene is the discovery of the "us," and by discovering the "us," we change our relation to the "other." In a community, commonality is a creative process of discovery, not a presupposition. So we do both, but we do it having the community in mind, the community as a mode of engagement with the other. (2002, p. 14)

But what about the national state? Sam Gindin (2002) argues that the state is no longer a relevant site of struggle if by struggle we mean taking over the state and pushing it in another direction. But the state is still a relevant arena for contestation if our purpose is one of transforming the state. He writes:

> Conventional wisdom has it that the national state, whether we like it or not, is no longer a relevant site of struggle. At one level, this is true. If our notion of the state is that of an institution which left governments can "capture" and push in a different direction, experience suggests this will contribute little to social justice. But if our goal is to transform the state into an instrument for popular mobilization and the development of democratic capacities, to bring our economy under popular control and restructure our relationships to the world economy, then winning state power would manifest the worst nightmares of the corporate world. When we reject strategies based on winning through undercutting others and maintain our fight for dignity and justice nationally, we can inspire others abroad and create new spaces for their own struggles. (p. 11)

John Holloway's (2002a, 2002b) premise is similar to that of Gindin. He argues that we must theorize the world negatively as a "moment" of practice as part of the struggle to change the world. But this change cannot come about through transforming the state through the taking of power but rather must occur through the dissolution of power. This is because the state reproduces within itself the separation of people from their own "doing." In our work as critical educators, Holloway's distinction between power to do (potentia) and power over (potestas) is instructive. Power over is the negation of the social flow of doing. Power to is a part of the "social flow of doing," the construction of a "we" and the practice of the mutual recognition of dignity. We need to create the conditions for the future "doing" of others through a power to do. In the process, we must not transform power to into power over, since power over only separates the "means of doing" from the actual "doing," which has reached its highest point in capitalism. In fact, those who exercise power over separate the done from the doing of others and declare it to be theirs. The appropriation of the "done" of others is equivalent to the appropriation of "the means of doing," and allows the powerful to control the doing of others, which reaches its highest point in capitalism.

The separation of doing from the doers reduces people to mere owners and nonowners, flattening out relations between people to relations between things. It converts doing into being. Whereas doing refers to both "we are" (the present) and "we are not" (the possibility of being something else), being refers only to "we are." To take away the "we are not" tears away possibility from social agency. In this case, possibility becomes mere utopian dreaming while time itself becomes irrefragably homogenized. Being locates the future as an extension of the present and makes the past into a preparation for the present. All doing becomes an extension of the way things are. The rule of power over is the rule of "this is the way things are," which is the rule of identity. When we are separated from our own doing, we create our own subordination. Power to is not counterpower (which presupposes a symmetry with power) but antipower. We need to avoid falling into identification, to an acceptance of what is.

Holloway (2002a, 2002b) reminds us that the separation of doing and done is not an accomplished fact but a process. Separation and alienation is a movement against its own negation, against anti-alienation. That which exists in the form of its negation—or anti-alienation (the mode of being denied)—really does exist, in spite of its negation. It is the negation of the process of denial. Capitalism, according to Holloway, is based on the denial of "power to," of dignity, of humanity, but that does not mean power to (countercapitalism) does not exist. Asserting our power to is simultaneously to assert our resistance against being dominated by others. This may take the form of open rebellion, of struggles to defend control over the labor process, or efforts to control the processes of health and education. Power over depends upon that which it negates. The history of domination is not only the struggle of the oppressed against their oppressors but also the struggle of the powerful to liberate themselves from their dependence on the powerless. But there is no way in which power over can ultimately escape from being transformed into power to because capital's flight from labor depends upon labor (upon its capacity to convert power to into abstract value-producing labor) in the form of falling rates of profit.

Holloway's (2002a) work is an important advance in theorizing the nature of power but it remains highly problematic. Asking the revolutionary subject to forego revolutionary movements and their historical importance in class struggle worldwide in favor of becoming a Marxist phenomenologist is not exactly the most pragmatic way forward. Forms of power over are unavoidable and in some cases desirable, at least in the limited context of developing a revolutionary organization with some form of direct or representative democracy. I agree with Michael Löwy that direct democracy at the horizontal level of local assemblies works well for factories or universities or communities or barrios. Even though the state is admittedly part of the network of capitalist domination, beyond the local level, regional and national levels of representation are necessary, such as a body, network, or federation based on direct democracy or council democracy (Löwy 2004). A revolutionary council democracy from below, combining direct and representative forms, needs to be struggled for, a new form of political power that can bring about the supercession of the capitalist system (Löwy 2004).

Clearly, the revolutionary praxis driven by a Marxist-Humanist pedagogy, and articulated throughout this book, has faith in overcoming commodity fetishism through a dialectical approach to self and social transformation, an approach grounded in the self-emancipation of everyday class struggle.

Another attempt to theorize resistance to the commodity fetishism of capital—inferior to that of Holloway—has been put forward by Michael Hardt and Antonio Negri in their book *Empire* (2000). The argument advanced by Hardt and Negri—that we live in a post-imperialist, decentered global network or empire populated by multinational corporations that have no loyalties to any nation, only to profit-making, an empire characterized as a smooth, evenly developed space where class conflict is outdated and replaced by a homogenization of the laboring process and where the imperial state is in decline, and the "immaterial labor" of service and information production reigns supreme—needs to be roundly rejected (see Hudis 2003a, 2003b, in press). Their position woefully ignores the continuing dominance of global industrial development concentrated in Western Europe, the United States, and Japan; the internationalization of lean production characterized by labor-intensive, low-wage production and accompanied by deskilling, outsourcing, and union bashing; and the combined and uneven development and growing gaps in income and production between the advanced capitalist north and the developing countries of the south, and the strengthening of the nation-state as a means of facilitating the dismantling of barriers to the goals of the transnational corporations and the coordinating of multilateral and bilateral investment agreements and enforcing investment guarantees. Interimperialist conflict proceeds apace, with the United States playing the "alpha male" role in directing financial markets, even though the imperialists are all squarely united behind the politics of neoliberal free-market capitalism. Hardt and Negri clearly miss the mark in articulating and advancing their new revolutionary subject—the biopolitical production of the multitude.

Keening the death of Marxism will do little more than momentarily stir the ghost of the old bearded devil. Clearly, present-day left educationalists need to rethink the state as a terrain of contestation while at the same time reinventing class struggle as we have been doing in the streets of Seattle, Porto Alegre, Prague, Quebec City, and Genoa. We have to keep our belief that another world is possible. We need to do more than to break with capital or abscond from it; clearly, we need to challenge its rule of value. Novel ingressions toward rebuilding the educational left will not be easy, but neither will living under an increasingly militarized capitalist state where labor-power is constantly put to the rack to carry out the will of capital and empire. While critical pedagogy may seem driven by lofty, high-rise aspirations that spike an otherwise desolate landscape of despair, where pockmarked dreams bob through the sewers of contemporary cosmopolitan life, they anchor our hope in the present. Here the social revolution is not reborn in the foam of avant-garde antifoundationalism, which only stokes the forces of despair, but emerges from the everyday struggle to release us from the burdens of political détente and democratic disengagement. It is anchored, in other words, in class struggle.

Revolutionary critical pedagogy must speak not only to those already far along on the path of dissent but to those wayfaring citizens who live Icarus-like lives of ascents and descents yet whose optimism of the will remains a constant source of strength, who seek ballast in the swirling eddy of political decision making but fear losing their faculties of critique, who desire to transform the sociopolitical terrain but lack a systematic language of social analysis, who outflank despair with steady resolve but long for more opportunities to build alliances around a coherent philosophy of praxis, who refuse to take refuge in some unnamable space, some fertile void or sublime metaphysical retreat where fungible epiphanies replace concrete struggles to transform the social relations of production, who resist official advice from the plenipotentiary of the state in favor of reflecting critically upon their own historical experiences, who refuse to turn the seminar room to a self-serving precinct of reflection safely ensconced from the absurdity of human existence and the turbid and restless sea of contemporary struggles against capital, who avoid the pitfalls of religious triumphalism but who long for inner revelation in life-affirming communal settings with like-minded citizens. Such a reaching out by critical educators is more imperative in today's social universe of exploitation than at any other time in our history. Building a base for renewed class struggle for a self-determining society without capitalism is both the origin and the destiny of the struggle ahead, for it is a struggle that is always in process, always moving forward as long as people are committed to keeping the dream alive.

ACKNOWLEDGMENTS

This chapter was previously published as "Critical Pedagogy in the Age of Neoliberal Globalization: Notes from History's Underside," *Democracy and Nature* 9, no. 1: 65-90. It appears here with permission. Some sections of this chapter are based on Peter McLaren and Nathalia E. Jaramillo, "Critical Pedagogy as Organizational Praxis: Challenging the Demise of Civil Society in a Time of Permanent War," in *If Classrooms Matter: Progressive Visions of Educational Environments*, ed. Jeffrey R. Di Leo and Walter R. Jacobs (London: Routledge), 75–92.

REFERENCES

Ahmad, A. May 1998–April 1999. "The Communist Manifesto and the Problem of Universality." *Monthly Review,* 50(2), 12–38.
Ahmad, A. 1997. "Culture, Nationalism, and the Role of Intellectuals: An Interview Conducted by Erika Repov and Nikolai Jeffs." In *In Defense of History: Marxism and the Postmodern Agenda*, edited by Ellen Meiksins Wood and John Bellamy Foster, 51–64. New York: Monthly Review Press.
Ainley, P. 1993. *Class and Skill: Changing Divisions of Knowledge and Labor.* London: Cassell.
Ali, Tariq. 2002. *The Clash of Fundamentalisms: Crusades, Jihads and Modernity.* London: Verso.
Allman, P. 1999. *Revolutionary Social Transformation: Democratic Hopes, Political Possibilities and Critical Education.* Westport, Conn.: Bergin & Garvey.
Allman, P. 2001a. *Critical Education against Global Capitalism: Karl Marx and Revolutionary Critical Education.* Westport, Conn.: Bergin & Garvey.

Allman, P. 2001b. "Education on Fire!" In *Red Chalk: On Schooling, Capitalism and Politics*, edited by M. Cole, D. Hill, P. McLaren, and G. Rikowski, 10–14. Brighton, England: Institute for Education Policy Studies.

Amin, Samir. 1996. "Imperialism and Culturalism Compliment Each Other." *Monthly Review*, 48(2), 1–11.

Amin, S. 2001. "Imperialism and Globalization." *Monthly Review*, 53(2), 6–24.

Bowers, C. A. 2001. *Educating for Eco-Justice and Community*. Athens: University of Georgia Press.

Bowers, C. A. 2003a. "Can Critical Pedagogy Be Greened?" *Educational Studies*, 34, 11–20.

Bowers, C. A. 2003b. *Mindful Conservatism: Rethinking the Ideological and Educational Basis of an Ecologically Sustainable Future*. Lanham, Md.: Rowman & Littlefield.

Bowers, C. A. In press. "How Peter McLaren and Donna Houston and Other 'Green' Marxists Contribute to the Globalization of the West's Industrial Culture." *Educational Studies*.

Callinicos, A. 1989. *Against Postmodernism: A Marxist Critique*. New York: St. Martin's Press.

Cleaver, H. 2000. *Reading Capital Politically*. Leeds, England: Antitheses and Edinburgh: AK Press.

Cole, M., and Hill, D. 1999. *Promoting Equality in Secondary Schools*. London: Cassell.

Cole, M., Hill, D., McLaren, P., and Rikowski, G. 2001. *Red Chalk: On Schooling, Capitalism and Politics*. Brighton, England: The Institute for Education Policy Studies.

Davies, S., and Guppy, N. 1997, November. "Globalization and Educational Reforms in Anglo-American Democracies." *Comparative Education Review*, 41(4), 435–459.

De Angelis, M. 2002. "From Movement to Society." *The Commoner*, 4(May), at www.commoner.org.uk/01-3groundzero.htm.

Dinerstein, A., and Neary, M. 1998. *Class Struggle and the* Communist Manifesto. Paper presented at the Conference to Celebrate 150 Years of the *Communist Manifesto*, Paris, May 1998.

Dinerstein, A., & Neary, M. 2001. *Marx, Labor and Real Subsumption, or How No Logo Becomes No to Capitalist Everything*. Unpublished paper.

Dunayevskaya, R. 2002. *The Power of Negativity: Selected Writings on the Dialectic in Hegel and Marx*. Edited by Peter Hudis and Kevin B. Anderson. Lanham, Md.: Lexington Books.

Dyer-Witheford, N. 1999. *Cyber-Marx: Cycles and Circuits of Struggle in High-Technology Capitalism*. Chicago: University of Illinois Press.

Ebert, T. 1996. *Ludic Feminism and after: Postmodernism, Desire, and Labor in Late Capitalism*. Ann Arbor: University of Michigan Press.

Ebert, T. 2001. "Globalization, Internationalism, and the Class Politics of Cynical Reason." *Nature, Society, and Thought*, 12(4), 389–410.

Ebert, T. 2002. *University, Class, and Citizenship*. Unpublished paper.

Elbaum, M. 2002. *Revolution in the Air: Sixties Radicals Turn to Lenin, Mao and Che*. London: Verso.

Feldman, Paul, and Lotz, Corinna. 2004. *A World to Win: A Rough Guide to a Future without Global Capitalism*. London: Lupus Books.

Fischman, G., and McLaren, P. 2000. "Schooling for Democracy: Towards a Critical Utopianism." *Contemporary Society*, 29(1), 168–179.

Foley, B. 1998. "Roads Taken and Not Taken: Post-Marxism, Antiracism, and Anti-communism." *Cultural Logic*, 1(2, Spring).

Forrester, V. 1999. *The Economic Horror*. Malden, Mass.: Blackwell Publishers.

Freire, P. 1998. *Pedagogy of the Heart*. New York: Continuum.

Gindin, S. 2002. "Social Justice and Globalization: Are They Compatible?" *Monthly Review*, 54(2, June), 1–11.

Giroux, H. 1983. *Theory and Resistance in Education: A Pedagogy for the Opposition*. South Hadley, Mass.: Bergin & Garvey.

Giroux, H. 1988. *Teachers as Intellectuals: Towards a Critical Pedagogy of Learning*. South Hadley, Mass.: Bergin & Garvey.

Giroux, H. A. 1981. *Ideology, Culture & the Process of Schooling*. Philadelphia, Pa.: Temple University Press.

Giroux, H., and McLaren, P. 1997. "Paulo Freire, Postmodernism and the Utopian Imagination: A Blochian Reading." In *Not Yet: Reconsidering Ernst Bloch*, edited by J. O. Daniel and T. Moylan, 138–162. London: Verso Press.

Goebbels, Joseph. 1934. *Der Kongress zur Nürnberg*. Munich: Zentralverlag der NS-DAP., Frz. Eher Nachf., 130–41. At www.calvin.edu/academic/cas/gpa/goeb59.htm.

Hardt, M., and Negri, A. 2000. *Empire*. Cambridge: Harvard University Press.

Hill, D. 2001. "State Theory and the Neo-Liberal Reconstruction of Schooling and Teacher Education: A Structuralist Neo-Marxist Critique of Postmodernist, Quasi-Postmodernist, and Culturalist Neo-Marxist Theory." *British Journal of Sociology of Education*, 22(1), 137–157.

Hill, D., and Cole, M. 2001. "Social Class." In *Schooling and Equality: Fact, Concept and Policy*, edited by D. Hill and M. Cole, 137–159. London: Kogan Page.

Hill, D., McLaren, P., Cole, M., and Rikowski, G. 2002. *Marxism against Postmodernism in Educational Theory*. Lanham, Md.: Lexington Books.

Hill, D., Sanders, M., and Hankin, T. 2002. "Marxism, Social Class and Postmodernism." In *Marxism against Postmodernism in Educational Theory*, edited by D. Hill, P. McLaren, & G. Rikowski, 167–206. Lanham, Md.: Lexington Books.

Holloway, J. 2002a. *Change the World without Taking Power: The Meaning of Revolution Today*. London: Pluto Press.

Holloway, J. 2002b. "Twelve Theses on Changing the World Without Taking Power." *The Commoner*, 4(May), at www.commoner.org.uk/04holloway2.pdf.

Houston, D., and McLaren, P. In press. "The 'Nature' of Political Amnesia: A Response to CA 'Chet' Bowers." *Educational Studies*.

Hudis, Peter. 1983. *Marx and the Third World: New Perspectives on Writing from His Last Decade*. Chicago: A *News & Letters* Publication.

Hudis, P. 2000. "The Dialectical Structure of Marx's Concept of 'Revolution in Permanence.'" *Capital & Class,* 70 (Spring), 127–142.

Hudis, P. 2000a. "Can Capital Be Controlled?" *News & Letters Online*, at www.newsandletters.org/4.00_essay.htm.

Hudis, P. 2003a. *The Future of Dialectical Marxism: Towards a New Relation of Theory and Practice*. A paper presented at Rethinking Marxism Conference, November 2003.

Hudis, P. 2003b. *Organizational Responsibility for Marxist-Humanism in Light of War, Resistance, and the Need for a New Alternative.* Report to National Plenum of News and Letters Committees, August 30, 2003.

Hudis, P. In press. "Marx among the Muslims." *Capitalism, Nature, Socialism.*

Jani, P. 2002. "Karl Marx, Eurocentrism, and the 1857 Revolt in British India." In *Marxism, Modernity and Postcolonial Studies,* edited by Crystal Bartolovich and Neil Lazarus, 81–97. Cambridge, England: Cambridge University Press.

Kagarlitsky, B. 2000. *The Return of Radicalism: Reshaping the Left Institutions.* Translated by Renfrey Clark. London: Pluto Press.

Kincheloe, J. 1998. *How Do We Tell the Workers? The Socioeconomic Foundations of Work and Vocational Education.* Boulder, Colo.: Westview Press.

Kovel, J. 2002. *The Enemy of Nature: The End of Capitalism or the End of the World?* London: Zed Books.

Krader, L. 1975. *The Asiatic Mode of Production.* Assen: Van Gorcum & Co.

Lather, P. 1991. *Getting Smart: Feminist Research and Pedagogy within the Postmodern.* London: Routledge.

Lather, P. 1998. "Critical Pedagogy and Its Complicities: A Praxis of Stuck Places." *Educational Theory,* 48(4), 447–498.

Lenin, V. 1951. *Imperialism: The Highest Stage of Capitalism.* Moscow: Foreign Language Publishing House.

Löwy, M. 2004. "Just an Answer to John Holloway." *New Politics,* IX(4, Winter), 142–143.

Luxemburg, R. 1919. *The Crisis in German Social Democracy: The Junius Pamphlet.* New York: The Socialist Publication Society.

Malik, K. 1996. "Universalism and Difference: Race and the Postmodernists." *Race & Class,* 37(3), 1–17.

Marx, K. 1844 [1977]. *Economic and Philosophical Manuscripts of 1844.* Moscow: Progress Publishers.

Marx, K. 1863 [1972]. *Theories of Surplus Value—Part Three.* London: Lawrence & Wishart.

Marx, K. 1865 [1977]. *Capital: A Critique of Political Economy—Volume 3.* London: Lawrence & Wishart.

Marx, K. 1866 [1976]. *Results of the Immediate Process of Production,* Addendum to "Capital," Vol.1. Harmondsworth: Penguin.

Marx, K. 1967. *Capital, Volume One.* Edited by Frederick Engels. Translated by Samuel Moore and Aveling. New York: International Publishers.

Marx, K. 1970. *A Contribution to the Critique of Political Economy.* New York: International Publishers.

Marx, K. 1973. *Critique of the Gotha Program.* New York: International Publishers.

Marx, K. 1988. *Economic and Philosophic Manuscripts of 1844.* New York: Prometheus Books.

Marx, K. 1993. Grundrisse: *Foundations of the Critique of Political Economy.* Translated by Martin Nicolaus. New York: Penguin Books.

Marx, K., and Engels, F. 1850, March. Address of the Central Committee to the Communist League, London. McChesney, R. W. 1999. "Introduction." In *Profit over*

People: Neoliberalism and Global Order, edited by N. Chomsky, 7–16. New York: Seven Stories Press.

McLaren, P. 1995. *Critical Pedagogy and Predatory Culture: Oppositional Politics in a Postmodern Era.* London: Routledge.

McLaren, P. 1997. *Revolutionary Multiculturalism: Pedagogies of Dissent for the New Millennium.* Boulder, Colo.: Westview Press.

McLaren, P. 1998a. *Life in Schools: An Introduction to Critical Pedagogy in the Foundations of Education* (3rd ed.). New York: Longman.

McLaren, P. 1998b. "Revolutionary Pedagogy in Post-Revolutionary Times: Rethinking the Political Economy of Critical Education." *Educational Theory,* 48(4), 431–462.

McLaren, P. 2000. *Che Guevara, Paulo Freire, and the Pedagogy of Revolution.* Boulder, Colo.: Rowman & Littlefield.

McLaren, P., and Farahmandpur, R. 1999a. "Critical Pedagogy, Postmodernism, and the Retreat from Class: Towards a Contraband Pedagogy." *Theoria,* 93, 83–115.

McLaren, P., and Farahmandpur, R. 1999b. "Critical Multiculturalism and Globalization. Some Implications for a Politics of Resistance." *Journal of Curriculum Theorizing,* 15(3), 27–46.

McLaren, P., and Farahmandpur, R. 2000. "Reconsidering Marx in Post-Marxist times: A Requiem for Postmodernism?" *Educational Researcher,* 29(3), 25–33.

McLaren, P., and Farahmandpur, R. 2001a. "Educational Policy and the Socialist Imagination: Revolutionary Citizenship as a Pedagogy of Resistance." *Educational Policy,* 13(3, July), 343–378.

McLaren, P., and Farahmandpur, R. 2001b. "Teaching against Globalization and the New Imperialism: Toward a Revolutionary Pedagogy." *Journal of Teacher Education,* 52(2, March/April), 136–150.

McLaren, P., and Farahmandpur, R. In press. *Teaching against Globalization and the New Imperialism: A Critical Pedagogy.* Lanham, Md.: Rowman & Littlefield.

McLaren, P., and Jaramillo, N. 2002. "Critical Pedagogy as Organizational Praxis: Challenging the Demise of Civil Society in a Time of Permanent War." *Educational Foundations,* 16(4, Fall), 5–32.

McMurtry, J. 1998. *Unequal Freedoms: The Global Market as an Ethical System.* West Hartford, Conn.: Kumarian Press.

McMurtry, J. 1999. *The Cancer Stage of Capitalism.* London: Pluto Press.

McMurtry, J. 2000. "A Failed Global Experiment: The Truth about the US Economic Model." *Comer,* 12(7), 10–11.

McQuaig, L. 2001. *All You Can Eat: Greed, Lust and the New Capitalism.* Toronto: Penguin Books.

Mészáros, I. 1986. *Philosophy, Ideology & Social Science: Essays in Negation and Affirmation.* New York: St. Martin's Press.

Mészáros, I. 1995. *Beyond Capital: Toward a Theory of Transition.* New York: Monthly Review Press.

Mészáros, I. 1999. "Marxism, the Capital System, and Social Revolution: An Interview with István Mészáros." *Science and Society,* 63(3), 338–361.

Mészáros, I. 2001. *Socialism or Barbarism: From the "American Century" to the Crossroads.* New York: Monthly Review Press.

Mészáros, I. 2003, June. "Militarism and the Coming Wars." *Monthly Review*, 55(2), 17–24.

Miranda, J. 1980. *Marx against the Marxists*. Maryknoll, NY: Orbis Books.

Neary, M. Forthcoming. "Travels in Moishe Postone's Social Universe: A Contribution to a Critique of Political Cosmology." *Historical Materialism: Research in Critical Marxist Theory*.

Neary, M., and Rikowski, G. 2000. *The Speed of Life: The Significance of Karl Marx's Concept of Socially Necessary Labour-Time*. Paper presented at the British Sociological Association Annual Conference 2000, University of York, April 17–20.

News & Letters Committee. 2002. "Confronting Permanent War and Terrorism. Why the Anti-War Movement Needs a Dialectical Perspective." A Statement from the Resident Editorial Board of *News & Letters* (pamphlet).

Ollman, B. 1976. *Alienation: Marx's Conception of Man in Capitalist Society* (2nd ed.). Cambridge: Cambridge University Press.

Ollman, B. 2001. *How to Take an Exam and Remake the World*. Montreal: Black Rose Books.

Panitch, L., and Gindin, S. 2001. "Transcending Pessimism: Rekindling Socialist Imagination." In *After the Fall: 1989 and the Future of Freedom*, edited by G. Katsiaficas, 175–199. New York: Routledge.

Parenti, M. 2001. "Rollback: Aftermath of the Overthrow of Communism." In *After the Fall: 1989 and the Future of Freedom*, edited by G. Katsiaficas, 153–158. New York: Routledge.

Parenti, M. 2002. "Global Rollback after Communism." *CovertAction Quarterly*, 72(Spring), 41–44.

Petras, J. 2000. *Globalization and Citizenship: Social and Political Dimensions*. Working Papers in Cultural Studies, 22, pp. 1–20. Pullman, Wash.: Department of Comparative American Cultures, Washington State University.

Petras, J., and Veltmeyer, H. 2001. *Globalization Unmasked: Imperialsim in the 21st Century*. London: Zed Books.

Post, C. 2002. *Review: Empire and Revolution*. Fourth International Press List.

Postone, M. 1996. *Time, Labour, and Social Domination: A Reinterpretation of Marx's Critical Theory*. Cambridge: Cambridge University Press.

Rikowski, G. 1999. "Education, Capital and the Transhuman." In *Postmodernism in Educational Theory: Education and the Politics of Human Resistance*, edited by D. Hill, P. McLaren, M. Cole, and G. Rikowski, 50–84. London: Tufnell Press.

Rikowski, G. 2000a. *That Other Great Class of Commodities: Repositioning Marxist Educational Theory*. Paper presented at the British Educational Research Association Conference 2000, Cardiff University, session 10.21, September 9.

Rikowski, G. 2000b. *Messing with the Explosive Commodity: School Improvement, Educational Research and Labour-Power in the Era of Global Capitalism*. Paper prepared for the Symposium on "If We Aren't Pursuing Improvement, What Are We Doing?" British Educational Research Association Conference 2000, Cardiff University, Wales, September 7.

Rikowski, G. 2001a. *The Importance of Being a Radical Educator in Capitalism Today*. A Guest Lecture in the Sociology of Education, The Gillian Rose Room, Department of Sociology, University of Warwick, Coventry, May 24.

Rikowski, G. 2001b. *The Battle in Seattle: Its Significance for Education.* London: Tufnell Press.

Rikowski, G. 2001c. *After the Manuscript Broke off: Thoughts on Marx, Social Class and Education.* A paper presented at the British Sociological Association Education Study Group, King's College London, June 23.

Rikowski, G. 2002. "Fuel for the Living Fire: Labor-Power!" In *The Labor Debate: An Investigation into the Theory and Reality of Capitalist Work,* edited by A. Dinerstein and M. Neary, 179–202. Aldershot: Ashgate.

Rikowski, R., and Rikowski, G. Forthcoming. "Against What We Are Worth." A paper to be submitted to *Gender and Education.*

Robbins, B. 1999. *Feeling Global: Inter-Nationalism in Distress.* New York: New York University Press.

Robinson, W. 1996. *Promoting Polyarchy: Globalization, U.S. Intervention, and Hegemony.* Cambridge: Cambridge University Press.

Robinson, W. 2000. "Social Theory and Globalization: The Rise of a Transnational State." *Theory and Society*, 30, 157–200.

Robinson, W. 2004. *A Theory of Global Capitalism: Production, Class, and State in a Transnational World.* Baltimore, Md.: Johns Hopkins University Press.

Robinson, W., and Harris, J. 2000. "Towards a Global Ruling Class? Globalization and the Transnational Capitalist Class." *Science & Society*, 64(1), 11–54.

Rochester, J. M. 2003. "Critical Demagogues: The Writings of Henry Giroux and Peter McLaren." *Education Next* (Fall) at www.educationnext.org/20034/pdf/77.pdf.

San Juan Jr., E. 1999. "Raymond Williams and the Idea of Cultural Revolution." *College Literature,* 26(2), 118–136.

San Juan Jr., E. 2002. *Racism and Cultural Studies: Critiques of Multiculturalist Ideology and the Politics of Difference.* Durham, NC: Duke University Press.

San Juan Jr., E. 2004. "Post 9/11 Reflections on Multicuturalism and Racism." *Axis of Logic*, November 13, at www.axisoflogic.com/artman/publish/article_13554.shtml.

Skolnik, J. 2004. "The Challenge of Anti-Humanism Today." *News & Letters*, (August–September), 5.

Teeple, G. 1995. *Globalization and the Decline of Social Reform.* Aurora, Ontario: Garamond Press.

Thompson, W. 1997. *The Left in History: Revolution and Reform in Twentieth-Century Politics.* London: Pluto Press.

Wilden, Anthony. 1980. *The Imaginary Canadian: An Examination for Discovery.* Vancouver, Canada: Pulp Press.

Wood, E. M. 1994. Identity crisis. *In These Times*, (June 13), 28–29.

Wood, E. M. 1995. *Democracy against Capitalism: Renewing Historical Materialism.* Cambridge, Cambridge University Press.

Wood, E. M. 2003. *Empire of Capital.* London: Verso.

Wypijewski, J. 2004. "Labor in the Dawn of Empire." In *Imperial Crusades: Iraq, Afghanistan and Yugoslavia*, edited by Alexander Cockburn and Jeffrey St. Clair, 289–298. London: Verso.

Žižek, S. 2001. *Repeating Lenin.* Unpublished paper.

2

Revolutionary Pedagogy in Postrevolutionary Times: Rethinking the Political Economy of Critical Education

Peter McLaren

Much (but of course not all) of the "mainstreamed" critical educational work in the United States, along with work in related fields, now appears woefully detached from historical specificities and basic determinations of capitalist society to be of much serious use in generating the type of critique and practice that can move education reform past its log-jam of social amelioration and into the untapped waters of social transformation. What is not on offer is an alternative social vision of what the world should and could look like outside the value form of capital. The construction of a new vision of human sociality has never been more urgent in a world of reemerging rivalries between national bourgeoisies and cross-national class formations where the United States seeks unchallenged supremacy over all other nation-states by controlling the regulatory regimes of supranational institutions such as the World Bank and the International Monetary Fund (IMF). It is a world where the working class toil for longer hours to exact a minimum wage that corresponds to pin money for the ruling elite. Even if the ruling class somehow felt compelled to reconfigure its tortured relationship with the working class, it could not do so and still extract the surplus value necessary to reproduce and maintain its own class formation built upon its historical legacy of class privilege and power. It is also a world undergoing an organic crisis of capital as domestic class fractions within the United States not only struggle to avoid membership in Marx's reserve army of labor, but are thrust, *nolens volens*, into service as the new warrior class destined to serve as capital's imperial shock troops expected to fight wars of preemption and "prevention" declared by the U.S. administration under the cover of the war on terrorism.

Over the last several decades, the exultant pronouncements and echolalic commentaries on the demise of socialism advanced by liberal and conservative propagandists of capitalism (including the growing ranks of post-Marxists) have helped to set in train the imperatives of a revitalized global order built around the logic of the free market. As rightist ideologues hoist the banner of unrestrained, frictionless, speculator capitalism while at the same time sound the requiem for Marxism in the catacombs of *realpolitik*, the U.S. left stands in disarray, currents of anxiety cascading through its ranks. The pivotal historical mechanisms leading the so-called end of ideology have resulted in the absence of a radical left able and ready to contest the neoliberal capitalist class. Even the tremulous excitement of the bourgeois liberals has disappeared. It's been out of sight since the 1960s. The educational left has not remained immune to the disorganization in the ranks of the Left in general, and the Marxist left in particular. While the educational left has made interesting advances with respect to the critique of postmodern culture, its performance has been prima facie discouraging in challenging the consolidation of global capitalist relations over the last several decades. The postmodern educational left has, for the most part, carefully ensconced itself within the educational establishment in an uneasy alliance that has disabled its ability to do much more than engage in hefty attempts at radical posturing, while reaping the benefits of scholarly rewards. This chapter discusses the dangerous triumph of global capitalism, advocates for a revitalized leftist critique of capital, and sketches provisionally a number of directions for critical education.

The globalization of labor and capital accompanied by technological innovation, its promise of structural equanimity and its paramystical guarantee of easy and endless consumption has brought about material shifts in cultural practices and the proliferation of new contradictions between capitalism and labor that progressive educators who work in schools of education have been hard-pressed to respond to, as opposed to react to, successfully.[1]

The current phenomenon of globalization has been described as the cannibalization of the social and political by the economy[2] and the "grand finale of the explosion of Western modernity."[3] Kleptocratic capitalism is afoot today, stealing from the poor to give to the rich. Welfare for the oppressed has been replaced by frontier-style subventions to capital by the government in the form of worldwide gunslinger entrepreneurialism. The political ideology of the times is legitimizing a traumatic suppression of labor income. One of the central contradictions of the new global economy is "that capitalism no longer seems able to sustain maximum profitability by means of commensurate economic growth and seems now to be relying more and more on simply redistributing wealth in favor of the rich, and on increasing inequalities, within and between national economies, with the help of the neoliberal state."[4] The poor living in our midst, sleeping in cardboard boxes and eating from garbage dumpsters, are as much a part of the global economy as Los Angeles's new

Mount Olympus, the shining new Getty Center atop the hill overlooking the luxury neighborhood of Bel Air.

It is undeniably the case today that capitalism has entered a global crisis of accumulation and profitability. Self-destructing as a result of intensified competition leading to overcapacity and overproduction and a fall in manufacturing profitability, the new era of flexible accumulation requires a number of ominous conditions: the total dismantling of the Fordist-Keynesian relationship between capital and labor; a shift toward the extraction of absolute surplus value; the suppression of labor incomes; a weakening of trade unions; longer working hours; more temporary jobs; and the creation of a permanent underclass, to name just a handful of developments. Western democracies are witnessing increasing numbers of individuals excluded from productive and distributive spheres. Such exclusion is not the result of a paralyzing abulia on the part of contemporary workers seeking decent jobs, but the structured exclusion of workers from the ranks of the employed. Unemployment is spreading misery and misfortune throughout all sectors of U.S. society; where employment opportunities are available, they are too often in the "second sector" of the economy where health insurance and pensions do not exist, and where few government regulations exist to protect workers. On a more global scale, we are witnessing the progressive division of "capitalist" and "proletarian" nations.

William Greider has noted in a recent issue of *The Nation* that: "In different ways, labor incomes are suppressed on both ends of the global system— usually by labor-market forces (including mass unemployment or temp jobs) in the advanced economies, often by government edict and brutal force in developing ones. Meanwhile, companies must keep building more production or locating factories to keep up in the cost-price chase"[5] According to Greider, we are returning to a form of prewelfare competitive capitalism that is driven by the motor of conservative political ideology—one that is capable of suturing together the discourses of freedom, family values, civic authority, nationalism, and patriotism. Of course, the term "freedom" is used in a decidedly and perniciously manipulative fashion. Only the market remains "free" and people must submit to the dictates of the market. This is most painfully evident in cases where the International Monetary Fund and the U.S. Treasury regularly impose forced-austerity terms on poor countries such as cutting wages and public spending and raising interest rates so that endangered banks can fix their balance sheets.[6] Thus Jorge Larrain is compelled to write that:

> unemployment is treated as laziness and pricing yourself out of a good job, workers' strikes are transformed into a problem of public order. Criminality and

new forms of violence are treated as the result of lack of authority in the family, not enough law and order, lack of Victorian values, and so on. Terrorism is successful because of the free press and the excessive leniency of the law. Divisions and forms of discrimination are partly blamed on immigration and partly conjured away by patriotism and jingoism.[7]

The global restructuring of industries and work organization has had devastating consequences for developing countries. The International Monetary Fund wants poor countries to improve their balance-of-payments position by liberalizing their economies, devaluing currencies, and increasing imports in proportion to exports. This has wrought nothing but havoc for the poor. And international trade conventions such as GATT have made the pursuit of ecologically sustainable food security increasingly more difficult.[8]

Today in the United States we are witnessing the emergence of a new dominant class bolstered by a technological aristocracy and a cadre of business executives who work in the interests of corporate share price.[9] Within this context, capital and the state are reconfiguring race and gender; a white male comprador labor aristocracy is giving way to more decentralized, local, and flexible means of using race and gender as "divide and rule" tactics. This follows from the fact that global capitalism is relying more and more on Third World labor and on Third World labor pools in First World spaces.[10]

With the advent of the Internet, inexpensive satellite communications, multibillion dollar global software corporations, online companies, and developments in biotechnology, nanotechnology, and alternative energy technology, the new world order is unfolding by evolutionary corporate design. The new operating matrix of the biotech-based technological revolution that is following in the wake of the mergers, consolidations, and acquisitions of the life-science industry by global commercial enterprises is creating the conditions for what Jeremy Rifkin describes as a "wholesale reseeding of the Earth's biosphere with a laboratory-conceived Second Genesis, an artificially produced bioindustrial nature designed to replace nature's own evolutionary scheme."[11] The logic of unfettered capitalism is being heralded as an amplification of nature's own principles, thus justifying the emerging corporate eugenics science as a second-tier evolutionary trend, one in which genes become the "green gold" that will drive the future of the world economy. The push for patent protection of gene pools—linked to projects such as the Human Genome Diversity Project—has witnessed clandestine attempts by the U.S. government to "privatize the human body"[12] by obtaining patents on the cell-lines of Panama's Guaymi Indians and populations in the Solomon Islands, Papua New Guinea, and India so that U.S. corporations can profit from global control over the genetic blueprints of human life.

Corporations such as Microsoft, Nike, and Disney are replacing human autonomy with the artificial needs and desires of mass consumption. Bill

Resnick notes that, "Nike's goal is an identity deeper and less accessible to rational critique, to become the stuff of consciousness, to become part of the definition of freedom and accomplishment, displacing other definitions and patterns."[13]

In a world where Michael Jordan is paid more for a single Nike advertisement than the combined wages of workers in a Southeast Asia Nike factory, is it any wonder that Mattel has brought out a new "Cool Shoppin' Barbie," the first doll with a toy credit card. The offspring of a Mattel and MasterCard initiative to secure a future generation of lifetime credit card addicts (similar to the way that the Joe Camel advertisement was designed to addict a generation of children to cigarettes), Cool Shoppin' Barbie is a shameless exploitation of children in a country in which 1.35 million people filed for bankruptcy in 1997 because of the easy availability of credit.[14] Is this any more ethically repulsive than the media's glorification of wealth, or celebration of violence, or its anointing of high-priced consumer items with a sacerdotal status, and its overall linking of consumption to identity? Is it any wonder that gun-obsessed children are feeling alienated and blowing away their classmates with high-powered rifles and then complaining that they can't order pizzas in their jail cells? Should we blink an eye at the fact that the former president and chairman of the Communist Party of the Soviet Union, Mikhail Gorbachev, was paid one million dollars by Pizza Hut to play his character on a TV commercial, where he is praised by the Russian people for introducing them to the delights of pizza, democracy, and Western-style freedom.[15]

The international division of labor characterized by vast inequalities has become so pronounced today that it excludes entire national and continental economies from the New World Order.[16] Propelled by a fragmentation of the mass market enabled by science and technology to be split into smaller submarkets and into customized niches where competition is focused on consumer "identity," the new "fast" capitalism makes competition fiercer, creating a small number of big winners (based on large short-run profits) and a large number of losers (competitors who come in second place face huge losses in a winner-take-all market). There is no place in America that isn't a stone's throw away from the dark certainty of unemployment.

We are faced with what Pierre Bourdieu refers to as the "gospel" of neoliberalism. This gospel is one that "leads to a combat *by every means*, including the destruction of the environment and human sacrifice, against any obstacle to the maximization of profit."[17] Bourdieu describes neoliberalism as:

a powerful economic theory *whose strictly symbolic strength, combined with the effect of theory, redoubles the force of the economic realities it is supposed to express*. It ratifies the spontaneous philosophy of the people who run large multinationals and of the agents of high finance—in particular pension-fund

managers. Relayed throughout the world by national and international politicians, civil servants, and most of all the universe of senior journalists—all more
or less equally ignorant of the underlying mathematical theology—it is becoming a sort of universal belief, a new ecumenical gospel. This gospel, or rather the
soft vulgate which is put forward everywhere under the name of liberalism, is
concocted out of a collection of ill-defined words—"globalization," "flexibility," "deregulation" and so on—which, through their liberal or even libertarian
connotations, may help to give the appearance of a message of freedom and liberation to a conservative ideology which thinks itself opposed to all ideology.[18]

Gangster politicians on the hustle are brokering the system for private industry at the expense of the public interest, public service, and public rights
and, in many recent instances such as California's Propositions 187 and 209,
at the expense of civil rights, and putting commercial interests before human
dignity and social justice, dismantling the Keynesian welfare state with such
a determinate fury that the concept of exploitation has been reduced to an
empty abstraction separated from the idea of living, breathing individuals
who suffer as a result of it. The seduction of capital is overwhelming, affect-
ing even the most well-intentioned groups of progressive educators. Davies
and Guppy remind us that "globalization is transforming education by
squeezing power from the middle. As power is being wrestled from education
professionals, teachers unions, and education officials, it is being redistrib-
uted upward to more senior state officials *and* downward to local groups."[19]

Out of the bourgeois salons of the "Red Vienna" of the early 1900s
emerged (along with the sherry and cigar smoke) the resilient thinking of
Fredrich Von Hayek, the prime *animateur* of neoliberal economics. The goal
of this Austrian economist and University of Chicago professor was to crush
socialism in his lifetime.[20] Von Hayek rejected unfettered, laissez-faire capitalism and instead urged active government involvement to protect the
smooth functioning of a free market. He advanced what he called "the catal-
laxy" or the spontaneous relations of free economic exchange between individuals. Under the influence of Ludwig Von Mises, secretary of the Vienna
Chamber of Commerce, and Carl Menger, founder of the Austrian School of
Economics, and the theories of knowledge developed by Ernst Mach and
Michael Polyani, Hayek developed his epistemology of citizenship in relation
to the figure of the global entrepreneur.

Hayek conceived of a monetarist economics of free-market constitutional
liberalism in order to fuel the engine of his ideological and moral crusade
against socialism based on the idea that there is no connection between human intention and social outcome, that the results of human activity are fundamentally haphazard, and that spontaneity must be protected by the strong
arm of tradition.[21] Hayek expressed faith—almost to the point of religious

zealotry—in the unregulated price mechanism as the means of economic co-ordination and argued that the role of the state must be to blunt human agency and protect the spontaneous social order from the persistently messy efforts of human design. As a philosophical naturalist, Hayek reveled in whatever transpired outside of the conscious attempt at social control; he abhorred what he believed to be the human engineering aspects of market intervention. Market ruthlessness was seen as the aggregate effort of consumer choices, and in Hayek's view it was more important to protect the spontaneity of the market—despite its often deleterious consequences for the poor—than it was to protect individuals or groups from the shameful effects of market justice.

Criticizing neoclassical equilibrium theory as too abstract, Hayek believed that business monopolies were always more benign than the monopolies of labor and the state.[22] Competition is what ensures the spontaneity of the market and this in turn is what creates necessary entrepreneurial opportunities that comprise the natural evolution of the market system, a natural evolution that must be safeguarded at all costs (and for Hayek, this meant that a *cognoscenti* of males over forty years of age would oversee the market and would be up for election every fifteen years). Under Hayek's scheme of free-market orthodoxy, the everyday citizen has no right to choose what is better for him or her. Only existing objective economic conditions can work as the motive force for choice, guided by a cadre of experts enforcing a "hands-off" policy of market protection.

The educational epistemology that follows from these neoliberal perspectives flows directly from the idea that knowledge is "constitutionally and irredeemably individual."[23] Ignoring the sociohistorical context of economic systems, Hayekian economic science depends upon statistical calculation, macroeconomic econometrics, and methodological individualism. Econometrics is a psuedoscience designed to promote profit at all costs. As Joel Spring notes, Hayek advanced a new form of totalitarianism where the individual is controlled in order to ensure favorable market conditions.[24] In both the United States and the United Kingdom, Hayek's ideals—namely, that markets are self-regulating—provided the underpinnings for discussions of school choice, national standards, and curricula, eliminating the welfare state and lifelong learning.

Hayek's ideals were adopted by his colleague at the University of Chicago, Nobel Laureate Milton Friedman, who put them to use in his support of government-financed vouchers for school choice. Hayekian economics underwrote both Thatcherism and the so-called Reagan revolution and eventually influenced global economic planning.[25] While classical liberals reject state intervention in economics and education, neoliberals in both economic and educational arenas advocate state intervention in order to ensure the operation of a free market and the unrestricted advance of capital. Neoliberal education policy is thus a conservative force, often blending Christianity, nationalism, authoritarian populism, and free-market economics and calling for such creations as a national history curriculum that celebrates the virtues of Christian values, minimal government regulation (except to ensure a "free market"), and individual freedom.[26] Educational criticalists who stress the social character of knowledge stipulate that people can, through cooperation, increase their understanding of the social consequences of their actions, even though they will never fully know their consequences. Stressing the socially constituted way in which knowledge is produced (a fundamental axiom among Freireans, for instance) provides a basis for questioning the values and mechanisms for regulating the social order. This, of course, contravenes Hayek's trenchant prohibition against human design and his valorization of the political neutrality of "accidental" market transactions.

In their new book *The New Work Order: Behind the Language of the New Capitalism*, James Paul Gee, Glynda Hull, and Colin Lankshear analyze the ways in which cognitive science has progressively shifted its concept of expertise from an association with disciplinary expertise in the academic sense to the worldview of the new capitalism with its focus on change, speed, flexibility, and innovation.[27] They also note the way in which the academic curricula in schools have been modified to link education more securely to the job requirements of "the new work order." In this sense, it is possible to view contemporary testing measures, institutional tracking, and efforts to link schools to the Internet not as strategies to prepare more creative and informed citizens, but as ways to assist in human resource planning for the global economy as we proceed apace in the new millennium.

Given current structural and conjunctural conditions such as the privatization of subjectively, free-market fundamentalism, and the moral collapse of social democracy after the defeat of communism, we need to rethink the nature and purpose of education according to the kind of "knowledge worker" proposed *by* the new capitalist order *for* the new capitalist order. This hidden curriculum or "pedagogical unsaid" is nothing new although the ideological state apparatuses have made it a more sophisticated enterprise. Its function is largely the same as it was during earlier phases of industrial capitalism: the attempt to de-form knowledge into a discreet and decontexualized set of technical skills packaged to serve big business interests, cheap labor, and ideological conformity. In fact, at a time in which real wages are being steadily ratcheted downward, students are being prepared to become custodians of the capitalist state—a state destablized by the constant deterritorialization and reterritorialization of capital and whose power is increasingly facilitated by the quick movement of information that permits instant turnover times within financial markets.

CRITICAL PEDAGOGY: A FRAGMENTATION OF VISION

About twenty years after the Cuban revolution, when "Che Guevara became the *prototype of a new revolutionary generation,*"[28] U.S. educational scholars on the Left began fighting the destructive logic of capital through the development of what has been variously called radical pedagogy, feminist pedagogy, and critical pedagogy. Critical pedagogy is a way of thinking about, negotiating, and transforming the relationship among classroom teaching, the production of knowledge, the institutional structures of the school, and the social and material relations of the wider community, society, and nation-state.[29] Developed by progressive teachers, literacy workers, and radical scholars attempting to eliminate inequalities on the basis of social class, it has sparked a wide array of antisexist, antiracist, and antihomophobic classroom-based curricula and policy initiatives. This follows a strong recognition that racism, sexism, and homophobia are exacerbated by capitalist exploitation.

Critical pedagogy has grown out of a number of theoretical developments such as Latin American philosophies of liberation; the pedagogy of Brazilian educator Paulo Freire;[30] the anti-imperialist struggle of Che Guevara and other revolutionary movements; the sociology of knowledge; the Frankfurt school of critical theory; feminist theory; and neo-Marxist cultural criticism. In more recent years it has been taken up by educators influenced by postmodern social theory and Derridean deconstruction and its somewhat more politically contestatory academic partner, post-structuralism.[31] Yet at the level of classroom life, critical pedagogy is often seen as synonymous with whole language instruction, adult literacy programs, and new "constructivist" approaches to teaching and learning based on a depoliticized interpretation of Lev Vygotsky's work and a tie-dyed optimism of "I'm okay, you're okay." While critics often decry this educational approach for its idealist multiculturalism and harmonious political vision, its supporters, including the late Paulo Freire, have complained that critical pedagogy has been frequently domesticated in practice and reduced to student-directed learning approaches devoid of social critique and a revolutionary agenda. Of course, this is due partly to the educational left's retreat from historical materialism and meta-theory as dated systems of intelligibility that supposedly have historically run their course, and the dislocation of power, knowledge, and desire brought on by the New Left's infatuation with more conservative forms of avant-garde apostasy found in certain incarnations of French postmodernist theoretical advances.[32]

Because many postmodern theorists and their post-structuralist companions operate from a theoretical terrain built upon a number of questionable assumptions—that is, they view symbolic exchange as taking place outside the domain of value; privilege structures of deference over structures of exploitation and relations of exchange over relations of production; emphasize local narratives over grand narratives; encourage the coming to voice of the symbolically dispossessed over the transformation of existing social relations; reduce models of reality to historical fictions; abandon the assessment of the truth value of competing narratives; replace the idea that power is class-specific and historically bound with the idea that power is everywhere and nowhere—they end up advancing a philosophical commission that propagates hegemonic class rule and reestablishes the rule of the capitalist class.[33] What this has done is precisely to continue the work of reproducing class antagonisms and creating a new balance of hegemonic relations favoring dominant class interests.[34] According to Glenn Rikowksi:

> the insertion of postmodernism within educational discourses lets in some of the most unwelcome of guests—nihilism, relativism, educational marketisation, to name but a few—which makes thinking about human emancipation futile. Left postmodernism, in denying the possibility of human emancipation, merely succeeds in providing complacent cocktail-bar academic gloss for the New Right project of marketising education and deepening the rule of capital within the realm of education and training.[35]

Here I am not attempting to adopt a conservative Marxist dismissal of postmodernism,[36] since, as Eagleton[37] reminds us (and as I myself have noted on numerous occasions), postmodernism, while limited as a critique of capitalism, has made considerable and important advances in explaining the construction of identity.[38] It has also contributed greatly to the construction of what has been called "radical democracy."

However, as Marxist and neo-Marxist educationalists (as well as other critical social theorists) continue to develop trenchant critiques of postmodernism, they are reinvigorating the debates over revolutionary class struggle within the current crisis of globalization in important and in urgent ways.[39] Nancy Fraser, herself a neo-Weberian—has put forward a convincing case that radical democracy, which utilizes postmodernist and post-structuralist analyses, "remains largely confined to the cultural-political plane" and continues to "bracket political economy" and work against the development of a social politics of resource distribution.[40] Because *both capitalism and postmodern education* find virtue in diversity, in the crossing of borders, in the disavowal of hierarchical control, in *droit à la différence* (the right to difference), in the emphasis on inclusion of everyone from workers to chief executives in meaningful work decisions of the business, and in the blurring of the boundaries between life inside and outside the workplace, the language of the new capitalism can often co-opt the language of the postmodern critique of capitalism.[41] It is relatively easy for the new capitalists to align themselves with postmodernist critics of capitalism and Western hegemony. For instance, British educationalist Andy Green reports that "the postmoderns argue that greater pluralism and 'choice' in education is good because it empowers individuals and subordinated cultures. They also suggest that it is somehow inevitable in the modern world because society and culture itself has become so fragmented."[42] In actual fact, notes Green, a radically relativist postmodern approach to cultural politics may appear on the surface to valorize the marginalized and the excluded but such an approach is unable to build solidarity or genuinely pluralist forms of curricula as an alternative to an exclusionary, monocultural, and national curricula. He concludes that "[w]hat we are left with in the end is a 'free market' in classroom cultural politics where the powerful dominant discourses will continue to subordinate other voices and where equality in education will become an ever-more chimerical prospect."[43] The applied barbarism of conservative postmodernism reduces identity to a psychogram, to an instance of discourse delinked from the social totality of capitalist relations of exploitation.

It is undeniably the case that the capitalist class is more odious and powerful today than in the days when anticapitalist guerrillas such as Che Guevara were struggling to cut capitalism at its joints with the revolutionary machete of armed guerrilla resistance. One explanation for the strength of the capitalist class in the current era of global economic restructuring is that its predatory power is more tenaciously fastened to the global commercial media system than at any other time in history. Capitalist discourses are coordinated by a small number of transnational media corporations that are mostly based in the United States.[44] This is a system, according to Robert W. McChesney, "that works to advance the cause of the global market and promote commercial values, while denigrating journalism and culture not conducive to the immediate bottom line or long-run corporate interests. It is a disaster for anything but the most superficial notion of democracy—a democracy where, to paraphrase John Jay's maxim, those who own the world ought to govern it."[45]

William Robinson is worth quoting at length on this issue:

> Global capitalism is predatory and parasitic. In today's global economy, capitalism is less benign, less responsive, to the interests of broad majorities around the world, and less accountable to society than ever before. Some 400 transnational corporations own two-thirds of the planet's fixed assets and control 70 per cent of world trade. With the world's resources controlled by a few hundred global corporations, the life blood and the very fate of humanity is in the hands of transnational capital, which holds the power to make life and death decisions for millions of human beings. Such tremendous concentrations of economic power leads to tremendous concentrations of political power

globally. Any discussion of "democracy" under such conditions becomes meaningless.

The paradox of the demise of dictatorships, "democratic transitions" and the spread of "democracy" around the world is explained by new forms of social control, and the misuse of the concept of democracy, the original meaning of which, the power (cratos) of the people (demos), has been disconfigured beyond recognition. What the transnational elite calls democracy is more accurately termed *polyarchy*, to borrow a concept from academia. Polyarchy is neither dictatorship nor democracy. It refers to a system in which a small group actually rules, on behalf of capital, and participation in decision-making by the majority is confined to choosing among competing elites in tightly controlled electoral processes. This "low-intensity democracy" is a form of consensual domination. Social control and domination is hegemonic, in the sense meant by Antonio Gramsci, rather than coercive. It is based less on outright repression than on diverse forms of ideological co-optation and political disempowerment made possible by the structural domination and "veto power" of global capital.[46]

In fact, what we are witnessing in countries such as the United States, is the development of a polyarchal capitalist culture underwritten by privileging hierarchies that resemble those of many so-called Third World countries.[47]

In the face of the current lack of real democracy and the postmodern assault on the unified subject of the Enlightenment tradition, the "old guard" revolutionaries such as Jose Marti, Camilo Torres, Augusto Sandino, Emiliano Zapata, Rosa Luxemburg, and Che Guevara would have a difficult time winning the sympathy of the postmodern left.[48] Yet when one examines the universal proletarianism that undergirded the vision of many of these revolutionaries, one confronts a necessary postnational journey toward socialism— and a profoundly dialectical journey at that—against the insurgent avantgardism of today's postmodern left, sunk into a despair brought on by a Nietzschean perspectivism and the political paralysis and semiotic inertia of a cultural politics that rarely criticizes the social relations of production, and one has an overwhelming sense that perhaps too much ground has been lost in order to rescue the revolutionary socialist project for education. Nevertheless, the "totalizing" vision of this project remains compelling and instructive, and indeed remains as urgent today as it was thirty years ago. Perhaps even more so. Not only have postmodern theorists cravenly insinuated that Marxist theory is inhospitable to issues of race, ethnicity, and gender, they have ignored the immeasurable richness of Marxist social theory that has been developed over the last several decades. Aijaz Ahmad takes issue with postmodernism's anti-Marxist assessment:

Marxism is today often accused of neglecting all kinds of "difference," of gender, race, ethnicity, nationality, culture, and so on. But it is not Marxism that recognizes no gender differences. These differences are at once abolished by capitalism, by turning women as much as men into instruments of production. These differences are also maintained through cross-class sexual exploitation, not to speak of the differential wage rate, in which women are paid less than men for the same work, or the direct appropriation of women's labor in the domestic economy.[49]

Let me make myself clear on this point. I believe that race/ethnicity, gender, and sexual orientation constitute an interconnected ensemble of social practices and relations and to a certain extent constitute different logics that arise from the same material relations of capitalist exploitation. My position is not a riposte to the relative autonomy thesis (in its various incarnations throughout the years) or to nonclass processes, but rather a criticism of postmodernism's petit-bourgeois–driven movement away from a "represented exterior" of signifying practices that renders an anticapitalist project not only unlikely but firmly inadmissible. Notwithstanding the slippage between Marxist categories and post-structuralist categories, I believe that postmodernist theories, in straddling uneasily the abyss between identity politics and class analysis, have relegated the category of class to an epiphenomena of race, ethnicity, and gender. I concur with Sherry Ortner who remarks that "class exists in America but cannot be talked about, that it is 'hidden,' that there is no language for it, but that it is 'displaced' or 'spoken through' other languages of social difference—race, ethnicity, and gender."[50] I agree with Ortner that while to a certain extent class, race, and ethnicity are separate but interacting dimensions of U.S. social geography and while they operate at least in part on different logics, *"at the level of discourse,* class, race, and ethnicity are so deeply mutually implicated in American culture that it makes little sense to pull them apart."[51] And while "there is no class in America that is not always already racialized and ethnicized" or racial and ethnic categories that are not always already class categories, the salience of race and ethnicity in the United States is such that when they are introduced into the discussion, they tend to "swamp" that of social class.[52] Ortner goes so far as to maintain that the persistent hiddenness of class "means that the discourse is muted and often unavailable, subordinated to virtually every other kind of claim about social success and social failure."[53] And when you mix this reality with the frenetic advance of contemporary global capitalist social relations, you have a recipe for the uncontested reproduction of global relations of exploitation.

Does this mean that I believe that the configuration of nonclass processes such as race, gender, and sexuality are unimportant? Far from it. Class relations deal with the process of producing, appropriating, and distributing surplus value. This view of class is not meant to downplay or deny the importance of power and property in the structure of contemporary society. In fact, allocations of power and property *follow from* the relationships that individuals have to the production and appropriation of surplus labor.[54] I certainly acknowledge that nonclass processes can compromise the conditions of existence of the fundamental class processes within capitalism. In other words, nonclass processes involving race and gender relations can provide changes in the condition for a transformation of the class processes of Western capitalist societies. Take gender as one example. Wolff and Resnick remark that:

> specific changes in social processes concerned with gender relationships would provide conditions for a change in the class processes of Western capitalist societies today. A change in popular consciousness about what "male" and "female" means (i.e., a change in certain cultural processes) alongside a change in the authority distribution process within families (a change in political or power processes) might combine with a change as women sell more of their labor power as a commodity (a change in the economic process of exchange) to jeopardize capitalist class processes. With other changes in still other social processes—which our class analysis seeks to identify—such altered gender relationships might provide the conditions of existence for a revolutionary change to a new social system including a different class structure.[55]

Class and nonclass processes fundamentally shape one another. My argument is not that class should subsume all other social and cultural processes, or that an analysis of class should outweigh an analysis of gender or race or sexuality, but that it should occupy a position of strategic centrality in educational reform efforts in the sense of taking into consideration the profound effects of globalized capitalist social relations.

I am no less in favor of the development of a critical cultural consciousness, or cultural criticism in general, in relation to questions of racial or ethnic or sexual identity than I have been over recent years. As someone who for thirty years has contributed to analyzing those very questions, such a shift in my position would be ludicrous. I am, however, more interested today in finding a *common ground* between cultural criticism and the movement for a transformation of productive relations. The process of capitalist globalization has given an increased urgency to what is at stake in the struggle for a pedagogy of liberation for me to do otherwise.

My position is that cultural criticism—accounting for the specific logics of noneconomic factors—for the most part has not adequately addressed the liberation of humankind from economic alienation linked to capitalist economic logics that serve as the motor force for transnational oligopolies and the reproduction of established social relations. I follow Samir Amin[56] in articulating a noneconomic-determinist interpretation of Marxism in which the capitalist mode of production is *not* reduced to the status of an economic

structure. In other words, the law of value governs both the economic reproduction of capitalism and all the aspects of social life under capitalism. Rather
than embrace Althusserian structuralism with its famously articulated concept
of "overdetermination" (i.e., each aspect of society is constituted as the effect
of all the others), I take the position adopted by Amin in his articulation of
"underdetermination." According to Amin, the determinations of economics,
politics, and culture each possess their specific logic and autonomy. There is
no complementarity among these logics within the system of underdetermination; there exist only conflicts among the determining factors, conflicts that
allow choice among different possible alternatives. Conflicts among logics
find solutions by subordinating some logics to others. The accumulation of
capital is the dominant trait of the logic of capitalism and provides the channels through which economic logic is imposed onto political, ideological, and
cultural logics. Precisely because underdetermination rather than overdetermination typifies the conflictual way in which the logics governing the various factors of social causation are interlaced, all social revolutions must
necessarily be cultural revolutions. The law of value, therefore, governs not
only the capitalist mode of production but also all the other social determinants. In order to move beyond—to overstep—contemporary capitalism that
is defined by its three basic contradictions of economic alienation, global polarization, and destruction of the natural environment, Amin charts out a project of social transformation that would initiate through its political economy,
its politics, and its cultural logics, a social evolution bent on reducing these
contradictions rather than aggravating them. Amin also argues convincingly
that postmodern criticism for the most part capitulates to the demands of the
current phase of capitalist political economy in the hope of making the system more humane—a happy capitalism. My position, as well as Amin's,
stresses the importance of contesting the unconstrained domination of capital
that masquerades as freedom, a domination that, with the help of its political
managers who pocket most of the cash, falsely sets itself up as the guarantee
of human emancipation.

CRITICAL EDUCATION FOR THE NEW MILLENNIUM

Both critical pedagogy and multicultural education need to address themselves to the adaptive persistence of capitalism and to issues of capitalist imperialism and its specific manifestations of accumulative capacities through
conquest (to which we have assigned the more benign term "colonialism"). In
other words, critical pedagogy needs to establish a project of emancipation
that moves beyond simply wringing concessions from existing capitalist

structures and institutions. Rather, it must be centered around the transformation of property relations and the creation of a just system of appropriation and distribution of social wealth. It is not enough to adjust the foundational level of school funding to account for levels of student poverty, to propose supplemental funding for poverty and limited English proficiency, to raise local taxes to benefit schools, to demand that state governments partly subsidize low-property-value communities, or to fight for the equalization of funding generated by low-property-value districts (although these efforts surely would be a welcome step in the right direction). I am arguing for a fundamentally broader vision based on a transformation of global economic relations—on a different economic logic if you will—that transcends a mere reformism within existing social relations of production and international division of labor.[57]

Marxist and neo-Marxist accounts have clearly identified imperialistic practices in recent movements toward global capital accumulation based on corporate monopoly capital and the international division of labor. The West has seen a progressive shift in its development that some liberals would champion as the rise of individuality, the rule of law, and the autonomy of civil society. Yet from a Marxist and neo-Marxist perspective these putative developments toward democracy can be seen, in effect, as "new forms of exploitation and domination, (the constitutive 'power from below' is, after all, the power of lordship), new relations of personal dependence and bondage, the privatization of surplus extraction and the transfer of ancient oppressions from the state to 'society'—that is, a transfer of power relations and domination from the state to private property."[58] Since the triumph of European capitalism in the seventeenth century, the bourgeoisie have acquired the legal, political, and military power to destroy virtually most of society in their quest for accumulation.[59] Capitalism in advanced Western countries must be transformed if extra-economic inequalities—such as racism and sexism—are to be challenged successfully. While it is true that people have identities other than class identities that shape their experiences in crucial and important ways, anticapitalist struggle is the best means to rearticulate identities within the construction of a radical socialist project. As Ellen Meiksins Wood notes, capitalism is more than just a system of class oppression, but rather constitutes a ruthless totalizing process which shapes our lives in every conceivable aspect, subjecting all social life to the abstract requirements of the market [60]

We need not accommodate ourselves to capitalist law of value, as István Mészáros reminds us.[61] The challenge ahead is to work toward the expropriation of the capitalists but also to ensure that the socialist project remains steadfast and self-critical. The struggle for a socialist democracy, it should be noted, is intractably linked to the struggle against racism. Critical educators need to consider how racism in its present incarnations developed out of the dominant mode of global production during the seventeenth and eighteenth centuries, particularly out of colonial plantations in the New World with slave labor imported from Africa to produce consumer goods such as tobacco, sugar, and cotton.[62] How the immigrant working class has been divided historically along racial lines is a process that needs to be better understood and more forcefully addressed by multicultural educators. How, for instance, does racism give white workers a particular identity that unites them with white capitalists? [63]

Critical pedagogy as a partner with multicultural education needs to deepen its reach of cultural theory and political economy and expand its participation in social-empirical analysis in order to address more critically the formation of intellectuals and institutions within the current forms of motion of history. Critical pedagogy and multicultural education need more than good intentions to achieve their goal. They require a revolutionary movement of educators informed by a principled ethics of compassion and social justice, a socialist ethos based on solidarity and social interdependence, and a language of critique that is capable of grasping the objective laws of history. [64] This is an especially difficult task, given that educational imperatives that link to corporate initiatives often use the language of public democracy to mask a model of privatized democracy.[65] Given current U.S. educational policy with its goal of serving the interests of the corporate world economy—one that effectively serves a de facto world government made up of the IMF, World Bank, G-7, GATT, and other structures—it is imperative that critical and multicultural educators renew their commitment to the struggle against exploitation on all fronts.[66] In emphasizing one such front—that of class struggle—I want to emphasize that the renewed Marxist approach to critical pedagogy that I envision does not conceptualize race and gender antagonisms as static, structural outcomes of capitalist social relations of advantage and disadvantage but rather locates such antagonisms within a theory of agency that acknowledges the importance of cultural politics and social difference. Far from deactivating the sphere of culture by viewing it only or mainly in the service of capital accumulation, critical pedagogy and multicultural education need to acknowledge the specificity of local struggles around the micropolitics of race, class, gender, and sexual formation. But in doing so it must not lose sight of the global division of labor brought about by the forces of capitalist production and accumulation. A critical pedagogy based on class struggle that does not confront racism, sexism, and homophobia will not be able to eliminate the destructive proliferation of capital.

The critical pedagogy to which I am referring needs to be made less informative and more performative, less a pedagogy directed toward the interrogation of written texts than a corporeal pedagogy grounded in the lived experiences of students. Critical pedagogy, as I am re-visioning it from a Marxist Humanist perspective, is a pedagogy that brushes against the grain of textual foundationalism, ocular fetishism, and the monumentalist abstraction of theory that characterizes most critical practice within teacher education classrooms. I am calling for a pedagogy in which a revolutionary multicultural ethics is performed—is lived in the streets—rather than simply reduced to the practice of reading texts (although the reading of texts with other texts, against other texts, and upon other texts is decidedly an important exercise). Teachers need to build upon the textual politics that dominater most multicultural classrooms by engaging in a politics of bodily and affective investment, which means "walking the talk" and working in those very communities one purports to serve. A critical pedagogy for multicultural education should quicken the affective sensibilities of students as well as provide them with a language of social analysis, cultural critique, and social activism in the service of cutting the power and practice of capital at its joints. Opportunities must be made for students to work in communities where they can spend time with economically and ethnically diverse populations—as well as with gay and lesbian populations—in the context of community activism and participation in progressive anticapitalist social movements.

Students need to move beyond simply knowing about criticalist multiculturalist practice. They must also move toward an embodied and corporeal understanding of such practice and an affective investment in such practice at the level of everyday life such that it is able to deflect and transform the invasive power of capital.

CRITICAL PEDAGOGY IN THE AGE OF GLOBALIZATION

As the public sphere continues to be devalued and depoliticized, transformed more and more into the culture of the shopping mall, the ongoing withdrawal of commitment to the public sphere is eroding the conditions for public schools to survive, let alone build a new social order. Defense of personal "enclaves" rather than public and collective spaces is the trend today and such enclave localism scarcely enables a macropolitics linked to the modern project of radical socialist transformation. Given the conditions of global capitalism described throughout this chapter, which is more falsely utopian, socialism or democratic capitalism? To me it would appear to be the latter, and by far. Yet while it is unlikely that schools by themselves can serve as anything more than necessary but not sufficient public spaces of potential political, cultural, and economic transformation, there are some initiatives that are, nevertheless, worth struggling to achieve. Consequently, I wish to specify in more detail the challenge—and the possibilities—that a philosophy of revolutionary struggle poses for critical educators.

First, critical pedagogy must reflect upon the historical specificity of its own categories so that it does not come to portray its own economy of desire as representing the nature and needs of all humankind. This is crucial if critical pedagogy is going to be able to challenge the patriarchal and Eurocentric assumptions within its own ranks. As critical pedagogy has learned from feminist pedagogies, and pedagogies associated with Latin American theologies of liberation, the African diaspora, and North American pedagogies of resistance, it must disclaim any false allegations of universality that speak only or mainly to white, male, Western, working-class heterosexuals. Where critical pedagogy claims to articulate a universal position on liberation and human rights, its premises must not remain vulnerable to a masculinist, Eurocentric perspective. It is important to keep in mind that the new agent of democratic socialism is not a being predetermined by social relations but is one that is never complete, one that is formed dialectically through social relations and the development of a politics underwritten by revolutionary praxis.

Second, critical pedagogy must speak to local issues and context-specific antagonisms but at the same time it must be careful not to limit itself only to local accounts.[67] As ludic postmodern educational analysis continues to communicate better and better about itself, it appears to have less and less to say about the world and how to change it. Enlisting itself as the propaganda arm of capital, while at the same time denouncing Marxism as fixated on class struggle in a demonic, world-capitalist system abducted from its more democratic local aspects, ludic postmodern educationalists have established the importance of provisional knowledge and multiple sites of power and resistance. Yet in doing so they have severed the relationship between critique and action. What needs to be incorporated more fully into critical pedagogy is the trenchant work being done in materialist feminist analysis, and the "red" feminism and pedagogy advanced by scholars such as Teresa Ebert and Rosemary Hennessy.[68] This work not only complements the Marxist pedagogy that I am advocating, but also troubles the counterpolitical ludic postmodernism found in so much contemporary social critique.

Critical pedagogy needs to move into the direction of challenging new carceral systems of social control through the development of a critical pedagogy of space. Following the lead of critical urban geographers such as Edward Soja, critical pedagogy should be encouraged to explore the spatiality of human life and couple this with its historicality-sociality, especially the genderizing and racializing of rural and urban cityspaces through the trialectics of space, knowledge, and power.[69]

Third, critical pedagogy must continue to speak to basic human needs, but it must do so without falling prey to a biological foundationalism or the falsely generalizing and ethnocentric tendencies of modern, Western grand theories that teleologically privilege certain historical or philosophical end-points to the human condition such as "the end of history" or "the end of ideology" or which sound the death knell of political agency such as "the death of the subject." Such grand theories imply the redundancy of any discourse projected into the future that attempts to hold humanity accountable for its present condition. And while we should abandon the epistemological closure stipulated by "grand theories," I do not wish to suggest by any means that we should no longer see history as a series of determinative effects or fail to view the social order in its "totality." A relentless randomness to history is affirmed in many postmodern articulations of critique, with little possibility held out for the success of struggles against patriarchy or racism or class exploitation. And as I hope I have made clear in chapter 1, I do not consider Marx as the author of grand Eurocentric narratives of the type that anti-Marxists such as C. A. Bowers and Patti Lather rail against with such bloated determination.

Fourth, critical pedagogy must continue to challenge normative associations of intelligence and the ways in which "reason" has been differentially distributed so that it always advantages the capitalist class. Knowledge, as we have come to know, is regularly serviced in systems of representation that a priori fix its meaning in preordained ways in order to serve special interest groups. Criticalists must never cease emphasizing that there exist determinate relations between the systems of intelligibility produced within public school institutions and those who occupy the dominant culture that houses such institutions. One of the political effects of knowledge production is to legitimate the voices of certain groups and to accord them credibility over voices of less privileged groups. In other words, a critical pedagogy must not concede any ground with respect to the position that asymmetrical relationships of power and privilege in any society have determinate effects on who will succeed and who will not. Who gets into universities, for instance, is not controlled by merit; if that were the case, then one would have to make the absurd argument that the capitalist class are conceptually more gifted. However, we could easily concede that the capitalist class is considerably gifted insofar as it is able to control the definition of what counts as legitimate knowledge (through test measures, official knowledge in textbooks, lack of challenges to "official" versions of history, etc.) and to make sure that such knowledge serves the interests of the global economy. As criticalists have pointed out, official knowledge, the ruling hierarchy of discursive authority, sovereign epistemes, and the official social transcripts of the capitalist class all contraindicate in some manner or another the pursuit of freedom and conspire against social justice.

Within the official transcript of United States citizenship there exists a fierce resistance even to the insinuation that there exists a presumption in favor of the view that only the white Euro-American elite are capable of achieving a universal point of view and speaking on behalf of all groups. Yet we know from Paulo Freire and other critical educationalists that the conditions of knowledge production in the "act of knowing" always involve political relationships of subordination and domination.[70] Criticalists need to excavate the coded meanings that constitute knowledge and bring to light the rhetorical and formal strategies that go into its interpretation. Further, criticalists need to acknowledge the complex acts of investiture, fantasy, and desire that contribute to the social construction of knowledge. Dominant knowledge forms must be challenged and so must claims that purify or (if I may use a noun as a verb for effect) "innocent" knowledge formations of their ideological and epistemic assumptions.

Human capital ideas presently underwriting neoliberal educational policy fetishize education and reduce the pursuit of knowledge to the logic of commodification tied to future employment opportunities, to schoolings' power of economic return, to its investment in human labor. To ensure favorable returns, education slavishly prostrates itself before the dictates of the labor marketplace and the Brain Lords of the corporate elite. These "dictates" can, in the dank hands of neoliberal bureaucrats, raise university tuition to reduce the number of college graduates or establish quotas for certain subjects if those subjects are perceived to further the economic growth of the nation as a whole. In order to motivate lifelong learning among workers, corporations can cut benefits and job security so that workers are forced to keep up with the changing demands of the labor market[71] and to maintain corporate barons in their luxury homes ensconced in gated communities. This neoliberal ideology only ensures the eternal return of injustices and patchwork remedies, exploitation, and compensatory programs. Gee, Hull, and Lankshear argue against the vision and practices of the "new capitalist school reformers" by disavowing their consumer determinism, by making social criticism "necessary to real learning and thus as part and parcel of critical thinking and the empowerment of workers,"[72] and by reinvigorating local politics "as against the 'faux' local of the new capitalism"[73] so that a global community can be established "in which the interests and well-being of all become the concern of all."[74] The authors urge a critical understanding of the complex forces of the new work order that can "unmask greed and manipulation hiding behind systems and their assorted rationalizations."[75]

Fifth, criticalists must rethink the issues of "modes of production" so that educators can take into account the shift from industrialized public life to contexts of flexible specialization within global capitalism. Yet they must do so in a manner that revises and does not diminish the importance of the category of social class and that does not suggest—as many conservative postmodernists do—that exploitation is somehow more subjective or less concrete or severe than it was during more industrialized regimes.[76] The reproduction of economic and discursive advantage is not coincidentally functional in school sites for the success of the capitalist project of maximizing resources and controlling the wealth in the interests of the white majority population. The exploited, the immiserated, and the wretched of the earth— *les damnés de la terre*—did not suddenly appear as a group of zombified volunteers enlisting in the ranks of the disenfranchised and destitute millions. Whether educators follow Marx's labor theory of value or other economic explanations, it cannot be disputed that positive profits within capitalism require corresponding rates of exploitation and that this uneven distribution of wealth is unjust.

As one (albeit modest) measure of resistance, teachers can incorporate into their curriculum units and lessons dealing with the global sweatshop.[77] Bill Bigelow reports that students from Monroe High School in Los Angeles organized to get a resolution passed by the school board committing the district not to buy soccer balls from countries that allow child labor. He also teaches against the myth that it is permissible to pay workers in undeveloped countries low wages because living expenses in those countries are much lower. He notes that milk in Haiti is 75 cents; in New York, 65 cents; eggs in Haiti are $1.50; in New York, $1.39; cereal in Haiti is $1.90; in New York, $1.60; gas in Haiti is $2.20; in New York, $1.26.[78] Such resistance is a daunting task in the face of the recent invasion into our schools by the Barons of Capital who devise pro-capitalist strategies such as Virtual Trade Mission now in use in growing numbers of U.S. classrooms. Backed by the Clinton administration and sponsored by the likes of MCI, Boeing, Hughes, and UPS (as well as by developing nations such as Indonesia and Singapore), the Virtual Trade Mission (VTM) curriculum initiative makes available to approximately fifty thousand students across ten states, "educational" videos and workbook exercises. The videos show business executives extolling the virtues of free trade and the advantages of selling military and other industrial and commercial wares to developing countries. The VTM program also includes guest lecturers by corporate officials and diplomats and provides a study plan called Export Challenge. For instance, students role-play marketing executives who wish to expand their business overseas or to developing countries. To cite one example, students at the Chattanooga Arts and Sciences School helped to craft a strategy to increase Boeing's share of the Chinese commercial aircraft market.[79] With the exception of one workbook exercise produced by the International Brotherhood of Electrical Workers that provides a small amount of contrast by discussing the social dimensions of trade, the VTM program presents for students an overwhelmingly glowing picture of the world of free trade. There is no mention of sweatshops, the exploitation of female workers, the environmental devastation, and the creation of a world of asymmetrical relations of power and privilege based on race, class, gender, and sexual orientation.

Critical pedagogy must be critical of capital as a social relation, which includes being critical of labor as the subject of capital. The struggle against capital is, after all, the main game. "We" as educators are also capital; capital is not just something "out there" but partially constitutes our subjectivity.[80] We are divided against ourselves, and within ourselves—as labor within (but also against) capital. Teacher unions must not shift their political center of gravity in order to appease free-market privateers but rather promote social policies and social movements that address the perils of global capitalism. They can accomplish this through political coalitions with parents, students, and community groups.

Sixth, critical pedagogy must be antiracist, antisexist, and antihomophobic. Currently whiteness, heterosexuality, and maleness stand together as a leitmotif of major significations within capitalist democracy while blackness and brownness function together as a sovereign indicator of racialization. This must be challenged, and done so as forcibly as possible.

Seventh, critical pedagogy must center around meeting the basic needs of human beings for survival and well-being in the struggle for a socialist democracy. This means "decent housing at affordable cost for all citizens, free education for students at all ages, employment for those who can work and average pay for those who cannot, equality of treatment and opportunity for women, equality in all areas for black and minority ethnic citizens, free health care at all levels and types of treatment, dignity in old age through pension provision at average income and free care, safe and nutritious food at affordable prices, [and] access to cultural and personal development opportunities" (Feldman and Lotz, in press).

There are material needs that must be satisfied consequent upon the common constitution of human beings as requiring food, adequate clothing, protection from the elements, and achieving self-worth and dignity. While it is surely true that needs are historical and are altered somewhat from context to context, I nevertheless continue to maintain that critical pedagogy must admit to a standard of minimum material needs and human rights as integral to its socialist vision and that such needs can serve as a transhistorical standard generally applied throughout the world. Self-realization and emancipation (while admittedly contingent, conjunctural, and never finished) are not possible without agreeing upon a basic standard to human capacities and surely there has be some type of limit-concept of what we name to be relations of domination, oppression, or exploitation. Or else we will have to entertain the idea that a white Beverly Hills physician is just as exploited as a Mexican migrant worker in the San Joaquin Valley if both of them experience a reduction of their salaries by one-half. I am not appealing here for a transcendental theory of justice; I wish instead to urgently underscore the fact that as neoliberal democracy's oxygen, capitalism is predicated upon relations of uneven and unequal exchange and in order to stipulate a moral basis for a pedagogy of liberation, one must, in a strategically universalist sense at least, rely on a transhistorical claim with respect to the distribution of social wealth insofar as we are compelled to acknowledge that people suffer cruelly and die needlessly as a result of capitalist exploitation. By stressing the economic here, I am not arguing that the world of signs, symbols, and other representations can never be freed from the thrall of capital or that the theater of discourse does not matter when the temper of the times calls for class struggle. After all, it is through discourse that we "live" social relations and make sense of them. When discourses are rendered meaningful and deconstructed for the way in which their meanings "live" through human activity, and when signs and symbols become intensified, they not only arch toward the development of critical understanding but can become hammer blows on the real. However, when discourses and interpretations become leeched of their social critique by capital-friendly policy makers, they become easily transformed into political advertisements for the neoliberal agenda.

Nor am I attempting to denigrate spiritual insight and activity. Here I agree with Roger Gottlieb (1992) that the Marxist tradition "pre-supposes—with little or no argument—that human fulfillment results from the proper arrangement of social relations and consumption" (p. 1999). Gottlieb is correct in drawing attention to the predominance of the "ego" as it is presently historically and socially constructed and asserting that the addictions to power of the nonoppressed will not be easily pacified in contexts in which basic physical needs are satisfied. Marxists need to consider modes of spirituality that can integrate the ego into a more comprehensive personal identity that is attentive to social suffering, openness to the truth, and a committed involvement with others. This is not a call to engage in traditional religious practice or pop spirituality but is a summons "distinct from dogmatic religious attachments to particular rituals, creeds, or organizations" (Gottlieb 1992, p. 203).

Here I agree with Gottlieb (1992) that "a variety of political *and* spiritual practices—from consensus decision making to being self-conscious about racism, from learning to appreciate what we have to learning to get a distance on our anger—can help create a new sense of subjectivity and the possibility of a new society" (p. 206). This does not mean we need to search for the psychic plasma of the demiurge to understand how to act, or to ascend into the perfect fullness of the pleroma of love in order to fulfill our revolutionary duty. It does mean that we need to understand and transcend the limitations of the capitalist ego and in doing so, we should not rule out how spiritual practices might help us in our efforts.

Eighth, critical pedagogy must involve a politics of economic and resource distribution as well as a politics of recognition, affirmation, and difference. In other words, it must be a politics that speaks both to a transformative politics and to a critical and feminist multiculturalism.[81] To be colorless is to be white, and whites—in particular, white males—currently function as the colorless, normative standpoints of humanity. The social benefits in our pseudodemocracy—our emergent global polyarchy—are always the greatest the less black or brown you happen to be. The fact remains that the teaching profession is mostly white while the student population in many of our major cities is populated increasingly by students of color. Questions that must be answered in this scenario include: How are racial formations essentially social constructions? Yet, more importantly, how are these social constructions taken up, lived, and played out in capitalist societies with devastating consequences for people of color? How are individuals and groups positioned inexorably by pseudoscientific classifications related to questions of biology or of culture both in terms of gender and ethnicity? How are these systems of classification defended by the imperatives of capitalism to exploit human labor and locate groups within the global division of labor?

The real problem is the internal or dialectical relation that exists between capital and labor within the capitalist production process itself—a social relation in which capitalism in intransigently rooted. This social relation—essential to the production of abstract labor—deals with how already existing value is preserved and new value (surplus value) is created (Allman 2001). If, for example, the process of actual exploitation and the accumulation of surplus value is to be seen as a state of constant manipulation and as a realization process of concrete labor in actual labor time—within a given cost-production system and a labor market—we cannot underestimate the ways in which "difference" (racial as well as gender difference) is encapsulated in the production/reproduction dialectic of capital. It is this relationship that is mainly responsible for the inequitable and unjust distribution of resources. A deepened understanding of this phenomenon is essential for grasping the emergence of an acutely polarized labor market and the fact that disproportionately high percentages of "people of color" are trapped in the lower rungs of domestic and global labor markets (McLaren and Farahmandpur 1999). "Difference" in the era of global capitalism is crucial to the workings, movements and profit levels of multinational corporations but those types of complex relations cannot be mapped out by using truncated post-Marxist, culturalist conceptualizations of "difference." To sever issues of "difference" from class conveniently draws attention away from the crucially important ways in which "people of color" (and more specifically "women of color") provide capital with its superexploited labor pools—a phenomenon that is on the rise all over the world. Most social relations constitutive of racialized differences are considerably shaped by the relations with production and there is undoubtedly a racialized and gendered division of labor whose severity and function vary depending on where one is situated in the capitalist global economy (Meyerson 2000).

In stating this we need to include an important caveat that differentiates revolutionary critical pedogogy from those who invoke the well-worn race/class/gender triplet which can sound, to the uninitiated, both radical and vaguely Marxian. It is not. Race, class, and gender, while they invariably intersect and interact, are not co-primary. This "triplet" approximates what the "philosophers might call a category mistake." On the surface the triplet may be convincing—some people are oppressed because of their race, some as a result of their gender, others because of their class—but this "is grossly misleading" for it is not that "some individuals manifest certain characteristics known as 'class' which then results in their oppression; on the contrary, to be a member of a social class just *is* to be oppressed" and in this regard class is "a wholly social category" (Eagleton, 1998, p. 289). Furthermore, even though "class" is usually invoked as part of the aforementioned and much vaunted triptych, it is usually gutted of its practical, social dimension or treated solely as a cultural phenomenon—as just another form of "difference." In these instances, class is transformed from an economic and indeed, social category to an exclusively cultural or discursive one or one in which class merely signifies a "subject position." Class is therefore cut off from the political economy of capitalism and class power severed from exploitation and a power structure "in which those who control collectively produced resources only do so because of the value generated by those who do not" (Hennessy and Ingraham 1997, p. 2).

Such theorizing has had the effect of replacing a *historical materialist class analysis with a cultural analysis of class*. As a result, many post-Marxists have also stripped the idea of class of precisely that element which, for Marx, made it radical—namely its status as a universal form of exploitation whose abolition required (and was also central to) the abolition of all manifestations of oppression (Marx 1978, p. 60). With regard to this issue, Kovel (2002) is particularly insightful for he explicitly addresses an issue which continues to vex the Left—namely the priority given to different categories of what he calls "dominative splitting"—those categories of "gender, class, race, ethnic, and national exclusion," etc. Kovel argues that we need to ask the question of *priority* with respect to what? He notes that if we mean priority with respect to *time*, then the category of gender would have priority since there are traces of gender oppression in all other forms of oppression. If we were to prioritize in terms of *existential significance*, Kovel suggests that we would have to depend upon the immediate historical forces that bear down on distinct groups of people—he offers examples of Jews in 1930s Germany who suffered from brutal forms of anti-Semitism and Palestinians today who experience anti-Arab racism under Israeli domination. The question of what has *political priority*, however, would depend upon which transformation of relations of oppression are practically more urgent and while this would certainly depend upon the preceding categories, it would also depend upon the fashion in which all the forces acting in a concrete situation are deployed. As to the question of which split sets into motion all of the others, the priority would have to be given to *class* since class relations:

> entail the state as an instrument of enforcement and control, and it is the state that shapes and organizes the splits that appear in human ecosystems. Thus class is both logically and historically distinct from other forms of exclusion (hence we should not talk of "classism" to go along with "sexism" and "racism," and "species-ism"). This is, first of all, because class is an essentially man-made category, without root in even a mystified biology. We cannot imagine a human world without gender distinctions—although we can imagine a world without domination by gender. But a world without class is eminently imaginable—indeed, such was the human world for the great majority of our species' time on earth, during all of which considerable fuss was made over gender. Historically, the difference arises because "class" signifies one side of a larger figure that includes a state apparatus whose conquests and regulations create races and shape gender relations. Thus there will be no true resolution of racism so long as class society stands, inasmuch as a racially oppressed society implies the activities of a class-defending state. Nor can gender inequality be enacted away so long as class society, with its state, demands the super-exploitation of women's labor. (Kovel, 2002, p. 123–124)

Contrary to what many have claimed, Marxist theory does not relegate categories of "difference" to the conceptual mausoleum; rather, it has sought to reanimate these categories by interrogating how they are refracted through material relations of power and privilege and linked to relations of production. Moreover, it has emphasized and insisted that the wider political and economic system in which they are embedded needs to be thoroughly understood in all its complexity. To the extent that "gender, race, and ethnicity are all understood as social constructions rather than as essentialist categories" the effect of exploring their insertion into the "circulation of variable capital (including positioning within the internal heterogeneity of collective labor and hence, within the division of labor and the class system)" must be interpreted as a "powerful force reconstructing them in distinctly capitalist ways" (Harvey, 2000, p. 106). Unlike contemporary narratives which tend to focus on one or another form of oppression, the irrefragable power of historical materialism resides in its ability to reveal (i) how forms of oppression based on categories of difference do not possess relative autonomy from class relations but rather constitute the ways in which oppression is lived/experienced within a class-based system and; (ii) how all forms of social oppression function within an overarching capitalist system.

This framework must be further distinguished from those who invoke the terms "classism" and/or "class elitism" to (ostensibly) foreground the idea that "class matters" (cf. hooks, 2000) since we agree with Gimenez (2001, p. 24) that "class is not simply another ideology legitimating oppression." Rather, class denotes "exploitative relations between people mediated by their relations to the means of production." To marginalize such a conceptualization of class is to conflate an individual's objective location in the intersection of structures of inequality with individual's subjective understandings of who they really are based on their "experiences."

Ninth, critical pedagogy needs to pursue the ideal of communicative democracy within a larger vision of socialist democracy. In the age of global capitalism, when so-called democratic schooling has become a laughable appellation, Iris Marion Young's concept of communicative democracy can prove instructive. Democracy, in Young's view, is not simply about registering one's preferences in a vote, but about becoming critically reflexive about one's preferences. This entails a move from motivated self-interest to collective interest, through examining the social knowledge available in a context free of coercion.[82] Criticalists such as Young also acknowledge that white people have the advantage in lobbying and organizing for their constituencies. And even when this constitutes majoritarian democracy, one has to acknowledge that communication is often restricted in this case. We know, for instance, that white males are now more vulnerable than ever in a global economy and that this is one of the major reasons why affirmative action is being rolled back in states such as California. Governor Arnold Schwarzenegger, like his predecessors Gray Davis and Pete Wilson, wants to protect the considerable advantage that whites already hold. What makes this even more shameful is that he claims the moral high ground as an immigrant who has achieved the American dream. Yet criticalists understand that to abolish "preferences" for people of color is, given the present sociopolitical state of affairs in the United States, to argue for affirmative action for white people. Some of the problems currently facing us can be ameliorated by group representation and by giving voice to formerly silenced and devalued needs and experiences of oppressed groups.

And tenth, critical pedagogy must articulate its politics with a profound respect for the lived experiences and standpoint epistemology of the oppressed. This means, for instance, acknowledging the power of religion in impacting the lives of the poor. Here I am referring not only to liberation theology and the way it has been taken up in the pastoral hinterlands of the Third World, but also to the growth of Pentecostalism. Witness the efforts of nongentrified, grassroots Pentecostals in addressing the depredations of poverty created by global capitalism in the slums of Latin America and Africa. In the social vacuum created by the withdrawal of state social services, Pentecostal networks—which can be reactionary as well as liberatory—populated by those who live outside the formal economy in the shadow world and liminal urban spaces of informal niche economies are taking up the roles of social activism once played by socialist organization during the early days of industrial capitalism (see Davis 2004). These are voices from below that need to be taken seriously.

Yet at the same time, criticalist pedagogy must reject the all-too-familiar stance that experiences speak for themselves. This is consistent with an emphasis on gaining theoretical grounding through self-education as a means of understanding and transforming one's experiences. Experiences of the oppressed must not be silenced, they must be given voice. And a critical pedagogy must also ensure that they are heard. While a standpoint epistemology "from below" is vitally important for the perspectives that it offers, it still must be defensible and interpreted with explanatory power. This is not to say that some events are not self-evident at certain basic levels; it is, however, to argue that frameworks for interpreting experiences and building theories from those experiences is a pressing and important task. We must strive for interpretive frameworks that permit the most persuasive explanations and justifications from both ethical and epistemological pivot points. Sometimes this calls for complex theory and sometimes it does not. However, often progressive educators and activists resist complex theory outright as elitist. For some, this is partially due to a false conception of experience as transparent and, I would argue, additionally results from a reluctance to engage in the arduous and labor intensive task of critical theorizing. Indeed, if all experiences and relationships were politically, psychologically, and ethically self-evident, then social analysis would not be necessary. Interpretations of experience are undeniably colonized by particular definitions of what is normal from the perspective that most serves the interests of the ruling elites. Theories of liberation challenge these commonsense definitions, systems of classification, and social and material relations as being socially and historically motivated to serve the interests of the capitalist class. What is important about these theories is not their complexity, but rather their explanatory and argumentative power as well as their rhetorical persuasiveness. Critical pedagogy negates the language of commonsense description by providing a language of analysis that seeks to explain those structures of representation that give commonsense reality its "natural" appearance. This is not political advocacy in the realm of the cultural imaginary alone. If necessary, we must follow the enslaved and the toilers of the world as they take to the streets.

In a world where the latest commodity fashion and the promise of the perpetually new and different has become democracy's aphrodisiac, a call for a self-conscious return to an earlier and restorative vision of social change may seem provincial, like a player who continues to play a game already abandoned by those considered to be the trendsetters. To call for a return to a theory grounded by a reflexive relation to practical application may seem a quaint—if not politically naive—maneuver in the new Nietzschean playground of the grammatologists. However, in contrast to the conservative postmodernists' game of infinite postponement of meaning, of infinite deferral of the real, of ever-recurring promises of a future that is unattainable, the revolutionary praxis undergirding the politics of critical pedagogy speaks to an *eschaton* of peace and labor, of final victory for the oppressed.

What I would like to underscore is that the struggle over education is fundamentally linked to struggles in the larger theater of social and political life. For instance, the struggle over education is linked to efforts to bring about a more sustainable economic system while at the same time drastically trying to change the parameters of social ownership and control in the direction of socialist society. This is because capital supports ecofriendly business practices through which it rehabilitates the logic of capital accumulation and reproduces ecological destruction under the "green" mantle of political progressivism (Feldman and Lotz in press). Since justice is alien to the sphere of production, our coevolution with nature can occur only when we dismantle private ownership of the forces of production, ending our alienated relationship with nature and production, all the while recognizing that human society is a part of nature. The answer is not the capitalist desire for absolute mastery and domination of nature or a naïve Green withdrawal to the most pristine preserves of nature, but rather to maximize our interactions with nature in a serious and sophisticated way while ending production based on capital accumulation, thereby dramatically transforming our ecology and ushering in the end of what Marx called our "unconscious pre-history" and the beginning of real human history (see Feldman and Lotz in press). The struggle that occupies and exercises us as school activists and critical educators should entertain global and local perspectives in terms of the way in which capitalist social relations and the international division of labor are produced and reproduced. While I am largely sympathetic to attempts to reform school practices at the level of policy, curriculum, and classroom pedagogy, such attempts need to be realized and acted upon from the overall perspectives of the struggle against capitalist social relations.

Schools must become sites for the production of both critical knowledge and sociopolitical action. Any institution worthy of the appellation "school" must educate students to become active agents for social transformation and critical citizenship. More than at any other time in world history, school practices need to address the objective, material conditions of the workplace and labor relations within global capitalism. This is an urgent task because the important challenge ahead is to educate a citizenry capable of overcoming the systemic exploitation of so many of the world's populations. Schools should provide students with a language of criticism and a language of hope. These languages should be used in order to prepare students to conceptualize systematically the relationship among their private dreams and desires and the collective dreams of the larger social order. New generations of students must be capable of analyzing the social and material conditions in which dreams are given birth, and are realized, diminished, or destroyed. More importantly, students need to be able to recognize which dreams and which dreamers are dangerous to the larger society, and why this is the case.

Schools need to foster collective dreaming, a dreaming that speaks to the creation of social justice for all groups, and the eventual elimination of economic exploitation, racism, sexism, and homophobia. This can occur only if schools are able and committed to help students analyze the ways in which their subjectivities have been ideologically formed within the exploitative forces and relations of globalized, transnational capitalism.

It is clear that if educators are to follow the example of a Marxist-inspired critical pedagogy, there must be a concerted effort to construct a social order that is not premised upon capital. As Kovel warns:

> [C]apital must go if we are to survive as a civilization and, indeed, a species; and all partial measures and reforms should be taken in the spirit of bringing about capital's downfall. Nothing could seem more daunting than this, indeed, in the current balance of forces, it seems inconceivable. Therefore the first job must be to conceive it as a possibility, and not to succumb passively to the given situation. Capital expresses no law of nature; it has been the result of choice, and there is no essential reason to assume it cannot be un-chosen. Conceiving things this way is scarcely sufficient. But it is necessary, in both a moral and a practical sense.[83]

The state has not diminished in importance with respect to the fashioning and management of political power, as some global analysts assert. In fact, critics such as Ellen Meiksins Wood believe that capital needs the state more today than ever before.[84] If this is indeed the case—and I believe that it is—then the working class may now be in an excellent position to challenge capital across nation-states on a global basis. Now is a precipitous time for educators to help develop the kind of critical citizenry capable of such a challenge. In the final analysis, educators need to renew their commitment to the oppressed—not in historical-teleological terms, most certainly—but in ethicopolitical terms that can guide political action and create the conditions for dreams to take root and liberatory praxis to be carried forward by an undaunted faith in the oppressed.

ACKNOWLEDGMENTS

To my comrades in Britain: Paula Allman, Mike Cole, Dave Hill, and Glenn Rikowski. This chapter was previously published in *The Journal of Educational Theory* 48, no. 4 (1998), pp. 431–62. © Board of Trustees at the University of Illinois–Urbana and the Journal of Educational Theory. Reprinted with permission.

NOTES

1. Peter McLaren, "Critical Pedagogy in the Age of Global Capitalism: Some Challenges for the Educational Left," *Australian Journal of Education*, 39, 1 (1995), 5:21. See also Peter McLaren and Ramin Farahmanpur, "Introduction," in *Charting New Terrains in Chicana(o)/Latina(o) Education,* ed. Carlos Tejeda, Zeus Leonardo, and Corinne Martinez (Creskill, N.J.: Hampton Press, 2002).

2. Jacques Adda, *La Mondalisation de L'Economie*, 2 vols. (Paris: Decouverte, 1996), 62.

3. Philippe Engelhard, *Principes d'une Critique de l'Économie Politique* (Paris: Arléa, 1993), 543. Cited in Alain de Benoist, "Confronting Globalization," Telos, no. 108 (1996), 117–137. Benoist is a radical conservative commentator.

4. Ellen Meiksins Wood, "Class Compacts, the Welfare State, and Epochal Shifts: A Reply to Frances Fox Piven and Richard A. Cloward," *Monthly Review*, 49, 8 (1998), 25–46. The regional and liberalization pacts that emerged in the past decade—the World Trade Organization (WTO), the North American Free Trade Agreement (NAFTA), the European Union, Latin America's Mercosur, and the recent negotiations of the Organization for Economic Cooperation and Development (OECD) surrounding the Multilateral Agreement on Investment—are shaping the New World Order in accordance with the most ideal investment conditions for

transnational corporations. Anything hindering foreign investment—that is, rules and regulations that protect workers and jobs, public welfare, environment, culture, and domestic businesses—will be removed. The World Trade Organization (which was created on January 1, 1995, following the signing of the GATT global free trade agreement in 1994) and the IMF both work to obtain trade concessions from those countries whose economies are in distress and to gain access to unprotected sectors of Third World economies. The WTO, the IMF, the OECD, the International Chamber of Commerce, the European Round Table of Industrialists, the Union of Industrial and Employers Confederation of Europe, the United States Council for International Business, the International Organization of Employers, the Business Council on National Issues, the World Business Council for Sustainable Development, the United Nations Commission on Trade and Development, the Business and Industry Advisory Committee, all work to ensure market control and assist transnational corporations in becoming some of the largest economies in the world. In the United States, research centers in Silicon Valley, Route 128 in Boston, the Research Triangle in North Carolina (Raleigh/Durham), and Fairfax County, Virginia, and other locations throughout the country are not only facilitating possibilities for electronic commerce, but are creating technological contexts for corporate mergers and takeovers.

5. William Greider, "Saving the Global Economy," *The Nation*, 265, 20 (1997), 12.

6. Greider, "Saving the Global Economy," 11–16.

7. Jorge Larrain, "Stuart Hall and the Marxist Concept of Ideology," in *Stuart Hall: Critical Dialogues in Cultural Studies*, ed. David Morely and Kuan-Hsing Chen (London: Routledge, 1996), 68.

8. Larrain, "Stuart Hall and the Marxist Concept of Ideology," 68.

9. David Ashley, *History without a Subject* (Boulder, Colo.: Westview Press, 1997).

10. Ashley, *History without a Subject*.

11. Jeremy Rifkin, "The Biotech Century: Human Life as Intellectual Property," *The Nation*, 266, 13 (1998), 12.

12. Rifkin, "The Biotech Century."

13. Bill Resnick, "Socialism or Nike? Just Do It!" *Against the Current*, X11, 3 (1997), 12–15.

14. Vanessa Hua, "Parents Give Credit Card Barbie a Low Rating," *Los Angeles Times*, Section D, April 2, 1998, D5.

15. In schools throughout the United States, commercial banners can be rented and hung in hallways and auditoriums for the entire calendar year; computer screen savers mix motivational messages with sales pitches for fast food and soft drink companies; Channel One, the in-school television advertising network, is in 40 percent of the nation's schools and has daily access to eight million elementary school children. See Cynthia Peters, "The Politics of Media Literacy," *Z Magazine* (February 1998), 25–30. See also Shirley Steinberg and Joe Kincheloe, *Kinderculture: Corporate Constructions of Childhood* (Boulder, Colo.: Westview Press, 1997).

16. Manuel Castells, *The Rise of the Network Society* (Maiden, Mass.: Blackwell Publishers, Inc., 1996). See also Peter McLaren, "Introduction: Traumatizing Capital: Pedagogy, Politics, and Praxis in the Global Marketplace," in *Critical Education in the New*

Information Age, ed. Manuel Castells, Ramón Flecha, Paulo Freire, Henry A. Giroux, Donaldo Macedo, and Paul Willis (Boulder, Colo.: Rowman & Littlefield, 1999), 1–36.

17. Pierre Bourdieu, "A Reasoned Utopia and Economic Fatalism," trans. John Howe, *New Left Review,* 227, (January/February 1998), 126. Italics in original.

18. Bourdieu, "A Reasoned Utopia," 126.

19. Davies and Guppy, "Globalization and Educational Reforms," 459. Italics in original.

20. See Hayek's most influential book, *The Road to Serfdom* (Chicago: The University of Chicago Press, 1994) . See also Milton Friedman, *Capitalism and Freedom* (Chicago: University of Chicago Press, 1962).

21. Hilary Wainwright, *Arguments for a New Left: Answering the Free Market Right* (London: Blackwell, 1994).

22. Wainwright, *Arguments for a New Left.*

23. Wainwright, *Arguments for a New Left,* 60.

24. Joel Spring, *Education and the Rise of the Global Economy: Sociocultural, Political and Historical Studies in Education* (Mahwah, N.J.: Lawrence Erlbaum Associates, 1998).

25. Spring, *Education and the Rise of the Global Economy.*

26. Spring, *Education and the Rise of the Global Economy.*

27. James Paul Gee, Glynda Hull, and Colin Lankshear, *The New Work Order: Behind the Language of the New Capitalism* (St. Leonards, Australia: Allen and Unwin, 1996).

28. James Petras, "Latin America: Thirty Years After Che," *Monthly Review,* 49, 5 (October 1997), 8–21.

29. See Peter McLaren, *Critical Pedagogy and Predatory Culture* (London: Routledge, 1995); Peter McLaren, *Revolutionary Multiculturalism: Pedagogies of Dissent for the New Millennium* (Boulder, Colo.: Westview Press, 1997); Peter McLaren, *Life in Schools: An Introduction to Critical Pedagogy in the Foundations of Education* (New York: Longman, Inc., 1997); Henry Giroux and Peter McLaren, *Between Borders: Pedagogy and the Politics of Cultural Studies* (New York: Routledge, 1994).

30. Peter McLaren and Peter Leonard, *Paulo Freire: A Critical Encounter* (London: Routledge, 1993); Peter McLaren and Colin Lankshear, *Politics of Liberation: Paths from Freire* (London: Routledge, 1994); Henry A. Giroux and Peter McLaren, "Paulo Freire, Postmodernism, and the Utopian Imagination: A Blochian Reading," in *Not Yet: Reconsidering Ernst Bloch,* ed. Jamie Owen Daniel and Tom Moylan (London: Verso, 1997), 138–162.

31. See Stanley Aronowitz and Henry Giroux, *Postmodern Education* (Minneapolis: University of Minnesota Press); Patti Lather, *Getting Smart: Feminist Research and Pedagogy within the Postmodern* (London: Routledge, 1991); William Doll Jr., *A Post-Modern Perspective on Curriculum* (New York: Teachers College Press, 1993); Joe Kincheloe, *Towards a Critical Politics of Teacher Thinking: Mapping the Postmodern* (Westport, Conn.: Bergin and Garvey, 1993); Robin Parker Usher and Richard Edwards, *Postmodernism and Education* (London: Routledge, 1994); Andy Hargreaves, *Changing Teachers, Changing Times* (New York: Teachers College Press, 1994);, Henry Giroux and Peter McLaren, *Between Borders: Pedagogy and the Poli-*

tics of Cultural Studies (New York: Routledge, 1994); and Richard Smith and Philip Wexler (eds.), *After Post Modernism* (London: Falmer Press, 1995).

32. See the discussion in Steven Best and Douglas Kellner, *The Postmodern Turn* (New York: Guilford Press, 1997). See also Steven Best and Douglas Kellner, *Postmodern Theory: Critical Interrogations* (New York: Guilford Press, 1991).

33. Morton Wenger, "Decoding Postmodernism: The Despair of the Intellectuals and the Twilight of the Future," *Social Science Journal*, 28, 3 (1991), 391–407. See also Morton Wenger, "Idealism Redux: The Class-Historical Truth of Postmodernism," *Critical Sociology*, 20, 1 (1993–94), 53–78.

34. See E. San Juan Jr., *Beyond Postcolonial Theory* (New York: St. Martin's Press, 1998).

35. Glenn Rikowski, "Left Alone: End Time for Marxist Educational Theory?" *British Journal of Sociology of Education*, 17, 4 (1996), 442.

36. Judith Butler, "Merely Cultural," *New Left Review*, 227 (January/February 1998), 33–44.

37. Terry Eagleton, *The Illusions of Postmodernism* (Oxford, UK: Blackwell Publishers, 1996). See my analysis of the distinction made by Teresa Ebert between "ludic postmodernism" (that celebrates the free-floating articulation of signifiers in the construction of lifestyle discourses that are viewed for the most part as decapitated from external determinations) and "resistance postmodernism" (which draws upon post-structuralist advances in understanding signification but views language as the product of history and links signification to class struggle through the Formalist linguistics of Mikhail Bakhtin and V. N. Volosinov and a sociological analysis of language associated with Lev Vygotsky and G. Plekhanov). See Peter McLaren, *Critical Pedagogy and Predatory Culture* (New York: Routledge, 1995).

38. See Vered Amit-Talai and Caroline Knowles (eds.), *Re-Situating Identities* (Peterborough, Canada: Broadview Press, 1996); Etienne Balibar and Immanuel Wallerstein, *Race, Nation, Class,* trans. Chris Turner (London: Verso, 1991); Judith Butler, *The Psychic Life of Power* (Stanford, Calif.: Stanford University Press, 1997); Iain Chambers, *Migrancy, Culture, Identity* (London: Routledge, 1994); James D. Faubion (ed.), *Rethinking the Subject* (Boulder, Colo.: Westview Press, 1995); Stuart Hall, David Held, and Tony McGrew, *Modernity and its Futures* (Cambridge, Mass.: The Open University, Polity Press, 1992); Stuart Hall and Paul du Gay (eds), *Questions of Cultural Identity* (London: Sage Publications, 1996); Michael Keith and Steve Pile (eds), *Place and the Politics of Identity* (London: Routledge, 1993); John Rajchman (ed.), *The Identity in Question* (London: Routledge, 1995); Jonathan Rutherford (ed.), *Identity: Community, Culture, Difference* (London: Lawrence & Wishart, 1990).

39. See Dave Hill and Mike Cole, "Marxist State Theory and State Autonomy Theory: The Case of 'Race' Education in Initial Teacher Education," *Journal of Educational Policy*, 10, 2 (1995), 221–232; Glenn Rikowski, "Left Alone," 415–451; Mike Cole, Dave Hill, and Glenn Rikowski, "Between Postmodernism and Nowhere: The Predicament of the Postmodernist," *British Journal of Educational Studies*, 45, 2, (June 1997), 187–200; Andy Green, "Postmodernism and State Education," *Journal of Education Policy,* 9 (1994), 67–83.

40. Nancy Fraser, *Justice Interruptus* (New York: Routledge, 1997), 181. For a different assessment, see Iris Marion Young, "Unruly Categories: A Critique of Nancy Fraser's Dual Systems Theory," *New Left Review*, 222 (March/April 1997), 147–160. Also see Mas'ud Zavarzadeh and Donald Morton, *Theory as Resistance* (New York: Guilford Press, 1994); and Teresa L. Ebert, *Ludic Feminism and After* (Ann Arbor: University of Michigan Press, 1996). See also Peter McLaren, "Beyond Phallogocentrism: Critical Pedagogy and its Capital Sins: A Response to Donna LeCourt," *Strategies,* 11/12 (Fall 1998), 34–55 and Carole A. Stabile, "Postmodernism, Feminism, and Marx: Notes from the Abyss," in *In Defence of History,* ed. Ellen Meiksins Wood and John Bellamy Foster, 134–148 (New York: Monthly Review Press, 1997).

41. Gee, Hull, and Lankshear, *The New Work Order.*

42. Andy Green, "Postmodernism and State Education," *Journal of Education Policy*, 9, 1(1994), 67–83.

43. Green, "Postmodernism and State Education," 81.

44. Douglas Kellner, *Media Culture* (New York: Routledge, 1995).

45. Robert W. McChesney, "The Global Media Giants," *Extra!*, 10, 6 (1997), 11.

46. William Robinson, "Globalisation: Nine Theses On Our Epoch," *Race and Class*, 38, 2 (1996), 20–21.

47. Alan Toneleson, "Globalization: The Great American Non-Debate," *Current History: A Journal of Contemporary World Affairs* (November 1997), 359.

48. See Peter McLaren, *Che Guevara, Paulo Freire and the Pedagogy of Revolution* (Lanham, Md.: Rowman & Littlefield).

49. Aijaz Ahmad, "The *Communist Manifesto* and the Problem of Universality," *Monthly Review*, 50, 2 (1998), 22.

50. Sherry Ortner, "Identities: The Hidden Life of Class," *Journal of Anthropological Research*, 54, 1 (Spring 1998), 8–9.

51. Ortner, "Identities," 9.

52. Ortner, "Identities," 4.

53. Ortner, "Identities," 14

54. Richard Wolff and Stephen Resnick, "Power, Property, and Class," *Socialist Review*, 16, 2 (1986), 97–124.

55. Wolff and Resnick, "Power, Property, and Class," 120.

56. Samir Amin, *Specters of Capitalism: A Critique of Current Intellectual Fashions* (New York: Monthly Review Press, 1998). See also Samir Amin, *Capitalism in the Age of Globalization* (London: Zed Books, 1997); and Samir Amin, *Eurocentrism* (New York: Monthly Review Press, 1989).

57. Joe Kincheloe, *How Do We Tell the Workers?* (Boulder: Westview, 1998).

58. Ellen Meiksins Wood, *Democracy against Capitalism; Renewing Historical Materialism* (Cambridge: Cambridge University Press, 1995), 252.

59. James Petras and Morris Morely, *Latin America in the Time of Cholera: Electoral Politics, Market Economies, and Permanent Crisis* (New York: Routledge, 1992).

60. Ellen Meiksins Wood, *Democracy against Capitalism*, 262–263.

61. István Mészáros, *Beyond Capital: Toward a Theory of Transition* (New York: Monthly Review Press, 1995).

62. Alex Callinicos, *Against Postmodernism* (Cambridge: Polity Press, 1989).

63. Callinicos, *Against Postmodernism.*

64. E. San Juan Jr., *Mediations: From a Filipino Perspective* (Pasig City, Philippines: Anvil Publishing, Inc., 1996).

65. David T. Sehr, *Education for Public Democracy* (Albany: SUNY Press, 1997).

66. David Gabbard, "NAFTA, GATT, and Goals 2000: Reading the Political Culture of Post-Industrial America," *Taboo*, II (Fall 1995), 184–199.

67. Joe Kincheloe and Shirley Steinberg, *Students as Researchers* (London: Falmer Press, 1998).

68. See Teresa Ebert, *Ludic Feminism and after* (Ann Arbor: University of Michigan Press, 1996); and Rosemary Hennessy, *Materialist Feminism and the Politics of Discourse* (New York: Routledge, 1993). The critique of postmodern discourses that I am employing is not an assault on feminist critique. It is a critique of those critical attempts—feminist, post-Marxist, and otherwise—that do not challenge sufficiently the ruling frameworks of patriarchal capitalism that deploy sexual difference to justify the unequal distribution of wealth and power. The Marxist-feminist critique I am employing locates patriarchal exploitation beyond the rhetoricization and troping of capitalism and within class, gender, and ethnic divisions of property relations and the struggle over profit and surplus labor. See Ebert, *Ludic Feminism and after.*

69. Edward Soja, *Postmodern Geographies* (London: Verso, 1989). See also David Harvey, *Justice, Nature & the Geography of Difference* (Cambridge, Mass.: Blackwell Publishers, 1996).

70. McLaren and Leonard, *Paulo Freire: A Critical Encounter*; McLaren and Lankshear, *Politics of Liberation.*

71. Spring, *Education and the Rise of the Global Economy.*

72. Gee, Hull, and Lankshear, *The New Work Order*, 166.

73. Gee, Hull, and Lankshear, *The New Work Order*, 166.

74. Gee, Hull, and Lankshear, *The New Work Order*, 152.

75. Gee, Hull, and Lankshear, *The New Work Order*, 167.

76. Rikowski, "Left Alone"; Cole, Hill, and Rikowski, "Between Postmodernism and Nowhere."

77. Bill Bigelow, "The Human Lives Behind the Labels: The Global Sweatshop, Nike, and the Race to the Bottom," *Rethinking Schools*, 11, 4 (1997), 1–16.

78. Bigelow, "The Human Lives Behind the Labels," 1–16."

79. See the discussion by Luke Mines, "Globalization in the Classroom," *The Nation*, 266, 20 (1998), 22–23.

80. See Rikowski, "Left Alone." See also Jack Amariglio and Antonio Calari, "Marxian Value Theory and the Problem of the Subject: The Role of Commodity Fetishism," in *Fetishism as Cultural Discourse*, ed. Emily Apter and William Pietz (Ithaca, NY: Cornell University Press, 1993), 186–216; William Pietz, "Fetishism and Materialism: The Limits of Theory in Marx," *Fetishism as Cultural Discourse*, ed. Emily Apter and William Pietz (Ithaca, NY:: Cornell University Press, 1993), 119–151; and Jean Baudrillard, "The End of the Millenium or The Countdown," *Theory Culture & Society*, 15, 1, (February 1998), 1–9.

81. See McLaren, *Critical Pedagogy and Predatory Culture*; and McLaren, *Revolutionary Multiculturalism.*

82. Iris Marion Young, *Justice and the Power of Difference* (Princeton, NJ: Princeton University Press, 1990).

83. Joel Kovel, "The Enemy of Nature," *Monthly Review*, 49, 6 (1997), 14. See also Peter McLaren, "Introduction: Traumatizing Capital"; Peter McLaren, "Critical Pedagogy in the Age of Global Capitalism."

84. Wood. *Democracy against Capitalism.*

REFERENCES

Allman, P. 2001. *Critical Education Against Global Capitalism: Karl Marx and Revolutionary Critical Education.* Westport, Conn.: Bergin & Garvey.

Davis, M. 2004. "Planet of Slums." *New Left Review*, 26 (March–April), at www.newleftreview.net/NLR26001.shtml.

Eagleton, T. 1998. "Defending the Free World." In *The Eagleton Reader,* edited by Stephen Regan, 285–293. Malden, Mass.: Blackwell.

Feldman, P., and Lotz, C. In press. *A World to Win: Ideas for a Future without Global Capitalism.* London: Movement for a Socialist Future.

Gimenez, M. 2001. "Marxism and Class, Gender and Race: Rethinking the Trilogy." *Race, Gender & Class*, 8(2), 23–33.

Harvey, D. 2000. *Spaces of Hope.* Berkeley: University of California Press.

Hennessy, R., and Ingraham, C. (eds.). 1997. *Material Feminism: A Reader in Class, Difference, and Women's Lives*, 1–14 New York: Routledge.

hooks, b. 2000. *Where We Stand: Class Matters.* New York: Routledge.

Kovel, Joel. 2002. *The Enemy of Nature: The End of Capitalism or the End of the World?* New York: Zed Books.

Marx, K. 1978. *The Marx-Engels Reader*, 2d ed. Edited by R. Tucker. New York: W.W. Norton & Company.

McLaren, P., and Farahmandpur, R. 1999. "Critical Pedagogy, Postmodernism, and the Retreat from Class: Towards a Contraband Pedagogy." In *Postmodernism in Educational Theory: Education and the Politics of Human Resistance,* edited by D. Hill, P. McLaren, M. Cole, and G. Rikowski. London: Tufnell Press.

McLaren, P., and Farahmandpur, R. 2001. "Marx after Post-Marxism: Reclaiming Critical Pedagogy for the Left." *Working Papers in Cultural Studies No. 25.* Pullman, Wash.: Department of Comparative American Cultures, Washington State University.

Meyerson, G. 2000. "Rethinking Black Marxism: Reflections on Cedric Robinson and Others." *Cultural Logic*, 3(2), at eserver.org/clogic/3-1%262/ineyerson.html.

Robinson, W. I. 1996. *Promoting Polyarchy: Globalization, U.S. Intervention, and Hegemony.* Cambridge: Cambridge University Press.

Robinson, W. I. 2003. *Transnational Conflicts: Central America, Social Change, and Globalization.* London and New York: Verso.

Robinson, W. I. 2004. *A Theory of Global Capitalism: Production, Class, and State in a Transnational World.* Baltimore, Md.: Johns Hopkins University Press.

Roy, A. 2004. "Tide? Or Ivory Snow? Public Power in the Age of Empire," at www.democracynow.org/static/Arundhati_Trans.shtml.

II

ON CLASS, CULTURE, AND DIFFERENCE

3

Paul Willis, Class Consciousness, and Critical Pedagogy: Toward a Socialist Future

Peter McLaren and Valerie Scatamburlo-D'Annibale

Paul Willis's *Learning to Labor*, published in 1977, marked a pivotal moment in the history of educational criticism.[1] As Stanley Aronowitz acknowledged in his introduction to the book, Willis's work represented a significant contribution to radical and Marxian-inspired analyses of the function of schools while nonetheless challenging some of their basic presuppositions. In what was to be acknowledged as one of the most significant ethnographies of working-class youth culture, a pathfinding work that connected a humanistic study of everyday life with a sophisticated macropolitical analysis of the workings of ideology and social power, Willis sought to understand how ordinary, everyday mainstream cultures were produced and to explore the expressions of resistance that were aimed at dominant social forms. *Learning to Labor* describes in compelling detail the ideological tensions between an oppressed group (working-class "lads") and the status quo (middle-class, white-collar "ear'oles") in order to demonstrate the dynamic relationship of the production, reproduction, and resistance of cultural meanings that constitute class-based ideology. Scuppering much of the ethnographic conventions of the time, Willis's ethnographic study, both in theory and method, demonstrated how lived culture and the rituals of everyday school life among primarily nonelite groups contributed to the shaping of capitalist structures of power and privilege. One of the most noteworthy aspects of Willis's work was its openness to "experience" as well as its attempt to explore a theoretical basis for activist struggle.

Willis argued that the lads' culture drew upon the broader working-class and factory cultures to which these young men had been introduced and exposed to in their homes, neighborhoods, and communities. Their resistance to and contempt for the "official" knowledges presented to them in school were derived from and influenced by the features of Hammertown's broader working-class tradition. Contrary to the many myths ensconced in the rhetoric of "meritocracy," the lads were consciously aware that their own cultural and economic context was the best guide to their futures—they realized, in short, that they would probably not get "good" jobs. The lads' culture, therefore, led them to "reject, ignore, invert, make fun of, or transform most of what they [were] given in careers lessons" (Willis 1977, p. 92). Rather than treating the lads as passive subjects deprived of agency, Willis contended that the lads were not simply channeled into jobs but rather were actively (if not defiantly) embracing their future in the realm of "unskilled" labor. Paradoxically, their resistance to the conformity encouraged within the educational setting also functioned to reproduce them as laborers in the workforce—in other words, the cultural practices that were interpreted as expressions of resistance in school situations were concomitantly serving as forms of accommodation to working-class futures. The pioneering aspect of Willis's work, however, was that he insisted that the processes by which working-class youths ended up with working-class jobs were far more complex than previous theorists had suggested. But more than this, Willis argued that the ability and eagerness of the lads to resist demonstrated at least a partial (if not sufficient) recognition of their social locatedness and the way in which they were economically situated as members of an oppressed class. This, of course, created at least the possibility of attaining the kind of class consciousness that would refuse to capitulate to capitalism's requirements.

Willis's *Learning to Labor* was, of course, one of several projects conducted under the auspices of the Birmingham Centre for Contemporary Cultural Studies during the 1970s. At the time of the work, the Centre as a whole was undoubtedly influenced by Marxism. In virtually all of its work, class was a central concept that was considered and analyzed not only in terms of its cultural aspects (i.e., people's beliefs, values, practices) but also *in relation to economic realities*. The earliest manifestations of cultural studies were, therefore, shaped substantially by social class and its attendant issues/concerns. Since then, as contemporary cultural studies have assumed an increasingly postmodern coloration, class (along with Marxism) has been generally consigned to the "discard tray labeled 'modernity'" (Milner 1999, p. 114). While the conflation of Marxism with modernity is, in and of itself, problematic enough given that Marx was one of the sharpest critics of liberal modernity (cf. Wallerstein 1995), the dismissal of class as a so-called modernist category is even more disturbing since class as a category was never really dissolved in the bubbling vat of postmodernity despite claims to the contrary. Nonetheless, the category of class has been marginalized not only within the prevailing precincts of cultural studies but also in what routinely passes for "radical" social theory. Talking about class is "unpopular" and presumably not "sexy enough for the intelligentsia," whose members seem more enthralled by the "intellectual eroticism" of studying difference (Munt 2000, pp. 3, 7). As Collini (1994) has aptly noted, in the "frequently incanted quartet of race, class, gender and sexual orientation, there is no doubt that class has been the least fashionable . . . despite the fact that all the evidence suggests that class remains the single most powerful determinant of life-chances" (p. 3).

Discussions of the working class, so central to Willis and other founding figures of cultural studies, now tend to "stick in the throat like a large chunk of stale Hovis" (Anthony, cited in Munt 2000, p. 3) and academics seem particularly squeamish when the subject is raised. To speak of the working class and/or working-class culture at a time when the topic of social class has been deemed defunct by the sentinels of intellectual fashion is often viewed as somewhat naïve, nostalgic, even perverse. Issues of class and explorations of class consciousness belong, or so we have been told, to an earlier era; notions of class are no longer "central to the current fashion in cultural studies" (Lave, Duguid, and Fernandez 1992, p. 258). In a presumably "posteverything" society, the problem of class has been supplanted by new concerns with identity and difference—categories that are considered more appropriate to the postmodern condition. Today, a rather uncritical and ahistorical postmodern "pluralism" reigns supreme.

As a partial result of the conceptual shift within social theory, and cultural studies in particular, it is not surprising that Willis's study subsequently became a target of criticism. *Learning to Labor* was critiqued for its class reductionism and its almost exclusive focus on working-class males and their experiences and their forms of resistance. It has also been accused by positivists of not constituting an adequate sample for making generalizations across wider communities and groups and feminists have charged that the study ignored cultural forms of patriarchy. Additionally, Willis's classic study has been plagued by charges of romanticizing working-class culture. The alleged structural functionalism (or functional structuralism, take your pick) of his theorizing has been traced to an epistemic essentialism and dualism. His sweeping dialectic of freedom/determination has been chastised for its presumed ahistoricism and utopianism. Yet despite these criticisms—and possibly, in part, because of them—*Learning to Labor* continues to be his most influential text—one that (a) represented a landmark in the annals of critical educational discourse, (b) created a seismic shift in the tectonic plates of educational ethnography, and (c) foregrounded the centrality of class issues/relations in the analysis of school cultures, pedagogical practices, and material conditions. We are not, however, interested in rehashing the critiques of Willis's work with the intent of defending it or contributing to its ongoing critique. Rather, we are concerned with identifying some political trajectories that emanate from Willis's work for he has provided some interesting fodder for radical educationalists committed to engaging (rather than cavalierly dismissing) the legacy of Marxism at a time in U.S. history when Marxism has all but disappeared as a legitimate problematic out of which analysis and action can proceed.

THE ABIDING CENTRALITY OF CLASS

Despite the lack of attention accorded to the category of class in contemporary narratives, everyday life is saturated with class relations. Class never went "away" and its marginalization in the academy and in realm of educational and cultural studies "merely alludes to the success of entrenched beliefs in liberal pluralism" (Munt 2000, p. 10). This marginalization is, of course, a symptom of the larger tendency—namely the suppression of Marxism—by erstwhile post- and ex-Marxists. Indeed, for years, Marxism has been maligned by the prevailing centers of intellectual power that tend to reject it as "totalizing," "reductionist," and even "repressive." Today, the critique of Marxism by cultural studies has "become a series of unthinking reflexes and slogans that are mobilized to dismiss historical materialist critique as quickly as possible" (Katz 2000, p. 51). In many respects, class has actually been hidden from analytic and political view by the "postmodern" turn in cultural studies. While we would not dispute that cultural studies have made great inroads in addressing the previous dearth of cultural investigation into gender, sexuality, race, and ethnicity, it has come at a considerable cost and has led to an evacuation of the key concern that gave birth to cultural studies in the first place—namely a profound commitment to questions of class. Recently, Andrew Milner (1999, pp. 10–13) has addressed the abandonment of class in academic and political discourses, despite the array of empirical data that provides ample evidence of the continued existence of class and people's identification with it (in both a positive and negative sense); where the daily realities of inequality in society speak not only to deep structural divides but also to economic and cultural exploitation and oppression. Milner (1999) in fact argues that the more class has become theoretically abstract and/or dealt with in a meta-theoretical sense, the more it has been marginalized and, in some instances, completely obliterated from the theoretical and political canvas. The vogue is toward textual readings of class at the expense of grounded, ethnographic investigations.

We view this as a disturbing theoretical and political development for it seems to emasculate the radicalism that informed the earliest manifestations of the cultural studies project. Rather than posing a challenge to dominant ideological formations and indeed to capitalism, post-Marxist, postmodern cultural studies (at least in the American academy) has become "an Establishment organon" (San Juan Jr. 2002, p. 222) and has evolved into an apologetic narrative that reinscribes the banality of liberal pluralism. Our own work in recent years has attempted to redress this tendency (McLaren 1998, 2000; McLaren and Farahmandpur 1999, 2000; Scatamburlo-D'Annibale and McLaren 2003). Our approach has not been one of defeatism nor triumphalism but one of emphasizing the strategic centrality of class in theorizing the "social." We argue that given the entrenchment of neoliberal globalization practices and the global dominance of U.S. military and economic power, class is as important a category as it ever was, perhaps even more so. We believe that the ongoing significance of Willis's work can point us in the direction of a more sustained emphasis on class consciousness and class struggle within educational research. In this context, Palmer's (1997) comments could not be more apposite:

> Class, as both a category of potential and becoming and an agency of activism has thus reasserted its fundamental importance. More and more of humanity now faces the ravages of capitalism's highly totalizing, essentializing, and homogenizing impulses. . . . There are no answers separate from those of class struggle, however much this metanarrative of materially structured resistance intersects with special oppressions. Class has not so much fallen as it has returned. It had never, of course, gone anywhere. *Identified* as simply one of many plural subjectivities, class has actually been obscured from analytic and political view by poststructuralism's analytic edifice, erected at just the moment that the left is in dire need of the clarity and direction that class, as a category and an agency, a structure and a politics, can provide. The legacy of Marxism in general, and of historical materialism in particular, is to challenge and oppose this obfuscation, providing an alternative to such material misreadings, building an oppositional worldview that can play some role in reversing the class struggle defeats. (p. 72)

We reject the notion put forward by postmodernists and poststructuralists that class is simply about habits and behavior, cultural status, or social prestige, or that is primarily a language sign whose meaning is overpopulated with referents and therefore, "undecidable." Class is both a lived culture and an objective entity. It has an objective existence as an empirical category and a subjective existence in terms of the way in which it is lived.[2] The progenitors of cultural studies well understood this even though they tended to emphasize (and in some cases, overemphasize) the subjective dimensions of class in response to the perceived economism of certain versions of Marxist theory. Yet in their rush to avoid the "capital" sin of "economism," many contemporary cultural and educational theorists have fallen prey to an uncritical and ahistorical culturalism that has severed the links between culture and class in a profoundly problematic manner. Unlike earlier theorizations, which bridged a cultural approach and the Marxist concept of class struggle, the very notion of class struggle and the very idea that Marxism still has something to teach us is considered passé. In the contemporary post-Marxist climate, those who dare speak of class tend to be Weberians who largely "ignore discussions of capital and labour"; as such there has been a "tendency to depoliticize class analysis so that it naturalizes social divisions" and replaces the "engine of protest" with a "resigned, imperceptible social organism" (Munt 2000, p. 3). Since there is no evidence that class has withered away in either the United States or Britain, there is no convincing argument that class analysis can be consigned to the proverbial dustbin of history. On the contrary, at a time when we are in the midst of returning to the "most fundamental form of class struggle" (Jameson 1998, p. 136) in light of global conditions, class analysis must be foregrounded. This can and must be done at different levels. On the one hand there is a need to return to concrete sites of class experience and to theorize out of them for they represent forms of situated knowledges that may provoke the forms of class consciousness necessary in the struggle against capitalist exploitation.

On the other hand, we cannot discard the notion of class as an objective phenomenon. Dominant post-al formulations tend to view class as one among a diversity of semiotically constructued identities and just another form of difference. In other instances, class is associated with the process of consuming commodities as a lifestyle event or focuses on their circulation. Against such innocuous conceptualizations, we believe it is imperative to acknowledge that class is directly connected to where a person is located within the capitalist division of labor and that it is labor that is the source of value. Capitalism is a system based on the imposition of "universal commodification, including, centrally, the buying and selling of human life-time" (Dyer-Witheford 1999, p. 9). Furthermore, class is not simply another ideology that serves to legitimate oppression. Rather, class denotes "exploitative relations between people mediated by their relations to the means of production" (Gimenez 2001, p. 24). While all categories are social, "class is the quintessence of the social"; unlike other categories, class cannot be determined "except by the position of the individual in society, and cannot be reproduced except through participation in the functioning of the economic system. . . . Class . . . was created by capitalism and is reproduced together with it, and for this reason poses a real danger to it" (Kagarlitsky 2000, p. 95).

Such an understanding of class has largely been marginalized in excessively "culturalist" narratives that confuse class (which has an objective status) with class consciousness, which is undoubtedly shaped and conditioned by social and cultural factors. Acknowledging this dimension of class does not undermine the subjective aspects of class as lived culture and lived experience but it does point out that classes do not simply come into being by subjective fiat. Furthermore, the "objectivity of capitalist exploitation" cannot be relativized by "treating it as a mere reflex of hermeneutic self-understanding" (Harvey 1998, p. 9) or as a mere discursively articulated subject position.[3] Unfortunately, educational discourse on the "left" has been awash in "postmodern" platitudes that sublimate class, valorize uncritical and fetishized notions of "difference" while marginalizing socialist alternatives to the social universe of capital. In an effort to counteract what we perceive to be politically domesticating and depotentiating tendencies in North American educational criticism, we argue elsewhere (Scatamburlo-D'Annibale and McLaren 2003; McLaren and Farahmandpur 2000) for the increasing relevance of Marxist analysis by locating the struggle for educational reform within current struggles against the globalization of capitalism, the conditions that produce the material armature of the imperial state, and the importance of working toward the socialization of productive property. Despite post-Marxist claims to the contrary, Marxist theory still has a key role to play in generating ideas that challenge intellectual orthodoxies and rationalizations for educational inequalities.

EXPRESSIVE PRACTICES AND
A GROUNDED MARXIST AESTHETICS

Throughout Paul Willis's innovative and expansive *oeuvre*, he has not only demonstrated an abiding interest in class consciousness and its potential role as a weapon against capital but he has also revealed an unyielding conviction that Marxist criticism can bring about a world less populated by economic exploitation and social injustice. These features of Willis's work operate dialectically within his overall project as a Marxist scholar: Working-class consciousness can be educated by Marxist theory, while Marxist theory can, at the same time, be both bodied forth as well as conceptually deepened by those emboldened in their daily praxis by working-class consciousness. For Willis, understanding human action stipulates grasping its dialectical relation to social and symbolic structures. He has been especially attentive to how systems of intelligibility are produced within cultural formations and how ideological hegemony is maintained internally to specific group cultures within identifiable historical moments, such as the present era of disaggregated and fragmented identities. Of course, he is most concerned with ways of challenging existing ideologies, hegemonic relations, and institutional orthodoxies through the creative operations of nondominant cultural formations.

To engage in a systematic and detailed examination of the production and reproduction of conflictual and contradictory cultural formations exercised by various social classes at specific historical moments, and to preoccupy oneself with how these formations contribute to the reproduction of and resistance to existing capitalist social relations, is a lifelong research endeavor, and it is no surprise that Willis often takes pains to clarify and revise his work when the occasion demands. Few theorists comprehend as well as Willis what is at stake politically when, at the metropolitan heart of the capitalist empire, the commodity reigns supreme. Willis understands only too well that commodities are always produced in excess of human need, and this poses a specific problem for the reproduction of cultural life and for the reproduction of capitalist social relations in particular. Specifically, Willis is interested in the dynamism constitutive of cultural production resulting in what he calls "sensuous meaningfulness" or "the bodily oil of lived presence" (2000, p. 31). He is concerned most of all with what he terms "expressive practices" linked to "living cultures." While these cannot be apodictically linked to the immanent and historically produced situations and logics of economic production, it is, nevertheless, highly likely that such practices are connected to these logics. His work has led him to formulate moments of resistance as forms of "embedded logics in rebellious impulses or social counter-forces" (1990, p. x). It is within these impulses and forces that capitalism as a living dynamic, rife with contradictions, can best be understood.

Willis comprehends the contradictions of capitalism as sites for both cultural struggles as well as other types of nondiscursive struggles, and also as "sources for change and expansion" (1990, p. x). Here Willis sees the prickly processes of cultural reproduction tied up in the development and maintenance of "the 'teeth-gritting' harmony of capitalist formations" while at the same time, paradoxically, operating as "critical resistant or rebellious forces" (1990, p. xi). Willis reveals how working-class students produce living critiques of their identity formation within capitalist culture and in doing so explains how their "penetrations" cannot always be understood as a form of critical reflexivity. In fact, they most often take expressive forms communicated in and through their bodies. As Willis (1990) argues:

> I would never argue that the lads' culture in *Learning to Labor* is socialist though I would argue that it contains materials that must be dealt with in any socialist reconstruction. The point of my ethnography was precisely to show the

profane complexity of cultural experience, only a small part of which—partially, selectively, differently at different moments of the argument—is explicable in our theoretical forays. For me culture is a very commodious and profane conceptual bag. It is much, much broader than ideology. I would never equate the two. My notions of cultural practices and cultural production . . . produce *living* critiques and penetrations of dominant ideology only as a small (though critical) part of their total effective presence. They often do so in eccentric, collectively unspoken rather than individually verbal ways, and almost as the byproduct of the application of sensuous human capacities to immediate ends. I hesitate to use the word "cognition" at all to describe such processes. Furthermore, the inbuilt limiting structures here embedded as they are in sensuous, concrete forms are not in any conceivable sense a question of "false consciousness." It is not a mistaken or false perception, for instance, to experience class exploitation as concretely mediated and mitigated (for white men) and changed through gender and race power. These things are "real," too. (p. x)

Central to cultural reproduction of the social relations of capitalist societies is the process of cultural production, a process that undergoes various stages of transformation. Cultural formations and expressive modalities are the shape-shifters of the postindustrial era, although not in a metaphysical sense; rather, they are continually transforming themselves into something else, only to return again, like the proverbial rag-and-bone shop of the repressed, in an expanded and enlarged aspect of their original state, refleshed, resignified, recathected, often with a vengeance. Willis is keenly interested in the internal relations of expressive practices—enacted while on the dole, in dance clubs, in the mall, in the classroom, or in the local pub—focusing on their critical content, their cultural production, and how cultural production is implicated in the larger process of social reproduction. His center of inquiry can be said to revolve around the following axis: How do cultural commodities relate to the creative capacities and practices of the individuals who create them, and to the process of commodification in general?

In *Common Culture*, Willis and colleagues (1990) discuss "symbolic work" (work that rests on the development of expressive labor power) to draw attention to the active and productive nature of cultural consumption, the "making whole" through binding fragments together, thereby defetishizing (remaking) commodities. We engage in symbolic work through our cultural practices of purchasing commodities. Our identification with the object appears to be the product of the commodity in itself that is purchased but in reality it is the social effects of the purchase that we mistake for the magical attributes of the commodity. In other words, we often confuse the effects of the purchase of a commodity for the identity that we believe the commodity bestows upon us. We mistake our self-identity achieved through our purchase of the commodity for the effects of our expressive labor-power. What people often confuse with the act of purchasing is, in reality, a purchasing effect, which is not a quality of their own symbolic labor. Symbolic work, as theorized by Willis, involves the transformation of commodities through the process of productive consumption; this involves the expenditure of expressive human labor to produce expanded value. In this process, alienated and fetishized meanings are converted into new contextual meanings and embodied satisfactions that were not previously available to the consumer. This process functions to expand the use value of the commodity over its exchange value through a form of defetishization. When we are faced with the production of expanded expressive labor power through the productive consumption of cultural commodities that is at odds with the repressive disciplines of the labor process, we have, according to Willis, participated in an act of resistance.

Willis has always been interested in communicative action, in the culturalization of the body, but it is in his later works, *Common Culture* and *The Ethnographic Imagination*, that these interests are most fully explored. Willis begins with the assumption that no commodity is ever completely fetishized. If this were the case, communication would be impossible. He ends with the conviction that communication is only truly possible when fetishization breaks down. In other words, a given commodity must be defetishized in order to offer communicative and cultural use values. Cultural commodities, observes Willis, possess an in-built stability, there is a "double naturing" or self-repairing quality about them; they are continually extinguished and renewed, never escaping the process of fetishization, but never being reduced to that process, either. Cultural commodities are for use, not for ownership. They seduce, they offer the promise of community but never deliver on that promise. As consumers, we become addicted to the failure of the commodity, by their fraudulent claims, by their enticing promises. You can't get them to sign a contract, but you still take them up on their offer. What makes them creative is that they remain unfettered by historical norms of consumption and they are preloaded with expressivity. Words are never eaten the same way, and they taste differently depending upon the combinations that are put in the mouth; but the best part is that they can be spit out and stripped of their dominating power before they arrive at their final destination in the stomach. Commodities are linked to the logic of capitalist production in terms of their availability within contexts of prior communicative meaning and symbolic appropriation—that is, in relation to their specific human role within communicative and cultural meaning systems that are inherently social.

Willis achieves a theoretical dynamism in *The Ethnographic Imagination* that surpasses much of his previous work. His writing appears less turgid and is crafted in a more self-consciously poetical style. On the one hand, his writing still betrays a textual heavy-handedness and arcane theorizing and trumpery that has become the signature of many postmodern writers, with ideas and concepts laboriously trowelled onto the surface of his text until it appears to collapse under the weight of its own ideas; on the other hand, there are moments when his own expressive style is refreshingly probing, resembling the wordplay of a loutish Leavisite hanging out with fellow word-smiths in the local pub, playing the theoretical dozens with the streetwise deftness of a homeboy from South Central Los Angles. *The Ethnographic Imagination* is a work that stalks the meaning of cultural objects and artifacts from the dark alleys of cultural criticism, cautiously approaching its subject matter from various theoretical angles and trajectories, yet never veering from the central question: How does human "praxis" rearrange the "objective possibilities" of a cultural object or material form? Carefully fashioning a transgressive aesthetic sensibility, Willis traverses the lost territory between particular signifiers and emotional expressivity with the hardscrabble earnestness of a shop steward. This is especially evident, for instance, in his discussion of working-class speech codes as a process of making words into fists, a process that is populated by a politics of subversion and freighted with creative alternatives to official representations and naturalized ideological accounts.

In *The Ethnographic Imagination*, Willis nominates resistance as a "grounded aesthetics." Grounded aesthetics is simply a modality of living through a creative defetishization of cultural commodities and the relocation of their social meaning. Grounded aesthetics highlights how "vertical" structures within capitalism that employ abstract reason and mentalized communication and that treat human beings as objects to control can be detached for "lateral" use and circulation for expressive resistance. Willis is able to boast an optimism of the will precisely because he is absolutely sold on the fecundating power of human creativity and on ethnography as a means of understanding how such creativity works in commercialized human culture. Willis sees ideological and institutional processes as producing the alienated individual of postmodern culture from above but symbolic work as producing the subject from below. He also sees the expanding and creative nature of expressive labor-power as a basis for critiquing instrumental labor-power, thereby challenging the capitalist labor processes and forming a basis for collective organization and a struggle on behalf of common interests. This can only occur when symbolic work is made less invisible. Because cultural production is not self-conscious enough of its own constitutive processes, informal meaning-making can help strengthen mental/manual divisions characteristic of capitalist societies.

A CRITICAL PEDAGOGY OF CLASS CONSCIOUSNESS

Willis undoubtedly ranks among the most prominent Marxist cultural theorists, especially in terms of the relevance of his work for education. Nonetheless, we would be remiss if we did not share some reservations we have concerning the overall trajectory of his work. In attempting to examine social life from the inside out, Willis is, at times, overly preoccupied with the expressive nature of meaning-making, particularly within the semi-autonomous spaces of mediated cultural formations, or structures of mediation. There often tends to be an undialectical overemphasis on abstract labor and the production of fetishized social relations (both mediated aspects of communicative activity and resistance to reified or alienated aspects of the same activity). These fetishized social relations are tied up with the alienation produced between the worker and the commodity he or she produces but also, as Marx pointed out in his labor theory of value, with those that enable individuals to misperceive everyday social intercourse as a relation between things. This, in our view, causes Willis to at times elevate cultural formations responsible for "alienation effects" over and above material relations of production.

Although Willis is clearly aware that such cultural formations are "structured" by capitalism as a specific system of social/production relations, these relations appear much less central to his work. We don't believe that capital can be defeated through fighting within and against its mediated forms. Resistance requires more than the defetishization of commodities. It requires the very overturning of the generalization of commodity production itself and the de-reification of capital and the nation-state; that is, it requires overturning the historical and material conditions that shape bourgeois ideology and our imprisonment within it. It requires creating the social and material conditions that can help to shape and educate class consciousness in the pursuit of socialist futures. Especially at a time of deepening social and economic crisis, punctuated by imperialist wars of aggression and conquest, resistance requires a democratic and centralized class struggle in order to transform state power and abolish the very value form of labor that not only gives class society its ballast, anchoring it in the process of commodification, but also its conditions of possibility.

We believe that Willis's grounded aesthetics needs to be complemented by a larger strategy for socialist transformation, one that proceeds from an assessment of the objective factors and capabilities latent in the current conditions of class struggle. The worldwide social movement against anticorporate globalization as well as the anti-imperialist/antiwar movements preceding and following the U.S. invasion of Iraq have provided new contexts (mostly through leftwing independent publications and resources on the Internet) for enabling various publics (and nonpublics beyond the institutions that serve majority groups) to become more critically literate about the relationship between current world events and global capitalism. Following an engagement in these new opportunities for analysis, it is possible to forge a vision of possible futures for humanity and the development of an understanding of what, exactly, stands between us and the realization of that vision. It is likely that the changes that we seek will not be possible without a massive social revolution consolidated around the wider struggle against imperialism and in support of human rights, and a search for a socialist alternative to capital. This will require a socialist education of working-class consciousness. And this, in turn, means challenging the mediated social forms in which we live and learn to labor.

One way of scrutinizing the production of everyday meanings so that they are less likely to provide ballast to capitalist social relations is to study working-class consciousness. It is here that Willis's work can be especially productive. Bertell Ollman (1993) notes that more systematic and effectively theorized studies of working-class consciousness remains to be done given that most current studies of working-class consciousness have been derived from non-Marxist approaches. A key point to remember, according to Ollman, is that class consciousness is much more than individual consciousness writ large. The subject of class consciousness is, after all, class. Viewing class consciousness from the perspective of the labor theory of value and the materialist conception of history, as in Ollman's account, stipulates that we view class in the context of the overall integrated functions of capital and wage labor. And while people can certainly be seen from the functionalist perspective as embodiments of social-economic functions, we need to expand this view and understand the subjective dimensions of class and class consciousness. Ollman follows Marx's advice in recommending that in defining class or any other important notions, we begin from the whole and proceed to the part (see also the writings of Ilyenkov 1977, 1982a, 1982b). Class must be conceived as a complex social relation in the context of Marx's dialectical approach to social life. It is important in this regard to see class as a function (from the perspective of the place of a function within the system), as a group (qualities that are attributed to people such as race and gender), and as a complex relation (that is, as the abstracted common element in the social relationship of alienated individuals). A class involves, therefore, the alienated quality of the social life of individuals who function in a certain way within the system. The salient features of class—alienated social relation, place/function, and group—are all mutually dependent.

Class as function relates to the objective interests of workers, class as group relates to their subjective interests. Subjective interests refer to what workers actually believe to be in their own best interests. Those practices that serve the workers in their function as wage laborers refer to their objective interests. Ollman (1993) summarizes class consciousness as:

> one's identity and interests (subjective and objective) as members of a class, something of the dynamics of capitalism uncovered by Marx (at least enough to grasp objective interests), the broad outlines of the class struggle and where one fits into it, feelings of solidarity toward one's own class and of rational hostility toward opposition classes (in contrast to the feelings of mutual indifference and inner-class competition that accompany alienation), and the vision of a more democratic and egalitarian society that is not only possible but that one can help bring about. (p. 155)

Ollman underscores (correctly in our view) the notion that explaining class consciousness stipulates seeking what is not present in the thinking of workers as well as what is present. It is an understanding that is "appropriate to the objective character of a class and its objective interests" (1993, p. 155). But in addition to the objective aspect of class consciousness, we must include the subjective aspect of class consciousness, which Ollman describes as "the consciousness of the group of people in a class in so far as their understanding of who they are and what must be done develops from its economistic beginnings toward the consciousness that is appropriate to their class situation" (1993, p. 155). But what is different between this subjective consciousness and the actual consciousness of each individual in the group? Ollman (1993) writes that subjective consciousness is different from the actual consciousness of the individual in the group in the following three ways:

> (1) It is a group consciousness, a way of thinking and a thought content, that develops through the individuals in the group interacting with each other and with opposing groups in situations that are peculiar to the class; (2) it is a consciousness that has its main point of reference in the situation and objective interests of a class, viewed functionally, and not in the declared subjective interests of class members (the imputed class consciousness referred to above has been given a role here in the thinking of real people); and (3) it is in its essence a process, a movement from wherever a group begins in its consciousness of itself to the consciousness appropriate to its situation. In other words, the process of becoming class conscious is not external to what it is but rather at the center of what it is all about. (p. 155)

Class conscious is therefore something that Ollman (1993) describes as "a kind of 'group think,' a collective, interactive approach to recognizing, labeling, coming to understand, and acting upon the particular world class members have in common" (p. 156). Class consciousness is different from individual consciousness in the sense of "having its main point of reference in the situation of the class and not in the already recognized interests of individuals" (1993, p. 157). Class consciousness is something that exists "in potential" in the sense that it represents "the appropriate consciousness of people in that position, the consciousness that maximizes their chances of realizing class interests, including structural change where such change is required to secure other interests" (1993, p. 157). Ollman stresses that class consciousness "exists in potential," that is, "class consciousness is a consciousness waiting to happen" (1993, p. 187). It is important here not to mistake class consciousness as some kind of "abstract potential" because it is "rooted in a situation unfolding before our very eyes, long before understanding of real people catches up with it" (1993, p. 157). Class consciousness, then, is not something that is fixed or permanent but is always in motion, always aborning. The very situatedness of the class establishes its goal—it is always in the process of becoming itself, if we understand the notion of process dialectically. Consequently, we need to examine class from the perspective of Marx's philosophy of internal relations, as that "which treats the relations in which anything stands as essential parts of what it is, so that a significant change in any of these relations registers as a qualitative change in the system of which it is a part" (Ollman 2003, p. 85).

Willis (2000) captures this dynamics of class when he writes:

> Nonclass categories may tell you more empirically about a person, but they do not "move" or develop by themselves. To understand principles of change or how those categories combine or develop over time, to make sense of the picture, to historicize it we need the dynamism of economic relations. To be crude, class explains more about them than they can explain about it. Socially received and atavistic, often still unnamed or analyzed, categories provide the sea, class the currents. Class and productive relations and commodity production provide nodal points of influence, confluence, and change that allow us to organize and see the empirical "wholes" in more ordered and interlinking ways. (p. 112)

It is precisely in mapping out and explaining these "nodal points" that Willis's work can offer us a deeper understanding of the formation and education of class consciousness. While the former nodal points Willis (2000) describes as "manual wage labor and masculinity, spatial concentration, white collar/blue collar, work/leisure, collectivity," the new nodal points that interest him include the conditions of cultural practices such as "different relations to language and to embedded forms of sensuous meaning; different access to and different types of relationships, with resources available for symbolic work and for the development of the expressive self" (p. 112). But again, too often Willis's focus on how capital is "lived" in the sensuous domain of the fetishized cultural object and its dialectical relation to individual and group identity fails to account sufficiently for the role of production in generating the value form in which labor is produced. It is here that Willis's work could benefit from a more dialectical approach like the one pioneered by Ollman. Willis's work as it stands could be more effectively deployed as a strategic weapon in the struggle against capital if it assumed a more world-historical, international, multicultural, and anti-imperialist perspective. Such a perspective would still be grounded in the social dimension of meaning-making but within the context of a wider counteroffensive against economic and environmental degradation brought about by globalized capitalism's imperial blitzkrieg. The glimmerings of what a postcapitalist socialist society might look like are as yet unbirthed in Willis's overall political project.

Having said this, where Willis's work can provide an especially significant contribution to the existing work on class consciousness resides in the challenge of according "sufficient weight to the social relations in which people produce and reproduce the means of material life without reducing everything to these" (McNally 2001, p. 113). Here Willis's empirical and theoretical work can help to establish what David McNally (2001) calls "the dialectical determination among the internally related elements that constitute a social whole" (p. 113). Willis's contributions to our understanding of commodity fetishism can be especially fruitful in helping us fathom the dialectical relationship that obtains between ideological class divisions and the forces of production and between the inner laws of capital and cultural and subjective processes. In the broadest sense, it can enable us to situate with more analytic precision the struggle over the meaning and the inner dialectical quality of the commodity within wider social, cultural, and historical processes and formations (keeping in mind that there are aspects of Willis's work that could themselves be improved with a more directed focus on the totality of capitalist social relations). In this regard, Willis emphasizes the importance of linguistic translation in helping to uncoil the hidden processes of symbolic work both as a means to resist the deleterious aspects of ideological fetishism and as a way of creating new inroads to political self-fashioning. Here we recognize in Willis's work a suggestive strategy for taking received meanings from bourgeois commodity culture and, as Volosinov (1986) would put it, contesting their "tenure." In this context, Willis's work provides a crucial avenue for exploring the formation and functioning of the conflicting ensembles of social and cultural relations, moral assumptions and obligations, and forms of social activity and discourse that make up the contemporary "moral economy" among working-class groups (see Thompson 1963, 1991). We suggest that much of the contemporary work on commodity culture and class consciousness could be deepened if undertaken with an eye to exploring the connections between

Willis's work and those of the Bakhtin School of the 1920s that includes V. N. Volosinov (1986), M. M. Bakhtin (1981, 1984), and P. N. Medvedev (Medvedev and Bakhtin 1985). We also discern a fruitful complementarity between Willis's use of aesthetics as a form of resistance and the work of Walter Benjamin (1968, 1999), especially in light of Benjamin's materialist theory of language and his understanding of how, in the words of McNally (2001), "bourgeois society tries to efface the human body, beginning with the fetishism of the commodity" (p. 224). Like Benjamin, Willis believes that degraded bodies in our society can trouble significantly the formation of capitalist commodification and become sites for resistance and revolt. McNally (2001) notes appositely, after Benjamin, that "a precondition of emancipation is that repressed desires must enter into the language of everyday life and that the latter must recover the language of the body and of things" (p. 225). If it is true that the pathways to liberation must make their way through the language of the body, then surely these bodies, and the way they are enfleshed with the capacity to recall memories long repressed and dreams long forgotten, constitute the most important resource in forming the larger collective body of class conscious workers necessary for class struggle to achieve its goal.

Because Marx lays bare "relations among what is, what could be, what shouldn't be, and what can be done about it," Ollman (2003, p. 82) argues that Marxism constitutes "science, critique, vision, and recipe for revolution" simultaneously "with each of these qualities contributing to and feeding off the others" (p. 82). It is by approaching Marxism with this description in mind that can best assist educators in exploring the causeways of revolutionary consciousness and praxis. It is precisely by utilizing Marx in this fashion that Willis's work can be strategically employed by radical educators bent on developing cultural strategies within forms of lived culture that can move defetishization into new creative contexts for sundry ad hoc struggles alongside, within, and against commodity culture. The key for critical educators is not only to become involved in making the process of cultural commodification less invisible to those whose subjectivities are formed within it, but to become involved in creating the kinds of social, political, and educational conditions that not only can assist in the defetishization of cultural practices but also can shape the development of working-class consciousness.

So much that we have learned about the ethnographic imagination from Willis's work can be brought to bear in new and productive ways on the study of class consciousness and its transformation into new forms of socialist resistance. Such an engagement can afford educators new ways of broadening the struggle for new resources of meaning-making and self-making, extending the norms for social transformation, and advancing the struggle for a socialist future.

NOTES

Valerie Scatamburlo-D'Annibale is associate professor in the communication studies department of the University of Windsor, Canada. This chapter was previously published in Nancy Dolby and Greg Dimitriadis (with Paul Willis), eds., *Learning to Labor in New Times* (New York: Routledge/Palmer, 2004), pp. 41–60. Reprinted with permission.

1. Many of us have viewed ourselves as fellow travelers of Willis, on the bumpy and uncharted road to liberation—what Raymond Williams called *The Long Revolution*—which can most effectively be brought about by socialist renewal. Willis had been riding the rails of socialist research for years while many of us were still cutting our graduate school teeth on his *Profane Culture*, delighting ourselves in his theoretical renditions of the Teddy Boys, Mods, and Rastas and debating the strengths and weaknesses of indexical, homological, and integral levels of cultural relations among motorbike-boy culture (not to mention integral circuiting). During the British invasion of graduate schools of education in the 1980s, commandeered by the Birmingham School of Contemporary Cultural Studies, any radical doctoral student worth her salt who was not familiar with the works of Paul Willis, Phil Corrigan or his brother, Paul, Stuart Hall, Richard Johnson, Angela McRobbie, or Dick Hebdige was unable to participate with any credibility in the weekly brown bag seminars or lunchtime conversations in the graduate student lounge. Those of us who were lucky enough to have our doctoral work read and encouraged by Willis, or other visitors from the UK to the radical campuses of the day, felt more than lucky: We were blessed.

2. In *The 18th Brumaire of Louis Bonaparte*, Marx proposed a clear distinction between the objective fact of class position and the subjective fact of class consciousness. In this discussion of the French peasantry, Marx (1984) argued that:

> In so far as millions of families live under economic conditions of existence that separate their mode of life, their interests and their culture from those of the other classes, and put them in hostile opposition to the latter, they form a class. In so far as there is merely a local interconnection among these small-holding peasants, and the identity of their interests begets no community, no national bond and no political organization among them, they do not form a class. (p. 124)

3. For a lengthier exposition of our approach, see Scatamburlo-D'Annibale and McLaren 2003.

REFERENCES

Allman, P., McLaren, P., and Rikowski, G. 2003. "After the Box People: The Labor-Capital Relation as Class Constitution and its Consequences of Marxist Educational Theory and Human Resistance." In *Yesterday's Dreams: International and Critical Perspectives on Education and Social Class,* edited by J. Freeman-Moir and A. Scott, 149–179. Christchurch, New Zealand: Canterbury University Press.

Bakhtin, M. M. 1981. *The Dialogic Imagination: Four Essays.* Edited by Michael Holquist. Translated by Caryl Emerson and Michael Holquist. Austin: University of Texas Press.

Bakhtin, M. 1984. *Problems of Dostoevky's Poetics.* Edited and translated by Caryl Emerson. Minneapolis: University of Minnesota Press.

Benjamin, W. 1968. *Illuminations.* Edited by Hannah Arendt. New York: Schocken Books.

Benjamin, W. 1999. *Selected Writings, Volume 2: 1927–1935.* Edited by Michael Jennings, Howard Eiland, and Gary Smith. Cambridge, Mass.: The Belknap Press of Harvard University Press.

Collini, S. 1994. "Escape from DWEMsville." *Times Literary Supplement,* May 27.

Dyer-Witheford. 1999. *Cyber-Marx: Cycles and Circuits of Struggle in High-Technology Capitalism.* Chicago: University of Illinois Press.

Gimenez, M. 2001. "Marxism, and Class, Gender and Race: Rethinking the Trilogy." *Race, Gender & Class,* 8(2), 23–33.

Harvey, D. 1998. "The Practical Contradictions of Marxism." *Critical Sociology,* 24(1&2), 1–36.

Ilyenkov, E. V. 1977. *Dialectical Logic: Essays on its History and Theory.* Moscow: Progress Publishers.

Ilyenkov, E. V. 1982a. *The Dialectics of the Abstract and the Concrete in Marx's Capital.* Moscow: Progress Publishers.

Ilyenkov, E. V. 1982b. *Leninist Dialectics and the Metaphysics of Positivism.* London: New Park Publications.

Jameson, F. 1998. *The Cultural Turn.* London: Verso.

Kagarlitsky, B. 2000. *The Return of Radicalism.* London: Pluto Press.

Katz, A. 2000. *Postmodernism and the Politics of "Culture."* Boulder, Colo.: Westview Press.

Lave, J., Duguid, P., and Fernandez, N. 1992. "Coming of Age in Birmingham: Cultural Studies and Conceptions of Subjectivity." *Annual Review of Anthropology,* vol. 21.

Marx, K.. 1869 [1984]. *The 18th Brumaire of Louis Bonaparte.* New York: International Publishers.

McLaren, P. 1998. "Revolutionary Pedagogy in Post-Revolutionary Times: Rethinking the Political Economy of Critical Education." *Educational Theory,* 48(4), 431–462.

McLaren, P. 2000. *Che Guevara, Paulo Freire, and the Pedagogy of Revolution.* Boulder, Colo.: Rowman & Littlefield.

McLaren, P., and Farahmandpur, R. 1999. "Critical Pedagogy, Postmodernism, and the Retreat from Class: Towards a Contraband Pedagogy." *Theoria,* 93, 83–115.

McLaren, P., and Farahmandpur, R. 2000. "Reconsidering Marx in Post-Marxist times: A Requiem for Postmodernism?" *Educational Researcher,* 29(3), 25–33.

McNally, D. 2001. *Bodies of Meaning: Studies on Language, Labor, and Liberation.* Albany: State University of New York Press.

Medvedev, P. N., and Bakhtin, M. 1928 [1985]. *The Formal Method in Literary Scholarship: A Critical Introduction to Sociological Poetics.* Translated by Albert J. Wherle. Cambridge, Mass.: Harvard University Press.

Milner, A. 1999. *Class: Core Conceptual Concepts*. London: Sage Publications.

Munt, S., ed. 2000. *Cultural Studies and the Working Class*. London: Cassell.

Ollman, B. 1971. *Alienation: Marx's Conception of Man in Capitalist Society*. Cambridge: Cambridge University Press.

Ollman, B. 1993. *Dialectical Investigations*. New York: Routledge.

Ollman, B. 2003. "Marxism, This Tale of Two Cities." *Science & Society*, 67(1, Spring), 80–86.

Palmer, B. 1997. "Old Positions/New Necessities: History, Class, and Marxist Metanarrative." In *In Defense of History: Marxism and the Postmodern Agenda*, edited by Ellen Meiksins Wood and John Bellamy Poster, 65–73. New York: Monthly Review Press.

San Juan Jr., E. 2002. *Racism and Cultural Studies: Critiques of Multiculturalist Ideology and the Politics of Difference*. Durham, NC: Duke University Press.

Scatamburlo-D'Annibale, V., and McLaren, P. 2003. "The Strategic Centrality of Class in the Politics of 'Race' and 'Difference.'" *Cultural Studies/Critical Methodologies*, 3(2), 148–175.

Thompson, E. P. 1963. *The Making of the English Working Class*. London: Gollancz.

Thompson, E. P. 1991. *Customs in Common*. London: Merlin.

Volosinov, V. N. 1986. *Marxism and the Philosophy of Language*. Translated by Ladislav Matejka and I. R. Titunik. Cambridge, Mass.: Harvard University Press.

Wallerstein, I. 1995. *After Liberalism*. New York: The New Press.

Willis, P. 1977. *Learning to Labor*. New York: Columbia University Press.

Willis, P. 1978. *Profane Culture*. London: Routledge and Kegan Paul.

Willis, P. 1990. "Foreword." In *Learning Capitalist Culture: Deep in the Heart of Tejas*, edited by Douglas E. Foley, vii–xii. Philadelphia: University of Pennsylvania Press.

Willis, P. 2000. *The Ethnographic Imagination*. Cambridge: Polity.

Willis, P., Jones, S., Canaan, J., and Hurd, G. 1990. *Common Culture: Symbolic Work at Play in the Everyday Cultures of the Young*. Boulder, Colo.: Westview Press.

4

After the Box People: The Labor–Capital Relation as Class Constitution and Its Consequences for Marxist Educational Theory and Human Resistance

Paula Allman, Peter McLaren, and Glenn Rikowski

For those interested in exploring relations between education and social class from a Marxist perspective, or, more accurately, examining education as an *aspect* of "class," these are interesting times. First, as Simon Clarke (1999) notes, we witness the virtual abandonment of the notion of the working class—not just by erstwhile postmodernists, but also by mainstream social scientists. Most people who analyze social class today do no such thing; rather, they have social inequality and stratification in view. Social class itself is evaded and avoided. This bad seed at the heart of capitalist society, indeed its existence at capital's structural core, is covered in mounds of obfuscation even though "we live it. . . . It is part of our lives, all around us," as Dave Hill extemporizes (Hill, in Cole, Hill, McLaren, and Rikowski 2001, p. 19).

Second, viewed as the class relation, the labor–capital relation, the real situation tallies with Hill's gut reaction: Class *is* everywhere, is *all around us*, and *within us* (as human capital)—as we live in capital's social universe whose substance is *value* (Rikowski 2000a, 2001a, 2002; Neary and Rikowski 2000). Class taken as the capital relation is inescapable, unavoidable, for there is no hiding place as we live in a specific social universe (the social universe of capital) that is premised upon the tragic antagonism between labor and capital.

Thus, within contemporary social theory in general and class analysis in particular there is a "reality gap." There is a chasm between "class as social inequality and stratification" in theory, and class as an element of the constitution of a world of struggle in practice. The violent relation at the heart of our social world is the *capital relation*, the struggle between labor and capital that is *everywhere*. Looked at in this way, what role does education play?

The argument of this chapter is that education plays a key role in the perpet-
uation of the capital relation; this is the skeleton in capitalist education's dank
basement. This is just one of the many reasons why, in contemporary capitalist society, education assumes a grotesque and perverted form. It links the
chains that bind our souls to capital. That it is uncomfortable for educational
theorists, researchers, activists, and practitioners to talk about such unsavoury
topics is not surprising. However, only by uncovering the lid on this issue can
Marxist science hope to advance.

SOCIAL INEQUALITY AND STRATIFICATION,
OR SOCIAL CLASS: OUT OF THE MAINSTREAM

Today, most social and educational theorists and researchers, rather than work
with a notion of social class actually operationalize and utilize notions of social
inequality and stratification. On the basis of skill, occupational status, and income, individuals are ascribed to various *strata* that are then taken as proxy social classes. Dave Hill and Mike Cole (2001) are meticulous in describing this
as the basis for the UK Registrar General's classifications of social class and
other academic definitions and frameworks. When we, as social and educational
theorists and researchers or political pollsters, utilize these classifications we become "box people." We collude in the attempt to mirror, or map, in true Ptole-
maic fashion, the relative social statuses of persons. As educational theorists and
researchers we then use these categories of persons to attempt to "explain" (in
practice this simply amounts to more mapping) what is going on in education
(e.g., qualifications outcomes, higher education participation rates, and the like).

At one level, the whole process is incredible. Having ranked people on a
range of disadvantage/advantage, it seems strange that we might then expect
those in the lower strata to rise above all these and perform well in other areas. Of course, some do—there are always exceptions—and the rate at which
people buck debilitating trajectories expected of them can be measured. But
on the grand scale, research that "discovers" that those in the upper strata
tend, on average, to do better than those in the lower strata (in education, for
example) almost qualifies as nonresearch. Thus, papers delivered at a conference on social class and education at King's College London in the summer
of 2000 were not saying anything really new or different from what was being written on class and education in the 1980s, or even the 1960s. Only historical details were different. Working-class school students seem to be
doomed; they appear to be perennially prone to "underachievement" in education relative to their more privileged middle-class peers. But it's a rigged
game. Of course, there is some value in trying to explain why it is that

middle-class pupils do better on average; such studies tell us things about the constitution of capitalist society and the generation of market inequalities. They can also generate explanations regarding the origins of social inequality, worth, and social validation, for example (see Rikowski and Rikowski 2002). However, we maintain that they tell us nothing about social class, for, as was noted earlier, the base categories are not social class ones at all but categories of social stratification founded on the combination and aggregation of various measures of social inequality and relative social status.

To get a real grip on social class and education we need to jump out of the mainstream, to get our feet muddy on the banks of Marxist theory. From a Marxist perspective, what is so wrong with the neo-Weberian view of social class that predominates in educational theory and research and its technicist accompaniments (e.g., the UK Registrar General's classification of occupations)? Hill and Cole (2001) summarize some of the key points. As they note, the occupations at the heart of conventional social class categories are based "not only on income, but also on notions of status and associated consumption patterns and lifestyles derived from the work of sociologist Max Weber" (p. 151). Furthermore, note Hill and Cole, "while the classifications may be interesting sociologically," Marxists would criticize them on three grounds (p. 151). The first shortcoming of conventional neo-Weberian outlooks on social class is that:

> they ignore, indeed hide, the existence of the capitalist class—that class which dominates society economically and politically. This class owns the means of production (and the means of distribution and exchange)—i.e. they are the owners of factories, transport companies, industry, finance, the media. In other words, these consumption-based patterns mask the existence of capitalists, including the super rich and the super powerful: the ruling class. (Hill and Cole 2001, p. 151)

Second, and more significantly for Hill and Cole:

> consumption-based classifications of social class gloss over and hide, the fundamentally *antagonistic* relationship between the two main classes in society, the working class and the capitalist class. In Marxist analysis, the working class includes not only manual workers but also millions of white-collar workers— such as bank clerks and supermarket check-out operators . . . whose conditions of work are similar to those of manual workers. (Hill and Cole 2001, p. 152, emphasis ours)

Hill and Cole's third criticism of neo-Weberian and technicist conceptions of "class" is that:

> by segmenting the working class, they both hide the existence of *a* working class and they also serve the purpose of "dividing and ruling" the working class—that,

by segmenting different groups of workers, for example white collar and blue collar workers, and workers in work and the so-called "underclass" workers. These subdivisions of the working class can be termed class fractions or segments (after Ainley 1993). Such classifications *hide and work to inhibit* or disguise the common interests of these different groups comprising the working class. They serve, in various ways, to inhibit the development of a common (class) consciousness against the exploiting capitalist class. (Hill and Cole 2001, pp. 152–153—our emphasis)

Thus, Hill and Cole's powerful Marxist critique of the mainstream neo-Weberian perspective on social "class" indicates that this conventional classification is basically *ideological* in nature. It functions to mask and subvert attempts to analyze class from a critical social scientific perspective concerned with the constitution of capitalist society. Mainstream views on "class" fail to capture it as a concept that expresses the deep antagonism within the heart of capitalist society. However, as Hill, Sanders, and Hankin (2002) note, "whilst the class war still rages the working class in general has been . . . demobilized and only the capitalist class knows itself to be in uniform" (p. 166). While conventional class analysis and research misreads the nature and significance of "class," capital relentlessly oppresses us, and human representatives of capital cheerfully (with their stock options, bonuses, and public-sector rip-offs) plot the extension of capital's rule over society. Unfortunately, a great deal of Marxist, and socialist, theory is guilty of the same type of misreading.

The problem at the heart of an unspoken alliance between certain classical Marxist theorizing of class (such as that evidenced in the writings of Erik Olin Wright and Nicos Poulantzas) and mainstream sociological theories is founded on the basis that they both rest upon a "box person" mentality. This is based on allocating persons to status groups. While the "box person" outlook is easy to see in social class frameworks such as the UK Registrar General's and those emanating from mainstream sociologists (such as John Goldthorpe), it is less understandably also present within far too many Marxist theorizations of class.

Bonefeld (1999) argues that "the comprehension of 'class' and therewith 'class struggle' can go forward *only in and through a critique of 'capital' as the dominant production relation*" (p. 3—our emphasis). For Bonefeld, this entails theorizing class as an aspect of the critique of political economy, and, in the process, providing a *critique* of class. Thus:

The aim, then, is to go beyond the notion of class as a thing-in-itself and to see class as a constitutive social relationship that exists in and against itself. "Class" is not an affirmative concept but a critical concept. Such an understanding objects to the glorification of the working class, refuses to espouse it uncritically, and rejects any attempt to tailor theoretical understanding according to the supposed historical role of the working class. (Bonefeld 1999, p. 4)

Class theory, argues Bonefeld, is not a "flag-waving exercise" (1999, p. 5). It is not morally committed to viewing contemporary society through working-class eyes or from the "standpoint" of the working class. Class theory is an aspect of the exploration of the constitution of capitalism that is premised upon a project for its abolition. It is an integral part of Marxism as a theory *against* capitalist society, and not just a theory *of* it. Class theory is therefore concerned with the *abolition* of class (Marx's position) and the opening up of human history from the desolation of its pre-history (Dinerstein and Neary 1998).

Before moving on to the critical concept of class, it should be noted that a critique of social inequality is not deemed unimportant. The gross social inequalities we witness today (between individuals, between social status groups, and between the advanced and developing countries) are widening and have intensified over the last twenty years. The critique and analysis of these is crucial. However, our argument on social inequality is similar in form as to that on class: In general, the explanation of social inequality has not been undertaken as a form of *critique* of existing social relations. In this sense, it has not been embarked upon seriously. At stake is the uncovering of the forces that *generate* social inequality. This type of analysis is not content just to describe and tabloidize (in postmodernist or liberal left mode) the empirical manifestations of these forces as concrete forms of social inequality, the fare of much mainstream sociology. Such a critique must go to the roots of capitalist society, vis-à-vis the labor–capital relation.

The analysis of this section has provided the groundwork for uncovering social class. The next section draws back the cloth and pursues the class relation (as capital relation). Eventually, we explain that the antagonistic relation between labor and capital that rests on a particular *form* of labor (the value form) resides not only within the capitalist labor process, the work situation. It exists throughout the whole of capital's social universe. We return to this point after considering a critical concept of class.

MARX'S CRITICAL CONCEPT OF CLASS

To say that class is the major irony or contradiction of the human condition as we enter the third millennium is putting it far too mildly—tragedy 2000 would be much more *apropos*. Today, class is the major factor of social division throughout the globe, as Marx so presciently predicted it would be. It is therefore ironic that many socialists and others who remain desirous of social transformation are swarming toward various new, as well as more traditional, social movements in the desperate attempt to find a radical force capable of replacing the class movement as the agent of social change. Others have refocused their attention on the so-called Third World, not through any laudable or critical reasoning but because they think that this is the only location in which the "true" working class can still be found in any abundance. And of course the greatest tragedy of all is that many others have forfeited their hope—often their desire even—for social transformation.

It is a constant source of amazement and frustration to us that so many socialists, and here we are thinking particularly of those who profess to be Marxists, totally ignore what we consider to be the most essential component of Marx's class analysis—his dialectical concept, or conceptualisation, of class. We have also grown weary of the perpetual battery of excuses: for example, those who blame history or specific political conditions pertaining at specific historical conjunctures, and especially those who blame Marx for his lack of clarity. No one would deny that there are bits of Marx's *oeuvre* that are difficult, but his concept of class is not one of these. However, since it appears to be widely misunderstood or ignored and also because it is absolutely fundamental to all sorts of political—including educational—struggles, it is important to discuss this concept. It must be kept in focus as we discuss other aspects of our collective strategies for global social transformation.

As Ollman (1976) argues, any analysis of Marx's thought should begin with recognition of his concept, or as Ollman calls it, his philosophy, of *internal relations*. The concept of internal relations is the key that unlocks the purported difficulty of Marx's thought. This philosophy, or concept, pertains to a particular form of relational thinking. Although academia is still replete with examples of categorical thinking and analysis, a great deal of intellectual endeavor involves relational thinking and analysis. However, there are two distinct types of relational thinking and they are paradigmatically as far removed from one another as relational thought is from categorical thinking. Tolman (1981) stresses that all of these modes or paradigms of thinking are necessary for the elucidation of social relations and phenomena. However, as people become increasingly immersed in a particular field of study, they are frequently driven to deepen their understanding by shifting to a more sophisticated or complex mode of thinking about the topic or phenomenon they are studying. In other words, each of these ways of conceptualizing the subject is valid and serves a function, but at the same time will eventually prove inadequate to a full understanding or intellectual penetration of the phenomenon one is seeking to understand. Once people saturate their ability to comprehend a field of study in terms of categorical thinking, they recognize that the phenomenon they are studying does not exist in isolation but rather in inter-action with various other entities. Therefore, they begin to focus their atten-tion on the result, or results, of these interactions. These results—whether we think of the outbreak of war or the formation of a chemical compound—are normally a synthesis of the interacting phenomena, a result of the bringing to-gether of some number of the attributes internal to each phenomenon or situ-ation. To analyze events or phenomena in this way is to think of them in terms of their *external* relations. Two or more entities might come together and in-teract, but the change that occurs is external to the entities. It is a result that has a separate and independent existence from the original entities once it has come into existence. Just as when a male and a female of some species pro-duce an offspring that continues to exist even when the parents do not.

Clearly, thinking in terms of external relations adds greater complexity to our understanding and is absolutely essential to the advancement of the hu-man intellect. Indeed, in the understanding of certain phenomenon and events it may offer a completely adequate level of comprehension. However, this is not always the case and Marx certainly found that although helpful it was far from sufficient when it came to understanding the material reality of capital-ism. This is why he employed a different form of relational thinking in a great deal of his analysis.

We doubt very seriously if Marx was fully aware that his analysis implied this paradigm shift. In fact, he argued that his dialectical "method" was dic-tated not by some a priori method of thought but by the actual—the mate-rial—reality of capitalism, itself. Therefore, if Marx explains capitalism in terms of internal relations—the type of relations that are central to his dialec-tical conceptualization of capitalism—it is because he found this type of re-lation in the real world of capitalism. Of course, this was not the world of cap-italism that we experience daily but the reality of capitalism that Marx was able to reveal through his penetrating analysis of the surface phenomena—those that constitute our immediate and illusory experience—of capitalism. That Marx found capitalism—his subject of analysis—to be a system com-prised of various internal relations is not all that unusual. There are many other areas of our material world—that is, real phenomena or entities—that are also involved in internal relations and that, as a consequence, can only be fully comprehended when analyzed accordingly. And those people who seek to deepen their understandings of these phenomena will of necessity be driven, just as Marx was, to adopt a new, more sophisticated, or complex, way of perceiving them. We are sure that at least a few will come to mind as you read the following explanation of internal relations.

When we conceptualize the internally related nature of something, or, to use Ollman's terminology, when we apply a philosophy of internal relations to our subject of study, we focus on the relation and how it is responsible for the past and present existence of the related entities. These entities are the opposites in the relation. Second, we focus simultaneously on the ongoing *internal development* within the related entities. We might also find that the relation leads to the development of a third entity, or something that appears to be similar to the result of an external relation. However, there is an important difference. The results of internal relations do not obtain a separate existence, despite the fact that they often appear to have done so. If the original entities/opposites cease to exist, which can only occur if the relation is abolished, then the result also ceases to exist. Furthermore, once this result of an internal relation is formed it aides and abets the continuing existence of the internal relation by helping to bind, or mediate the related opposites, or entities, within the relation. We will give you the most important example of this as soon as we move on to explaining Marx's dialectical concept of class—that is, the concept of class that is derived from grasping class as an internal relation. First, however, there is a point about terminology—that is the use of, as well as relation between, concepts—that we should make.

We have already suggested a strong connection between dialectical conceptualization and thinking in terms of internal relations. Indeed, the connection is so strong that for many intents and purposes they can be considered to be synonymous. However, there are distinctions that must be made. At the heart of dialectical thought—its focus or raison d'être—is the dialectical contradiction. A dialectical contradiction should not be confused with a logical contradiction, even though there is a relation between them—we hasten to add, however, that this is an external relation. Logical contradictions have to do with the errors in thought or the presentation of one's thinking and also errors in one's behavior that occur when one utterance or action does not follow logically from a previously stated utterance or a previously executed behavior. Dialectical contradictions often lead to these contradictory situations, but this is a matter of their consequences rather than a depiction of their form. All dialectical contradictions are internal relations—a relation of two opposite entities/phenomena that could not exist, continue to exist, or have come into existence in the absence of their internal relation to one another. Both externally and internally the very nature—past, present, and future—of each of the opposites is shaped within its relation to the other opposite. The opposites could not be what they are or what they are to become outside of this relation. When this is an antagonistic relation, the existence of each opposite is variously constrained or hampered by virtue of the fact that it is in an internal relation with its opposite; however, one of the opposites, despite these limitations, actually benefits from the relation. It is in the interest of this opposite—often referred to as the positive—to maintain the relation. The other opposite—the negative—although it can better its circumstances temporarily within the relation, is severely limited by its relation to its opposite and sometimes to the point of devastation; therefore, it is in its interest to abolish the relation. This abolition is referred to as "the negation of the negation." The individuals constituting the negative opposites do not cease to exist, but they do cease to exist as the negative, and inferior, opposite they have been due to their existence within an internal relation/dialectical contradiction—hence this is called the "negation of the negation." The relationship between a dialectical contradiction and an internal relation is not a mutually exclusive relation. By this we mean that while all dialectical contradictions are internal relations it does not follow that all internal relations are dialectical contradictions. Another term that can be used for a dialectical contradiction—a term that is actually a descriptive phrase—is a "unity of opposites." We tend to use this term when we want to emphasize the internally related nature of the dialectical contradiction. Having dealt with this terminology, we can now move on to that most important example of an internal relation/dialectical contradiction/"unity of opposites": the relation between labor and capital that constitutes the class relation.

According to Marx's analysis of capitalism, the dialectical contradiction that lies at the heart of capitalism is the relation between labor and capital. This relation, together with the internal relation between capitalist production and circulation/exchange, constitutes the *essence* of capitalism (Allman 2001a). The labor–capital relation, however, is our focus. It is the relation that produces the historically specific from of capitalist wealth—the *value form* of wealth. The most accurate and encapsulating way to describe this relation is to posit it as a relation of valorization. To explain fully what is meant by each of these statements, we must take you on a brief journey through the historical development of capitalism. This will be a selective tour in that there were several preconditions that led to the development of capitalism, but we focus only on those that pertain specifically to Marx's dialectical concept of class.

Human beings have a long history of struggling against scarcity, or struggling to overcome scarcity. Therefore, one of the age-old motivators for further development, and indeed the very survival of various communities, has been the need to increase human productivity. For a long period of human history, the goal was to fulfill the needs of individuals, families, and communities; therefore, if individuals or family units produced a surplus to their own requirements, it was shared or traded in kind within the community. As the productive abilities of people increased, trade between communities became possible and rudimentary markets in certain goods grew in importance. However, it is only with capitalism that all production becomes production for the market. With the exception of very primitive markets where exchange of people's products took place through barter or trade in kind, production for market exchange necessitates a more systematic and reliable basis for exchange. People need to find some common element inherent in what they produce that can become the basis for their exchanges. If we think of their products as commodities, which all products of human labor become once capitalism is fully established, we can conceptualize them as a unity of a use value with an exchange value. Clearly, the use values of different commodities cannot be considered a common factor or a factor that can be used to establish their relative equivalencies. What we need to discover is the factor—a factor that can be represented in measurable units—that determines their exchange value. The only factor that all commodities share in common is that they are all the result of human labor, and the only external or observable aspect of human labor that can be reduced to measurable units is the time that it takes to produce the commodity.

However, labor-time as the common factor remains problematic because if it were the basis for establishing the equivalency of commodities, then the slowest and probably least skilled workers producing a particular commodity would produce the most value. Once products are produced for the market, they must be produced in what Marx calls the "socially necessary labor-time" for the production of a particular commodity. This means that they must be produced in the socially *average* time and with the *average* degree of skill that it takes to produce the commodity at a particular time. That is, they must be produced in at least this amount of time if they are to command a price that reflects the value they contain. In capitalist societies, wealth is measured in labor-time rather than in use values. It is therefore an abstract rather than concrete form of wealth. Individuals or communities must possess this abstract form of wealth in order to obtain the use values, or real objects and services they need—objects such as food, clothing, and shelter and services, such as health care and education. What we are describing here is what Marx calls "The Law of Value" and the historically specific from of wealth to which it leads. This law only comes into full effect once capitalism is fully established, and capitalism can only be established when a very special commodity becomes available on the market. This is the commodity that Marx calls *labor-power*.

When capitalists purchase labor-power, they obtain people's capacity to labor, but if this were all they received, there would be no capitalism. What capitalists actually receive when they purchase labor-power is people's ability or capacity to create a value greater than their own replacement value—a value greater than their wages or salaries. When people's labor is utilized within the labor–capital relation—and when they, therefore, constitute the dialectical opposite of capital—they enter into a value-creating process. This value-creating process is comprised of two parts, which Marx calls necessary labor and surplus labor, or if we focus specifically on value, necessary labor-time and surplus labor-time.

Marx calls the second part of this process the valorization process. It is within the valorization process that surplus value—the lifeblood of capital—is created. Marx also conceptualized labor, itself, as a dialectical contradiction, or an internal relation of two opposites—concrete labor and abstract labor. People's concrete labor produces use values—objects or services that are supposed to meet human needs. Their abstract labor, that takes place simultaneously with their concrete labor, constitutes the substance of value, a substance measured in labor-time. Once people produce the value of their own labor-power (expressed as the wage), then any excess labor-time produces the surplus value that is the driving force of capitalist production. The capitalist's profit is a portion of surplus value (as state revenues, insurance, rent, and other calls on surplus are drawn off, leaving the remainder as profit).

Marx takes great pains to explain that it is not the type of concrete labor one performs that determines one's class position, but instead one's internal/dialectical relation with capital. Therefore, the idea that it is only manual, or physiological, labor that produces surplus value is totally erroneous as is the idea that it is only this type of labor that positions one within the working class, or proletariat. A passage that makes this crystal clear is in volume 1 of *Capital*, where Marx stresses with his customary wit:

> The only worker who is productive is one who produces surplus value for the capitalist . . . [who] contributes towards the self-valorisation of capital. If we may take an example . . . from outside the sphere of material production, a schoolmaster is a productive worker when, in addition to belabouring the heads of his pupils, he works himself into the ground to enrich the owner of the school. That the latter has laid out his capital in a teaching factory, instead of a sausage factory, makes no difference to the relation. (1867, p. 644)

The most obvious conclusion that can be drawn from Marx's dialectical concept of class is that the dialectical opposite of capital—that is, the working class, or the proletariat—increased exponentially during the last decades of the twentieth century. This is one of the most important and dramatic effects of globalization. And the rapid growth in the numbers of people who constitute the working class will continue this rapid growth as long as capitalism exists. It is not just the millions upon millions of peasants who have become agricultural workers for the giant multinational agribusinesses and the producers of handicrafts and menial services in the developing world that are being drawn into the labor–capital relation. An increasing number of professional services—including in some places education or parts of the education service—have been

turned into commodities, in other words use values that are dialectically insep-
arable and unobtainable until the point of purchase from an exchange value—
a price. Once the results of one's labor are commodified, then one's labor itself
becomes vulnerable to incorporation, or as Marx calls it, *subsumption* within
the labor–capital relation—vulnerable to becoming the commodity Marx calls
labor-power. One's labor becomes a potential source of surplus value—of capital—and thus subject to the same experiences of exploitation and alienation
that have plagued industrial workers since the inception of capitalism. As a consequence, if we may expand upon the most obvious conclusion: Never before
has the potential—indeed the reason—been greater for humanity to unite
against capitalism.

Unfortunately this unity will not happen without critical education, or what
we prefer to call *revolutionary critical education* (see Allman 1999, 2001a).
It won't happen, or at least not in a way that has any chance of defeating capital. This is because our concept of class—a limited, distorted, and undialectical concept—is so entrenched that most people, including a considerable
number of stalwart Marxists, think that class has become, at best, a secondary issue, or factor in transformational/revolutionary struggles. This problem
is compounded by the fact that subsumption within the labor–capital relation
takes place relatively slowly and also unevenly, especially within professional areas of work. People going through the process complain that their
work is being deintellectualized and has become subject to bureaucratic or
tighter managerial control and supervision. Increased paperwork, or "paper
pushing," is frequently the focal point in employees' moans concerning the
quality of their working lives. Increased levels of stress and stress-related ab-
senteeism are rife in many areas of work. Yet if workers understood how capitalism actually functions—something that will only happen when and if revolutionary critical education becomes widespread—they would understand
both what is happening to them and why it is happening. And educators, one
of the professions experiencing this process, would also be able to better understand what is happening to those they teach—how not only they but the labor-power of the future is being groomed for the needs of capital. To cut short
a long explanation of a complex situation that is fraught with a multitude of
contradictions, one of capital's needs, on a global scale, is millions of young
people with a similar level skill—often a very high level. This is not because
there are jobs for all of these people. Rather, their level of skill will make
them eligible to compete with one another for the jobs that *do* require this
level of skill, thereby, as is true of all competition, driving down the value of
their labor-powers expressed as wages.

Given this situation and all the dilemmas it poses to our professional lives,
what can we do? Instead of striking out against an endless succession of

windmills in the fashion of that famous Spanish knight, those who are currently being shaped and molded to capital's requirements could join forces and begin to challenge and eventually unite with others in the struggle to abolish the real enemy. As has been argued elsewhere and in more detail, the real enemy is capitalism (Allman 2001a). While we applaud those who have begun to challenge globalization and its institutional minions, such as the World Trade Organization (WTO), the World Bank, and the International Monetary Fund (IMF), we hasten to warn that we will make little progress for humanity until we first understand and then confront, challenge, and eventually defeat the real enemy. This enemy is capitalism, or rather global capitalism, and its historically specific form of wealth—a form of wealth, which regardless of the level of human productivity, guarantees humanity a future tormented by the perpetual existence of scarcity and escalating divisions between the rich and the poor. Capitalism depends upon the existence of scarcity—the callous denial of human needs—and also the proliferation of various forms of social division for its very survival. Clearly, humanity's survival will demand its abolition.

THE VIOLENT RELATION WITHIN CAPITAL'S SOCIAL UNIVERSE

According to the analysis of the previous sections, the generation of capital's social universe, whose substance is value, is based on the antagonistic relation between labor and capital. The class relation *is* the labor–capital relation, and it forms a violent dialectic that generates value. Human representatives of capital (e.g., owners, managers, shareholders, and so on) drive laborers on to produce surplus value so that their profits are maximized. Various forms of worker resistance ensue to limit the depredations of capital in the labor process (e.g., oppressive intensification of work through management strategies), to increase wages to heighten living standards (thus increasing the value incorporated as necessary labor) and to enhance working conditions. Hence, the *production of value and surplus value is struggle based on antithetical social drives*; the relation between labor and capital *is* class, indeed, *is the constitution of class as a social relation of production*. Thus, class is the capital relation: the dynamic, contradictory, antagonistic relation that generates and maintains the social universe of capital. No "class" in *this* sense implies no capital, and a different social universe.

Traditionally, Marxism has focused on the class struggle at the point of production. Some Marxists make a fetish out of strike statistics note Bonefeld (1999) and Holloway (1999). If there were no strikes at all this would not mean the termination of class or the class struggle. Strikes constitute only one form of the concretization of the social antagonism that is at the heart of capitalist society. As capital, with value as its social substance, constitutes a veritable social universe, *it is everywhere*; and, therefore, *the class struggle is everywhere too*. The whole social universe is subject to the "violent relation" between capital and labor. This section seeks to demonstrate this.

Capital's social universe is an expanding one. This expansion takes three main forms (Rikowski 2001c). First, spatially (globalization) as capital fills all known sociophysical space (and this is not just confined to this planet). This is its *extension*. Second, capital expands as the differentiated form of the commodity, through the invention of new types of commodity. It expands through variegated and differentiated examples of itself. This is its *differentiation*. Third, capital expands through *intensification*; it deepens and develops within its own domain.

An appropriate example of capital's rapid expansion is what is happening today in education in England. Contemporary education is being *capitalized* at an increasing speed (Rikowski 2001b). The WTO education agenda is to speed up the capitalization of education through its commercialization, privatization, liberalization, and marketization (Rikowski 2001b). In England, this involves capital's *extension* in particular (into new fields through the Private Finance Initiative, competitive tendering, and so on in the United Kingdom), *differentiation* (especially through the development of new information and technology products designed specifically for educational institutions, something universities themselves are engaged in), and *intensification*. Empirical and historical research could explore these developments; though it is unlikely research funders would stump up the money for Marxist research that seeks to contribute toward changing the world and not just researching it.

On this analysis, Marx (1844) was correct to speak of the "becoming" of capital. The social universe existing today is a specific form of totality in constant, restless development. Capital, as a social force, progressively permeates all that there is and intensifies its existence wherever it moves. In doing this, it is simultaneously *powered by* and *establishes the class relation*. The tragedy is that our labor, already divided against itself, assists at each and every stage in this process of bringing the class relation to life, extending its domain and intensifying its operation. The upside is that we, *as labor*, also exist not just in capital, but also *against capital*. Capital's drive for social intensification can be blocked, subverted, and delayed (e.g., Seattle late-1999 and the struggle against the WTO, the IMF, and the World Bank post-Seattle). However, the social drive for its expansion reasserts itself, and if capital could speak directly to us it would always say: "I'll be back! Though perhaps in different clothes."

There are no exceptions to capital's expansion. There are no islands of safety, no special cases. This proposition offends the sensibilities of liberal left educational theorists and researchers most when it is taken to the limit and "the human" itself is included. But this final step must be made; in capital's social universe "the human" is capitalized too (Rikowski 2001d). Thus, the concept of "human capital," rather than being the subject of mirth and derision, rejected as a hopeless "bourgeois" concept, actually expresses something real and horrific: the capitalization of the human.

The important point to note is that *the class struggle is also within the "human."* The struggle between the human as capital (and this also implies the incorporation of capital's *contradictions* into the human too) and the human as "not capital" takes place within individuals, intersubjectively and collectively. What is required to get to the bottom of this is a *psychology of capital*, a psychology that explores capital as a form of the human, and the human as a form of capital (Rikowski 2001d). Class within the human can best be viewed as a "clash of force and drives" within the human that engage with other contradictory drives and social forces within personhood as an aspect of the totality. These are expressed in and through our "everyday lives." Thus, empirical study of these expressions of the "class struggle within the human" is possible in principle. We should not be deterred by the fact that it is unlikely that research funders would encourage such subversive research.

Marx discusses two types of laborer. There are those who produce value in the labor process that is incorporated in commodities, on the one hand. On the other hand, there are those who socially produce labor-power (e.g., teachers), maintain labor-power (e.g., health workers), or socially reproduce the labor-powers of the future (e.g., those who labor in the home, the family, and those such as child-minders). The reality of capitalist social existence indicates that laborers take on *both* characteristics. Thus, the great rift *within labor as a form of social existence within capitalist society* is not between two great groups of laborers. The split is founded on the basis of a relation *internal to labor itself*, labor as value-producer and labor as labor-power developer. This relation is internal to all labor, an aspect of the social existence of all laborers. This is a point that is crucial for political clarity.

The next two sections indicate how education fits into the arguments so far advanced. It follows from what has been said that capitalist education and training are implicated in the constitution of class as the relation between labor and capital. This is because capitalist education and training constitute key processes within the social production of labor-power in capitalism today. The following section pinpoints the significance of this.

EDUCATION AND THE TRAGEDY OF LABOR:
SOCIAL CLASS AND EDUCATION

The social production of labor-power was a process that Marx never discussed in great depth. Its social existence was only rudimentary in his time, with state schooling just emerging. Indeed, its lack of social definition in Marx's day led him to conclude that, "Labor, as a social and natural force does not develop within the valorization process as such, but within the actual labor process. It presents itself therefore as a set of attributes that are intrinsic to capital as a thing, as its use value" (1866, p. 1056).

Thus, the labor process itself is a force that develops labor-power. Marx (1863, p. 148; 1865, p. 292) distinguishes between the costs of production of specific labor-powers and their reproduction, but the social production of labor-power in general remains shadowy. As argued elsewhere by Rikowski (1999), there are basically two aspects to the social production of labor-power:

> First, there is the development of labor power potential, the capacity to labor effectively within the labor process. Secondly, there is the development of the willingness of workers to utilize their [abilities], to expend themselves within the labor process as value-creating force. This is manifested in all the studies that pinpoint work attitudes as the most sought after and significant attribute of workers in recruitment studies, and the exhortations of employers that schools must produce "well motivated" young people, with sound attitudes to work and recruits who are "work-ready" and embody "employability" —though these points would need to be driven home through focused empirical and historical studies. (p. 77)

The social production of labor-power refers to a process that is fragmented in capitalist society. Today, it typically includes compulsory education. However, it can include training (on and off the job), various forms of personal development programs, further and higher education, computer-based training, and many other elements. It also develops through labor itself, in the labor process—as Marx notes earlier. This last is labor-power's "automatic" production, though various "learning company" strategies are attempts to formalize it.

In mainstream sociology, education and training are approached as sites of the production of multiple dimensions of social, market, and economic status and identities—including these as they relate to social class. Here, however, the focus is on the social production of the commodity that makes the class relation possible, and hence makes *capitalism* possible: *labor-power.* The transformation of labor-power into labor in the capitalist labor process creates value, capital's social substance. Education and training, in turn, shape and develop labor-power. They are vital supports to, and developers of, the class relation, the violent labor–capital relation that is at the core of capitalist society and development.

However, because education and training socially produce labor-power, and there are real limits to this process, this is a source of labor's strength as well as its tragic predicament. On the latter, the tragedy of labor results from the fact that labor creates its own opposite (capital) that comes to dominate it (Postone 1996). Indeed, it creates something that permeates its own soul in the form of human capital. On the other hand, teachers and trainers are implicated in socially producing the single commodity—labor-power—on which the whole capitalist system rests. This gives them a special sort of *social power*. They work at the chalkface of capital's weakest link: labor-power. Hence, they have the capacity to work with *Red Chalk* (McLaren 2001; Cole et al. 2001): to open up visions of alternatives to capitalism in the classroom, or at least provide vital critiques of its violent class relation and market inequalities. Teachers are in a special position regarding their capacity to disrupt and to call into question the capitalist class relation. Furthermore, teachers can also insert principles of social justice into their pedagogy, principles that are antithetical to the generation of the class divide and also market and social inequalities (as articles in Cole and Hill [1999] indicate). This is essential, for as Peter McLaren (2000) has argued, the task of forging new forms of pedagogy that clash against capital's limited forms of social life involves making "liberation and the abolition of human suffering the goal of the educative enterprise itself" (p. 185). For:

> Regardless of the personal, epistemological, ontological, and moral paths that we choose to take as educators, at some point we have to come face-to-face with the naked reality of capitalist social relations in both local and global contexts. We cannot ignore these relations, and if we are to engage in a revolutionary educational praxis, we need to do more than rail against the suffering and tribulations of the oppressed and instead seek ways of transforming them. (McLaren 2000, p. 190)

Clearly, education is an aspect of the class relation; it is involved in generating the living commodity, labor-power, whose consumption in the labor process is a necessary condition for the social existence of the class relation between labor and capital in contemporary capitalism. This is tragic, but also yields educators a special sort of social power, for education also has "the potential to provide a spark that can ignite the desire for revolutionary democratic social transformation throughout the world" (Allman 2001b, p. 10). In this way, education can be the foundation of a politics of human resistance to the capitalization of humanity and also one of the forces playing a key role in the development of forms of labor *not* tied to the value form.

REVOLUTIONARY PEDAGOGY: EDUCATION AS HUMAN RESISTANCE AND THE DISSOLUTION OF THE CLASS RELATION

Critical pedagogy has had a tumultuous relationship with the dominant education community both in North America (McLaren 1997) and the United Kingdom (Allman 1999, 2001a) for the past twenty-five years. We do not wish to rehearse this vertiginous history here, since we assume that most progressive educators have at least some sense of its presence or lack thereof in the particular precincts where they practice their pedagogy. In the mid-1970s to mid-1980s the role of critical pedagogy was much more contestatory with respect to dominant social and economic arrangements. That it was often conflated with liberation theology in Latin America and with anti-imperialist struggle worldwide accounts for its failure to be preconized in the cultural chambers of the ruling elite. The direction of our own research and activism—what Paula Allman (2001a) has termed "revolutionary critical pedagogy"—increases the stakes for critical education studies that, over the years, have become increasingly domesticated and depotentiated. Rejecting the progressive diktat that reform must be incremental and gradual, we take the position that critical pedagogical work must up the ante by taking the critique of political economy seriously and by imagining what life outside the social universe of capital would be like.

Unscrolling the present state of critical pedagogy and examining its depotentiated contents, processes, and formations puts progressive educators on notice in that few contemporary critical educators are either willing or able to ground their pedagogical imperatives in the concept of labor in general, and in Marx's labor theory of value in particular. This is certainly more the case in North American educational settings than it is in the United Kingdom, the latter context having had a much more serious and salutary engagement with the Marxist tradition in the social sciences, and in one of its professional offshoots: adult education.

While it certainly remains the case that too many teachers take refuge in a sanctuary of assertions devoid of reflection, it would be wrong to admonish the educational activism of today as a form of pedagogical potvaliancy. Courageous attempts are being made in the struggle for educational reform on both sides of the Atlantic. In this case, we need to be reminded that the lack of success of the educational left is not so much the result of the conflicted sensibilities of critical educators as it is a testament to the preening success of

Western Cold War efforts in indigenizing the cultural logic of capitalism, the fall of the Eastern Bloc nonprofit police states, and the degradation and disappearance of Marxist meta-narratives in the national-popular agendas of decolonizing countries. It can also be traced to the effects of the labor movement tradition, which keeps labor-left educators struggling inside the labor–capital antagonism by supporting labor over capital, rather than attempting to transcend this divide entirely through efforts to implode the social universe of capital out of which the labor–capital antagonism is constituted.

We believe that the concept of labor is axiomatic in theorizing the school/society relationship and thus for developing radical pedagogical imperatives, strategies, and practices for overcoming the constitutive contradictions that such a coupling generates. The larger goal we have stipulated for radical educationalists involves direct participation with the masses in the discovery and charting of a socialist reconstruction and alternative to capitalism. However, without a critical lexicon and interpretative framework that can unpack the labor–capital relationship in all of its capillary detail, critical pedagogy is doomed to remain trapped in domesticated currents and vulgarized formations. The process whereby labor-power is transformed into human capital and concrete living labor is subsumed by abstract labor is one that eludes the interpretative capacity of rational communicative action and requires a dialectical understanding that only historical materialist critique can fully provide. Historical materialism provides critical pedagogy with a theory of the material basis of social life rooted in historical social relations and assumes paramount importance in uncovering the structure of class conflict as well as unravelling the effects produced by the social division of labor.

In this interregnum, in particular, where the entire social universe of capital is locked up in the commodity form, where capital's internal contradictions have created a global division of labor that appears astonishingly insurmountable, and where the ecological stakes for human survival have shifted in such seismic proportions, creating a vortex in which reactionary terrorism has unleashed its unholy cry, we lament the paucity of critical/pedagogical approaches to interrogating the vagaries of everyday life within capital's social universe.

Our purpose in this section is not to develop a comprehensive perspective on or programmatic architectonic of critical pedagogy, something that has already been accomplished in the works of Allman and others. Our intention is much more modest in scope but is nevertheless crucial if critical pedagogy is ever to release itself from the current grip of its left-liberal masters who wield it not as a tool for liberation but rather as an enfeebled teaching mechanism for resignifying capitalist social relations in a register that has the appearance of liberation but that works to reproduce the rule of capital. Our modest purpose therefore is to uncoil some of the conceptual tensions that exist in linking up the concept of critical pedagogy to that of class struggle. In doing so we must develop at the very least a number of provision points: (1) a sense of what constitutes critical agency and revolutionary praxis, and (2) a nuanced notion of what liberation means at this particular historical juncture.

In developing further the concept of revolutionary critical pedagogy and its specific relationship to class struggle, it is necessary to repeat, with a slightly different emphasis, some of the positions we have discussed earlier on in the chapter and in some preceding chapters. We follow the premise that value is the substance of capital. Value is not a thing. It is the dominant form that capitalism as a determinate social relation takes. Following Dinerstein and Neary (2001), capital can be conceived as "value in motion." Marx linked the production of value to the dual aspect of labor. Workers do not consume what they produce but work in order to consume what others have produced. Labor is thus riveted in both use value and exchange value (see also Allman 1999, 2001a; Rikowski 2000b, 2001a, 2001c). Domination in this view is not so much by other people as by essentially abstract social structures that people constitute in their everyday social intercourse and sociopolitical relations. In the *Grundrisse,* Marx emphasised that "society does not consist of individuals; it expresses the sum of connections and relationships in which individuals find themselves. . . . [Thus,] to be a slave or to be a citizen are social determinations" (cited in San Juan 1996, p. 248). Labor, therefore, has a historically specific function as a social mediating activity.

Labor materializes itself both as commodified forms of human existence (labor-power) and structures that constitute and enforce this process of generalized social mediation (such as money and the state) against the workers who indirectly constituted them. These determinate abstractions (abstract labor) also constitute both human capital and the class struggle against the exploitation of living labor and the "capitalization" of human subjectivity.

This split within capital-labor itself is founded on the issue of whether labor produces value directly or labor-power. Following Dinerstein and Neary (2001), we adopt the premise that abstract labor is underwritten by value in motion, or the expansive logic of capital (referring to the increases in productivity required to maintain capitalist expansion). Abstract labor is a unique form of social totality that serves as the ground for its own social relation. It is socially average labor-power that is the foundation of the abstract labor that forms value (Rikowski 2001d). In the case of abstract labor, labor materializes itself twice—first as labor and the second time as "the apparently quasi-objective and independent structures that constitute and enforce this process of generalized social mediation: money (economics) and the state (politics) against the workers who constituted them" (Neary 2001, p. 7; see also Postone 1996). This value relation—captured in the image of the capitalist juggernaut driving across the globe for the purpose of extracting surplus value (profit)—reflects how the abstract social dimension of labor formally arranges (through the imposition of socially necessary labor-time) the concrete organization of work so that the maximum amount of human energy can be extracted as surplus value. Here, concrete labor (use value) is overwhelmed by abstract labor (value in motion) so that we have an apparently *noncontradictory unity*. That is to say, capital's abstract-social dimension dominates and subsumes the concrete material character of labor and so becomes the organizing principle of society—the social factory where labor serves as the constituent form of its own domination. This is the process of "real subsumption" where humanity's "vital powers" are mightily deformed. This helps to explain how workers become dominated by their own labor. Labor becomes the source of its own domination. The subsumption of concrete labor by abstract labor or value in motion is what Dinerstein and Neary (2001) refer to as Disutopia. Disutopia captures vividly the current time in which students and teacher toil. They write:

> Disutopia is the most significant project of our time. It is not the temporary absence of Utopia but the celebration of the end of social dreams. Social dreams have become a nightmare in which it is impossible to materialize our desires into a collective thought. Disutopia should not be confused with the form in which it appears: indifference. Disutopia entails an active process involving simultaneously the struggle to control diversity and the acclamation of diversity; the repression of the struggles against Disutopia and celebration of individual self-determination. The result of this is social schizophrenia. Insofar as diversity, struggle, and contradiction cannot be eliminated by political or philosophical voluntarism, Disutopia has to be imposed. The advocates of Disutopia spend a huge amount of time in deconstruction, repentance, denial, forgetfulness, anti-critique, coupled with academic justifications and the scientific classification of the horrors of our time. Whilst the reality of capitalism is destroying planet earth, Disutopia pictures Utopia as a romantic, naïve and old-fashioned imaginary that is accused of not dealing with the real world. However, our point is that Disutopia can only be sustained by denying the real content of life, i.e., the foundations of the real world. The result of all this together is mediocrity. (p. 4)

Yet the contradictory logic of this production of real abstraction takes concrete forms—such as teachers fighting against pay cuts, workers fighting for their jobs or antiglobalization struggles unleashed in the streets. These types of struggles disconnect themselves from the struggle they claim to be representing because they are still positing capital against labor. Here, class struggle follows the value form of labor. Following Dinerstein and Neary (2002), we are making an immanent critique derived from the idea of the subsumption of concrete labor by abstract labor and in so doing are making the additional claim that capital is not against labor so much as capital constitutes an impossible human society. Thus, it is not enough to critique capital but we must critique in and against capital. Our pedagogical struggle must be anti–value in motion. In sum, *all pedagogical struggle must be linked to class struggle*, which in turn must be linked to the relation internal to all labor, the split or rift within labor as a form of social existence within capitalist society. *Class struggle as both the source and the effect of critical pedagogy is therefore implicated in the tragic truism that labor creates its own opposite (capital) that comes to dominate it.* As Dinerstein and Neary (in press) make clear, the issue of class struggle needs to be approached from the perspective *of a critique of capital and its value form of labor.*

Rikowski's (1999, 2000a, 2000b) adaptation of Marx's value theory of labor, which reveals how education is implicated in the social production of labor-power in capitalism, becomes crucial here. Rikowski's premise, which is provocative yet compelling (and perhaps deceptively simple), can be summarized as follows: Education is involved in the direct production of the one commodity that generates the entire social universe of capital in all of its dynamic and multiform existence: labor-power. Within the capital's social universe, individuals sell their capacity to labor—their labor-power—for a wage. In fact, the only thing that workers can sell in order to obtain their own necessities is their labor-power; thus, they have only one life-sustaining commodity to sell as long as they are trying to survive within capitalist social relations. Within this process labor provides an important use value for capital. Furthermore, as human will or agency is partially incorporated within labor-power (though never totally, as the human will is also an aspect of ourselves constituted as *labor against capital*), and because it is impossible for capital to exist without labor-power, this strange living commodity is therefore *capital's weakest link.* The unique, living commodity that capital's social universe depends upon for its existence and expansion, labor-power, is subject to an aspect of the human will that is antagonistic to capital's depredations and demands: ourselves *constituted as labor against capital.* This aspect of our social existence as laborers drives us on to maximize the quality of our existence within capitalist life: better wages, better working conditions, fewer working hours, and so on. As labor against capital, workers yield labor-power conditionally, at times grudgingly, and in extreme circumstances (e.g. strikes) not at all. This creates massive insecurities for human representatives of capital. Such insecurity is expressed in management and business studies through attention to the perennial problem of workers' attitudes and studies on the "motivation" problem regarding workers' willingness to expend their precious commodity by transforming their capacity to labor into *actual* labor in the labor process.

As capitalist education is involved in the production of labor-power it can be redesigned within a social justice agenda that will reconfigure labor-power for socialist alternatives to human capital formation. This reconfiguration is simultaneously an aspect of the overall drive for social transformation and the struggle for socialism. It is not just a case of reclaiming labor-power (and also capitalist education and training on which its development partly depends). Rather, in a project of radical social transformation, labor-power (and by implication education and training) must be reconfigured as aspects of this broader and more general social transformation. In this process, labor-power is de-commodified and *rehumanized*, and developed for a new society—with the laborers, the possessors of labor-power, being active participants and democratic shapers of all the new forms of labor-power developed.

Today, labor-power is capitalized and commodified and education plays a tragic role in these processes. According to Rikowski, education "links the chains that bind our souls to capital. It is one of the ropes comprising the ring for combat between labor and capital, a clash that powers contemporary history: 'the class struggle'" (2001c, p. 2). Schools therefore act as vital supports for, and developers of, the class relation, "the violent capital-labor relation that is at the core of capitalist society and development" (2001c, p. 19).

As a consequence of this, we need to devise forms of labor-power expenditure and development *not tied to the value form of labor.* In the meantime, teachers are in a structural position to subvert the smooth flow of labor-power production by inserting principles in opposition to the domination of capital (Rikowski 2001a). Rikowski asserts that while teachers are surely helpful in reproducing the ideological fabric of capitalism, they are also potentially "dangerous to capital and its social domination" (2001a, p. 38). He argues that educators constitute the "guardians of the development of the one commodity that keeps capitalism going [labor-power], whilst also being in a structural position to *subvert the smooth flow of labor-power production by inserting principles antagonistic* to the social domination of capital. Such principles include social justice, equality and solidarity for progressive social change" (2001a, p. 38—original italics).

Let us expand upon the idea of subverting labor-power production for a moment because it forms the basis of our revolutionary critical pedagogy. The concept of liberation that informs our project here stipulates that the logic of emancipation is contained within the apparent noncontradictory unity of the commodity (Neary 2001). Critique cannot be derived from the standpoint of labor (i.e., whether such derivation is ontological, normative, metaphysical, or romantic). This is because the oppressed under capitalism are always circumscribed by a determined totality; they are always already implicated in capitalist social relations as the necessary ground of capitalist exploitation such that they—as workers—exist primarily and permanently as commodified labor. Thus, they have no point of reference with which to articulate a counterpraxis to capital, or a counterprinciple to capitalist society. Labor is the source of its own domination even though conflict and struggle are structurally endemic to the labor–capital relation. Any critical pedagogy that wants to move beyond reformism must recognize that in order to achieve emancipation for the oppressed the social relations out of which labor's antagonistic relation to capital (i.e., the structuring principles of capital's contradictory constitution) must be smashed outward or imploded inward (or both).

Revolutionary critical pedagogy adopts a theory of agency that sees subjectivity not as wholly determined by capital in some mechanically deterministic way; rather, the contradictions among the social forces that are constitutive of subjectivity provide the cracks in capital's armour, forming apertures through which directions and opportunities for contesting capital can be gleaned (as long as critical consciousness is sufficiently present). Contesting capital takes the form of class struggle.

In our formulation of revolutionary critical pedagogy, we are using the term "class struggle" after Rikowski (2001c), as a social relation that exists between labor and capital. It is one of the primary phenomena integral to the existence of capitalist society, "an element of the constitution of a world struggle" (2001c, p. 1) that is constituted everywhere that capital's hydra-headed tentacles are able to effect a slithering grasp on social life. There is no escape from it. Rikowski's perspective that the class relation simply *is* the labor–capital relation that forms the "violent dialectic" that in turn generates all value becomes a bedrock assumption in the revolutionary critical pedagogy we are attempting to advance here. Class struggle is born out of the antagonistic relation between labor and capital. In fact, Rikowski argues that class struggle occurs *intersubjectively* as well as collectively as a clash of contradictory forces and drives within the social totality. Rikowski notes that:

> The class relation runs through our personhood. It is internal to us; we are labor, and we are capital. We are social beings incorporating antithetical social drives and forces. This fact sets off contradictions within our lives, and their solution can only come from the disintegration of ourselves as both capital and labor and our emergence as a new, non-capitalized life-form. (2001c, p. 20)

The struggle among what Marx called our "vital powers," our dispositions, our inner selves and our objective outside, our human capacities and competencies and the social formations within which they are produced, *ensures* the production of a form of human agency that reflects the contradictions within capitalist social life. Yet these contradictions also provide openness regarding social being. They point toward the possibility of collectively resolving contradictions of "everyday life" through revolutionary/transformative praxis (Allman 1999). Critical subjectivity operates out of practical, sensuous engagement within social formations that enable rather than constrain human capacities. Here, critical pedagogy reflects the multiplicity and creativity of human engagement itself: the identification of shared experiences and common interests; the unravelling of the threads that connect social process to individual experience; rendering transparent the concealed obviousness of daily life; the recognition of a shared social positionality; unhinging the door that separates practical engagement from theoretical reflection; the changing of the world by changing one's nature. Critical pedagogy is able to nourish free-conscious activity in the "species-character" of working-class men and women because of what Andy Merrifield (2001) calls the "prodigious power of human dissatisfaction" and the "drive to attain justice and class vengeance" (p. 80).

Andy Merrifield summarizes this power as follows:

> For Marx, problems of our world—real social dilemmas—are approachable and resolvable only in a practical way, "only through the practical energy of man." The "reality of our essential powers" is especially tangible in our "species-activity," in our own "everyday, material industry." The way we toil, the way we struggle every day, shaping our lives, consciously and thoughtfully, makes us special, takes us beyond other animals. We are special because we are equipped with what Marx calls—and italicizes—"vital powers." (Marx emphasizes this point because he knows that for many people, for many working-class people especially, these vital powers are denied, enervated, abused; numbed by deadening routine, by repetitive work without content, by lousy housing, by junk food.) These powers exist in all of us as "dispositions," "capacities," and "drives," irrespective of our social class. They energize us as human beings, define our nature, spur us on somehow. At the same time, the "objects of these drives are objects that exist outside us, exist independent of us, yet are "indispensable to the exercise and confirmation of our essential powers." We've got to have them, and as we try to get them, we become sensuous. (pp. 79–80)

Practicing revolutionary critical pedagogy is not the same as preaching it. Revolutionary critical educators are not an apocalyptic group; they do not belong to a predicant order bent on premonizing the capitalist crisis to come. Revolutionary critical pedagogy is not in the business of presaging as much as it is preparatory; it is in the business of pre-revolutionizing: preparing students to consider life outside the social universe of capital—to "glimpse humanity's possible future beyond the horizon of capitalism" (Allman 2001a, p.219). What would such a world be like? What type of labor would be—should be— carried out? But revolutionary critical pedagogy is not born in the crucible of the imagination as much as it is given birth in its own practice. That is, revolutionary critical education is decidedly more praxeological than prescored. The path is made by walking, as it were. The principles that help to shape and guide the development of our "vital powers" in the struggle for social justice via critical/revolutionary praxis have been discussed at length by Allman (2001a, pp. 177–186). These include: principles of mutual respect, humility, openness, trust, and cooperation; a commitment to learn to "read the world" critically and expending the effort necessary to bring about social transformation; vigilance with regard to one's own process of self-transformation and adherence to the principles and aims of the group; adopting an "ethics of authenticity" as a guiding principle; internalizing social justice as passion; acquiring critical, creative, and hopeful thinking; transforming the self through transforming the social relations of learning and teaching; establishing democracy as a fundamental way of life; developing a critical curiosity; and deepening one's solidarity and commitment to self and social transformation and the project of humanization.

To summarize: The revolutionary critical pedagogy we are envisioning operates from the premise that capital in its current organizational structure provides the context in which working-class struggle develops. Revolutionary critical pedagogy in this sense can be viewed as a form of human resistance to the "classification" of our souls, our lives, our relationships with others and social life in toto. As such, revolutionary pedagogy is a vital weapon in uncovering the ground of our being as social entities necessarily shot though with "class": the labor–capital relation. But class struggle must move well beyond a struggle for redistributing rights, responsibilities, or resources within the established world of capital. Such struggles—while often important in themselves—do little to bring about a dismantling of capital's predacious rule or its privileging hierarchies linked to the international social division of labor. And in some cases, by disguising themselves as socially democratic transformative practices, reformist struggles actually serve to reproduce dominant social relations—putting brass knuckles on the velvet fist of neoliberalism. Nor do such practices sufficiently contest the labor–capital relation that condemns working-class labor as the founding form of its own domination. This is because, as we have argued, concrete labor (use value) is overwhelmed by abstract labor (value in motion) resulting in *a noncontradictory unity*. Facing such a predicament, Rikowski (2001a) notes that: "If labor-power is the weakest link in the domination of capital's rule and at the heart of socialist transformation then the question of *critical pedagogy* is crucial" (p. 21). The soil out of which labor sprouts is the apparent noncontradictory unity of the commodity that embodies the two dimensions of capital: use value and exchange value. However, value contains its own demon-seed because while it undeniably increases the productive power and knowledge of humanity in alienated form, it also points to a nonalienated reappropriation of such knowledge by the oppressed. Consequently, revolutionary critical educators need not affirm the labor of the oppressed but rather scorch the earth that provides nourishment for labor—that is, abolish the social relation based on the two forms of labor—in order that the human capacities and vital forces of our species-being can take root in the soil of nonalienated social formations.

Revolutionary critical pedagogy encourages students and teachers to move beyond the domination of capital's rule embodied in the apparent noncontradictory unity of the commodity form by asking: What is the maximum damage can we do to the rule of capital, to the dominance of capital's value form? Ultimately, the question we have to ask is: Do we, as radical educators, help capital find its way out of crisis, or do we help students find their way out of capital? The success of the former challenge will only buy further time for the Bushites and the Blairites to continue their war on the world's working class; the success of the latter will determine the future of our planet, or whether or not we will have one.

Working-class struggle becomes the seedbed of revolutionary praxis and transformation only when it directs its struggle from *within and against* labor—and not from the standpoint *of* labor—so that it can manifest itself beyond the horizon of capital and instantiate new forms of freely associated labor outside of capital's value-producing social factory (i.e., so that it can bring about new socialist futures of nonalienated labor). We need a pedagogy, therefore, that can help students reconstruct the objective context of class struggle by examining the capitalist mode of production as a totality, a process that includes Marx's labor theory of value. This mandates teaching students to think dialectically, to think in terms of "internal relations," such as creating an internal relation between diversity and unity, and between our individuality and our collectivity (Allman 2001a). Here we must work "toward establishing a counter-capitalist, pro-humanity form of worldwide togetherness, or universality, as an alternative and a challenge to capital's pseudo-universalism" (Allman 2001a, p. 221). Here the radicality of Marx's work is not implicit in the categories through which he writes—the working class, capital, and so on—so much as it is to be found within the process out of which the categories are formed and the method with which he uncovers the development of that process. This critical approach points to the significance of the commodity form in Marx's work, the process of commodity fetishism, and the reinterpretation of Marx's work as a theory of social form (Neary 2001).

Following from Marx's idea of labor's value form, we need to move beyond neo-Weberian notions of social class. As Merrifield (2001) notes, Marx:

> never looked upon class as an occupational category or as a rigid, quantifiable numbers game, assessed by any census. For him, class is always a dynamic process, an intricate battle of roles and relationships, in which individuals become "bearers" of economic categories and interests, interests that are changeable over time and space. For Marx, the role played by the group he christened the "modern working class" was—as it still is—necessarily complex. Sometimes, for instance, the role and interests of its members are ambiguous; sometimes their constitution changes, their "personification" of labor-power has them wear many hats, dress in different clothes, live in pretty suburban houses as well as squalid inner city tenements. As an experiential being, the working class uses its brains, hands, and feet to make something useful or to provide a service for somebody else in exchange for a wage. Other times, the working class's enslavement to capital is "concealed by a variety of individual capitalists to whom it sells itself." None of this, however, annuls the fact that its members must labor in some way to earn a living. (pp. 74–75)

Practicing revolutionary critical pedagogy in a global context of increasing violence, poverty, and horror requires a considerable dose of hope, and even more if the attempt is to develop alternative proposals to the current process of intensification of teachers' work. Paulo Freire reminds us that we cannot generate hope from the past but must set our sights on tomorrow. For it is tomorrow that holds the promise of today's vision and promise of a new world. He writes:

> Without a vision for tomorrow, hope is impossible. The past does not generate hope, except for the time when one is reminded of rebellious, daring moments of flight. The past understood as immobilization of what was, generates longing, even worse, nostalgia, which nullifies tomorrow. Almost always, concrete situations of oppression reduce the oppressed's historical time to an everlasting present of hopelessness and resignation. The oppressed grandchild repeats the suffering of their grandparent. (1998, p. 45)

In our struggle to defeat capital, we must ensure that hope is not left as a metaphysical or mystical abstraction or as an attempt to summon a prelapsarian or pre-exilian world of the unsullied. Hope must be made practical and despair impractical. What is currently lacking among the educational left is what Daniel Bensaid calls "strategic reason" and the "strategic art of the possible." He writes:

> In the art of decision, of the right moment, of the alternatives open to hope, is a strategic art of the possible. Not the dream of an abstract possibility, where everything that isn't impossible will be possible, but the art of a possibility de-

termined by the concrete situation: each situation being singular, the instant of the decision is always relative to this situation, adjusted to the goal to be achieved. (cited in Callinicos 2001, p. 55)

The key to resistance, in our view, is to develop a revolutionary critical pedagogy that will enable the working class to discover how the use value of their labor-power is being exploited by capital but also how working-class initiative and power can force a recomposition of class relations by challenging capital as a social relation in all of its complexity. This will require critical pedagogy not only to plot the oscillations of the labor–capital dialectic, but also to reconstruct the objective context of class struggle to include schools as major sites of resistance and transformation. Teachers, students, and community activists must challenge capital's control of the creation of new species of labor-power through current attempts to commodify and privatize the process of schooling and social life in general (Cleaver 2000; see also Rikowski 2001b).

REFERENCES

Paula Allman is an Honorary Research Fellow in the School of Continuing Education at the University of Nottingham, England. Glenn Rikowski teaches at University College Northampton, UK. This chapter was previously published in John Freeman-Moir and Alan Scott, eds., *Yesterday's Dreams: International and Critical Perspectives on Education and Social Class* (Christchurch, New Zealand: Canterbury University Press, 2003), pp. 149–79. Reprinted with permission.

Ainley, P. 1993. *Class and Skill: Changing Divisions of Knowledge and Labor.* London: Cassell.
Allman, P. 1999. *Revolutionary Social Transformation: Democratic Hopes, Political Possibilities and Critical Education.* Westport, Conn.: Bergin & Garvey.
Allman, P. 2001a. *Critical Education against Global Capitalism: Karl Marx and Revolutionary Critical Education..* Westport, Conn.: Bergin & Garvey.
Allman, P. 2001b. "Education on Fire!" In *Red Chalk: On Schooling, Capitalism and Politics,* edited by M. Cole, D. Hill, P. McLaren, and G. Rikowski, 10–14. Brighton, England: Institute for Education Policy Studies.
Bensaid, D. 2001. *Les Irreductibles*. Paris: Textuel.
Bonefeld, W. 1999. *Capital, Labor and Primitive Accumulation: Notes on Class and Constitution.* Paper presented at "The Labor Debate" Seminar, Centre for Comparative Labor Studies, University of Warwick, Coventry, February 24, and developed further as Bonefeld, W. 2002. "Capital, Labor and Primitive Accumulation: On Class and Constitution." In *The Labor Debate: An Investigation into the Theory and Reality of Capitalist Work,* edited by A. Dinerstein and M. Neary, 65–88. Aldershot: Ashgate.
Callinicos, A. 2001. "Tony Negri in Perspective." *International Socialism*, 92 (June-July), 32–61.

Clarke, S. 1999. *The Labor Debate.* Paper presented at "The Labor Debate" Seminar, Centre for Comparative Labor Studies, University of Warwick, Coventry, February 24, and developed further as Clarke, S. 2002. "Class Struggle and the Working Class: The Problem of Commodity Fetishism." In *The Labor Debate: An Investigation into the Theory and Reality of Capitalist Work,* edited by A. Dinerstein and M. Neary, 41–60. Aldershot: Ashgate.

Cleaver, H. 2000. *Reading Capital Politically.* Leeds & Edinburgh: Anti/Thesis & AK Press.

Cole, M., and Hill, D. 1999. *Promoting Equality in Secondary Schools.* London: Cassell.

Cole, M., Hill, D., McLaren, P., and Rikowski, G. 2001. *Red Chalk: On Schooling, Capitalism and Politics.* Brighton, England: Institute for Education Policy Studies.

Dinerstein, A., and Neary, M. 1998. *Class Struggle and the* Communist Manifesto. Paper presented at the Conference to Celebrate 150 Years of the *Communist Manifesto.* Paris, May 1998, at http://www.espaces-marx.eu.org/Archives/Marx_98/Contrbutions/Autre.../Dinerstein.htm (accessed July 7, 2001).

Dinerstein, A., and Neary, M. 2001. *Marx, Labor and Real Subsumption, or How No Logo becomes No To Capitalist Everything.* Unpublished paper.

Dinerstein, A., and Neary, M. 2002. "Anti-Value-in-Motion: Labor, Real Subsumption and the Struggles against Capitalism." In *The Labor Debate: An Investigation into the Theory and Reality of Capitalist Work,* edited by A. Dinerstein and M. Neary, 226–239. Aldershot: Ashgate.

Freire, P. 1998. *Pedagogy of the Heart.* New York: Continuum.

Hill, D., and Cole, M. 2001. "Social Class." In *Schooling and Equality: Fact, Concept and Policy,* edited by D. Hill and M. Cole, 137–159. London: Kogan Page.

Hill, D., Sanders, M., and Hankin, T. 2002. "Marxism, Social Class and Postmodernism." In *Marxism against Postmodernism in Educational Theory,* edited by D. Hill, P. McLaren, & G. Rikowski, 159–194. Lanham, Md.: Lexington Books.

Holloway, J. 1999. *Class and Classification.* Paper presented at "The Labor Debate" Seminar, Centre for Comparative Labor Studies, University of Warwick, Coventry, February 24, and developed further as Holloway, J. 2002. "Class and Classification: Against, in and beyond Labor." In *The Labor Debate: An Investigation into the Theory and Reality of Capitalist Work,* edited by A. Dinerstein and M. Neary, 27–40. Aldershot: Ashgate.

Marx, K. 1844 [1977]. *Economic and Philosophical Manuscripts of 1844.* Moscow: Progress Publishers.

Marx, K. 1863 [1972]. *Theories of Surplus Value—Part Three.* London: Lawrence & Wishart.

Marx, K. 1865 [1977]. *Capital: A Critique of Political Economy—Volume 3.* London: Lawrence & Wishart.

Marx, K. 1866 [1976]. *Results of the Immediate Process of Production*, Addendum to "Capital," Vol. 1. Harmondsworth: Penguin.

Marx, K. 1867 [1976]. *Capital: A Critique of Political Economy—Volume 1.* Harmondsworth: Penguin.

McLaren, P. 1997. *Life in Schools.* New York: Longman, Inc.

McLaren, P. 2000. *Che Guevara, Paulo Freire, and the Pedagogy of Revolution.* Lanham, Md.: Rowman & Littlefield.

McLaren, P. 2001. "Gang of Five." In *Red Chalk: On Schooling, Capitalism and Politics,* edited by M. Cole, D. Hill, P. McLaren, and G. Rikowski, 3–9. Brighton, England: Institute for Education Policy Studies.

Merrifield, A. 2001. "Metro Marxism, or Old and Young Marx in the City." *Socialism and Democracy*, 15(2, Fall), 63–84.

Neary, M. 2001. "Travels in Moishe Postone's Social Universe: A Contribution to a Critique of Political Cosmology." Unpublished paper, Department of Sociology, University of Warwick, UK.

Neary, M., and Rikowski, G. 2000. *The Speed of Life: The Significance of Karl Marx's Concept of Socially Necessary Labor-Time.* Paper presented at the British Sociological Association Annual Conference 2000, University of York, April 17–20.

Ollman, B. 1976. *Alienation: Marx's Conception of Man in Capitalist Society*, 2nd ed. Cambridge: Cambridge University Press.

Postone, M. 1996. *Time, Labor, and Social Domination: A Reinterpretation of Marx's Critical Theory.* Cambridge: Cambridge University Press.

Rikowski, G. 1999. "Education, Capital and the Transhuman." In *Postmodernism in Educational Theory: Education and the Politics of Human Resistance,* edited by D. Hill, P. McLaren, M. Cole, and G. Rikowski, 50–84. London: Tufnell Press.

Rikowski, G. 2000a. *That Other Great Class of Commodities: Repositioning Marxist Educational Theory.* Paper presented at the British Educational Research Association Conference 2000, Cardiff University, session 10.21, September 9.

Rikowski, G. 2000b. *Messing with the Explosive Commodity: School Improvement, Educational Research and Labor-Power in the Era of Global Capitalism.* Paper prepared for the Symposium on "If We Aren't Pursuing Improvement, What Are We Doing?" British Educational Research Association Conference 2000, Cardiff University, Wales, September 7.

Rikowski, G. 2001a. *The Importance of Being a Radical Educator in Capitalism Today.* Guest lecture in the Sociology of Education, The Gillian Rose Room, Department of Sociology, University of Warwick, Coventry, May 24.

Rikowski, G. 2001b. *The Battle in Seattle: Its Significance for Education.* London: Tufnell Press.

Rikowski, G. 2001c. *After the Manuscript Broke off: Thoughts on Marx, Social Class and Education.* Paper presented at the British Sociological Association Education Study Group, King's College London, June 23.

Rikowski, G. 2002. "Fuel for the Living Fire: Labor-Power!" In *The Labor Debate: An Investigation into the Theory and Reality of Capitalist Work,* edited by A. Dinerstein and M. Neary, 179–202. Aldershot: Ashgate.

Rikowski, R., and Rikowski, G. 2002. "Against What We Are Worth." Guest lecture in Sociology of Education, University of Warwick, Coventry, May 9.

San Juan Jr., E. 1996. *Mediations: From a Filipino Perspective.* Pasig City, Philippines: Anvil.

Tolman, C. 1981. "The Metaphysics of Relations in Klaus Reigel's Dialectics of Human Development." *Human Development*, 24, 33–51.

5

Revolutionary Ecologies: Ecosocialism and Critical Pedagogy

Peter McLaren and Donna Houston

> To make the earth an object of huckstering—the earth which is our one and all, the first condition of our existence—was the last step toward making oneself an object of huckstering.
>
> —Frederick Engels[1]

Clearly, time and capital have made a sweetheart deal and there is little evidence that the relationship will terminate anytime soon. This is especially true in the United States, a country whose debt-financed economy is keeping the global economy afloat, a country that relies on a permanent "war economy" (in which risk can be socialized and profit privatized) to carry out its domestic war on the working class and to crush "rogue states" that refuse to submit their natural resources and markets to structural adjustment programs imposed by the International Monetary Fund (IMF) and other international financial powers that ultimately work on behalf of U.S. corporate rule. The willing participants in this transnational accord involve more than shady business leaders in the thrall of corporate power, or industrialists that Bush *hijo* has put into environmental posts, or politicians unmolested by the nuisance of foresight, but all those who have contributed to the ecosystemic destructiveness that has resulted from the current domination of humanity and nature by capital.

It is difficult to ignore the Bush administration's hijacking of environmental protections and the criminal environmental record of the president's administration, unarguably the worst administration on environmental issues in the history of the United States. Just recently, for instance, the Sierra Club, the Natural Resources Defense Council, and the Center on Race,

Poverty and the Environment under the Freedom of Information Act have sued the Bush administration. These organizations have demanded that the Bush administration divulge information about its closed negotiations with the livestock and poultry industries that would exempt giant factory-farm polluters from violations of the Clean Air Act and the Superfund hazardous waste law and allow them to continue polluting without any threat of prosecution. It is important, too, to acknowledge that the attitude of the Bush administration to environmental issues (beginning with its opposition to the Kyoto Accord and followed by an all-out war on the environment in the interests of capital accumulation) is tied to a larger social logic that we have come to associate with the project of neoliberalism and the championing by big business of the unfettered movement of capital throughout the globe. The inevitability of capital's ingress into the organs of everyday life was predicted by Marx and the solution that he presented—class struggle and socialist revolution—is as relevant today as it was in Marx's time.

As critical educators and activists involved in the development and practice of critical pedagogy—or what we have recently termed "revolutionary critical pedagogy" (after Paula Allman 2001)—we are all too aware that the field of critical pedagogy is bereft of a conscious ecological dimension, a revelation consistently and forcefully made by opponents of critical pedagogy, most famously by anti–critical pedagogy pundit C. A. Bowers (1995, 1997, 2001). Not only opponents of critical pedagogy, but also its most fervent supporters, have long insisted that critical educators in the industrialized West have failed to address environmental issues in their work. Edgar Gonzalez-Gaudiano, former director of Environmental Education in the National Institute of Ecology, Mexico City, and professor at the Autonomous University of Mexico, has presciently remarked:

> It doesn't surprise me to see educational theorists who form the vanguard in industrialized countries sidestepping the environmental problem, omitting it as a central element in their profile of the complex situation which needs to be addressed. Because even though the environmental problem diminishes their quality of life, for the time being it still doesn't threaten their very survival—which is what's already occurring in many other parts of the world. (see Gonzalez-Gaudiano and McLaren 1995, p. 73)

In this chapter, we argue that escalating environmental problems at all geographical scales from local to global have become a pressing reality that critical educators can no longer afford to ignore. Given the complicity between global profiteering, resource colonization, and the wholesale ecological devastation that has become a matter of everyday life for most species on the planet, we argue that radical pedagogy grounded in Freirean and Marxist traditions, with its already well-developed critique of exploitative economic conditions, provides a rich theoretical landscape to address issues of ecological and environmental justice in educational theory and practice. Our intention here is to link revolutionary critical pedagogy with an entire interdisciplinary field of ecosocialist scholarship that has emerged over the past two decades, to become one of the most exciting areas of engagement between ecological philosophy, green politics, radical history, and political economy (see Williams 1980; Smith 1984; Harvey 1996; Benton 1996; O'Connor 1998; Low and Gleeson 1998; Davis 1999; Burkett 1999; Foster 2000, 2002; Castree and Braun 2001). In doing so, we do not set out to significantly reengineer the DNA of revolutionary critical pedagogy as much as adjust its political optic to include what Richard Kahn (2003) calls "a critical dialogue between social and eco-justice." Although Marx clearly loathed ethical discourse and moral entreaties, arguing that capitalism had destroyed morality and that socialism should be grounded in challenging the underlying causes of social misery in the processes of material production rather than fostering socialist ideas on the basis of moral precepts, his refusal to countenance a socialist ethics of justice need not lead us to disqualify Marxism from operating in the realm of ethics. There clearly exists an ethical substratum to Marxism that concerns how human beings—in the process of coming-into-being—ought to live. Although Marx contends, correctly in our view, that capitalist society has perverted the essence of social creativity and prevented the development of human freedom through successive modes of production that have enslaved humanity over the centuries, there is an ethical dimension that is immanent in his social theory (Wilde 1998). In fact, Marx engages in a form of moral realism that reveals the gap between appearance of liberal social justice claims and the reality of class despotism (Wilde 1998). His approach here is decidedly dialectical.

ECOLOGIES OF DISSENT: ENVIRONMENTAL AND ECOLOGICAL JUSTICE IN EDUCATION

The lexicon of environmental crisis and its social and spatial consequences have been one of the most fundamental preoccupations of late-twentieth-century global culture. Increasingly, the politics of the environment, which includes a palimpsest of social and ecological ills, has been translated onto the terrain of justice for humans as well as toward nonhuman nature. The idea of "justice," much like the idea of "nature," has had a long and varied tradition in Western philosophy and carries within its genealogy a great deal of historical and conceptual baggage. Indeed, the shifting of the idea of justice onto the terrain of ecology, environment, and place has not diminished its historical specificity and cultural weight, but rather, has challenged scholars to think critically about how justice is emplaced in particular social and spatial contexts and to examine what consequences it holds for whom and in relation to what (Young 1990; Harvey 1996). Educators such as David Gruenewald (2003) have recently illuminated such questions by arguing for the significance of place-based critical pedagogy as a site of ecological ethics, social justice, and political engagement both inside and outside of the classroom. Of particular concern for Gruenewald and an increasing number of educators concerned with environmental issues has been the ways in which place-based critical pedagogies foreground questions of ecojustice.

Drawing upon the work of Bowers, Gruenewald (2003, p. 6) outlines an ambitious project for ecojustice that embodies the complex histories of what he calls "dissident" ecological traditions, ranging from relations across human and nonhuman borders to environmental racism, issues of sustainability in urban and rural contexts, to the revitalization of indigenous cultures and environmental practices. For Gruenewald, what holds these dissident ecological traditions together and gives them their cultural and historical specificity is their intimate relationship with place-based knowledge grounded in the local and particular but global in its outreach. He writes, "people must be challenged to reflect on their own concrete situationality in a way that explores the complex interrelationships between cultural and ecological environments" (2003, p. 6).

While we fully support Gruenewald's recommendation for critical pedagogy to be attuned to the local nuances of ecology, place, and environment, we would also like to caution against framing the kinds of dissident ecologies he describes under an encompassing category of ecojustice. Drawing on the work of the political ecologists Nicolas Low and Brendan Gleeson (1998, p. 2), we would like to propose a modest template for a "dialectics of justice" as they are produced through collective struggles over and for the environment. This entails, in Low and Gleeson's view, two relational aspects of justice as it has been shaped by the politics of the environment: "the justice of the distribution of environments among peoples, and the justice of the relationship between humans and the rest of the world" (Low and Gleeson 1998, p. 2). While clearly two sides of the same coin, the distinction between environmental justice (unequal distribution of harmful environments between people) and ecological justice (justice toward nature) nevertheless remains important because it highlights the situatedness of environmental conflict in particular events and places without undermining their structural processes and historical production (Low and Gleeson 1998, pp. 20–21). In what follows we attempt to map out what a dialectics of environmental and ecological justice might look like for critical and revolutionary educators by examining how justice toward those exploited under the capitalist class system is increasingly shaped by environmental concerns. In particular, we examine schooling as one site of environmental injustice before embarking on a wider discussion of how justice toward nature more broadly may be linked to the objectives of revolutionary critical pedagogy.

SCHOOLING AS A SITE OF ENVIRONMENTAL
AND ECOLOGICAL INJUSTICE

Environmental justice as both a diverse grassroots movement and field of academic research explicitly makes connections between race, class, environmental degradation, and political economy in order to tacitly link the poisoning of workplaces, communities, and children to the geography of capitalism (Pulido 2000; Faber 1998; Horfrichter 2002). Nowhere is this more evident than on a dusty construction site within view of the steel and glass corporate citadel of Bunker Hill in downtown Los Angeles, the location of the unfinished Belmont Learning Center, widely reported to be the nation's most expensive public school. Situated in the largely immigrant Latino neighborhood of Temple Beaudry (one of the poorest in L.A. County), plans for the school complex included state-of-the-art technology and learning facilities for four thousand students in addition to a mix of residential and commercial amenities designed to bring much-needed investment opportunities for revitalizing the neighborhood's struggling economy.

For many Latino civic leaders and many residents of nearby neighborhoods, the Belmont Learning Center was seen as a desperately needed salve for both the severe overcrowding that has plagued the Los Angeles Unified School District (LAUSD) and as an important step toward cauterizing decades of economic and political bloodletting and malign neglect suffered by the poorest residents of L.A.'s urban core. However, by the summer of 1999, the Belmont Learning Center was no longer being publicly hailed as a local "Taj Mahal" of educational initiative and community redevelopment. Instead, it had become the "Belmonster" that ate a neighborhood (Anderson 2000). Financed in 1997 with nonvoter-approved, tax-exempt bonds known as Certificates of Participation (COPs), it has cost $175 million to date, with Los Angeles School Board approval for an additional $110 million for remediation for environmental hazards. To say that Belmont blazed onto the heady landscape of L.A. city politics in a conflagration of racial, environmental, and economic controversy, after it was discovered that the school stood upon an abandoned oil field and industrial site containing "active methane leaks and soil contaminated with carcinogenic compounds," is something of an understatement (see Pastor Jr., Sadd, and Morello-Frosch 2002). This in itself was bad enough to place Belmont prominently on the map of Southern California's ever-expanding "riskscape," and when it was further revealed that LAUSD officials and developers had prior knowledge of the school's potentially deadly toxicity, it raised many questions about the relationship between schooling and environmental injustice in our inner cities and urban areas (Morello-Frosch and Pastor Jr. 2001).

Although the civic uproar around Belmont sparked fresh concerns about the local geographies of environmental inequity and crisis in schools, it would seem that the spectre and reality of ecological distress and injustice has been haunting educational theory and practice for some time. The toxic risk to children in schools is an important place to begin a discussion about educating for and about environmental and ecological justice because it addresses fundamental questions about the relationship between place, equity, and opportunity for children who already face a lifetime of social and economic barriers. As Morello-Frosch and Pastor Jr. (2001) observe, children are far more vulnerable to the adverse health effects of pollution than adults. The development of severe medical conditions such as asthma related to environmental pollution and toxic exposure can lead to prolonged absences from school, which ultimately place one more obstacle in the path of children already faced with overcrowded classrooms, underfunded schools, and in the case of inner-city Los Angeles, one of the most park-deprived areas in the nation. In examining patterns of cancer and respiratory risk associated with pollution exposure from small manufacturers and traffic near schools in Los Angeles, Morello-Frosch and Pastor Jr. (2001) also found that "the fifth of the schools with the cleanest air were nearly 30 percent Anglo (in a school district that is less than 15 percent white), while the fifth of the schools with the most polluted air were 92 percent minority."

On the whole, the question of environmental inequity in schools and within school districts has not been given substantive attention to by educators.[2] The lesson that can be taken from Belmont and many other schools around the nation where children on a daily basis are exposed to a noxious brew of indoor and outdoor hazards including ambient air pollution, pesticides, and heavy metals, is that it is quite difficult to sever questions of environmental and ecological justice from the more familiar terrain (for critical pedagogues at least) of social and economic justice. This is because no matter how pervasive the increasingly inescapable florescence of environmental risks may seem in our everyday lives, they do not *take place* just anywhere. The example of the Belmont Learning Center is but one point on what is now an alarmingly familiar map of environmental injustice in the United States that links the poorest and least white places with the worst and most deadly pollution (Commission for Racial Justice, United Church of Christ [UCC] 1987). The production of unhealthy places entails far more than the unequal distribution of environmental problems, but a whole range of economic, historical, and geographical processes that have diminished the everyday opportunity and social mobility of poor and minority people and constrained them to "places" that are adjacent to factories, Toxic Release Inventory sites, hazardous waste facilities, mining tailing ponds, and a whole plethora of locally undesirable land uses and work-related environmental hazards (Pulido 2000). It is imperative that critical pedagogies engaged in place-based approaches remain carefully attuned to the sociospatial practices, historical relations, and economic processes that contribute to environmental inequity. The lived reality of environmental injustice is not news to the children and parents of Suva Elementary in Los Angeles, to draw on another example from Morello-Frosch and Pastor Jr. (2001), located next to a chrome-plating plant blamed for a cancer cluster among both students and teachers. In this regard, places are not simply social constructions or containers for human attachment and meaning, they are also *made* through circuits of social, political, and economic power that are more often than not profoundly shaped through the extractive politics of capital.

NATURE POLITICS: CRITICAL PEDAGOGY, ECOSOCIALISM, AND ITS DISCONTENTS

Precisely what a dialectics of ecological and environmental justice illuminates, then, is how the malign interaction between capitalism, imperialism, and ecology has created widespread environmental degradation and has dramatically escalated with the expansion regimes of free markets into new territories of production and accumulation. Moreover, it reveals how such conditions require that the most economically exploited and socially vulnerable people and places on the planet bear the greatest burden of ecocide on their bodies, livelihoods, and communities. This, of course, is by no means constrained to the human world (see Wolch and Emel 1998; Whatmore 2002). The present historical conditions of global capitalism also threaten nonhuman nature. To name but a few examples—the poisoning of ecosystems by industrial and military wastes, the fragmentation and destruction of habitats leading to the extinction of species as a result of the relentless quest for land and resources, and through the super exploitation of animals for the mass production of food, pharmaceuticals, and cosmetics.

The significantly deep ecological impress of capitalism on much of the earth's surface has yielded a dynamic field of green, Marxist philosophy, and activism, which we argue ought to become an important site of dialogue between "green" and "red" critical pedagogies. After all, more than a century and a half ago it was Marx and Engels who ruthlessly critiqued the historical conditions underlying the socially and environmentally unsustainable system of capitalism (Foster 1997). As Marx (1967) famously observed in *Capital, Volume One*, "Capitalist production . . . develops technology, and the combining together of various processes into a social whole, only by sapping the original sources of wealth— the soil and the laborer" (p. 475). Indeed, Marx's work highlights several important ways for how an ecosocialist critical pedagogy may proceed. His account of how nature is transformed and transforms capitalist circuits of production and consumption provides us with the conceptual architecture for an analysis not of separation between humans and nature, but of how what Margaret FitzSimmons (1989) calls "social nature" is produced, represented, and contested through everyday cultural, economic and ecological registers.

Understanding the material and ideological production of nature (and indeed environmental crisis) as a social and historical process highlights how our ideas of what *matters* as nature is never fixed, uniform, or stable. What an ecosocialist project illuminates is precisely how the present state of nature is neither inevitable nor desirable—that ecologically and socially just alternatives exist. The deeply embedded histories of imperialism that have gone hand in hand with the resource colonization of Indigenous lands and the global commons must be recognized. As Sandy Grande (in press) notes, "issues of power and cultural diversity (are) . . . intimately related to biodiversity and sustainment of the Earth as a life source; ecocide [is] intimately related to genocide." While Indigenous struggles over the environment are certainly about preserving cultural integrity and traditional knowledge, they are also fundamentally connected to struggles for territory, sovereignty, and social justice (see Trask 1993; LaDuke 1999; Grande and McLaren 2000).

What we wish to emphasize here is that as Peluso and Watts (2001) observe, "the environment is an arena of contested entitlements, a theater in which conflicts and claims over property, assets, labor, and the politics of recognition play themselves out" (p. 25). It is in this sense that we need to address issues of the cultural *domination* of nature as much as we need to address the conditions of its economic exploitation. This requires a dialectical and historical approach to understanding relations between humans and across the society-nature interface—since such relations operate in both discursive (the ideological production of nature) and material (the economic exploitation of nature) fields. Ecosocialist critical pedagogies in both theory and praxis involve an understanding of how real geographies of uneven capitalist development produce discursive and material "natures" that obscure the historical contexts and origins of environmental crisis and its deadly effects.

"Pollution; famine; ozone depletion; putative declines in biodiversity; human, plant, and animal epidemics; and staggering inequalities in wealth are local, global, and transterritorial" writes Cindy Katz (1995, pp. 278–279). She further notes that "they are endemic not to 'human nature' but to a specific mode of organizing social production and consumption: global capitalism" (1995, pp. 278–279).

This certainly requires paying careful attention to how knowledge about nature is historically contingent and socially produced through discursive and material practices (including noncapitalist ones). The sheer enormity of ecological distress both at home and abroad has left conservatives and liberals alike with little time for so-called environmental doomsayers, ecofreaks, or as George W. Bush once called them, "the green, green lima beans."[3] The domestication of the environmental crisis into our everyday vocabularies is a story many educators choose to ignore, but it is an extraordinarily important one. What is erased are strategies for collective knowledge of social nature that might construct a dialectic of environmental and ecojustice and a relational ethics of "species being" for humans and nonhumans—one that, as Donna Haraway (1992) powerfully appeals—ought not include either reification or possession.

TOWARD A GREEN REVOLUTIONARY CRITICAL PEDAGOGY

Anticapitalist initiatives undertaken by critical educators cannot ignore the relationship between capital and the abuse of environmental and human rights, including the right to a healthy school environment, equitable access to greenspace and ecologically sustainable communities, or the plight of those activists who expose this connection and organize for change. It becomes imperative that, in the words of Gruenewald (2003), "ecological educators and critical pedagogues must build an educational framework that interrogates the intersection between urbanization, racism, classism, sexism, environmentalism, global economics, and other political themes" (p. 6). From our perspective, however, the central theme around which all of these concerns pivot is that of class exploitation.

Contrary to what many have claimed, Marxist theory does not relegate categories of "difference" to the dumpster of bourgeois mystification; rather, it has sought to reanimate these categories by interrogating how they are refracted through material relations of power and privilege and linked to relations of production. Moreover, it has emphasized and insisted that the wider political and economic system in which they are embedded needs to be thoroughly interrogated in all its complexity. Although perhaps undertheorized in an educational setting, green Marxist perspectives explicitly make the connection between the alienation of workers *and* nature under an exploitative class system. Such a perspective does not seek to externalize or objectify nature as being "out there," but rather views humans as dialectically and spiritually linked to natural processes in a mutually transformative capacity.

Unlike contemporary narratives which tend to focus on one or another form of oppression, the irrefragable power of historical materialism resides in its ability to reveal (a) how forms of oppression based on categories of difference do not possess relative autonomy from class relations but rather constitute the ways in which oppression is lived/experienced within a class-based system and (b) how all forms of social oppression function within an overarching capitalist system (see Scatamburlo-D'Annibale and McLaren 2003). To this we would also add a dialectics of justice, which takes into account ethical relations with the nonhuman world as well as the conditions of its superexploitation. This framework must be further distinguished from those who invoke the terms "classism" and/or "class elitism" to (ostensibly) foreground the idea that "class matters" (cf. hooks 2000) since we agree with Gimenez (2001) that "class is not simply another ideology legitimating oppression" (p. 24). Rather, class denotes relations of exploitation between people mediated by their particular relationship to the means of production (Gimenez 2001). To marginalize such a conceptualization of class is to conflate an individual's objective location in the intersection of structures of inequality with individual's subjective understandings of who they really are based on their "experiences." Our stress on the strategic centrality of class here can be further explained by contrasting our development of an ecosocialist revolutionary critical pedagogy with that of environmentalism. Kovel (2002) elaborates on this distinction by drawing attention to the differences between environmentalism and what he calls "a prefigurative ecosocialism":

> Where environmentalism seeks first of all to protect *external nature from assault*, a prefigurative ecosocialism *combines this goal with anti-capitalist activity*— which implies, as we have seen, anti-imperialist and anti-racist activity, and all that devolves from these. In the great wealth of interstitial openings the general rule is that whatever has promise of breaking down the commodity form is to be explored and developed. This can extend from organizing labor (re-configuring the use-value of labor-power), to building cooperatives (ditto, by a relatively free association of labor), to creating alternative local currencies (undercutting the value-basis of money), to making radical media (undoing the fetishism of commodities). In every instance, the challenge is to build small beach-heads— liberated zones that can become the focal points of resistance and combine into larger ensembles. (pp. 251–252)

How can teachers recognize the important role they play in the battle between capital and nature? How can they develop an ecosocialist pedagogy?

Part of the answer to these questions will depend upon the ability of teachers to cultivate the potential of schools as sites for capacity building and democratization and for fostering a spirit of popular activism and socialist militancy. Critical pedagogy in this instance must be broadened to include working outside the precincts of the classroom and alongside new social movements (such as the Pachakutik Indigenous Movement in Ecuador, the *piquetero* movement in Argentina, the Bolivarian movement in Venezuela, the Landless Workers' Movement in Brazil, and the Zapatistas in Mexico) that have regional, national, and global reach. Critical pedagogy needs to flee from the seminar room and to make its eyrie in the hearts of all those who struggle for freedom and against the practices of capitalist exploitation. Approaching social transformation through the optic of ecosocialist pedagogy deepens this pedagogical project since it challenges teachers to recognize their embeddedness in globalized social relations of exploitation and how these relations are linked to an embodied social and political geography of environmental inequity and crises.

Within such an approach, an ecosocialist focus on the dialectics of justice can help us replenish the soil of universal human endeavor by bringing to the attention of students the intractable connection between capitalism and ecological devastation. Capitalism's requirement for its own self-expansion and growth is destructive to environmental balance. While environmental relationships are usually discussed in terms of the way that they intersect with class and race relations—that is, the disproportionate number of toxic waste dumps in poor and minority neighborhoods or the poisoning of workers in the workplace—it is important to stress the fact that both the working class and the privileged elite—not to mention their future generations—are at risk from acid rain, from global warming, and from a host of other spectres of ecosystemic breakdown.

What we support is a pedagogy that is premised upon what John McMurtry (2002) calls a "life economy." According to McMurtry (2002), "a functioning life economy consciously selects for life goods, rather than against them. At the most basic, it selects for life capital—means of life that produce more means of life . . . all life is a process and this process always follows the pattern of the life sequence of value" (p. 139). Life capital is wealth that produces more wealth, with wealth in this instance referring to "*life capabilities and their enjoyments* in the individual, the bio-regional, or the planetary form" (2002, p. 139). Life capital is the "*life-ground in its economic form*" (p. 142) and in capitalist society it is subjugated to money-sequence capital.

An ecosocialist pedagogy begins by connecting the globalization of capital to the existence of a world ecology and in doing so recognizes that the economic sphere and the biosphere operate according to different logics. An ecosocialist pedagogy is related to the concept of social justice insofar as it recognizes that without a critique of political economy, the political concept of social justice that drives many approaches to environmental education (including environmental education that adopts the mantle of critical pedagogy) is enfeebled beyond redemption.

Many of the progressive critiques of education that fall under the banner of social justice, including those addressing issues of environmental justice, reprise the debates over educational reform in a lamentably predictable fashion: The problem is ultimately a lack of diversity, a lack of material resources, a disproportionate degree of inequality suffered by people of color or those living in working-class communities, or a failure to equalize material resources. Within such a logic, the most one can do is maximize minimal well-being for the poor and the powerless. Relative improvement in conditions for the subaltern, for society's poor and powerless, for the castaways, for *los olvidados*, is, of course, expected to fluctuate. This is to be expected within a capitalist society preoccupied, for the most part, by the logic of reformism. In this instance, when the production of inequalities begin to affect the weakest, only then do liberal theories of justice consider an injustice to have occurred. There is little hope for a fructuous future on the wings of liberal theories of justice.

Liberal theories of justice attempt to harmonize individual interests in the private sphere. But Daniel Bensaid (2002) points out, correctly in our view, that one cannot allocate the collective productivity of social labor individually; the concept of cooperation and mutual agreement between individuals is a formalist fiction. We cannot reduce social relations of exploitation to intersubjective relations any more than we can locate subjectivity as a reflex of objective class position. In the Rawlsian conception of the social contract, its ideology is circular, as its conclusions are built into its very premises. Bensaid argues that within progressive liberal theories of justice, the concept of inequality is tied to the notion of "mutual advantage," to the idea of creating a fair climate of equality of opportunity that will benefit the least advantaged in society. Yet it is still possible for inequality to be considered legitimate as long as such inequalities make a functional contribution to the expectations of the least advantaged. Bensaid (2002) puts it thus: "This hypothesis pertains to an ideology of growth commonly illustrated as the 'shares of the cake': so long as the cake gets bigger, the smallest share likewise continues to grow, even if the largest grows more quickly and the difference between them increases" (p. 149). However, the political conception of justice doesn't hold in the face of real, existing inequality premised on the reproduction of the social relations of exploitation.

The political theory of justice only makes sense in a world devoid of class conflict, that is, in a world primarily driven by intersubjectivity and communicative rationality as opposed to capitalist relations of production. According to Bensaid (2002), "As long as the variable sum of the 'game' increases and allows for a relative improvement in the condition of the worst-off, the theory of justice legitimates exploitation. Injustice begins only when exploitation contributes to increasing inequalities to the detriment of the weakest" (p. 156). Here, class relations and property relations are dissolved in a formal world of interindividual juridical relations. This viewpoint accepts a priori the despotism of the market; the whole question of production is displaced, in fact, is evaded. Let us quote Bensaid again, who writes: "Capitalist exploitation is unjust from the standpoint of the class that suffers it. There is thus no theory of justice in itself, only a justice relative to the mode of production that it proposes to improve and temper, sharing the old and false commonsensical view that it is pointless to redistribute the wealth of the rich, as opposed to helping them perform their wealth-creating role better, with a view to increasing the size of the common cake!" (p. 156). As long as distribution remains the one-sided focus— as is the case with many apologists for the capitalist class—you create a cover, an alibi in fact, for the social relations of production, for the exploitation of workers by capitalists, and for the devastation of the environment. Bensaid concludes: "Theories of justice and the critique of political economy are irreconcilable" (p. 158). The same can be said with respect to a critique of political ecology.

According to Bensaid (2002), "The critique of political ecology can reinforce that of political economy" (p. 355). Both of them can form a productive relationship because both of them start from different temporalities. Take the case of capital, a social relation that "cannot change scale and dimension without convulsions, because it is incapable of yielding the new social measures that make it possible to harmonize human beings' relations with one another and with nature." The focus here should be a critique of political ecology that demands, in Bensaid's terms, "more free responsibility and responsible freedom for humankind as 'human natural beings'" (p. 352). Here Marx develops an approach that brings together natural science and human science, "involving a mutual envelopment in which natural science 'subsumes' the human science that 'subsumes' it" (Bensaid 2002, p. 353). In fact, this approach stipulates an immanent moral economy rather than a transcendent conception of justice that "cannot be measured in exclusively monetary or energy terms" (Bensaid 2002, p. 354). It renounces both an integral socialization of nature as well as an integral naturalization of humankind, but holds both these illusions in a dynamic tension in a way that mandates democratic choice. The antimony between economics and ecology is bound to the question of "whether a *moral and ultimately political economy* can harmonize the rhythms of renewal of natural resources, official levies, and environmental self purification, while awaiting the discovery of novel renewable forms of energy, or the means of recycling the great mass of energy that is dissipated unproductively" (Bensaid 2002, p. 355).

Working within the tension pitched by such a challenge, we are able to avoid the dangers of a radical naturalism that rejects humanist values (such as a rejection of contraception and abortion in the name of nature as opposed to artifice) and distinguish between ecodevelopment (a conscious and collective mastery of science, technology, and decisions about production and consumption) and ecocracy (a reformist technocratic environmentalism). Ecodevelopment is grounded in a concept of socialist democracy that does not reduce ecology to the role of a simple crutch for a failed progress whereas ecocracy strips citizens of their responsibility in decision-making on the pretext of expertise (Bensaid 2002).

For Marx, equal right in a socialist society would be a distinct advance on bourgeois society and would point to a distributive principle of the higher phase of communist society: from each according to abilities and to each according to needs. We don't work toward this goal by utilizing universal or transhistorical principles of justice whose formulations are necessarily suprahistorical. Rather, we follow Marx in calling for the examination of the specific historical development of moral ideas (as he did in *The German Ideology*). Marx's position is meta-ethical in that it does not deliver a moral code or decision procedure for ethical judgment but rather reintegrates ethics into the constitution of the dynamics of communal life (Wilde 1998).

The issue of Belmont offers a good instance for raising ecosocialist issues among students and community members. Straddling an earthquake fault and sitting atop a former oil-well field seeping toxic and explosive gases, the Belmont Learning Center will require costly environmental remediation. Who will suffer the greatest burden of such costs? What economic price can be put on the toxic polluting of the commons? Students need to recognize that ecology does not escape politics. Further, they need to ask what it means to have membership in nature, including human nature, and whether this is possible within the present value form of capital that commodifies both nature and humanity rather than enriching them both. This raises more urgent questions: How are the natural and the human united in their specific histories as students of color living in urban downtown Los Angeles? How have students been assimilated—as a class, as an ethnic and as a gendered group—into the instrumental evolution of an urban environment subject to the globalization of capital? How have their subjectivities been commodified, and capitalized? In the case of the prospective students of Belmont, a large number of whom are Chicano/Chicana, teachers could invite them to trace their family histories from Mexico to the United States in the context of the larger crisis of global capitalism and link those histories to the effects that neoliberal globalization (and more specifically, the North American Free Trade Agreement) have had on the Mexican economy.

Escaping the pollution that the United States has "exported" to Mexico, their families now find themselves in a similar position "downtown" relative to the Anglo population living on the west side of Los Angeles. Prospective students, along with their parents, could be invited to evaluate the recent plan advanced by school board member Jose Huizar, City Councilman Ed Reyes, and the Santa Monica Mountains Conservancy that would feature a park with a fishing pond, play area, and nature-education stations on fourteen acres of the site bounded by Toluca, Colton, and West First streets. And they could be invited to respond to the claim that the risk at Belmont does not so much concern the production of carcinogens or a pollution standard, but a possible future explosion from leaking methane gas. They need to ask: Who makes the decision on such a risk? Do students and parents choose to bear the risk? Or is such a risk delegated to them by politicians? What recourse do we have to challenge or eliminate such a risk? How can we fight for a stronger role in the decision-making process? After all, students would face the risk of exploding methane gas over a three-year period, while teachers would face the risk over as long as a thirty-year period. According to some reports, Beverly Hills High School has similar problems. If this turns out to be the case, then how did the Beverly Hills community deal with the issue of methane gas? What was the history of that struggle and how did it compare to the current debate over the Belmont Learning Center?

Students might also want to explore the history of America's best-known toxic site—Love Canal—but also lesser known sites in black communities such as the Altgeld Gardens housing project in Chicago, which was constructed over a toxic waste dump and surrounded by polluting factories, and Longview Heights in Memphis, where a chemical plant was placed adjacent to a residential neighborhood (Alan 2003). And students could be invited to study the history of nationally supported protests against environmental racism, which first took place in rural Warren County, North Carolina, in 1982, where five hundred protestors were jailed for blocking trucks taking toxic PCB-laden soil to a landfill (Alan 2003).

Students might also want to investigate how environmental activism is being reconfigured post–9/11. Students could be invited to study the case of Jeffrey Luers, a political prisoner serving a twenty-two-year prison sentence for actions that did not physically threaten or harm anyone. A popular community activist in Eugene, Oregon, Luers was active in forest defense and anti-police brutality activism. He was arrested in June 2000, after leaving the scene of a fire at a Romania car dealership in Eugene, Oregon. He was initially charged with three counts of first degree arson for setting fire to three Sports Utility Vehicles (SUVs) at the car dealership (he admits this but took precautions to make sure nobody was injured) and later received additional charges of attempted arson and conspiracy to commit arson at Tyree Oil Company (he denies this charge). Luers has been labeled by the FBI and corporate press as an "ecoterrorist." This label has been used by the Oregon Department of Corrections to justify placing Mr. Luers at Security Threat Group status—a designation typically reserved for white supremacists and gang members. Students might question why Luers received a sentence greater than those for the crimes of rape, manslaughter, and attempted murder.

In working within a larger Marxist-driven ecosocialism, we are not claiming that Marx's anticipatory and prefigurative work on ecological theory (such as his equilibrium-based work on metabolic rift) has not been outpaced by nonlinear advances in deep ecological or liberal environmental approaches that are based upon conditions of disequilibria (see De Kadt and Engel-Di Mauro 2001). Rather, our purpose is to situate critical pedagogy within a larger ecological Marxism and political ecology that takes as its primary focus a critique of the accumulation and concentration of dead labor through the exploitation of living labor. We also believe that a critique of political ecology is fundamental since historical materialism alone cannot reconcile the incommensurablility of heterogeneous temporalities such as the cycle of capital and natural cycles, as well as temporal relations between generations (Bensaid 2002). This requires a dialectical approach to social justice that encompasses both a critique of political economy and a critique of political ecology. The central goal of an ecosocialist pedagogy is to work toward a society of associated producers who collectively control production instead of being controlled by it, brought about when the working class transforms itself into a class "for itself." The objective is to create a society in which we are free from physical need so that we can engage in work free from coercion and obligation to capital. Only then can we inhabit a society in which our human sociality and creativity can flourish.

CONCLUSION

It is clear that educators of all theoretical traditions can no longer neglect the ways in which educational policy, politics, and critical praxis is increasingly shaped by and through ecological imaginaries. If anything can be taken from the examples like the Belmont Learning Center or the countless school-children exposed to harmful environmental risks across the nation it is that educating for and about environmental and ecological justice must entail far more than teaching kids about recycling or undertaking field trips to the "wilderness." Indeed what ecosocialist critical pedagogies reveal is the extent to which the social imaginaries and material production of places are integrated in capitalist processes, neoliberal economies of scale and geographies of imperialism. In this regard the development of ecosocialist critical pedagogies should be grounded in the collective knowledge of places as sites of environmental struggle, activism, and cooperation in addition to an objective understanding of how places and communities are entangled within the wider totality of flexible and uneven production and capitalist accumulation. This requires a dialectic of justice grounded in a relational ethics of care toward each other and to the nonhuman world that does not erase the analysis and ultimate transformation of the collective historical conditions of injustice produced by capital and its value forms under a rubric of a "new" green paradigm or recently reimagined ecological "past." As the environmental historian William Cronon (1996) asserts, there is such a thing as "getting back to the wrong nature" and critical and revolutionary educators must carefully interrogate the claims that "greening" their respective theoretical traditions register. Having said this, green revolutionary pedagogy ought not diminish its radical and transformative intent, but rather provide a map for how we might resist the current zeitgeist of "Hummer" pedagogy and its adherents who insist on teaching U.S. citizens that civilization is tantamount to free access to capitalist investment and the creation of a habitus most congenial to the ascendant bourgeoisie whose robust faith in the market is only superceded by their faith in the apparent endless capacity of the earth's ecosystems to support U.S. global hegemony and the kill ratio of its military technology.

ACKNOWLEDGMENTS

The authors would like to thank Kathryn Ross Wayne and David Gruenewald for their keen editorial insights and thoughtful suggestions; any shortcomings of this chapter are entirely our own.

Donna Houston is lecturer at the School of Environmental Planning at Griffith University, Nathan Campus, Australia. This chapter was previously published in *Educational Studies* 36, no. 1 (2004), pp. 27–44. Reprinted with permission.

NOTES

1. This quote from Engels is cited in John Bellamy Foster (1997, p. 153).

2. At the time of writing this chapter, there remains a dearth in epidemiological studies on the relationship between the academic performance of schoolchildren and environmental inequity. Although see Morello-Frosch and Pastor Jr. (2001) and Pastor Jr. et al. (2002) for an empirical analysis of the demographic distribution of potentially hazardous facilities and health risks resulting from ambient air pollution among schoolchildren in the L.A. Unified School District.

3. This quote from Bush appeared in a fascinating article about the current administration's environmental policy: Michael Shnayerson, "Sale of the Wild," *Vanity Fair*, September 2003, pp. 328–353.

REFERENCES

Alan, J. 2003. *Dialectics of Black Freedom Struggles: Race, Philosophy, and the Needed American Revolution.* Chicago, Ill.: News and Letters.

Allman, P. 2001. *Critical Education against Global Capitalism: Karl Marx and Revolutionary Critical Education.* Westport, Conn.: Bergin & Garvey.

Anderson, S. 2000. "The School That Wasn't." *The Nation.* June 5, at www.thenation.com/doc.mhtml?i=20000605ands=anderson (accessed on July 25, 2003).

Bensaid, D. 2002. *Marx for Our Times: Adventures and Misadventures of a Critique.* Translated by Gregory Elliot. London: Verso.

Benton, T., ed. 1996. *The Greening of Marxism.* New York: Guilford Press.

Bowers, C. A. 1995. *Educating for an Ecologically Sustainable Culture: Rethinking Moral Education, Creativity, Intelligence and Other Modern Orthodoxies.* Albany: State University of New York Press.

Bowers, C. A. 1997. *The Culture of Denial: Why the Environmental Movement Needs a Strategy for Reforming Universities and Public Schools.* Albany: State University of New York Press.

Bowers, C. A. 2001. *Educating for Eco-justice and Community.* Athens: University of Georgia Press.

Burkett, P. 1999. *Marx and Nature: A Red and Green Perspective.* New York: St. Martins Press.

Castree, N., and Braun, B. 2001. *Social Nature: Theory, Practice, and Politics.* Malden, Mass.: Blackwell.

Commission for Racial Justice, United Church of Christ (UCC). 1987. *Toxic Wastes and Race in the United States: A National Report on the Racial and Socioeconomic Characteristics of Communities with Hazardous Waste Sites.* New York: Public Data Access Inc.

Cronon, W. 1996. "The Trouble with Wilderness; or, Getting Back to the Wrong Nature." In *Uncommon Ground: Rethinking the Human Place in Nature,* edited by William Cronon. New York: WW Norton and Company.

Davis, M. 1999. *Late Victorian Holocausts: El Niño Famines and the Making of the Third World*. London: Verso.

De Kadt, M., and Engel-Di Mauro, S. 2001. "Failed Promise." *Capitalism, Nature, Socialism*, 12, 50–56.

Faber, D., ed. 1998. *The Struggle for Ecological Democracy: Environmental Justice Movements in the United States*. New York: Guilford Press.

FitzSimmons, M. 1989. "The Matter of Nature." *Antipode*, 21, 106–120.

Foster, J. B. 1997. "Marx and the Environment." In *In Defense of History: Marxism and the Postmodern Agenda*, edited by Ellen Meskins Wood and John Bellamy Foster, 150–162. New York: Monthly Review Press.

Foster, J. B. 2000. *Marx's Ecology: Materialism and Nature*. New York: Monthly Review Press.

Foster, J. B. 2002. *Ecology against Capitalism*. New York: Monthly Review Press.

Gimenez, M. 2001. "Marxism and Class, Gender and Race: Rethinking the Trilogy." *Race, Gender and Class*, 8, 23–33.

Gonzalez-Gaudiano, E., and McLaren, P. 1995. "Education and Globalization: An Environmental Perspective—An Interview with Edgar Gonzalez." *International Journal of Educational Reform*, 4, 72–78.

Grande, S. In press. *Red Pedagogy: Critical Educational Theory and Native American Geographies of Identity and Power*. Boulder, Colo.: Rowman & Littlefield.

Grande, S., and McLaren, P. 2000. "Critical Theory and Indian Geographies of Identity, Pedagogy and Power: An Interview with Sandy Marie Anglás Grande." *International Journal of Educational Reform*, 9, 70–73.

Gruenewald, D. A. 2003. "The Best of Both Worlds: A Critical Pedagogy of Place." *Educational Researcher*, 32, 3–12.

Haraway, D. 1992. "The Promises of Monsters: A Regenerative Politics for Inappropriate/d Others." In *Cultural Studies*, edited by Cary Nelson, Paula Treichler, and Lawrence Grossberg, 295–337. NewYork: Routledge.

Harvey, D. 1996. *Justice, Nature and the Geography of Difference*. Malden, Mass.: Blackwell.

Hofrichter, R., ed. 2002. *Toxic Struggles: The Theory and Practice of Environmental Justice*. Salt Lake City: University of Utah Press.

hooks, bell. 2000. *Where We Stand: Class Matters*. New York: Routledge.

Katz, C. 1995. "Under a Falling Sky: Apocalyptic Environmentalism and the Production of Nature." In *Marxism in the Postmodern Age: Confronting the New World Order*, edited by Stephen Cullenberg, Carole Biewener, and Antonio Callari, 276–282. New York: Guilford Press.

Kahn, R. 2003. "Paulo Freire and Eco-Justice: Updating Pedagogy of the Oppressed for the Age of Ecological Calamity," at www.paulofreireinstitute.org/freire online/volume1/1kahn1.html (accessed November 12, 2003).

Kovel, J. 2002. *The Enemy of Nature: The End of Capitalism or The End of the World?* London: Zed Books.

LaDuke, W. 1999. *All Our Relations: Native Struggles for Land and Life*. Cambridge, Mass.: South End Press.

Low, N., and Gleeson, B. 1998. *Justice, Society and Nature: An Exploration of Political Ecology*. London: Routledge.

Marx, K. 1967. *Capital, Volume One*. Edited by Frederick Engels. Translated by Samuel Moore and Aveling. New York: International Publishers.

McMurtry, J. 2002. *Value Wars: The Global Market versus the Life Economy*. London: Pluto Press.

Meszaros, I. 2003. "Militarism and the Coming Wars." *Monthly Review*, 55, 17– 24.

Miranda, J. 1980. *Marx against the Marxists*. Maryknoll, NY: Orbis Books.

Morello-Frosch, R., and Pastor Jr., M. 2001. "Pollution, Communities, and Schools: A Portrait of Environmental Justice on Southern California's 'Riskscape.'" *Different Takes*, 12 (Spring). At hamp.hampshire.edu/~clpp/popdev.html (accessed on July 25, 2003).

O'Connor, J. 1998. *Natural Causes: Essays in Ecological Marxism*. New York: Guilford Press.

Pastor Jr., M., Sadd, J. L., and Morello-Frosch, R. 2002. "Who's Minding the Kids? Pollution, Public Schools, and Environmental Justice in Los Angeles." *Social Science Quarterly*, 83, 263–280.

Peluso, N., and Watts, M. 2001. *Violent Environments*. Ithaca: Cornell University Press.

Pulido, L. 2000. "Rethinking Environmental Racism: White Privilege and Urban Development in Southern California." *Annals of the Association of American Geographers*, 90, 12–40.

Scatamburlo-D'Annibale, V., and McLaren, P. 2003. "The Strategic Centrality of Class in the Politics of 'Race and Difference.'" *Cultural Studies/Critical Methodologies*, 3, 148–175.

Smith, N. 1984. *Uneven Development: Nature, Capital, and the Production of Space*. Oxford: Blackwell.

Trask, H. 1993. *From A Native Daughter: Colonialism and Sovereignty in Hawai'i*. Monroe, Mich.: Common Courage Press.

Whatmore, S. 2002. *Hybrid Geographies: Natures, Cultures, Spaces*. London: Sage Publications.

Wilde, L. 1998. *Ethical Marxism and its Radical Critics*. London: MacMillan Press.

Williams, R. 1980. *Problems in Materialism and Culture*. London: Verso.

Wolch, J., and Emel, J. 1998. *Animal Geographies: Place, Politics, and Identity in the Nature-Culture Borderlands*. London: Verso.

Young, I. M. 1990. *Justice and the Politics of Difference*. Princeton: Princeton University Press.

III

NEOCONS AND NEOLIBERALISM

6

The Legend of the Bush Gang: Imperialism, War, and Propaganda

Peter McLaren and Gregory Martin

> The lie can be maintained only for such time as the State can shield the people from the political, economic and/or military consequences of the lie. It thus becomes vitally important for the State to use all of its powers to repress dissent, for the truth is the mortal enemy of the lie, and thus by extension, the truth is the greatest enemy of the State.
>
> —attributed to Joseph Goebbels

> Gout begins in the little finger of a hand or in the big toes, but once on the way it goes right to the heart.
>
> —Trotsky (1940)

> The profound hypocrisy and inherent barbarism of bourgeois civilization lies unveiled before our eyes, moving from its home, where it assumes respectable form, to the colonies, where it goes naked.
>
> —Karl Marx (1853)

Especially since September 11, 2001, the United States has been behaving more and more like a nation-state pushed to the limits of imperial expansion, where fascism and war have become the preferred methods of choice to stave off economic collapse and to relieve the agonizing tension of its underlying contradictions. Operating under an official philosophy that maintains its military power should remain "beyond challenge" and that asserts the unimpeachable right to act unilaterally by means of "preventative" military strikes when feeling threatened, the United States is busy looking for further proof to justify its punishment of Iraq, while at the same time seeking out every nook and cranny of the globe for surplus-value extraction. Here it likens its path to Empire to a benevolent paternalism as the seeds its sews in the name of capital's inevitability are sprouting into grotesque bloom resembling mustard-colored clouds from its bunker-buster bombs wafting slowly skyward or shimmering bursts of radioactive dust kicked up after a hail storm of depleted uranium shells pulverized some luckless Muslim wedding party celebrating with AK-47s.

The grim reality is that as monopoly interests are imposed on other countries and peoples, underdeveloped client states are being crushed by trade deficits and debt burden, especially through the "tough love" policies of the International Monetary Fund (IMF) and the World Bank. The confounding complexity of capitalist social relations in this so-called bastion of free enterprise democracy cannot be erased by the mere realization of its existence but needs to be branded with the designation it has deservingly earned: imperialist exploitation. Exposed as the Benedict Arnolds of the so-called age of democracy are the spin doctors and purveyors of "free-market" globalization, who claim that monopoly capitalism, under the influence of the much ballyhooed "information revolution," spreads capitalist development, boosts the prosperity of the working class, and blots out features of uneven development amongst national economies (Foster 2001, 2003; Sison 2003). Clearly, behind this high-rise rhetoric, nothing is further from the overflowing sewers of truth, its stench-filled tributaries leading from the outsourced factories of Mexico's *maquiladoras* to the poisonous smokestacks of China's sprawling factories. As Jan Nederveen Pieterse (2003) points out, "the American combo of 'private wealth and public squalor' is gradually being transferred to the global domain" (p. 315). In the 1990s, "Overall human development, measured by the UN as an amalgam of income, life expectancy and literacy, fell in 21 countries during the 90s. By contrast only four countries suffered falling human development in the 80s" (Elliot 2003).

Like the doomed sailors on the unsinkable Titanic, workers in capitalism's flagship economy are fast sinking under the weight of recurrent budget expansion and a historically unprecedented military budget. What is important to recognize here is that despite the frantic, last-ditch efforts of the Bush gang and its criminal accomplices, the same historical laws and processes operate in the home citadels of imperialism as in other nations and regions of the world: the laws of capitalist decline. This is the case despite the cunning efforts of U.S. corporations and banks to exercise international leverage (i.e., via the World Trade Organization [WTO]) and regional arrangements so as to consolidate their world leadership, and institutionalize their advantage, in order to maintain U.S. hegemony (Pieterse 2003). This happens regardless of whether we are living in the stakeholder capitalism of an earlier Keynesian era or today's Anglo-American shareholder capitalism. Today, this endemic feature of imperialism finds its sharpest expression in the downward spiral of the falling rate of profit, which is the germ of other crisis tendencies (e.g., the overproduction of capital and the spectacular financial collapses we have witnessed in home markets, for instance Enron, WorldCom). Scandal-ridden corporations fall apart like Humpty Dumpty, only in their case, they are destined to reappear again because the structures that enable them to exploit are the same as those that enable the public to forget. Pieterse (2003) remarks:

> As if in a vast project of self-colonization Americans have surrendered their forums of public engagement. The reactions of the Enron episode, the corporate scandals and loss of trillions of dollars illustrate the power of the status quo. It has led to a weaker stock market and prompted moves to achieve greater corporate accountability. Yet the indications are that these changes will be marginal because influential players from the Business Roundtable to the Democratic Party have no interest in major reform. (p. 317)

In the United States, the sharp drop in the rate of profit has discouraged business spending, with the indebtedness of corporations at an all-time record and defaults on corporate bonds and bank loans running high (Despeignes 2003). At the same time, the slump in U.S. manufacturing has resulted in the biggest drop in jobs since the Great Depression, with unemployment and poverty rates getting worse among African Americans, married couples, and suburbanites, particularly in the heartland of the United States, the Midwest. With people forced to deplete their hard-earned savings just to survive, consumer credit and mortgage debt has soared sky-high, with household debt running at 120 percent of disposable income in early 2001 (Despeignes 2003; Lahart, 2003; Sison 2003). Forget the bluster encapsulated in Bush's slickly packaged "No Child Left Behind," which actually threatens to condemn students to educational poverty by punishing schools that do not measure up (literally) to criteria set by standardized tests. In 2002, 12.1 million children were officially living in poverty, which is a staggering 16.7 percent of all children ("Poverty Rate Rises" 2003). The year 2003 has been a year of record homelessness in New York City, with numbers reaching 38,357, almost double the number five years ago, and reports show that families with children are the fastest growing segment of the homeless (Bovino 2003, p. 25). According to a recent report by the Associated Press (2003), the Agriculture Department has revealed that more and more American families are hungry or unsure whether they can afford to find food, as nearly 3.8 million families were so hungry that someone in the family had to skip meals because the family could not afford to purchase food. Not only this, but the United States is falling into out-of-control budgetary deficits due to corporate tax cuts and big increases in military and homeland-security spending, the burden of which will fall upon the working class (Sison 2003).

Long before the tragic events of September 11, when the United States would begin treating future attacks as if they had already happened, the steady culmination of crisis tendencies at the heart of the profit system was guiding U.S. foreign policy toward "hyperpower" status through the use of military force. As Pieterse (2003) notes: "As a hyperpower it [the United States] acts on a narrow understanding of power as military force" (p. 316). Without the counterweight of the former Soviet Union, the United States, under both the Republicans and the lesser "evil" Democrats, was acting like the world's bullyboy to acquire long-term security for its imperial interests (McLaren and Martin 2003). Led by Vice President Dick Cheney, a cabal of hawks—what Ritt Goldstein (2003) calls "an extra governmental network operation outside normal structures and procedures"—have hijacked the U.S. government and are running "a shadow foreign policy, contravening Washington's official line." Karen Kwiatkowski, a former Air Force lieutenant-colonel and recently retired Middle East specialist in the office of the Undersecretary of Defense for Policy, remarked with grave alarm: "What these people are doing now makes Iran-Contra look like amateur hour . . . it's worse than Iran-Contra, worse than what happened in Vietnam . . . George Bush isn't in control . . . the country's been hijacked" (Goldstein 2003). Kwiatkowski went even further in her condemnation, describing what she saw as "a subversion of constitutional limits on executive power and co-option through deceit of a large segment of the Congress" (Goldstein 2003).

The American strategy, which finds its unabashed expression in a number of U.S. imperial foreign policy "think-tank" memos and articles as well as official U.S. policy statements, advocated the use of global mechanisms such as the WTO, IMF, and the World Bank to achieve "informal control," with the invisible hand of the market backed up by the iron clenched fist of the military, if deemed necessary (Socialist Democracy 2003). Do not forget: The last decade began with Bush padre's Gulf War and ended with Clinton's NATO bombing of Serbia (Beam 2003). In fact, the latest wars of aggression in Afghanistan and Iraq are simply an intensification of the United State's distinctly neoliberal agenda, which is to impose old-school American values of capitalist exploitation through a policy of "peace through strength." The most comprehensive statement of this deranged outlook came in September 2002, when the Bush administration published its *National Security Strategy of the United States of America*, which asserted the right of the United States to use its military might preemptively anywhere in the world, against any perceived enemy that it believes may at some point become a threat to American interests (Socialist Democracy 2003).

Imperial statecraft has become the guiding fist of American foreign policy. In their response to the social distress brought on by 9/11, and their project of

rethinking the ongoing reconstruction of the capitalist world order, ultranationalist geopolitical strategists have become the new heralds of fascism, fus-
ing national security with the re-creation myth of perpetual rebirth through
perpetual war: the purging of decadent anti-American "traitors"—especially
those from Hollywood—and the conquest of the black-turbaned barbarian
hordes. This is presented to the public as a journey toward the transformation
of the Homeland into a new moral order premised on the pillars of Judeo-
Christian faith. With the exception of a few politicians who share an understanding of and commitment to democracy, everyone in Washington is
jumping on board for the giddy ride to fully incapacitate its capitalist rivals and
make the future conform to its current interests. We are not dealing here with
the unfolding of abstract laws but a historically specific process of a developing capitalism and capitalist state (Panitch and Gindin 2003). Here the "dynamism of American capitalism and its worldwide appeal has combined with
the universalistic language of American liberal democratic ideology to under-
pin a capacity for informal empire far beyond that of nineteenth century
Britain's" (Panitch and Gindin 2003). Latin America is particularly hard hit by
the ideology and practices of U.S. imperialism. Saul Landau (2004) writes:
"Democracy in Latin America might also prove nice if the United States would
allow it to occur. . . . Indeed, U.S. concern about democracy shows only when
that ancient Greek form begins to function for the poor. In Chile in the early
1970s and in Venezuela today, the wealthy change 'democracy' only when tax
policies designed to help the poor threaten their fortunes" (pp. 1, 47).

Whether or not Osama bin Laden was responsible for the bombing of the
World Trade Center and the Pentagon, it is clear that the Bush gang seized
upon the sympathy and fear afforded by that day's tragic events to push their
preexisting reactionary agenda: imperialist aggression abroad and fascism at
home, an agenda not even remotely connected to terrorism (McLaren and
Martin 2003). Like Hitler, who used the burning of the German Reichstag
(parliament) to justify his goals in 1933, September 11 gave Bush the pretext
to arrogantly declare: "You are either with us or for the terrorists." With for-
malities out of the way, the Bush gang is waging an unapologetic crusade on
a number of different fronts (e.g., Afghanistan, Columbia, Iraq, the Philippines, Cuba, Venezuela, and the United States), which is supposed to be all
about protecting "our way of life" and defending the "free world" from evil-
doers ("The Dictatorship of Capital" 2002). But beneath this craven attempt
at fear-mongering lurks what Joseph Goebbels, Hitler's propaganda chief, in-
famously termed the art of the "Big Lie." The simple logic of the Big Lie is
that people will generally accept a lie as truth if it is a really big one told often enough by authoritative sources. Whereas Goebbels' lie laid the foundations for the Holocaust, the Bush regime is manipulating the U.S. population

into an epoch of imperialist war that threatens to kill millions of the world's poorest people (McLaren and Martin 2003). We agree with John Bellamy Foster when he writes: "Rather than generating a new 'Pax Americana' the United States may be paving the way to new global holocausts" (2003, p. 14).

It staggers the imagination to look back at all of the lies cooked up by the Bush administration to deceive the American public, which have been repeated, spun, and "sexed-up" by its coalition of big (United Kingdom) and little (Australia) imperialist supporters (Beam 2003). Before the invasion of Iraq, U.S. Secretary of State Colin Powell presented evidence from the CIA and U.S. intelligence community to the United Nations Security Council that Iraq was armed to the teeth with alleged "weapons of mass destruction." The so-called clear proof (satellite photographs, intercepted voice recordings, and crudely forged documents) was calculated to create support for a war, deemed in violation of international law. Yet six months after Bush declared the war officially over, an official report compiled by David Kay, the CIA's chief weapons hunter in Iraq, suggests that weapons of mass destruction have vanished like a mirage in the desert. No matter. The U.S. public has blindly lapped up and ingested the lie.

Australian investigative journalist John Pilger claims to have proof that Colin Powell and Condoleezza Rice in early 2001 publicly expressed confidence that Saddam Hussein had been contained and disarmed by the UN sanctions (Mulvey 2003). Yet after September 11, the Bush administration obviously decided to wage war on Saddam because he was found to be armed by weapons of mass destruction. Pilger claims to have uncovered video footage of Colin Powell in Cairo on February 24, 2001, saying, "He [Saddam Hussein] has not developed any significant capability with respect to weapons of mass destruction. He is unable to project conventional power against his neighbors." Two months later, Condoleezza Rice is reported to have said: "We are able to keep his arms from him. His military forces have not been rebuilt." Clearly, the Bush administration suddenly changed its tune about Iraq's status as a military threat when the attacks of September 11 provided them with an opportunity to invade Iraq.

As Dean Rusk, Vietnam-era secretary of state, conceded, the mass media plays a vital role in determining the outcome of a war (Cohn 2002). Shaping public opinion, of course, is crucial to creating discipline and support for the Bush gang's crazed and totalizing ambitions. Even before the illegal invasion of Iraq began, the mass media's twenty-four-hour-a-day "no spin zone" techniques of ideological manipulation and control played a critical role in getting people to subjectively identify with ideas that were not objectively in their interests (e.g., nationalism, racism, and war) (McLaren and Martin 2003). The cold hard truth is that the embedded corporate media was not "duped" or "outwitted" by the highly choreographed machinations of Bush Junior's political advisor Karl Rove but rather worked in cahoots with the administration to placate and deceive the American people (North 2003). In this respect, what is most alarming is the roar of silence as reporters sit on their hands, even as the bloated facts and shredded corpses accumulate in Iraq. The problem is that real investigative journalism no longer suits the ad-based corporate and ideological interests of media barons' heinous ideologues such as Rupert Murdoch, the owner of the Fox Television Network. Pieterse (2003) writes that, "The strident conservatism in most U.S. media is so habitual that one hardly notices anymore" (p. 316). These days, it is not surprising that few reporters or editors attach much weight to the notion that government lying and skullduggery is something that needs to be exposed, unlike a short generation ago (e.g., Vietnam War and the Watergate Nixon era) when the term "credibility gap" was invented and popularized by the mainstream media (North 2003). As North (2003) remarks, the situation is so bad that even when political lies are eventually brought to light, the immediate reaction is not outright "condemnation, but new and even more insolent justifications in the media."

Media lies, in the form of spin maneuvers and disinformation campaigns, must be understood as part of a domestic psyop (psychological operation) aimed at producing ideological oxygen for Bush's war on Iraq and building support for any future adventures. Psyops, as they are called in the military, have always been an integral part of such campaigns in the psychological battle to sway public opinion and deceive adversaries (Leinwand 2003). Modern psyops include a vast range of actions that frequently cross the line between propaganda and outright deception (Leinwand 2003; Tyson 2002). Take for example the infamous baby-incubator "news" story in 1990, which was trotted out as a justification for passing the Senate resolution for Gulf War I under Bush padre. Afterward, it was discovered that this "legend" (spook or intelligence jargon for bogus story) was a complete lie manufactured by Hill & Knowlton (H & K), a public relations firm with a notorious record for disseminating and promoting media distortion. Early 2002, on February 19, the *New York Times* (Dao and Schmitt 2002) reported that "the Pentagon is developing plans to provide news items, possibly even false ones, to foreign media organizations as part of a new effort to influence public sentiment and policy makers in both friendly and unfriendly countries." In response to the ensuing controversy that erupted, Donald Rumsfeld told a Department of Defense news conference that he was going to close down the newly created Office of Strategic Influence, headed by Air Force Brigadier General Simon "Pete" Worden (Tyson 2002). Of course, that does not mean that the official Pentagon policy of lying has been forgotten; rather, this function has simply been outsourced to firms such as Hill & Knowlton and the Rendon Group, which are in the business of peddling lies and news-ready disinformation for the mass media (Berkowitz 2003; Miller and Rampton 2001). Leo Strauss, the avatar of the "noble lie," would give Bush's gang the highest grades since Strauss advocated that lying to the masses was a preferred strategy if it meant a small elite group of "worthier" minds could use the lies to advance their national agenda.

During the invasion of Iraq, Bush Junior reportedly watched with amusement the Iraqi information minister twisting reality into a political pretzel by claiming that the U.S. military had suffered a defeat at the hands of the Iraqi forces. As Maureen Dowd (2003) described the situation:

> "He's my man," Bush laughingly told TV anchor Tom Brokaw about the entertaining contortions of Mohammed Saeed al-Sahaf aka "Comical Ali" and "Baghdad Bob," who assured reporters, even as U.S. tanks rumbled in, "There are no American infidels in Baghdad. Never!" And, "We are winning this war, and we will win the war. . . . This is for sure."

Dowd now compares the discourse that Bush is using to describe the situation in Iraq to those of the former Iraqi information minister:

> Now Crawford George has morphed into Baghdad Bob. Speaking to reporters last week, Bush made the bizarre argument that the worse things get in Iraq, the better news it is. "The more successful we are on the ground, the more these killers will react," he said. In the Panglossian Potomac, calamities happen for the best. One could almost hear the doubletalk echo of that American officer in Vietnam who said: "It was necessary to destroy the village in order to save it."

It is interesting to see how the tables have turned. As the U.S. struggles to increase its control throughout Iraq, the American public is now growing increasingly skeptical and sour about the war. Officially, the number of troops killed in ambushes and attacks has surpassed the total number of casualties since Bush, sporting a flight suit that highlighted a set of bulging *huevos*, flew to the *USS Abraham Lincoln* to declare the end of major combat on May 1, against the backdrop a huge banner reading "Mission Accomplished." Faced with falling support in the polls, the Bush gang has undertaken a renewed propaganda campaign to gain "information superiority" in the mainstream media, which, it claims has failed to support the war against terrorism by refusing to adequately acknowledge the success stories in Iraq. Coinciding with this, eleven identical letters were published in newspapers in the United States over the signatures of eleven different soldiers, telling about the progress they have made in rebuilding Iraq (King 2003). When contacted by

Gannett News Service, none of the soldiers said that they wrote the letters submitted on their behalf to their hometown papers. Spokespersons for the military also denied any knowledge about the letter-writing campaign (King 2003). Needless to say, soldiers who spoke out against Donald Rumsfeld and the war in Iraq during the invasion were sternly warned that dissent would not be tolerated among the rank-and-file and those who did dare to speak out, especially against our commander in chief, would be officially reprimanded. It seems just slightly ironic that these young soldiers who are told that they are fighting against Hussein's tyrannical dictatorship to create a foothold for democracy in the region are denied the democratic right to express opinions critical of the Bush administration, defender of the world's mightiest and most celebrated democracy. To make matters worse, Bush has not attended memorials or funerals for any of the troops killed during his presidency, unlike his predecessors (Vann 2003). This is not a mere oversight. Dana Milbank (2003) of the *New York Times* reported that on the eve of the Iraq war, the Bush administration, recognizing the negative effect of dead solider "homecomings" in flag-draped caskets on public opinion, issued the following directive to the Pentagon: "There will be no arrival ceremonies for, or media coverage of, deceased military personnel returning to or departing from Ramstein (Germany) airbase or Dover (Del.) base, to include interim stops."

Why is there all this focus on the missing weapons of mass destruction in Iraq? Illegal weapons of mass destruction have indeed been found in Iraq, but they are part of the deadly arsenal of the U.S. military and tragically they will kill American soldiers as well as Iraqis. Depleted uranium (DU)—a radioactive byproduct used to coat tank shells and missiles—can create upon impact radioactive dust that, once ingested, can cause various cancers, paralysis, degenerative diseases, birth deformities, and death. Limbless, eyeless, and tumor-ridden infants are being born in Iraq and Afghanistan as a result of such DU warfare, which many critics charge is a war crime. The U.S. military also allegedly used "Mark-77" napalm—a bomb banned by the United Nations.

If the United States is the greatest world defender of democracy, then why over the last five decades has it funded, advised, and sponsored the overthrow of democratically elected reformist governments that attempted to introduce egalitarian redistributive economic programs in countries such as Guatemala, Guyana, the Dominican Republic, Brazil, Chile, Uruguay, Syria, Indonesia (under Sukarno), Greece, Cyprus, Argentina, Bolivia, Haiti, and the Congo? The U.S. government clearly continues to be intolerant of any rival alternative economic system. According to Michael Parenti (2002), "The intent behind Washington's policy is seen in what the U.S.-sponsored military rulers do when they come to power. They roll back any reforms and open their countries all the wider to foreign corporate investors on terms completely favorable to the investors" (p. 80).

Why, for instance, has the United States participated in wars of attrition that included terrorist attacks on "soft targets" such as schools, farm cooperatives, health clinics, and whole villages in places such as Cuba, Angola, Mozambique, Ethiopia, Portugal, Nicaragua, Cambodia, East Timor, Western Sahara, Egypt, Lebanon, Peru, Iran, Syria, Jamaica, South Yemen, and the Fiji Islands? Why, in the words of Parenti, does the United States have "a record of direct military aggression unmatched by any communist government in history" (p. 81) through invasions and assaults against Vietnam, Laos, the Dominican Republic, North Korea, Cambodia, Lebanon, Grenada, Panama, Libya, Iraq, Somalia, Yugoslavia, and Afghanistan? It doesn't matter whether or not the countries targeted by the United States are or have been populist military governments, Christian Socialist governments, social democracies, anticolonialist reform governments, Marxist-Leninist governments, Islamic revolutionary governments, or conservative militarist regimes: The goal is always the same. Parenti explains:

> The goal of U.S. global policy is the Third Worldization of the entire world including Europe and North America, a world in which capital rules supreme with no labor unions to speak of; no prosperous, literate, well-organized working class with rising expectations; no pension funds or medical plans or environmental, consumer, and occupational protectionism, or any of the other insufferable things that cut into profits. (p. 83)

Echoing the rise of fascism in Germany, the Bush regime and its bourgeois apologists are using ultranationalist propaganda to squelch dissent (McLaren and Martin 2003). Based on generalized fear (e.g., sudden Homeland color-coded terror alerts, stories about duct tape and domestic terrorist "cells") and programmed ignorance (e.g., monopoly control over content in the print and mass electronic media), the imperialist's propaganda machine is working to eliminate dissent by equating it with terrorism. As we have seen, a well-heeled cabal of feral right-wingers, media pundits, religious fundamentalists, and government officials are using McCarthyite methods to engage in a witch hunt and brand people who express opinions critical of U.S. foreign policy as unpatriotic and even as traitors who give "aid and comfort" to the enemy. Media thugs such as Bill O'Reilly, host of Fox's *The O'Reilly Factor*, are fuelling paranoia and hatred for antiwar demonstrators in the battle for "hearts and minds" (Hart 2003; Rendall 2003). Former MSNBC talk show host Michael Savage even called for the restoration of the Sedition Act to silence dissent. Community debate and dissent is being squeezed out with people expected, "on demand," as Alan Ramsey (2003) points out, "to join uncritically in simultaneous shows of mass grief and triumphal nationalism." Sean Penn had to pay around $125,000 to take out a full-page anti-Bush ad in the *New York Times*, and that is what it costs now to see dissent appear in the mainstream press. Let's not play naïve— it is obvious that Bush Junior and his right-wing backers do not love "free speech," for a host of reasons. Forget the sinister plots of conspiracy theorists and just look at the way that the Bush administration dished out vigilante justice to Joseph C. Wilson, former diplomat in Baghdad, after he cast doubt on claims that Iraq had attempted to buy yellowcake-uranium ore to develop nuclear weapons. Not only was he vilified but also his wife Valarie Plame's name was leaked as a CIA operative—all in the name of discouraging others from exercising their right of free speech (Harris 2003c). Witness the abominable character assassination of Richard Clarke, former White House counterterrorism chief, by the Bush gang for his criticism of the Bush administration's preparedness for the September 11 terrorist attacks.

The Bush gang seeks to stamp its foreign and domestic agenda with the imprimatur of biblical certitude. Disagreement with a literal interpretation of the Bible has become a political risk factor for politicians—especially Republican ones—with evangelical Christians casting at least two of every five Republican votes. We need to acknowledge that Bible study is structured into the president's weekly schedule, that Bush is regularly engaged in devotional study of Oswald Chamber's *My Utmost for His Highest*. To better understand Bush Junior, we need to recognize that he fervently believes that God wanted him to be president of the United States (Didion 2003; Harris 2003b). We need to recognize the implications of what it means for Bush Junior to trust in Providence. In his January State of the Union address, Bush urged the people of the United States to place their confidence in "the loving God behind all life, and all of history" and noted that America's "sacrifice" was "for the liberty of strangers." Its sacrifice was "not America's gift to the world" but "God's gift to humanity" (cited in Didion 2003, p. 11). When the smoke and uranium dust eventually clears over the Middle East, it might well turn out that Bush Junior is really Nicolae Carpathia, the Anti-Christ in the end-times Christian fundamentalist *Left Behind* book series. Wouldn't that be a twist for the Moral Majority? Maybe we'll see a repeat of the Bush Junior reported in Christopher Andersen's *George and Laura: Portrait of an American Marriage*, where the boy emperor, yet to be selected our leader by the Supreme Court, launches into an attack on Al Hunt, the Washington bureau chief of *The Wall Street Journal*: "You no good fucking son of a bitch! . . . I will never fucking forget what you wrote!" (cited in Didion 2003, p. 87).

We are living through a very dangerous, corrupt, and oppressive period in which imperialism has assumed its most mature and brutal character (Trotsky 1939). We are in the middle of Bush Junior's Christian crusade to civilize the

Arab world, an economic crisis made worse by the tragic events of 9/11, the huge corporate scandals of 2002, the invasions of Afghanistan and Iraq, and the pernicious right-wing assault on democratic freedoms in the name of homeland security. The most important aspect of this crisis is the surreal concentration of wealth and growth of social inequality, with homelessness, food "insecurity," and poverty skyrocketing (Shaft 2003). The Bush gang's solution is to mix unvarnished "neoliberal rapacity" with military Keynesianism: tax cuts for the rich, especially on dividends and capital gains, generous subsidies for military research and production, and lucrative purchase contracts in the sphere of military production (Sison 2003). But despite occasional epileptic fits including the recent jump in third-quarter GDP figures, monopoly state financing for military production and forces cannot but hope to generate a lot of employment or act as a stimulus for economic growth in a sustained way, not at least without "continual booster shots" (Gross 2003).

Unable to hold society in a state of equilibrium, especially after stealing the 2000 election, the unpopular Bush II administration declared its bankruptcy by resorting to fascist tactics and imperialist war. Its advance attack dogs include Rush Limbaugh, Fox TV News, and pundits within the corporate media apparatus. The parasitical character of imperialist societies, which boast of their higher standard of living (most people on this planet live on less than two dollars a day), is exposed through the plunder of oppressed nations, which is nothing short of essential for propping up this predatory system of exploitation. Yet every imperialist war ultimately comes home to roost, with military aggression abroad always met with political repression at home. As Martin Luther King Jr. said on April 4, 1967, in a speech in New York City, "The bombs in Vietnam explode at home" (cited in Cohn 2003). An important part of this is an acceleration of the Bush administration's offensive against the working class, which has a strong racial character in the United States. Take for example the killing of Alberta Spruill, a quiet church going fifty-seven-year-old black woman living in Harlem, under the pretense of fighting the "war on drugs." Spruill, a proud union member of DC 37 Local 1549, was preparing for work at 6 A.M. when NYC police, acting on a "tip" and using a "no-knock" search warrant, set off a deafening concussion grenade in her apartment. After the cops launched an all-out Gestapo-style commando raid, Spruill breathlessly explained that she had an acute heart condition but was dragged out of her home and handcuffed anyway before being taken to the hospital, where she was pronounced dead upon arrival (The Northstar Network 2003).

Spruill's death was not a "tragic mistake" but reflective of the shock-and-awe terror campaign being waged daily in inner-city neighborhoods throughout the United States, which must be understood as a domestic counterpart of the imperialist's invasion and colonial occupation of Iraq (McLaren and Martin 2003). At the very heart of this is the chilling fact that for the past twenty-five years, including the period in which Reagan was ranting and raving about an "evil" Soviet empire, the United States has been the world's most aggressive jailer, with a greater proportion of its population in prison than any other country, including Communist China—and it is growing, right alongside the prison-industrial complex (Goldberg and Evans 2002; "Prison and Beyond" 2002). A search for a substantive comparison would take us back to the Stalinist era, when the Soviet Union was under attack from the Nazis. To find a comparison with U.S. imprisonment of black people, one has to look to apartheid South Africa before Mandela became president (Goldberg and Evans 2002).

A brief look at recent historical experience in the United States is sufficient to draw the conclusion that the horror of fascism did not die with the madness of the Mussolini regime or Adolf Hitler in his Berlin bunker. As Trotsky (1940) stressed, fascism is a direct product of capitalist crisis, an extreme form of capitalist reaction, adopted as a last grasp to protect the same system of bourgeois rule. Under Bush Junior, fascism is a plebian movement that plays on the hearts and minds of NASCAR dads and is backed by monopoly capital as it eagerly overrides the remnants left of bourgeois democracy in order to reestablish conditions of profitability. Domestically, this means doing away with "old-fashioned" democratic freedoms (e.g., individual civil rights and liberties) that were once regarded as integral to the development of capitalism. With only a word or two of explanation, the government can flagrantly ignore the wishes of a significant minority of people. Indeed, armed with a vastly expanded police state apparatus, the government has proven its willingness to use the external "international crisis" as an excuse to break any domestic opposition, under the pretence of national security (Socialist Democracy 2003). A boulder-sized reminder of who is calling the shots is the repeated use of militaristic tactics at antiwar events such as when riot-equipped police hurled concussion grenades and fired wooden bullets and "sting bags," which send out a spray of BB-sized rubber pellets and a cloud of gas, to terrorize and injure antiwar protestors and longshoremen at the Oakland docks (Mendoza 2003). All of this domestic turmoil is occurring at a time when the United States is promising the Iraqi people that it will build up the infrastructure of Iraq—schools, hospitals, educational institutions—so that it can give the Iraqi people what it has been unable to give its own citizens.

With nary an obstacle in its path, the Bush gang is able to exercise the full power of the state to crush every adversary, including organized labor, just like the Nazis did when they formed the government (McLaren and Martin 2003). Strangely enough, advocates of free trade and competition such as Bush Junior have sought to differentiate U.S. capitalism from single-party "dictatorships" and all sorts of "totalitarian" regimes, with special attention now turned toward Cuba, where U.S. officials have stepped up their attempt to destabilize the Castro government by increasing the funding of "dissidents" on the island as well as ruthless terrorist groups of Cuban expatriates who walk the streets of Miami with impunity, and by practically eliminating the visa program for Cuban emigrants wishing to leave ("The Dictatorship of Capital" 2002). Yet with the building of a gigantic modern Gestapo-like "security state," what is exposed is a "Dictatorship of Capital," with the Bush regime operating by command rather than by openness and full-fledged participation. By extension, the concept of liberty and freedom for all is turned on its head, with the Living Dead mass of ordinary working people "freed" from the burden of secure employment, pensions, affordable housing, health care, and civil rights, while the ruling class rakes in grotesque amounts of money with no limit, regulation, or legal obstruction (McLaren and Martin 2003).

So we should not pretend in the aftermath of September 11 that "everything has changed" when the state is continuing to obstruct the dispensing of justice for its citizens at home, even as it wages multiple and enduring wars of "justice" and "liberation" abroad. If anything, the passage of the USA Patriot Act by Congress together with the recent slew of executive orders, mandates, and Orwellian security measures enacted by Bush, Ashcroft, and Company indicate that we have entered a reactionary period unprecedented since the 1950s, where every thought and activity is subject to preemptive action. Authorized by the draconian Patriot Act, the newly created Department of Homeland Security along with its secret thought police now has the right to wiretap anyone's phone it wants without a court order, to search any home without a warrant, to hold anyone in jail for thirty days or more without filing any charges (with no phone call "privileges"), and to snoop into people's lives by monitoring their finances, purchases, and library or Internet use with sophisticated electronic and computer eavesdropping equipment (McLaren and Martin 2003). The presence of Big Brother even extends to colleges and universities where the FBI has recruited campus police officers to monitor rogue students and faculty (Harris 2003a). It has even been reported in the press (Sniffen 2003) that the Pentagon, through the Defense Advanced Research Projects Agency (DARPA), is now soliciting bids to develop a digital super diary, known as Lifelog, that "records heartbeats, travel, Internet chats, everything a person does."

Every American should be gravely concerned about the erosion of civil rights in the United States, especially those prepared to speak out against this monstrous system (McLaren and Martin 2003). In the beginning, the repressive state apparatus was content to set its racist sights upon immigrants and people of color, especially Muslims, as evidenced by the Department of Homeland Security's plan called Operation Liberty Shield, enacted as bombs rained down on Iraq (Lawyers Committee for Human Rights 2003). Targeting precisely the kind of people who have been victims of regimes that the United States was formerly allied with in the past but has now vociferously singled out for condemnation, Operation Liberty Shield authorized immigration officials to round up and detain virtually all asylum seekers from a group of thirty-three countries including Iraq, Iran, Sudan, and Somalia (Amnesty International 2003). Stoking racism and hate crimes, such repressive measures were generally tolerated by the public (given that they were selectively applied) but are now being quickly integrated and expanded throughout the entire judicial system, sharply undermining the democratic rights of U.S. citizens and noncitizens alike (McLaren and Martin 2003).

Despite the hypnotic effect of prowar jingoism and propaganda, public opposition is escalating against the government's attacks on civil liberties, especially the USA Patriot Act (Ferguson 2003). The Act's curator, Attorney General John Ashcroft, was compelled to undertake a month-long propaganda tour across the country in support of it (Caruso 2003; Teather 2003). Timed to exploit the second anniversary of September 11, this tawdry road show was designed to convince the broad masses of people to submit to proposals that will even further reduce their civil liberties, with Bush requesting a big boost in law enforcement powers ("On Eve of 9/11" 2003). Typical of the administration's calculated style, Ashcroft gave a series of canned speeches, met only with friendly local officials, and granted select press interviews. At the same time, the Department of Justice was forced to admit that audiences at many public meetings were stacked almost entirely with law enforcement personal. Caruso (2003) reports the following strategy used to terrorize the public into supporting the government's actions, "As part of the campaign, all 94 U.S. attorneys around the country are being encouraged to hold town hall-style events to discuss the Patriot Act and its role in preventing terror."

If all this is not dire enough, the United States has grabbed the lion's share of the spoils in Afghanistan and Iraq, intensifying interimperialist rivalries (Sison 2003). Aside from ensuring U.S. hegemony, a strong motivation of the coin-operated Bush administration is to share the booty with contractors and backers that have close ties to the Republican Party. It was reported recently in the press that a study by the Washington-based group the Center for Public Integrity found, "Nearly every one of the 10 largest contracts awarded for Iraq and Afghanistan went to companies employing former high-ranking government officials or individuals with close ties to those agencies or Congress" ("Reconstruction Deals" 2003). With just perhaps a faint scent of oil and sewage, Halliburton, a company formerly run by Mr. Cheney, scooped up one of the biggest contracts, worth $US 2.3 billion, for its Kellogg, Brown and Root unit to rebuild Iraq's oil infrastructure. Other well-connected beneficiaries to share in the looting of Iraq include Bechtel Group Inc. (George Schultz, secretary of state under Ronald Reagan sits on its board of directors), which won a cool $1 billion deal to rebuild Iraq's infrastructure; the already bankrupt MCI Worldcom, which scored a scandalous no-bid contract for cell phone service in Iraq; and the union-busting Stevedoring Services of America, the lead company fighting the International Longshoremen's and Warehousemen's Union on the West Coast docks, which picked up a $4.1 million contract for operating the port of Umm Qsar (Teather 2003). Clearly, all these contracts offer high profits worth billions of dollars. Yet, Nordland and Hirsh (2003) of *Newsweek* report that mismanagement and corruption in the rebuilding of Iraq is rife. In the wake of such allegations, companies such as Halliburton are waging a public relations offensive, which has included asking its employees to either phone or write their local newspaper to stem public criticism and bad press about overspending and overcharging (Goldenberg 2003).

One of the Bush administration's major weapons in the "war on terror" is educating client populations to participate in transforming their nations into free-market democracies. The better they can be educated, the less likely the U.S. military will have to impose its will on them militarily. For instance, consider the State Department's International Military Education and Training Program. It is a program that arms and trains U.S. satellites and dependencies, preparing foreign soldiers to do the bidding of the United States without risking direct U.S. casualties. According to Chalmers Johnson (2003), in utilizing such a strategy, "responsibility is displaced and consequences diffused. This dislocation has roots in a much older phenomenon, in which empires sought to 'outsource' the enforcement of their political will" (p. 54). Johnson describes the development of this program over recent years:

> In 1990 it was offering military instruction to the armies of 96 countries; by 2002 that already impressive number had risen to 133 countries. There are 189 countries in the United Nations, which means that this single program "instructs" militaries in 70 percent of the world's nations. We train approximately 100,000 foreign soldiers each year—most of them officers who then can pass on American methods to their troops. In 2001 the U.S. military taught 15,030 officers and soldiers in Latin America alone. The Pentagon does this either by bringing them to one of the approximately 150 military educational institutions in the United States or by sending military instructors, almost always Army Special Forces, to the countries themselves. The "war on terror" has only accelerated these programs, in many cases replacing the "war on drugs" as a justification,

with no discernible difference in pedagogy. The United States claims that such training promotes American values. (2003, p. 55)

One area in which the U.S. military unquestionably reigns supreme is in its ability to deliver instant profits on its contracts. Business contracts cannot begin to compete with military ones. The reason that military contracts are the most profitable businesses in the country today is that they constitute no-risk, cost-plus deals that guarantee a profit because they operate outside the fluctuations of the marketplace:

> The largest contractors are the Vinnell Corporation of Fairfax, Virginia, which on July 2 received a $48 million contract to train a new Iraqi army; Military Professional Resources, Inc. (best known by its acronym, MPRI), located in Alexandria, Virginia, and owned by L-3 Communications; Kellogg, Brown & Root, the Texas company that, long before its merger with Kellogg, bankrolled Lyndon Johnson's political career and that is today a subsidiary of the Halliburton Corporation; DynCorp of Reston, Virginia, which became notorious during the late 1990s when it was discovered that some of its employees in Bosnia were keeping underage women as sex slaves and then selling them elsewhere in Europe; Science Applications International Corporation of San Diego, whose top five executives made between $825,000 and $1.8 million in salaries in 2001 and held more than $1.5 million worth of stock options each; BDM International of Fairfax, Virginia; Armor Holdings, Inc., of Jacksonville, Florida; Cubic Applications, Inc., of Lacey, Washington; DFI International (originally Defense Forecasts, Inc.) of Washington, D.C.; and International Charter Incorporated of Oregon. (Johnson 2003, p. 56)

Johnson reports that since 1975, Vinnell Corporation has been licensed by the government to train the Saudi National Guard, a 100,000-man force used to protect Saudi Arabia's violently repressive monarchy. Vinnell also constructs, runs, staffs, and writes doctrine for five Saudi military academies, seven Saudi shooting ranges, and a state-operated health care system. It trains and equips four Saudi mechanized brigades and five infantry brigades. Saudi Arabia funnels hundreds of millions of dollars into leading defense corporations to equip these forces. DynCorp provides personal protection for President Hamid Karzai of Afghanistan and will eventually take over the training of the Afghan army. Johnson describes how, since the 1990s, the Pentagon has been contracting out most of its services, as in the case of luxurious camp Bondsteel in the Balkans, built for the U.S. military on a thousand acres of farmland seized from private owners after the bombing campaign in Yugoslavia in 1999. It cost $36.6 million dollars to build and its annual operating expenses are $180 million.

The best business in the global marketplace these days appears to be the business of bombing the infrastructure of a country to the Stone Age and then receiving millions of dollars to rebuild it. When Dick Cheney became head of Halliburton in 1995, its subsidiary, Brown & Root, won government contracts worth $2.3 billion. According to Johnson (2003), "In the late 1990s, Halliburton rebuilt Saddam Hussein's war-damaged fields for some $23.8 million—fields Cheney, as secretary of defense during the first Gulf war, had been instrumental in destroying" (p. 57). Johnson notes, "When war becomes the most profitable course of action, we can certainly expect more of it" (p. 58). Therefore, it should come as no surprise that military contractors are also the biggest war boosters. Of course, this becomes easier to understand when you realize that, for them, the "liberation" of a country is synonymous with a "profit" for the military developers of the occupying power:

> The biggest of all munitions companies, the Lockheed Martin Corporation, played an important behind-the-scenes role in developing support for Bush's war with Iraq. In 2002 its former vice president Bruce Jackson became chairman of a "private" lobbying organization, the Committee for the Liberation of Iraq. Charter members include George Shultz and John McCain. (Johnson 2003, p. 58)

For many Americans who took to the streets to protest the invasion of Iraq, faith in the United Nations afforded a steady undertow to the imperialist advances of the United States. However, if there was ever a doubt that the United Nations serves as a paramount political instrument for the legitimization of U.S. foreign policy or is little more than a trembling quisling in the face of U.S. imperial strategy, that doubt should by now be erased. The United Nations clearly responds in the last instance only to military power, not the force of diplomacy or the interests of the oppressed. As Tariq Ali (2003) writes:

> As for the UN acting as an "honest broker," forget it—especially in Iraq, where it is part of the problem. Leaving aside its previous record (as the administrator of the killer sanctions, and the backer of weekly Anglo-American bombing raids for 12 years), on October 16 the security council disgraced itself again by welcoming "the positive response of the international community . . . to the broadly representative governing council . . . [and] supports the governing council's efforts to mobilize the people of Iraq." Meanwhile a beaming fraudster, Ahmed Chalabi, was given the Iraqi seat at the UN. One can't help recalling how the U.S. and Britain insisted on Pol Pot retaining his seat for over a decade after being toppled by the Vietnamese. The only norm recognized by the security council is brute force, and today there is only one power with the capacity to deploy it. That is why, for many in the southern hemisphere and elsewhere, the UN is the U.S.

In our contemporary urban world, a world that is "rushing backwards to the age of Dickens," that has approximately 921 million slum dwellers "nearly equal to the population of the world when the young Engels first ventured onto the mean streets of Manchester," and where, by 2020, "urban poverty in the world could reach 45 to 50 percent of the total population living in cities" (Davis 2004), how can we move forward? In our crumbling urban universe where the global informal working class "is the fastest growing and most unprecedented social class on earth" and where "only the slum remains as a fully franchised solution to the problems of warehousing the twenty-first century's surplus humanity" (Davis, 2004), how can we defeat the rock-ribbed custodians of capital? Capitalist globalization and its imperialist stepchildren cannot be defeated by cooperative efforts on the part of interimperialist rivals. It requires mass struggle by the working classes worldwide. To defeat capitalist globalization and the accumulation of corporate profits by private owners means developing a philosophy that can help us to organize praxis to this end.

Our position as revolutionary critical educators is to support continent-wide mobilizations against the neoliberal offensive and the Washington consensus whose objective is to turn back all the social rights achieved over the past half century. We advocate a gender-balanced, multiracial opposition to imperialism, to war, to capitalist globalization, to the law-and-order policies that have made a mockery of our democratic freedoms and that institutionalize violence against the most vulnerable groups in our society. We challenge the productivist model of development that puts the future of humanity at risk and we demand democratic control over choices of development and of production. In doing so, we steadfastly refuse to submit to social liberalism, which controls the institutions of the state in the interests of the minority who own all the wealth, and we work toward a socialist alternative to capitalism so that social needs are satisfied. Here we advocate the politics of internationalism, especially in light of the rise in power of social movements and continental social forums. We refer to diverse groups that include the *piqueteros* in Argentina, the *cocaleros* in Bolivia, the landless workers in Brazil, the Pachakutik Indigenous Movement in Ecuador, the Zapatistas in Mexico, and the Bolivarian Circles in Venezuela. The convergences necessary to give a true credibility to the conviction that another world is possible—a world released from the fetters of capital and all forms of social oppression and exploitation, where wealth will be measured in free time and value as freely associated labor and unbounded creativity, where the earth's biodiversity and ecological equilibria are protected—will not just happen on their own, they must be struggled for and guided by all of our efforts. Here we advocate a critical pedagogy as a means for reconnoitering the world of socialist politics and for casting off our vegetated product-oriented society and time-anchored façade of "everything has a price." What kind of challenges we put to capital today will set the terms for how we engage reality tomorrow. This is the challenge of researchers, scholars, and activists working together for global justice and peace.

POSTSCRIPT

Emblazoned across the American psyche like a movie advertisement on a Sunset Strip billboard, the phrase "We got him" will be forever etched on the template of American popular culture, similar to those indelible phrases "Bring it on," "Go for it," or "Make my day." In asserting that we are all safer now that Saddam has been captured, that the coordinated resistance has been made acephalous, that the tyrant finally has been felled, Bush accords reality with the dubious virtue of being its opposite in clever disguise. Bush neither chooses to be detained by honesty nor held captive by integrity. In politics, necessity renders truth nugatory. Bush was fully aware that Saddam was not a major threat to the safety of the United States when he ordered missiles and cluster bombs to rain down on the enemy, marinating flesh, severing limbs, and pulverizing bone. And when the shock troops were not chopping down Iraqis like twigs in a wood chipper, and disease and hunger ravaging the population, the truth of the Iraqi threat was kept from the public through vast networks of deceit and deception that is the common coin of the technobureaucratic elite, the White House, and the corporate media. While Bush knows that the U.S. occupation of Iraq and Afghanistan has most assuredly made the United States more vulnerable to terrorist attacks, he will never share this with the American people.

The spin doctors of the Bush administration think nothing of demoting analysis in favor of the propaganda value of blind assertion, that hypermasculinist assault on reason that claims that the more carnage we create, the closer we are to winning democracy and freedom for the Middle East. Will it come out during Saddam's "trial" that American corporations were happy to do business with him in the 1980s; that they sold him anthrax bacillus, botulinum toxin, and other toxic bacteria; that U.S. military intelligence helped him fight his enemies; or that the U.S. government remained friendly, even when he gassed his opponents, the Iranians and the Kurds (after the United States helped locate their positions for him via satellite images)? Will it come out that Donald Rumsfeld was happy to shake the mass murderer's hand in 1983? No doubt it will. But not in the mainstream U.S. media, which is owned and controlled by corporate interests. Will the United States make a quick exit from Iraq, now that the tyrant has been deposed? Very unlikely. It is too risky for the Bush gang to permit a genuine election to take place because a freely elected government might object to current U.S. efforts to sell off the country to foreign corporations, or to the continuing efforts to smash what is left of the Iraqi trade unions.

Even though the chairman of the independent commission who investigated the September 11 attacks—former New Jersey Governor Thomas Kean—stated that the attacks of September 11 could have and should have been stopped (he stopped short of putting the blame for such failure squarely on the shoulders of the Bush administration), it is unlikely that the Bush administration will open up its classified documents to show the public what it knew about the terrorist threat to the United States in the months preceding September 11, 2001. Clearly they know more than they have admitted. If Bush Junior loses his aura of the invincible war president, he will plummet from his marble balcony like a wounded eagle headlong into the thronging crowds he has so far been successful in captivating by the diplomacy of deception and lying.

REFERENCES

Gregory Martin is lecturer at the School of Education and Professional Studies, at Griffith University, Gold Coast Campus, Australia. This chapter was previously published in *Cultural Studies – Critical Methodologies* 4, no. 3 (2004), pp. 281–302. © 2004 by Sage Publications. Reprinted by permission of Sage Publications.

Ali, T. 2003. "Resistance Is the First Step Towards Iraqi Independence." *The Guardian* November 3, at www.guardian.co.uk/comment/story/0,3604,1076480,00.html (accessed October 12, 2004).

Amnesty International. 2003. News Release. At www.amnestyusa.org/news/ 2003/usa03182003_2.html (accessed March 18, 2003).

Associated Press. 2003, November 2. "More U.S. Families Hungry or Too Poor to Eat, Study Says." *NYTimes.com*. November 2, at www.nytimes.com/2003/11/02/ national/02HUNG.html (accessed November 3, 2003).

Beam, N. 20030. "The Political Economy of American Militarism." *World Socialist Web Site*. July 10, at wsws.org/articles/2003/jul2003/nb-j10_prn.shtml (accessed July 11, 2003).

Berkowitz, B. 2003. "Marketing the Invasion of Iraq New Book Documents Bush Administration's Use of PR Firms to Sell War to the American People." *Dissident Voice*. August 28, at www.dissidentvoice.org/Articles8/Berkowitz_Stauber-Rampton-Review.htm (accessed October 12, 2004).

Bovino, A. 2003. "Offering a Hand, and Hope, in a Year of Record Homelessness in New York." *The New York Times*, November 2, 25.

Caruso, D. 2003. "Ashcroft Begins Patriot Act Tour." *The Guardian*. August 20 at www .guardian.co.uk/uslatest/story/0,1282,-3050744,00.html (accessed August 21, 2003).

Cohn, C. 2002. "The Assault on Civil Liberties." *International Socialist Review*. March–April at www.isreview.org/issues/22/civil_liberties.shtml (accessed October 12, 2004).

Dao, J., and Schmitt, E. 2002,. "Pentagon Readies Efforts to Sway Sentiment Abroad." *New York Times.* February 19 at www.nytimes.com/2002/02/19/international/ 19PENT.html (accessed February 19, 2002).

Davis, M. 2004. "Planet of Slums." *New Left Review* 26. March–April, at www.usatoday .comnews/politicselections/nation/2003-09-28-economy-ideas_x.htm (accessed September 28, 2003).

Despeignes, P. 2003. "Few Options Left to Goose the Economy." *USA Today.* September 29, at www.usatoday.com (accessed October 12, 2004).

"The Dictatorship of Capital." 2002. *The Red Critique*, at www.geocities.com/ redtheory/redcritique/SeptOct02/thedictatorshipofcapital.htm.

Didion, J. 2003. "Mr. Bush & the Divine." *The New York Review of Books.* November 6, at www.nybooks.com/articles/16749 (accessed November 6, 2003).

Dowd, M. 2003. "Bush's War a Far Cry from the Real Thing." *Sydney Morning Herald.* November 3, at www.smh.com.au/articles/2003/11/02/1067708070552.html (accessed November 3, 2003).

Elliot, L. 2003. "The Lost Decade." *The Guardian.* July 9, at www.guardian.co.uk/ international /story/0,3604,994440,00,html (accessed October 12, 2004).

Ferguson, S. 2003. "New Yorkers Protest the Attorney General's Tour to Promote the Patriot Act: Bashcroft!" *The Village Voice.* September 10, at www.villagevoice.com/ print/issues/0338/ferguson.php (accessed October 12, 2004).

Foster, J. B. 2001. "Imperialism and 'Empire.'" *Monthly Review*, at www.monthly review.org/1201jbf.htm (accessed October 12, 2004).

Foster, J. B. 2003. "The New Age of Imperialism." *Monthly Review,* 55(3), 1–14. July–August, at www.monthlyreview.org/0703jbf.htm (accessed October 12, 2004).

Goldberg, E., and Evans, L. 2002. "The Prison Industrial Complex and the Global Economy," Global Exchange, at www.globalexchange.org/campaigns/usa/ pic.html (accessed October 12, 2004).

Goldenberg, S. 2003. "Employees Urged to Defend Iraq Contracts." *The Guardian.* October 27, at www.guardian.co.uk.print/0,3858,4783144-110878,00.html (accessed October 28, 2003).

Goldstein, R. 2003. "Cheney's hawks 'hijacking policy.'" *Sydney Morning Herald.* October 30, at www.smh.com.au/articles/2003/10/29/1067233251576.html (accessed October 30, 2003).

Goebbels, J. 2003. Quoted in Grant Wakefield. "Weapons of Mass Deception." *The Fire This Time*, at www.firethistime.org/weaponsofdeception.htm (accessed October 12, 2004).

Gross, D. 2003. "The Economy Just Had a Great Quarter. Does That Really Mean It's Booming." *Slate.* October 29, at slate.msn/id/2090498/ (accessed October 30, 2003).

Harris, P. 2003a. "Big Brother Takes Grip on America." *The Observer.* September 7, at www.guardian.co.uk/print/0,3858,4748382-110878,00.html (accessed September 7, 2003).

Harris, P. 2003b. "Bush Says God Chose Him to Lead His Nation." *The Observer.* November 2, at observer.guardian.co.uk/international/story/0,6903,1075950,00 .html (accessed November 2, 2003).

Harris, P. 2003c. "Bush Under Fire: Leaks, Scandal, War and a Floundering Economy Are Rocking the Foundations of a Once Invincible White House." *The Guardian.*

October 4, at www.observer.guardian.co.uk/worldview/story/0,11581,1056328,00 .html (accessed October 12, 2004).

Hart, P. 2003. "O'Reilly's War: Any Rationale—or none—Will Do." *Extra!* 16(3, June), 22–24.

Johnson, C. 2003. "The War Business: Squeezing Profits from the wreckage in Iraq." *Harper's Magazine*, 307(1842, November), 53–58.

King, L. 2003. "Many Soldiers, Same Letter." *The Olympian.* October 11, at www .theolympian.com/home/news/20031011/frontpage/121390_Printer.shtml (accessed October 12, 2003).

Lahart, J. 2003. "Spending Our Way to Disaster." October 3, at www.money .cm.com/2003/10102/markets/consumerbubble/ (accessed October 12, 2004).

Landau, S. 2004. "Is Venezuela Next?" *Progreso Weekly*, at www.progresoweekly .com/index.php?progreso=Landau&otherweek=1080194400 (accessed October 12, 2004).

Lawyers Committee for Human Rights. 2003. "'Operation Liberty Shield' Turns Liberty on Its Head Iraqi Asylum Seekers Targeted for Detention." March 18, at www.lchr.org/media/2003_alerts/0318b.htm (accessed March 20, 2004).

Leinwand, D. 2003. "U.S. Forces Drop Propaganda Bombs on Iraq." *USA Today.* At www.usatoday.com/news/world/iraq/2003-02-12-psyops_usat_x.htm (accessed February 12, 2003).

Marx, K. 1853. "The Future Results of British Rule in India." *New York Daily Tribune.* January 2, at www.marxists.org/archive/marx/works/1853/07/22.htm (accessed October 12, 2004).

McLaren, P., and Martin, G. 2003. "The 'Big Lie' Machine Devouring America." *Socialist Future Review* (Summer), pp.18–27.

Mendoza, M. 2003,. "Police Open Fire at Anti-War Protest, Longshoremen Injured." *Truthout.org.* April 7, at www.sfgate.com/cgi-bin/article.cgi?f=/news/archive/ 2003/04/07/state1145EDTOO63.DTL (accessed October 12, 2004).

Milbank, D. 2003. "Curtains Ordered for Media Coverage of Returning Coffins." *Refuse and Resist.* October 21, at www.refuseandresist.org/war/art.php?aid=1107 (accessed October 30, 2003).

Miller, L., and Rampton, S. 2001. "The Pentagon's Information Warrior: Rendon to the Rescue. *PRWatch.Org*, at www.prwatch.org/prwissues/2001Q4/rendon.html (accessed October 12, 2004).

Mulvey, P. 2003. "Journal Claims Proof of WMD Lies." *News.com.au.* September 23, at http:www.apfn.net/messageboard/9-27-03/discussion.cgi.71.html (accessed October 12, 2004).

Nordland, R., and Hirsh, M. 2003. "The $87 Billion Money Pit." *Newsweek*, CXL11(18), 26–30.

North, D. 2003. "War, Oligarchy and the Political Lie." *World Socialist Web Site.* May 7, at www.wsws.org/articles/2003/may2003/war-m07_prn.shtml (accessed) May 8, 2003.

The Northstar Network. 2003. "Death by Fear: The Case of Alberta Spruill." May 20, at www.thenorthstarnetwork.com/news/topstories/181948-1.html (accessed October 12, 2004).

"On Eve 9/11, Bush Makes Pitch for New Laws." 2003. *MSNBC*, at www .msnbc.com/m/pt/printthis_main.asp?storyID=964322 (accessed October 30, 2003).

Panitch, L., and Gindin, S. 2003. Global Capitalism and American Empire. *The Socialist Register*, at www.yorku.ca/socreg/Panitch%20and%206indin%2004.html (accessed October 12, 2004).

Parenti, M. 2002. *The Terrorism Trap: September 11 and Beyond.* San Francisco: City Lights Books.

Pieterse, J. N. 2003. "Hyperpower Exceptionalism: Globalisation the American Way." *New Political Economy*, 8 (3), 299–319.

"Poverty Rate Rises." 2003. *CNN.com.* September 26, at www.cnn.com/2003/US/09/26census.poverty.ap/index.html (accessed September 28, 2003).

"Prison and Beyond: A Stigma That Never Fades." 2002. *The Economist.* August 8, at www.theeconomist.comworld/na/displaystory.cfm?story_id=1270755 (accessed October 12, 2004).

Ramsey, A. 2003. "Forget Bush, the Joke Is on the Kelly Gang." *Sydney Morning Herald.* October 22, at www.smh.com.au/articles/2003/10/21/1066631429106.html (accessed October 22, 2003).

"Reconstruction Deals 'to Bush Backers.'" 2003. *The Australian.* October 31, at www.theaustralian.news.com.au (accessed October 31, 2003).

Rendall, S. 2003. "Dissent, Disloyalty & Double Standards: Kosovo Doves Denounced Iraq War Protest As 'Anti-American.'" *Extra!* 16(3, June), 25–26.

Shaft, J. 2003. "US Homelessness and Poverty Rates Skyrocket While Billions Are Spent Overseas on Occupation. Homeless and Starving in the Land of the Free." *Scoop.* August 31, at www.scoop.co.nz/mason/stories/HL0308/S00011.htm (accessed August 31, 2003).

Sison, J. 2003. "An Update on Imperialism, War and the People's Struggle." Defend Democratic Rights. March 3, at www.defendsison.be/archive/pages/03/0303/030303UpdateOnImperialism.html (accessed October 30, 2003).

Sniffen, M. 2003. "Super Diary Worries Privacy Activists." *The Guardian.* June, at www.guardian.co.uk/uslatest/story/0,1282,-2744985,00.html (accessed June 3, 2003).

Socialist Democracy. 2003. "The New Imperialism, 'Imperial America.'" *SocialistViewpoint.* January, at www.socialistviewpoint.org/jan_03/jan_03_11.html (accessed February 12, 2003).

Teather, D. 2003. "Civil Libertarians Prepare to Fight Bush Over Tougher Anti-Terror Laws." *The Guardian.* September 15, at www.guardian.co.uk/print/0,3858,4753400110878,00.html (accessed September 15, 2003).

Trotsky, L. 1939. *Lenin on Imperialism.* February, at www.marxists.org/archive/trotsky/works/1930-ger/400820.htm (accessed October 12, 2004).

Trotsky, L. 1940. "Bonapartism, Fascism, and War." Leon Trotsky Internet Archive. August 20, at www.marxists.org/archive/trotsky/works/1930-ger/400820.htm (accessed October 12, 2004).

Tyson, A. 2002. "Defining Propaganda, Illegal Deception." *The Christian Science Monitor.* February 22, at www.csmonitor.com/2002/0222/p02s02-usmi.html (accessed February 22, 2002).

Vann, B. 2003. "White House Bans News Coverage of Coffins Returning from Iraq." *World Socialist Web Site.* October 23, at wsws.org/articles/2003/oct2003/bush-o23.shtml (accessed October 23, 2003).

7

The Dialectics of Terrorism:
A Marxist Riposte

Peter McLaren

The law that authorises torture is a law that says: "Men, resist pain; and if nature has created in you an inextinguishable self-love, if it has granted you an inalienable right of self-defence, I create in you an altogether contrary sentiment: a heroic hatred of yourselves; and I command you to accuse yourselves, to speak the truth even while muscles are being lacerated and bones disjointed."

—Beccaria (1764)

PART ONE: REMEMBERING TO FORGET

Shortly after waking up one morning, and while I was still in a twilight frame of mind (what anthropologists sometimes call "liminal" state) between sleep and consciousness, a scene played out before me that involved our beloved ex-Attorney General John Ashcroft. A few days before I had gone to see Michael Moore's landmark film *Fahrenheit 9/11* and, as is often the case, I woke up thinking about the state of the world and our responsibilities for making it a better place. My usual reflections on Marxism, socialism, and grassroots activism were nudged out of frame by an arresting technicolor image of John Ashcroft, wearing his trademark all-American smile and marching in a Fourth of July parade. Dressed as Uncle Sam (although tarted up a bit with white pancake makeup, incarnadine lipstick, salmon-pink eyeshadow, turquoise earrings, and painted on beauty marks), and surrounded by tatterdemalions from a nearby squatters camp, he was walking on stilts and singing his signature song, the blockbuster Pentecostal paen "Let the Eagle Soar." Then the scene began suddenly to shift. Following the ritual he has performed each time he has been

213

sworn into office, he asks to be anointed with cooking oil (in the manner of King David). Pushing his top hat jauntily to one side so that I might apply unimpeded some Crisco oil to his forehead, I notice that his skin is the texture of latex, and that he is actually wearing over his head a condom. I glance downward at his flabalanche and notice that below the equator he is brandishing a large Statue of Liberty codpiece. Our (presumably) tumescent attorney general seems oblivious to the shocked looks on the faces of the suburban families who have lined the streets to enjoy the parade, listen to the attorney general's rich baritone voice, and anticipate the fireworks finale.

I am relieved when the image suddenly vanishes. Was the scene a lurid enactment of the animating ideal of evangelical Christianity's "family values," revealing the hypocrisy and fanaticism that has come to define the Bush Jr. administration? Was it repressed rage at Ashcroft's remark about the Iraqi people finally tasting liberation in their native land? Or, as Ebenezer Scrooge might put it, was it just an undigested piece of cheese that I ate the night before? In either case, it brings up one of the pervasive themes currently challenging our nation: What will happen to our hard-won civil rights when American values are defined by leaders in the fatidic thrall of evangelical Christian fanaticism and the value form of labor wrought by capitalist globalization? The short answer: They will be quashed.

We have entered a reality zone already captured by its opposite: unreality. It is a world where nobody really wanted to venture. It is a world where order has given way to disorder, where reason has given way to unreason, where reality is compromised by truth, where guilt is presumed over innocence, where the once noble search for explanations has been replaced by a dizzying vortex of plastic flags, stars-and-stripes rhinestone belts, coffee klatch war strategists, Sunday barbecue patrioteering, militant denunciations of war protestors, a generalized fear of whatever lies ahead, xenophobic hostility, and point-blank outrage. Thanks to the fawning obeisance of a population punch drunk on the fascist antics of a self-proclaimed "war president," the so-called "war on terror" continues apace, but few in the ranks of the patriotic faithful see it for what it is: an imperialist war of terror.

Soccer moms in SUVs festooned with images of Old Glory park in dimly lit alleys and then slink into the local sex shop in search of red, white, and blue thongs for couch potato husbands strangely rejuvenated by daily doses of carnage, courtesy of CNN. Public school teachers across the country eagerly prepare new courses on Western civilization. Politicians sporting American flag lapel pins plan ways to purge domestic political dissent. Hollywood producers hunker down in their studios and plan new war films. Retired generals shine in their new roles as political consultants, pronouncing the scenes in Iraq as invariably "fluid," which is a give-away that they don't know much more than their interviewers, and probably less. Adds for Radi-tect, "the first affordable radiation detector for your home, car, or office" airs on television and boasts it ability to warn us of radiation "long before it's on the news." Scandal-plagued Fifth Amendment capitalists appear in court as defendants, in an ironic reversal of the Fifth Amendment Commu-nists of the McCarthy era. Former secretary of education under Bush padre, William Bennett, has penned the jeremiad *Why We Fight: Moral Clarity and the War on Terrorism*, charging multiculturalists who hawk ethical rela-tivism with being prime enemies of the Homeland. Harvard Law School Professor Alan Dershowitz basks in the national limelight again, this time advocating the use of "torture warrants" in specified circumstances when the issue of "time" is crucial.

Their reason paralyzed by fear and replaced by the baleful logic of mob fury, American citizens eagerly give up their right of habeus corpus for gov-ernment assurances that terrorists will be tracked down and killed, or if they are captured, for assurances that they will be tried by secret tribunal, and then killed. The U.S. government proposed a plan to recruit one million domestic spies to report any suspicious behavior in our cites, towns, and neighbor-hoods, not unlike operations once put in place by Joseph Stalin, behind the Iron Curtain. Once the war on terror was announced, some doyens of the es-tablishment right must have been so thrilled at the prospect of limitless polit-ical and military opportunity that they were driven mad (unless, like Karl Rove, they were already over the edge), especially after the consentaneity of the public was secured, federal dragnets for rounding up suspicious Arabs were launched across the nation, wiretapping without warrants was put into effect, and a move to reverse a decades-old ban on government assassination signed by Gerald Ford in 1976 was floated by the Bush administration through Congress. With the National Endowment for Democracy pushing for another try at a coup in Venezuela and likely planning to undermine Lula's chances for winning the presidency of Brazil for a second time, I can imag-ine Henry Kissinger in his living room, wickedly brandishing a Clockwork Orange codpiece emblazoned with stars and stripes and dancing La Macarena in Imelda Marcos's ruby slippers. Go for it, Hank! Stud muffin (and Malekhamoues to nations hostile to U.S. vital interests) Donald Rumsfeld, endlessly searching for yet another known unknown, wishes that his support-ive visit to Saddam Hussein in Baghdad during the Iran–Iraq war on Decem-ber 20, 1983, would remain (at least with the American public) an unknown known.

The world has been transformed into pure intensity where to seek refuge in the sanctuary of reflection is to engage in an act of unpardonable treason. Where the governor of Florida can plot to disenfranchise tens of thousands of potential African American voters who traditionally vote Democratic in the guise of clearing felons off voter rolls and still preach the sanctity of democracy. Where previously silenced realities are now guaranteed never to be heard. Where America is above the law and proud of it. Where preaching democracy while destroying democracy and labelling this hypocrisy a Straussian virtue can get you a top job with the Bush administration. Where America Firstists can celebrate the U.S. attempt to block a new international protocol on torture, where they can champion a Farm Bill that will help U.S. farmers but drive millions of small farmers worldwide into destitution, where they can remain determined to keep America "free of entangling treaties and obligations" and encourage America to "wield its big stick and big wallet abroad because its national interests now span the globe and because the culture war against Judeo-Christian city on the hill has gone global" (Barry 2002, p. 3). Where they can exercise "power unconstrained by laws or norms" and play the role of the "self-deputized enforcer, the final arbiter of good and bad, the Lone Ranger" (Barry 2002, p. 3). Where state socialism survives only as naked militarism. Where our commander in chief encourages his boys to "smoke 'em out of their caves, to get 'em runnin' so we can get 'em" in order that we can ultimately "save the world from freedom" (cited in Tobin 2002, p. 42). Where banana republic militarism and authoritarian populism are exercised against those who would dissent against an arrogant and petulant self-appointed "wartime president" in the name of patriotism. It is truly a world turned, in the words of Eduardo Galeano, "upside down." It is a looking-glass world that "rewards in reverse: it scorns honesty, punishes work, prizes lack of scruples, and feeds cannibalism. Its professors slander nature: injustice, they say, is a law of nature" (Galeano 2000, p. 7). Within this looking-glass world, that world that exists upside down, there exists the "looking-glass school" that "teaches us to suffer reality, not to change it; to forget the past, not learn from it; to accept the future, not invent it. In its halls of criminal learning, impotence, amnesia, and resignation are required courses" (Galeano 2000, p. 8).

It is a world where even Colin Powell (who, in his speech to the United Nations, cited Iraqi defector Hussein Kamal's figures on chemical weapons produced by Iraq but failed to mention that Kamal had already told the U.S. authorities that these stockpiles had all been destroyed) is considered too moderate and is replaced by the more hawkish Condoleezza Rice. Where Douglas J. Feith and his staff at the rogue Office of Special Plans can mockingly ignore the traditional intelligence centers and cherry pick information about Iraq so that Bush Jr. can make his case for war. Where Karl Rove can plant as many microphones as he wants in as many campaign offices as he desires and where he can clandestinely orchestrate as many Swift Boat Veterans attacks on as many politicians as he sees fit, and no one will find his fingerprints, only perhaps detect a lingering stench of vermin breath. It is a world where we forbid the coffins of dead soldiers to be photographed, where we threaten to postpone a presidential election in the event of a terrorist attack, and where we contemplate excluding entire cities that have experienced uprisings against the U.S. occupation from voting to elect a "democratic" government in Iraq, where we threaten to shoot journalists covering "hot spots" in Iraq (and sometimes actually do shoot them) on the pretext that they are putting themselves in harm's way, and where we ban Al-Jazeera television from covering the U.S. occupation because we claim that its news reports are fomenting violence and dissent among the Iraqi people (meanwhile we continue to bomb their cities). It is a world where Operation Phantom Fury can level buildings in Fallujah and litter the streets with bodies of women and children, where U.S. soldiers can shoot unarmed and wounded insurgents, and where the U.S. news media can dutifully carry daily stories of how the troops are bringing democracy to Iraq. Where Kofi Annan can declare the U.S.-led invasion of Iraq to be illegal and have his statement be denounced by CNN's Lou Dobbs as "bizarre" and "astonishing." Truly, it is Dobbs's remark that is astonishing given that even the infamous neocon hawk Richard Perle admitted that the invasion violated international law—but that international law in this case stood in the way of what needed to be done. And where Sumner Redstone, CEO of CBS's parent company, Viacom, and a Bush supporter, can halt until after the election a *60 Minutes* story exposing the fraudulent documents that the Bush administration used to make the case that Saddam Hussein tried to buy uranium from Niger. Aren't we looking a lot like the dictatorships we criticized during the Cold War?

Yet we consider ourselves the vanguard of democracy. Do you think the truth is beginning to nibble on the soul of the U.S. citizenry? Have Bush the lesser and his State Department satraps so fueled hatred for "enemies of civilization" and manufactured blind acceptance that the capitalist transfer of the resources of the poor to the corporate accounts of the rich is tantamount to democracy that U.S. citizens will continue to permit their rage and fear to be hijacked by the shameful political opportunism of their leaders?

As the United States reorganizes itself in a double perspective of praising trade liberalization as the path to freedom while repressing its own popular movements, a disquieting incongruence arises between democracy and freedom. It is the reverse mirror image of the democracy that we thought we knew, a democracy for which many had fought and some had died. The United States as the global steward of benevolence has dropped its mask of civil comity to reveal its spectral Dorian Gray smile. While the

Office of Strategic Security—modeled after Reagan's infamous Office of Public Diplomacy that planted propaganda stories about the Contras in major U.S. media outlets (in order to provide misinformation to foreign media organizations) has been shut down, Otto Reich and John Negroponte still lurk in the shadows of White House policy. Reich, assistant secretary of state for western hemisphere affairs, who was found in 1987 by the comptroller general of the United States to have egregiously abused his State Department duties with the Reagan administration by engaging in prohibited covert propaganda activities, gleefully supports attempts to force Hugo Chavez from power in Venezuela and threatens to withdraw U.S. aid to Bolivia if they elect a socialist president.

Shortly after 9/11, concerns surfaced surrounding pronouncements from the Bush administration that similar powers given by Ronald Reagan to the Federal Emergency Management Agency (FEMA) with respect to internal dissent in the face of national opposition against a U.S. military invasion abroad (Reagan was considering an invasion of Nicaragua at the time) might be exercised by the Bush administration should there be sufficient opposition to the U.S. plan to invade Iraq. While Reagan's national plan was never fully disclosed (and is unlikely to be in the foreseeable future thanks to Bush's sealing of the Reagan presidential papers last year), we know from information made public during the Iran-Contra scandal that Oliver North helped FEMA to draft a plan that, on Reagan's executive orders, provided for a suspension of the constitution, internment camps, and the turning over of the government to the president and FEMA. The plan was found to be similar to the one that FEMA director Louis Guiffrida had allegedly drafted earlier to combat "a national uprising by black militants" and that provided for the detention "of at least 21 million American Negroes" in "assembly centers or relocation camps" (Goldstein 2002, p. 2). Louis Guiffrida's deputy, John Brinkerhoff, who handled the martial-law portion of the planning for FEMA under Reagan, is now with the Anser Institute for Homeland Security and has recently argued for the legality of deploying U.S. military troops on American streets—a position that challenges the Posse Comitatus Act of 1878. Tom Ridge, former director of Homeland Security, advocated a review of U.S. law regarding the use of the military for law enforcement duties. Already in place is the Northern Command to aid Homeland defense, created by the U.S. military (Goldstein 2002, p. 2). The current retreat of civil liberties is understood not as something imposed by the Bush-Cheney-Rice *junta*, that has rehired many of the participants in the Iran-Contra scandal of Reagan and Bush padre, but as something "natural" like the self-regulation of the stock market. Henry Weinstein, Daren Briscoe, and Mitchell Landberg, staff writers at the *Los Angeles Times*, explain it to the public this way: "American civil liberties are as fixed and steady an influence in national life as the stock market—and every bit as elastic. Like the market, the rights enjoyed by U.S. citizens have grown to an extent that the Founding Fathers probably never imagined. But in times of danger, civil liberties have shrunk, suffering what market analysts call a correction" (2002, p. A1).

Using the same market logic, Bush is looking toward more deregulated, technology-driven wars (i.e., employing "adaptive" nuclear capabilities, bunker-busting mininukes, and nuclear weapons that reduce "collateral damage") to ensure the United States's geopolitical dominance, so the country can feel secure enough to reverse the "contractions" in civil rights investment that occurred before September 11 and bounce back from our current civil rights recession. But the problem is not simply one of reselling the legacy of Martin Luther King in the language of a brokerage firm, but to pose the question: In an era defined as one of perpetual danger, as one of perpetual war, will we ever regain the rights that we have lost? Will a "hitting first" policy of preemption ever enable the United States to assume the moral high ground?

We can now put aside our fin de siècle existential anxieties about individual mortality and our financial worries about stock market investments and the bureaucratic parasitism of the federal government and lose ourselves in the sheer adrenaline rush of watching the daily carnage that only a new war can bring. As families across the country break out their beer and barbecue chips and sit concupiscently enthralled in front of their television sets watching bombs drop, rockets fire, and buildings explode, approvingly nodding their heads when the newscaster details (with the aid of computerized illustrations) how the BLU-82 "daisy cutter" bomb incinerates everything in its path while sucking up all the oxygen so that nothing will survive its wrath, thousands of Afghan and Iraqi refugees die ignominious deaths from hunger, freezing weather, and collateral damage. Following the invasions of Afghanistan and Iraq on Fox television is like watching a twenty-four-hour infomercial produced by Swift Boat Veterans, where images of death and destruction are accompanied by voiceover editorials that legitimize them as the regrettable but necessary price of freedom. And it's not as though our unqualified enthusiasm, rapt attention, and untempered bloodlust go educationally unrewarded. We are generously repaid, for instance, with technical knowledge. We learn that the ordinances we dropped on front-line troops were the size of Volkswagon Beetles—even bigger than those deployed by our most famous ex-Gulf War veteran, Holy Ghost Warrior, and domestic militia movement patriot Timothy McVeigh:

The BLU-82 combines a watery mixture of ammonium nitrate and aluminum with air, then ignites the mist for an explosion that incinerates everything up to

600 yards away. The BLU-82 uses about six times the amount of ammonium nitrate that Timothy McVeigh used in the bomb that blew up the Oklahoma City
federal building in 1995. (*Los Angeles Times* 2001, p. A10)

Imagine the limitless opportunities now available for high school science
teachers to capture the interest of their freshmen chemistry students.

While publishers in Alabama are stamping forty thousand biology textbooks with warning stickers, reminding students that evolution is a contro-
versial theory they should question, and while Bush hijo pushes for faith-
based programs (what he calls "armies of compassion") to provide social
services, and for tax breaks and other benefits for religious charities that
would entitle them to be the recipients of billions of dollars of government
funding, and while Christian talk-show hosts prone to lachrymose sermons on
the goodness of America continue to bless the war on terrorism "in Jesus's
name," one realizes that the United States functions as a covert theocracy.

Those disappointed that the apocalypse was not ushered in at the millennium's end are making up for it in their razor-edged celebration of the war on
terror. History has been split down the middle as if it had been sliced by a Taliban cane soaked in water. On the one side, modernity houses the transnational ruling class, whose dreams remain unbounded, rewinding time. On the
other side, the transnational working class takes refuge in modernity's refuse
heap of time unravelled and dreams dehydrated. Understanding how this
mighty division has been prepared by capital is the skeleton key that unlocks
the boneyard of reason where truth can be found amidst the charred ruins of
civilizations past and those yet to come. Once the needs of the ruling class are
satisfied, the appetite for other wants increases dramatically such that what
was once considered excess is now taken for granted and what was once a
plaintive longing becomes a fanatical quest.

The specter of world cataclysm is perilously close; it is hiding in the back
alley behind Macy's; in the offices of software programmers in Silicon Valley and Bombay; in the Art Deco Reading Room at Claridge's and the bar at
George's; in the corporate boardrooms of the international banks; in the factories of Prague; in the Parisian cafes of the Latin Quarter; in the French
Quarter of New Orleans; in the *maquiladoras* of Juarez and Mexicali; in the
bankrupt offices of Enron; in the shredding rooms of WorldCom; in the ship-
yards of Gdansk; in the Sky Bar on Sunset Boulevard; in St. Peter's Square;
under the flicking blue tongues of aging porno stars; in the rebarbative and ul-
cerative logic of a Bush Jr. speech; and in the ragged tufts of bin Laden's
beard. Here the contradictions we face vastly exceed the simple choice "between mullahs and the mall, between the hegemony of religious absolutism
and the hegemony of market determinism" (Barber 2002, p. 17). After all,

capitalism, whose intensity if presence is not uniform, is unrescuably contradictory in its own self-constitution, whose conditions of possibility foreclose any resolution between the labor–capital antagonism. Capitalism is predicated upon a failure to realize its truth in practice. It cannot survive outside of the truth of its own lies. It cannot realize its own truth in practice because it cannot do so and continue to survive as capitalism. It is a constitutive impossibility for capitalism to create equal access to education, to feed and clothe the poor, and to provide medical assistance to those who are ill. Denys Turner (1983) remarks that "Capitalism has to live its own morality ideologically, that is to say, it can sustain its moral convictions only as a way of recognizing the fact that it installs the very conditions under which those convictions are unrealizable. It cannot abandon the moral language it cannot live" (p. 151). In this era of casino capitalism, the house always wins.

The interests of corporations continue to be placed ahead of workers, as corporate lobbyists have successfully pressured key members of Congress to give Bush hijo Fast Track authority to negotiate in secret a Free Trade of the Americas Agreement—a move that, if passed into law, will give multinational corporations more power to use the World Trade Organization (WTO) to eliminate public interest safeguards and to increase their power to engage in the same abuses internationally for which they have been condemned by Congress for engaging in nationally. Developed and underdeveloped population groups occupying contradictory and unstable locations in an increasingly transnational environment coupled with cultural and religious antagonisms among the capitalist actors create conditions of desperation and anger among the fractions of the oppressed, most of whom are from developing countries. We do not say this to give credibility to terrorism as a response to such anger but to seek to understand and prevent the conditions in which terrorism is ignited. Manning Marable (2001a) warns: "The question, 'Why Do They Hate Us?' can only be answered from the vantage point of the Third World's widespread poverty, hunger, and economic exploitation" (p. 1). The same GOP operatives who order voter registration forms to be handed out to new citizens shortly after being sworn in by the U.S. government (with the party affiliation box already checked Republican) are those who work to swindle the governments of the very countries from which those citizens have emigrated.

We have entered a world where the concinnity between democracy and justice has been irreparably fractured. While Bush hijo gives stump speeches on the virtues of bringing democracy to Iraq, U.S. soldiers return from Iraq with stumps for limbs, wondering how long it will take to pacify Iraq with rockets and gunships. The events in the United States since September 11 despairingly record not only what John Powers (2002) calls the "Trumanizing of

George W. Bush" (p. 24) but also the remorseless widening of powers by hardliners, revanchists, and hawks over the average citizen, following in the wake of a constitutional coup d'etat in the form of the USA Patriot Act. Regrettably, the "vestigial spine" (Powers 2002) developed by the Democrats has done little to stem the tide of resurgent fascism and foreign policy fiasco. Bush hijo stands under the cover of popular political support that is as sturdy as an Augustan arch, even after his business betrothal to "Kenny Boy" came to an embarrassingly abrupt end. His dyslectic comments and bogus sincerity have been shielded from the American public (or at least buttressed) by media pundits that serve as little more than quislings for the Republican Party, solemnly carrying out their patriotic duty. His gee-whiz-I'm-just-folks bipartisan style has become cruelly calcified in tandem with the autocratic character that his presidency has now assumed. His Enronesque/Global Crossings/WorldCom ideology of loathing the little guys who should be squeezed like wet rag dolls if it will wring more profits from their labor-power has permeated the culture of the White House. Powers (2002) notes:

> Nobody wants to say it during wartime, but the cozy yet ruthless Texas business culture that produced Enron also produced our president. Bush takes pride in working like a CEO, and if you study his behavior, you find him duplicating, almost exactly, the culture of Enron. He displays the same obsession with loyalty (his number one virtue), the same habit of dishonest, short-term accounting (think of his lies about those tax cuts), the same blithe disregard for ordinary workers (his post-September 11 economic proposals all aimed at helping corporations) and the same pitiless certainty he's on the side of the free-market angels. (p. 17)

The smooth-shaven smile of the impish fraternity brother has given way to the permanent jaw-jutting sneer of the dictator. Bush's increasingly Nixon-like penchant for secrecy, his attempts to keep his and his father's presidential papers from public scrutiny (not to mention his own dealings with Harken), and his creation of drumbeat courts vitiate the very notion of the open society he was wont to celebrate before the unforgiving and unforgivable events of September 11. His aw-shucks dyslexic humor and light-minded reveries have given way to imperial declarations of war against all those who oppose his definition of civilization (i.e., whatever economic, legal, foreign, or domestic policies the United States chooses to undertake). As Donald Freed remarked, "He [Bush] looks taller when you are on your knees" (Mikulan 2001, p. 23). What was once thought to be Bush's political autism when it came to foreign policy has now been reevaluated as political psychosis. We have seen him mutate from an *ubermensch* raised on political junk food to a smirking avenging angel growing mean on a diet of corporate swindle served up at Enron executive lunches. As Bernard Weiner (2002) notes, "The Bush administration is like an Enron alumni reunion, with officials in charge of investigating Enron formerly working for Enron" (p. 6). Bush is our American Werewolf in Kabul and the proxy Emperor of Baghdad, lapping up the very lifeblood of the Afghan and Iraqi people and regurgitating it as condolences for those innocents killed by errant American bombs.

It has become dangerous to think, to ask too many questions, or to look beyond the face value of whatever commentary is served up to us by our politicians, our military, and our so-called intelligence agencies, summarized daily in the infantilizing screeds of daily media columnists who have disingenuously become their Beverley Hills lap dogs. Not only has dialectical thought been lamentably undervalued and shamefully underpracticed by these media commentators, but political propaganda in the name of Western Truth has been accorded supercelestial status. Gore Vidal (2004) writes: "Now in the year 2004, when we have ceased to be a nation under law but instead a homeland where the withered Bill of Rights, like a dead trumpet vine, clings to our pseudo-Roman columns, Homeland Security appears to be uniting our secret police into a single sort of Gestapo with dossiers on everyone to prevent us, somehow or other, from being terrorized by various implacable Second and Third World enemies" (p. 28).

It is a world where it is safer to engage in rehearsed reactions to what we encounter on our television screens. After all, domestic dissent has now acquired a police state translation that equates it with terrorism. It is safer to react in ways that newscaster/entertainers big on acrimonious scapegoating and short on analysis define for us as patriotic: applaud all actions by governmental authorities (especially those of the president) as if they were sacerdotal or morally apodictic. CNN declared that it was "perverse" to focus on civilian suffering (some reports have already placed the number of civilian Afghan casualties from U.S. bombing raids at three thousand five hundred and civilian and combatant Iraqi casualties at one hundred thousand before the second assault on Fallujah on November 4, 2004), exercising a racist arithmetic that deems civilian casualties in the United States as a result of the attacks of 9/11 to be more important than Afghan or Iraqi civilian dead. Death and destruction have become as faceless as a smoldering turban on the side of a dirt road.

Just as the *New York Times* participated in covering up the effects of radiation emanating from the use and testing of nuclear weapons after the success of the Manhattan Project, thus serving as little more than a propaganda vehicle for the U.S. military industrial complex and its Cold War warriors (see Keever 2004), so too in today's world does the corporate media serve a similar function as a cheerleader for corporate capital and its weapons industries. This is most clearly seen in the case of the electronic media, mainly television. Of course there is the infamous case of the Sinclair Broadcast Group and its plan to influence the 2004 U.S. presidential election with a preemptive programming strike on Senator John Kerry shortly before the election. More subtle is the use of political "centrists as stand-ins for the left" (Rendall and Kosseff 2004, p. 18), especially in the case of televised talk shows with political debate formats. Program executives, leashed to their corporate sponsors and owners, make sure that these centrists disguised as liberals are appropriately wishy-washy, vacillating milquetoasts—characters certain to be ridiculed when contrasted with their rock-ribbed, testosterone-fueled and hypermasculanized, neoconservative opponents. If the political culture of the United States moves anymore to the right as a result of these shows, then anyone who is caught using the words "civil rights" or "economic equality" will provoke such chest-heaving guffaws and thigh-slapping chortling that public debate will have merged with the fast-approaching media Dark Ages.

Those stubborn enough to break away from the media's unvarnished boosterism surrounding the war on terrorism and insist on understanding world events and their connection to the terrorist attacks of September 11 are implored to submit to the explanations provided by carefully chosen experts hired by our corporately owned and controlled media if for nothing else than fear of public humiliation via media-speak homiletics (author Susan Sontag and left-libertarian talk-show host Bill Maher being two prominent examples that most readily come to mind. It is a world best left to the television journalism experts to figure out. Who are we to question the people who, after all, must "know things" that we don't—like CBS anchorman Dan Rather? Or Fox TV's bullet-dodging Geraldo Rivera (who was rumored to be trekking around Afghanistan with scores and scores of private bodyguards)?

One of the primary ideological vehicles of the new totalitarianism is Fox News. Owned by Rupert Murdoch, Fox News is rapidly gaining a wide and committed audience on the basis of its appeal to right-wing white male viewers. Its political catechism is spiked with testosterone and rage and gives ballast to the logic of transnational capitalism and U.S. militarism. James Wolcott (2001) aptly describes this gang as the "Viagra posse":

> Relatively subdued in the first weeks after September 11, Chris Matthews, Geraldo Rivera, and the Viagra posse of Fox News refilled their gasbags and began taking turns on Mussolini's balcony to exhort the mob, their frog glands swelling like Dizzy Gillespie's cheeks. Agitating for the insertion of ground troops, hothead hosts and like-minded guests (many of them retired military of-

ficers now getting a chance to coach from the sidelines) scoffed at the overreliance on airpower before doing a nimble backflip and complaining that we weren't bombing enough, or in the right spots. Frustrated, indignant, and irate over the patty-cake pace of the Afghan campaign (talk shows serve strong coffee in the greenrooms), these masters of Stratego escalated their rhetorical heat as if hoping the bombing campaign would follow their lead, sounding riled enough to storm the fighter cockpit and get the job done themselves if these gutless wonders wouldn't. (p. 54)

Fox television's chief "no spin" angry white male, commentator Bill O'Reilly—his mind rarely burdened by a dialectical thought, which makes him the perfect spokesperson for the vile backlash politics of disenfranchised white men looking for scapegoats in the multitude of liberal girlie men and flip-flop politicians who can effectively be "feminized" as indecisive and inconsistent—berates with autocratic homilies those few guests he invites on his show who dare offer an explanation for the events of September 11. He enjoys sparing his audiences insight, and lifting from them the burden of comprehension, preferring instead a spectacle of self-congratulatory belligerence, Stygian anger, and a Sergeant Friday "just the facts" aura of credibility. Not to mention emitting a gutteral, Banshee-like screeching "shut up" when he wants to silence a particularly truculent opponent. The majesty of O'Reilly's self-regard is propped up by a stubborn conviction that unsupported opinions presented in a mean-spirited fashion are preferable to complex analysis. Proud of his simple patriotic (i.e., warmongering) advice to kill the enemy because the enemy is evil, he admonishes anyone offering critical analysis as giving evil credibility and as comforting our enemies. On a September 17, 2001, segment of his show, *O'Reilly Factor*, our no-spin host Bill put forth a plan for action if the Taliban did not hand over bin Laden:

If they don't, the U.S. should bomb the Afghan infrastructure to rubble—the airport, the power plants, their water facilities and the roads. This is a very primitive country. And taking out their ability to exist day to day will not be hard. Remember, the people of any country are ultimately responsible for the government they have. The Germans were responsible for Hitler. The Afghans are responsible for the Taliban. We should not target civilians. But if they don't rise up against this criminal government, they starve, period. (Hart 2001, p. 8)

O'Reilly also went on to say that the infrastructure of Iraq "must be destroyed and the population made to endure yet another round of intense pain" (Hart 2001, p. 8). He also disembarrassed himself from any humanitarian sentiments by calling for the destruction of Libya's airports and the mining of its harbors, crying: "Let them eat sand" (Hart 2001, p. 8). There is no spectacle of suddenly vanishing competence here, for his reasoning is as inexorably puerile as it is predictable. He was effectively asking for millions more Iraqi children and civilians to die at the hands of the United States (as if the U.S.-imposed sanctions had not killed enough), not to mention the tens of thousands of civilian casualties that would result from the kind of utter destruction of the infrastructure that he so perversely called for. We have heard this kind of advice before. It's underwritten by the same logic that spikes the Taliban's advice to their own followers. It is the logic of fascism, only this time it is *our fascism* sweetened and made more palatable by the nationalist arrogance and righteous indignation betrayed by O'Reilly and those of his stamp. With so many "attack poodles" and "media mutants" (Woolcott 2004) like O'Reilly in trouble these days (William Bennett admitting a major gambling problem, Rush Limbaugh admitting to drug addiction, and O'Reilly, having escaped becoming the Pee Wee Herman of the Right, by settling a lawsuit by a coworker who alleged that he harassed her with conversations of masturbation, vibrators, and invitations to participate in pornographic sex), neoconservatives spokespersons who position themselves on the moral high ground all the way to Mount Olympus are more prone than ever to accusations that they are sanctimonious and hypocritical for their attacks on Bill Clinton, John Kerry, and other liberals. The court of public opinion, a court located at ground zero of American political and cultural life, doesn't like phonies, Republican or Democrat. But it has a way of forgiving them and rationalizing their behavior. While the media can't heal this popinjay's broken wings, they can grow O'Reilly some new feathers to hide his injury, at least enough to ensure that his caterwauling will continue to attract loyal Fox television viewers.

We live in a world where neoconservative celebrities suffer image problems, but the polices that they continue to promote rage on. Some conservative parents, haunted by images of a tongue-flicking, drooling, naked Bill O'Reilly, may be given pause before purchasing Bill's best-selling book, *The O'Reilly Factor for Kids*, at the local Borders. Since Bill is an icon of conservative male masculinity, and a rich one at that, maybe they will just write it off as a "guy thing." Maybe they can no longer enjoy the oily harangues of Rush Limbaugh the way that they did before his drug addiction was made public. Or maybe they just write it off as a "guy thing." Maybe they are not as anxious as they once were to invite William Bennett, author of the best-selling *Book of Virtues*, as guest speaker at their Republican fund-raiser dinners (or at least want to offer him less than his usual fifty-thousand-dollar speaking fee), after learning that he loses more money each year to a high-stakes gambling addiction than it would take to provide health insurance to all the children of inner-city Baltimore. Or maybe they will just write it off as a "guy thing." Who knows? After all, what is the price of a few anal fissures, or gambling debts, or trips to drug clinics when you have the privilege in this country of supporting imperialist wars and tax breaks for the richest Americans? The corporate media will find a way to redeem you. After all, you're all just "guys."

Attempts to link September 11 to the crisis of global capitalism are left solely in the hands of leftist editors whose publications are marked by outlawed academics such as Noam Chomsky, Michael Parenti, James Petras, Edward Herman, Howard Zinn, and the "California Cassandra" and author of *Blowback*, Chalmers Johnson but also by modest and diminishing circulation numbers whereas the mainstream media is mining the entrails of academia for more comforting oracular theories such as those offered by Harvard professor Samuel Huntington. Huntington argues that the world is moving from a Cold War bipolar division to more complex multipolar and multicivilization divisions with greater potential for conflict. Here Islamic cultures conveniently collide with Western ones with the force of tectonic plates. John Pilger (1999) has appositely noted that "Huntington's language relies upon racial stereotypes and a veiled social Darwinism that is the staple of fascism. It is a vision of global apartheid" (p. 36).

It is not as if the flat-footed storm troopers have already arrived. It is more as if shimmerings of fascism have crossed our political landscape. Ghostly coruscations of negative energy are slowly crystallizing into holograms of Joe McCarthy hovering ominously over the White House. We are living in the moist flaps of Richard Nixon's jowls, drowning in the yellow ink of Steve Dunleavy's pen, sleepwalking on a Pirhandello stage, discovering ourselves as Ionesco characters in a Rod Serling nightmare. Unlike *The Twilight Zone*, the horror of the human condition won't disappear when we turn off our television sets. Bill O'Reilly's kerosene tongue will always be there, wagging obscenely on our television sets, or disguised in the mouths of everyday God-fearing folk from places like Murrieta, California, or Topeka, Kansas. When you see a red-faced young Republican at a campus demonstration screaming support for the Bush cabal's foreign policy, you are witnessing the likelihood of a mind ripped asunder by the ideological bombardment of a Bill O'Reilly, Rush Limbaugh, or Larry Elder and being conscripted into the ranks of warriors for "humanitarian imperialism" and "benevolent assimilation" that is part of our destiny and burden as the world's greatest democracy.

The Sword of Damocles that hangs over the American way of life glows blood-red. The act of patriotism has been shamelessly downgraded by making it compulsory. According to novelist John Le Carre (2001):

> it's as if we have entered a new, Orwellian world where our personal reliability as comrades in the struggle [against terrorism] is measured by the degree to which we invoke the past to explain the present. Suggesting there is a historical context for the recent atrocities is by implication to make excuses for them. Anyone who is with us doesn't do that. Anyone who does, is against us. (p. 15)

Edward Said echoes a similar sentiment:

> What terrifies me is that we're entering a phase where if you start to speak about this as something that can be understood historically—without any sympathy— you are going to be thought of as unpatriotic, and you are going to be forbidden. It's very dangerous. It is precisely incumbent on every citizen to quite understand the world we're living in and the history we are a part of and we are forming as a superpower. (Barsamian 2001b)

James Petras (2002b) perhaps says it best when he argues that we inhabit a veritable police state, at the cusp of a totalitarian regime. He writes:

> One of the hallmarks of a totalitarian regime is the creation of a state of mutual suspicion in which civil society is turned into a network of secret police informers. The Federal Bureau of Investigation (FBI) soon after September 11 exhorted every U.S. citizen to report any suspicious behavior by friends, neighbors, relatives, aquaintances, and strangers. Between September and the end of November almost 700, 000 denunciations were registered. Thousands of Middle Eastern neighbors, local shop owners, and employees were denounced, as were numerous other U.S. citizens. None of these denunciations led to any arrests or even information related to September 11. Yet hundreds and thousands of innocent persons were investigated and harassed by the federal police. (p. 10)

Also forbidding is the current wave of repressive government actions, including the ongoing racial profiling of Muslim U.S. citizens, the clearcutting of constitutional protections of immigrants, and a full-frontal assault on those civil liberties still standing after decades of strip-mining the hard-won gains made by courageous civil rights activists in the 1960s. Bush is transforming the war on drugs in places such as Colombia into counterterrorist laboratories at war with revolutionary movements.

The U.S. government has overrun the waterline of civil rights, drowning out protests in its assault on immigrants and dangerous classes with the creation of the so-called USA Patriot Act and setting the stage for propaganda "show trials" once reserved for military dictatorships who formerly were Cold War adversaries. The establishment of military tribunals by Bush hijo amounts to little more than legitimizing a network of ad hoc, "drumhead" or "kangaroo" courts that can safely bypass both Congress and the judiciary. If, for instance, President Bush believes that a long-term resident of the United States has aided a terrorist in some way, that resident can be tried in secret by a military commission and sentenced to death on the basis of hearsay and rumor, without any appeal to a civilian court. Even the Supreme Court will be out of reach.

The USA Patriot Act treats Islamic terrorism as a surrogate for Communism and brings to mind the inspiriting spectacle and ideological intoxication of the Red Menace and historical events burned by fear into the political unconscious of the country. Repressed by guilt and displaced into the crevices of historical memory, these events include the Espionage and Sedition Acts that were used against socialists, anarchists, and other groups opposed to the U.S. entry into World War I; the 1919–1920 Palmer raids that rounded up would-be Bolsheviks and those who sympathized with the 1917 Russian Revolution, but which were also used as a device to round up thousands of foreign-born radicals (including a number of U.S. citizens) and send them overseas; the 1940 Smith Act that was designed to go after Nazi sympathizers but also was used to imprison Trotskyites and leaders of the U.S. Communist Party; the World War II incarceration of one hundred twenty thousand Japanese Americans in concentration camps under the Roosevelt administration; the McCarran Act of 1950 that legitimized secret FBI record-keeping on political subversives and the deportation of noncitizens who had been Communists at any time in their lives; the McCarthy hearings of the 1950s that functioned as anti-Communist witchhunts targeting reds, union militants, and Hollywood screenwriters and that famously earned the opprobrium of the Left for generations that followed; "Operation Wetback" of the mid-1950s that rounded up and deported over one million Mexican men, women, and children; COINTELPRO operations that were put to use against leftists and black militants in the 1960s; the 1980s RICO "antiracketeering" laws that were developed to target organized crime but also were used to break strikes and exert complete control over unions like the Teamsters; and the creation of the 1984 plan by the Federal Emergency Management Agency to appoint military commanders to run state and local governments in the event of a national emergency (see *Workers Vanguard* 2001). While it appears a die-casting term reserved for the truly evil, the terrorism of the USA Patriot Act is actually an extortionate term packed in an aerosal can whose political mistiness enables the United States to declaim against the politics of any country, and to employ lethal force—preemptive strikes in contrast to defensive maneuvers—against anyone who opposes American vital interests anywhere in the world. When the Americanization of the foreign psyche through the mediation of Hollywood, popular culture, and official propaganda fails to create subjectivities pliant enough to turn all the world into decaffeinated Americans, then the way of the bomb becomes the method of choice for acquiring and maintaining strategic U.S. interests.

And now former CIA director James Woolsey is urging a reversal of U.S. policy prohibiting the use of foreign assets with abusive human rights records (established by CIA director John Deutch in 1996) after it was revealed that CIA informants were involved in kidnapping, torture, and assassination in Guatemala. Without consulting with Congress, Bush hijo signed executive order 13233 by which he seeks to modify the law and make it more difficult to make presidential papers and records available to the public. In his efforts to rule by executive fiat, he appears to be grasping beyond his executive powers under the Presidential Records Act of 1978, most probably to protect the public from gaining access to information during his father's vice-presidency and presidency. Not only does he want to protect his father but also others— like Dick Cheney—now working in Bush hijo's administration. Does the Bush administration and its imperial quartermasters want to hide something from the American public now or from now on—or both? And why is this happening just when information is being made public about the connections between the Taliban, the CIA, and Pakistani intelligence; the business dealings of the Bush and bin Laden families through the Carlyle Corporation; the corporate malfeasance of Bush and Cheney before they assumed their presidential duties; and the relationship between U.S. oil conglomerates and countries in the Caspian Sea region?

In the face of the particularly fierce hawkish administration of Bush hijo, and in the midst of widespread apprehension about the motives behind the U.S. war on terrorism among Third World peoples, is a particularly difficult time to call for rethinking the role that the United States plays in the global division of labor. The recent events of mind-shattering world-historical dimensions, the sudden unfolding nightmare that saw death and destruction unleashed upon thousands of innocent and unsuspecting victims in Washington and New York City, such that the gates of hell appeared to have been blown open, have made it difficult for many U.S. citizens to comprehend why their familiar world has suddenly turned upside down.

The practices of U.S.-backed client regimes in the Middle East such as Egypt, Algeria, Jordan, Israel, and Saudi Arabia, who are waging brutal campaigns of violence against their Islamic opposition, certainly provide a back-drop against which we can begin to analyze—but not justify, or rationalize, or legitimize—the events of September 11. The organizing, arming, funding, and training of Islamic groups (with the exception of the Shi'ites in Iran) against working-class rebellion and social revolution have been a cornerstone of U.S. foreign policy (Macdonald 2002). Certainly the alliance that the United States has maintained since World War II with the fundamentalist Wahhabite regime in Saudi Arabia has been a particular sore spot among many Islamic groups. But we shouldn't uncritically proclaim that U.S. actions were the *direct cause* of the attacks, because such a position is undialectical. For instance, the North Vietnamese, who suffered the tragic loss of millions of people at the hands of the United States, did not attack the U.S. populace in retaliation (Hudis 2001). The terrorist attacks required a certain willful "agency" that served to generate the terrorism—an agency that is context specific. Terrorism does not work on the basis of operant conditioning and is not teleologically inscribed in history as a reaction to U.S. foreign and economic policy. But it is surely the case that U.S. involvement in the Third World in general and the Islamic world in particular has created—and continues to create—the background conditions that are likely to lead to terrorism. Hasn't the time-tested modus operandi of the United States in its spread of democracy throughout the world been savage military assaults using the deadliest weapons known to humankind? The taproot of terrorism surely lies in the fertile soil of imperialism—both military and economic. It is nourished by the transnationalization of the productive forces and fertilized by the defeated dreams of the vanquished poor. The terrorism of 9/11 was rhizogenic—its roots and filaments interlaced with U.S. foreign policy and practices. The fact that terrorists are not nation-state actors (their nationalities are relatively incidental) but rather are agents that work in the liminal interstices of the international system, suggests that attacking sovereign nations in retaliation for acts of terrorism is woefully misguided and will lead only to more "blow-back."

The new totalitarian ambience in the United States can be sniffed in the malodorous words of prominent right-wing journalist Charles Krauthammer: "America is no mere international citizen. It is the dominant power in the world, more dominant than any since Rome. Accordingly, America is in a position to reshape norms—How? By unapologetic and implacable demonstrations of will" (cited in McMurtry 2001). Sound Nietzschean? Readers who are fans of *Zarathustra* might be emboldened by the words uttered by David Rockefeller at the June 1991 Bilderberg's meeting in Baden, Germany: a "supranational sovereignty of an intellectual elite and world bankers . . . is surely preferable to the national autodetermination practised in past centuries" (cited in McMurtry 2001). When you put Krauthammer and Rockefeller together, you complete the circuit of totalitarian logic of "full-spectrum dominance" or "absolute power" set in train by the juggernaut of globalized capital. James Petras (2001) warns that we must start to:

> recognise the barbarities committed today in the name of Western victories, hegemony, democracy and free markets: the premature death of ten million Russians, twenty million African AIDS victims denied medicine by Western pharmaceutical corporations backed by their governments, the killing of one million Iraqi children by the Anglo-U.S. war and blockade, the 300 million Latin Americans living in poverty, the tens of thousands of Colombians killed thanks to U.S. military training and aid. (p. 14)

While clearly U.S. economic policies and geopolitical strategies are a factor in creating an environment for terrorism—that is, Israeli treatment of the Palestinians and unyielding U.S. support for Israel, U.S. support for the repressive regimes of Saudi Arabia and Egypt, as well as the training of the military and death squads of numerous Latin American regimes who went on to murder hundreds of thousands of peasants—it is also clear that in the case of the attacks of September 11 that other factors are involved, like anti-Semitism, anti-Americanism (as against genuine anti-imperialism), and a reaction against the dimensions of "Western society" that every leftist should support: workers rights, feminism, gay rights, and so on (Hudis 2001). Peter Hudis (2001) is bracingly forthright in asserting that it is wrong to believe that bin Laden was simply responding to the same injustices as radical leftists, except that he used a method leftists would never condone and would find utterly abhorrent. Bin Laden loathes the masses, whom he is willing to use as canon fodder in the name of his holy war. Steve Niva (2001b) has rightly pointed out, for instance, that bin Laden's small, violent, and socially reactionary network—influenced by the socially reactionary Wahhabi school of Islam practiced in Saudi Arabia and the conservative Pakistani Islamist Party, *Jamiat-ul-Ulema-e-Islam*—is roundly antagonistic to social justice and differs in important ways with the wider current of Islamic activism in the Arab world and more globally.

The wider current of Islamic activism does have a social justice agenda on behalf of the poor and dispossessed, is more involved in party building and mass mobilization, and largely rejects the simplistic Islamic doctrines promoted by bin Laden's network. Moreover, Niva stresses that bin Laden's organization is disconnected from wider Islamic activist movements in that they do not locate their struggle in a national context, but rather in a global war on behalf of Muslims worldwide. It is problematic therefore to locate the attacks on September 11 in a natural reflex reaction to U.S. policies and practices. It is much more complicated than that. There is a difference between saying that the United States helps to foster conditions in which terrorism thrives and that the terrorist acts of September 11 were a causal reflex of U.S. foreign and economic policy—like billiard balls in a mechanical Newtonian universe. U.S. imperialism creates the potential for and probability of terrorist attacks but it does not ensure that they will occur. To say that U.S. imperialism caused the terrorist attacks skips over the notion that acts of terror are often the outcome of an irreducible plurality of causes and overlooks the fact that some forces, like the terrorist factions of Osama bin Laden, are as regressive as anything done in the service of U.S. imperialism (Hudis 2001). It forgets that there exist a great array of crimes that can be linked to world capitalism, that go beyond the participation of the United States. In fact, it is important to point out that Islamic fundamentalism (what Samir Amin calls political Islam) is, itself, an adaptation to world capitalism. As Amin (2001) notes, political Islam is in fact not a reaction to the abuses of secularism and little more than an adaptation to the subordinate status of comprador capitalism.

While there surely existed strong left-wing currents across the Muslim world in the 1950s, 1960s, and 1970s (i.e., Syria, South Yemen, Iraq, Somalia, Libya, and Ethiopia) and left-leaning populist leaders (such as Nasser), it is worth remembering that Islam persists today as the official ideology of some capitalist states and as an oppositional force in others. The Islamist movement is multilayered and nuanced, with competing Sunni and Shi'ite backers. But generally speaking, as Lisa Macdonald (2002) notes, "While veiled in religious garb, support for Islam is motivated by the self-interest of the capitalist class of each country." Macdonald asserts that:

> Even the most progressive of political Islamists put forward no clear alternative to capitalism. The best they can do is try to insert themselves into the secular national liberation struggles in their countries and point to the sections of the Koran that call for egalitarianism, equality, and "brotherhood" to defend their religious flank from attack by traditionalists. Since the basic tenets of Islam also uphold the right of private ownership, individual enterprise, and profit, the contradictions are unresolvable. (They are supposedly resolved through the *zaket*—a morally enforced levy on wealth which is given to the poor—but this amounts to no more than charity and is purely cosmetic in a capitalist economy.) (p. 17)

In many cases, Islamic fundamentalist vigilante groups, like their Christian counterparts, have become a major instrument of counterrevolution for the reactionary forces of state imperialism. Islamic fundamentalism's popular support has been aided by the failure of local bourgeoises to provide even basic development in the form of social welfare, public education, and other services and their failure to stem the increasing impoverishment of the majority of people in their respective countries (Macdonald 2002). While U.S. imperialism clearly contributes to the conditions that are likely to foster terrorism, the actual causes of terrorism are conjunctural; they are a multiple and complex articulation of forces and relations rooted in globalized capitalism.

Il N'ya Pas Hors du Monde

When former White House press secretary Ari Fleischer insisted that people now have to "watch what they say, watch what they do" it was not, as some have claimed, a flippant remark. Interestingly, but not surprisingly, Cuba is listed as a country that exports terror internationally. Since September 11, some members of Congress have tried to have Cuba removed from the terrorist list but the Cubans in Congress stopped this move in its tracks. Even though Fidel Castro roundly condemned the terrorist attacks on September 11, and offered to cooperate with Washington in combating terrorism, the State Department put forward an unconvincing case against Cuba by noting that Cuba harbors Basque separatists. But the truth of the matter is that they are there as the result of an agreement between the Spanish and Cuban governments and are not engaged in terrorist activities of any kind (Kawell 2001). The State Department can put forward specious reasons for putting Cuba on the list of countries that harbors terrorists but remains adept on ignoring its own local swamp for terrorist infestation: Florida. As Pilger (2001) notes, "There is no 'war on terrorism.' If there was, the SAS would be storming the beaches of Florida, where more terrorists, tyrants and torturers are given refuge than anywhere in the world" (pp. 2–3). Bertell Ollman (2001) echoes similar sentiments to those of Pilger when he writes:

> I'm still waiting for [Bush] to declare war on Florida. Miami is a haven for terrorists, it's the terror capital of the world. All these Latin American and Cuban terrorists go there to refresh, to retire, to conduct their business. If Bush wants to make a war on terror he should start by bombing Miami and arresting the governor of Florida, even if he is his brother. . . . And after he's successfully done away with terrorism in Miami, then we'll talk about the next step. (p. 8)

It is difficult to deny that the United States has a calculated penchant for ignoring its own terrorists (groups and individuals who have been trained and financed either directly or indirectly by the U.S. military); not just the *gusano* mafia in Florida (see McLaren and Pinkney-Pastrana 2001) but also fundamentalist Christian mass murderer General Efrain Rios Montt of Guatemala, Savimbi and Renamo in Angola and Mozambique, and the Nicaraguan Contras. Many people reject the idea that the United States exports terrorism. Some no doubt find it difficult to understand why a powerful nation such as the

United States would need to employ what are generally considered to be the weapons of the weak. Klare (2001a) asserts that, "Throughout history, the weapon of those who see themselves as strong in spirit but weak in power has been what we call terrorism. Terrorism is the warfare of the weak against the strong: if you have an army you wage a war; if you lack an army you engage in suicide bombings and other acts of terrorism. (Remember: this is exactly what the American Revolution looked like to the British, the strong force in 1775)." Chomsky (2001b) views this issue from a different angle. He explains that, far from being a weapon of the weak, terrorism is primarily the weapon of the strong:

> That is the culture in which we live and it reveals several facts. One is the fact that terrorism works. It doesn't fail. It works. Violence usually works. That's world history. Secondly, it's a very serious analytic error to say, as is commonly done, that terrorism is the weapon of the weak. Like other means of violence, it's primarily a weapon of the strong, overwhelmingly, in fact. It is held to be a weapon on the weak because the strong also control the doctrinal systems and their terror doesn't count as terror. (p. 11)

The late Eqbal Ahmad (1998) makes the point that the moral revulsion in response to terrorism is highly selective. He writes that, "We are to feel the terror of those groups, which are officially disapproved. We are to applaud the terror of those groups of whom officials do approve" (p. 3). In this context, it is impossible not to seriously question the odious role of the Western Hemisphere Institute for Security Cooperation, or Whisc, based in Fort Benning, Georgia (until January this year, Whisc was called the "School of the Americas," or SOA). Since 1946, SOA has trained more than 60,000 Latin American soldiers and policemen. Its graduates constitute a veritable rogues gallery of the continent's most notorious torturers, mass murderers, dictators, and state terrorists.

How can the United States condemn other countries for human rights abuses and acts of terror and not recognize that it houses, educates, and graduates some of the most notorious butchers in the Americas? If the United States really believes that supporting terrorists makes you as guilty as the terrorists themselves, then it would have to put on trial most of its military and political leadership over the last handful of administrations—and more. Alexander Cockburn (2001) reports that in recent years the United States has been charged by the United Nations and also by human rights organizations such as Human Rights Watch and Amnesty International with tolerating torture in its prison system. Methods of torture range from putting prisoners into solitary confinement in concrete boxes, twenty-three hours a day, for years on end, to activating 50,000-volt shocks through a mandatory belt worn by prisoners. The United States began serious experiments in torture during the Vietnam War. One experiment involved three prisoners being anesthetized and having their skulls opened up. Electrodes were planted into their brains. They were revived, given knives, and put in a room. CIA psychologists activated the electrodes in order provoke the prisoners to attack one another, but the prisoners did not respond as expected. So the electrodes were removed, the prisoners shot, and their bodies burned (Cockburn 2001). And, of course, what is global terrorism if not the doctrine of preemptive war, which, according to Gore Vidal (2004), is "based on a sort of hunch that maybe one day some country might attack us, so, meanwhile, as [President Bush] and his business associates covet their oil, we go to war leveling their cities to be rebuilt by other business associates" (p. 28).

PART TWO: UNVEILING THE PAST, EVADING THE PRESENT

For the last several years following some of the most heinous crimes ever to occur on U.S. soil, we have been told to remain on high alert, that more terrorist attacks by roving "sleeper" cells are imminent. Nobody seems to know where or when, exactly, the evil-doers will strike, or with what arsenal: Dirty bombs? Anthrax? Suitcase-size mininukes? Yet we are constantly reminded by the media to be afraid for ourselves and for our family members. Karate, kickboxing, and Kung-Fu clubs are packed with would-be defenders of the Homeland. And assault rifles are legal again and making a comeback. Citizens who live in fear will give the government a green light to do just about anything, from taking more money from the poor to give to the already filthy rich, to invading more Third World countries to get rid of terrorist cells, to increased racial profiling of Arab Americans, to militarizing the borders in order to seal them off against anyone who even bears a remote physical resemblance to Arab Americans.

Even in times of relative peace, the average American citizen has vigorously defended the capitalist state, which is regarded as the summit of human achievement. And this has been especially true in the years leading up to 9/11, even though the gap in income between the wealthiest Americans and the rest of the population—a level of inequality higher than in any other industrialized nation—has witnessed 47 percent of the total real income gain between 1983 and 1998 accruing to the top 1 percent of income recipients, 42 percent going to the next 19 percent, and 12 percent accruing to the bottom 80 percent (O'Brien 2001). Of course, this gap now can be conveniently blamed on the terrorist attacks, even though it has been growing steadily for many decades. And this has been especially true in the years leading up to 9/11 and can be directly linked to the internationalization of capital, the deregulation and liberalization of world markets and trade, the growing autonomy of finance capital and advances made in information technology, and the growth in power of multinational corporations.

If we want to understand the roots of terrorism, it is imperative to locate the current war on terrorism within the larger optic of the globalization of capitalism. When we do, we soon recognize that multinational corporations are still based predominately in advanced capitalist countries where they exercise enormous political influence. In fact, imperialist countries such as the United States wield disproportionate influence within international financial agencies. In contrast, the developing, so-called Third World countries are overwhelmingly low-wage areas, interest and profit exporters (not importers), and "virtual captives of the international financial institutions and highly dependent on limited overseas markets and export products" (Petras and Veltmeyer 2001, p. 30). The multinational corporations and banks located in the imperial states constitute the mainspring of transnational flows of capital and commodity trade. The International Monetary Fund (IMF) and the World Trade Organization (WTO) define their policies in accordance with imperial imperatives of free trade, free markets, and free flows of capital and serve mainly as staging areas where advanced capitalist states can do business, under the leadership of the United States.

While it is true that greater internationally integrated financial markets now exist, it is important to remember that capitalism is not a conglomeration of transnational capitalist corporations—capital is a relation constituted by its contradictory relationship with wage labor. Capitalism has certain conditions of reproduction that sets limits to the extent to which its structures can be reformed (Petras and Veltmeyer 2001). Most reforms operate well within the limits set by the requirements of capitalist production. As Petras and Veltmeyer (2001) note, the theory of imperialism (as distinct from the idea of globalization) can best explain the relationship between the growth of international flows of capital and the increase of inequalities between states and between CEOs and workers.

Petras (2002b) has persuasively argued that as the world's leading imperial state, the United States (as well as EU countries) continues to play a central role in the world political economy. Petras is correct in claiming that the role of the nation-state is far from over as we bear witness to numerous U.S. (and EU) practices: interventions to save multinational corporations and world financial systems; bail-outs in exchange for opening markets and foreign takeovers of basic industries; the conquest of foreign markets and the protection of local markets; the negotiation and enforcement of major trade agreements and bilateral, regional, multilateral trade pacts; the knocking down of trade barriers and the destabilization of nationalist regimes; the imposition of protective barriers; the subsidization of industries; the limiting of imports through quotas; and the prevention of exporting countries from entering certain markets. Although we witness the appearance of a transnational capitalist elite, we acknowledge that multinational corporations continue to have specific locations in particular nation-states, where mobility is contingent upon interstate relations. Clearly, as Petras notes, old nation-state governments have not been superceded by international financial institutions. The so-called information revolution has not eliminated state borders. The new economy remains highly speculative, driven by exorbitant claims of high returns in the absence of profits and sometimes even revenues. The United States exercises managed trade that combines the protection of home markets with aggressive intervention to secure monopoly market advantages and investment profits. The United States continues to operate a "selective" openness in designated product areas (with U.S. affiliates) while Euro-U.S. policy makers and their employees in the IMF-World Bank insist that countries in the so-called Third World eliminate all trade barriers, subsidies, and regulations for all products and services in all sectors. The United States preaches market fundamentalism to the Third World while protecting domestic economic sectors. The United States operates as the Alpha Male of a neomercantilist imperialism and uses its military might to back itself up. Petras (2002a) notes that:

> So-called globalization grew out of the barrel of a gun—an imperial state gun. To further protect overseas capital, the U.S. and the EU created a new NATO doctrine which legitimates offensive wars outside of Europe against any country that threatens vital economic interests (their MNCs). NATO has been expanded to incorporate new client states in eastern Europe and new "peace associates" among the Baltic states and the former republics of the USSR. In other words, the imperial state military alliances incorporate more states, involving more state apparatuses than before—to ensure the safe passage of Euro-U.S. MNCs into their countries and the easy flow of profits back to their headquarters in the U.S. and western Europe. (p. 5)

It is clear now that the spread of globalization has not helped the world's poor. From 1960 to 1980, the gross domestic product in Latin America grew by 75 percent per person, but from 1980 to 2000—a period of massive globalization, market liberalization, and international investment—the gross domestic product rose only 6 percent. In Africa, the gross domestic product rose by a third from 1960 to 1980 but over the next twenty years it lost nearly half of that gain (Fishman 2002). Ted Fishman (2002) comments:

> The lethal double dynamic begins with the dirt poor whom the spread of global capitalism has not helped. Half the planet lives on less than two dollars a day, a

billion people on half of that. For them, globalization has meant little in terms of real income gain. Oxfam recently recalculated the statistics in the World Bank study on developing countries, this time not weighted for population, and determined that incomes for people in countries that are pursuing a global program grew just 1.5 percent. For one in three of these countries, incomes actually rose more slowly than in states that resisted reforms. (p. 34)

In fact, the influx of capital and liberalization measures bring some countries closer to war, decimating large impoverished sections of the population. Fishman (2002) notes that most of the world's battles involve groups of capitalist profiteers struggling for competitive advantage, using offshore bank accounts and dummy corporations—that is, behaving like Enron—and fighting each other with cheap soldiers. He asks, "Should we be surprised, then, that the freeing up of world financial markets and world trade has spread an epidemic of violence? The dictators, warlords, corporate partners, banks, law firms, and nations that thrive on deadly business have known it all along" (2002, p. 41).

The United States is the largest arms dealer in the world and the coalition's weapons manufacturers stand to—forgive the metaphor—"make a killing" in the current war on terrorism. Currently, about eighty-five thousand private firms profit from the military contracting system. The Carlyle Group (which removed its Web site after the September 11 attacks), a privately owned, U.S. $12 billion international merchant bank or equity firm, and the eleventh largest defense contractor in the United States, invests heavily in the defense sector and makes its money from military conflicts and weapons spending. It retains Bush padre as a senior consultant (Bush has been allowed to buy into Carlyle's investments, which involve at least 164 countries). Carlyle's chairman and managing director is former U.S. secretary of defense Frank Carlucci (and former roommate of Donald Rumsfeld) and its partners include former U.S. secretary of state James A. Baker III, George Soros, Richard Darman (Reagan aide and GOP operative), and Fred Makek (Bush hijo's campaign manager). The Carlyle Group has in the past done business with the bin Laden family, including deals involving the aerospace industry.

Joseph Stiglitz of Columbia University, who was awarded the Nobel Prize in economics in 2001, recently admitted:

Clearly, terrorists can be people like bin Laden who come from upper-income families. Nevertheless, abject poverty and economies without jobs for males between the ages of 18 and 30 are particularly good breeding grounds for extremism. Solving the economic problems doesn't eliminate the risk of terrorism, but not solving them surely enhances it. (Press, 2002, p. 16)

Michael Klare situates the current danger facing us as one that puts the U.S. economy at the service of hypothetical future enemies, or actually creates those enemies by producing a climate of fear and hostility in anticipation of those enemies one day arising:

> The question facing all Americans, therefore, is whether the expenditure of hundreds (later thousands) of billions of dollars to defend against hypothetical enemies that may not arise until thirty or forty years from now is a sensible precaution, as contended by the president and defense secretary, or whether it eventually will undermine U.S. security by siphoning off funds from vital health and educational programs and by creating a global environment of fear and hostility that will produce exactly the opposite of what is intended by all these expenditures. (2002, p. 15)

But what about the new technologies that are supposedly bringing about what has been described as the "information economy"—an economy characterized as qualitatively different from the industrial capitalism theorized by Mr. Marx? It can be convincingly argued that the new technologies really have not changed the basic reproductive principles of advanced capitalism, since they remain embedded in preexisting classes and nation-states and within the structural dynamics of the capitalist system. The international division of labor has not been effectively transformed by these new technologies, since most of the industrial output in both Third World and imperial countries is for domestic consumption and is produced by domestic owners (Petras and Veltmeyer 2001). What these information technologies have been good at is bombarding us with the message that there is no alternative to capitalism and that any attempts to replace capitalism with an alternative will bring about rampant destruction. But what about possible alternatives to the globalization of capital—especially to the voracious, binge capitalism that currently engulfs us? Socialist planning has been discredited as a result of the collapse of the bureaucratic command economies of the Soviet Union—what Callinicos (2001) calls "economic statism" (p. 119). The only alternatives seemingly available are economic statism, neoliberalism, or the more progressive Rhineland model of regulated capitalism (see Callinicos 2001). I don't believe that it is possible for capitalist social relations to be "transformed" such that they can better serve the interests of the working class in developing countries, or those who live in relations of economic servitude to advanced capitalist countries (an argument that I do not have space to develop here). What needs to be replaced are the social logics of these alternatives with that of socialism.

Today's monopolist program of corporate power resembles Hannah Arendt's "omnipresent center" where the logic of capital accumulation is internalized as a public value-set (McMurtry 2001). In this context, the war on terror exemplifies what John McMurtry (2001) calls the logic of "the extortion racket of the neighborhood" writ large, "the symbolic male gangs in corporate logos" (p. 3). McMurtry writes that "[t]ransnational corporations have marketed and financed these political leaders to ensure that captive states serve them rather than the peoples governments are elected by, guaranteeing through state plenipotentiaries and transnational trade edicts that governments can no longer govern them in common interest without infringing the new trade and investment laws in which transnational corporations alone are granted rights" (2001, p. 4). He further points out that the "permanent war against 'terrorists' of the Third World is the cap of a continuous and historically unprecedented financial deregulation of markets and hemorrhages of transnationally mobile capital in and out of nations leading to meltdowns from Brazil and Mexico and Russia and Asia" (2001, p. 9). The invisible hand of the market is now a clenched fist wielding the sword of civilization, mercilessly punishing those who have disobeyed its laws.

McMurtry forcefully claims that the United States has effectively created a new form of totalitarianism. The old totalitarianism culture of the "Big Lie" is marked by "a pervasive overriding of the distinction between fact and fiction by saturating mass media falsehoods" (2001, p. 9). This Big Lie is an omnipervasive lie that "is disseminated by round-the-clock, centrally controlled multimedia which are watched, read, or heard by people across the globe day and night without break in the occupation of public consciousness instead of national territories" (2001, p. 9). McMurtry writes that "in the old totalitarian culture of the Big Lie, the truth is hidden. In the new totalitarianism, there is no line between truth and falsehood. The truth is what people can be conditioned to believe" (2001, pp. 9–10).

And conditioned they certainly are.

Of course, the culture of the new totalitarianism and the international division of labor produced by the globalization of capital cannot fully account for the creation of a climate for terrorism, or for the terrorist attacks against the United States. The remaining challenge is to understand how the new totalitarianism and the globalization of capital are related to the foreign policies and military activities undertaken by advanced capitalist nations, including covert operations. What is clear, however, is that we inhabit a world in which one can identify certain kinds of "terrorism from below" as well as examples of "terrorism from above." Joel Kovel (2002) clarifies this distinction thusly:

> For the oppressed, terror is the restitution of identity through violence against the oppressor; while for the latter, it becomes a "collateral damage." In this respect

the suicide bomber striking on behalf of a ravaged people has a certain moral advantage over the powerful nation who impersonally bombs a helpless population. The former may falsely deny that he is doing evil, but at least he knows he is being violent, and that he is willing to take violence to the limit of giving his own life. The terrorism from below is undoubtedly evil, because it strikes back at innocents to get back at an oppressor; but its evil is refracted through the objective reality of that oppressor. The terror from above, on the other hand, is nakedly of the oppressor himself, hurled down from the great heights of the Command and Control Center while its perpetrator looks forward to an evening at the mall, or thinks, if he is the president and has to give a press conference, of how good we are. (p. 17)

A Global Culture of Looking the Other Way

How wonderfully consistent history appears when the former hanging governor of Texas uses his powers as commander in chief of the armed forces to authorize, through a November 13 presidential directive, military tribunals with the power to execute terrorist suspects on the basis of secret deliberations. Do these not constitute the reverse mirror image of Stalin's show trials? Is this not Bush's own Court of the Star Chamber? With an icy wave of the presidential hand, Bush and his administration have brought the United States into the imperial ambit of a dictatorship. Bush and his administration are doing Texas line dancing over the Bill of Rights, their stomping cowboy boots echoing more like the goose-stepping jackboots of another time, another place.

The United States, along with other countries in the capitalist West, certainly help to create the global culture that nourishes and helps to sustain the virus of terrorism. But historical denial and the arrogance of our leaders in successive political administrations helped put blinkers on public awareness that America was anything other than America the Good. As Lewis Lapham (2001) remarks, "We didn't see the planes coming because we didn't think we had to look" (p. 41). It is striking how terrorism is sanctioned, condemned, and by whom. In 1990, George Bush padre released from house arrest the notorious Orlando Bosch, after Bosch had served two years for illegally entering the United States. Government officials in the United States believed that Bosch was involved in the bombing of a Cuban civilian airliner that killed seventy-three people and the Justice Department linked him to at least thirty acts of sabotage. The *New York Times* called Bosch "one of the hemisphere's most notorious terrorists" (cited in Bortfeld and Naureckas 2001, p. 14). It turns out that Bush's son, Jeb, who was at the time a burgeoning Republican leader trying to curry favor with Miami's anti-Castro Cubans (gusanos), had lobbied for Bosch's release (Bortfeld and Naureckas 2001).

A Central Contradiction

President Bush's central position around which his justification for the war pivots—that we're fighting for democracy, pluralism, and civil liberties—is plagued by a profound contradiction. In a speech before Congress he piously intoned that terrorists "hate what they see right here in this chamber: a democratically elected government." He went on to say: "They hate our freedoms: our freedom of religion, our freedom of speech, our freedom to vote and assemble and disagree with each other. They want to overthrow existing governments in many Muslim countries such as Egypt, Saudi Arabia, and Jordan." He ended his speech by saying: "This is the fight of all who believe in progress and pluralism, tolerance and freedom."

But how could this be true, since any coalition that includes the Bonapartist rulers and corrupt monarchs of countries in the Muslim Crescent such as Egypt, Saudi Arabia, or Jordan cannot with any seriousness include the principles stated by Bush in his speech. After all, each of these countries restricts freedom of speech, the press, assembly, association, religion, and movement. Jordan is a monarchy whose security forces, like Israel's and like Saddam's Ba'ath Party enforcers, engage in torture and "extrajudicial" killings. The establishment of political parties are prohibited in Saudi Arabia. In fact, they have a religious police force—the *mouttawa*—to enforce a very conservative form of Islam. Egyptian security forces regularly arrest and torture people under the banner of fighting terrorism. Clearly, Bush's characterization of the United States as the pinnacle of civilization and every country who does not support his preemptive strikes as enemies of freedom is wrong-headed. Has Bush been educated in a capitalist version of a *madrass*? One would think so after listening to what he said at an October 11 press conference: "How do I respond when I see that in some Islamic countries there is vitriolic hatred for America? I'll tell you how I respond: I'm amazed. I'm amazed that there's such misunderstanding of what our country is about that people would hate us. I am—like most Americans, I just can't believe it because I know how good we are" (cited in Kovel 2002, p. 17).

Of course, much of Bush's rhetoric is to be expected; it is, in fact, politically de rigeur. Instead of listening to the incredulous comments exercised for the television cameras by Bush, the American public would be better served by the feminist Muslim voices of women such as Nawal El Saadawi, Asma Jahangir, Fatema Mernissi and the Revolutionary Association of Women in Afghanistan (RAWA) who condemn the attacks of September 11 and urge the Muslim world to promote a culture of democracy and tolerance within their own countries but who also implore the U.S. government to consider the root causes of terrorism, such as international interventions by the United States (Afzal-Khan 2002).

The world is becoming more attuned to what it views as the perversely obstinate and unredeemably pernicious exercise of U.S. double standards, to what, in the words of Ahmad could be termed "a new pathology of power" (cited in Glendinning 2002, p. 42). American concepts of justice appear to be riven with a perfidiously stage-managed spin. How else can you explain how the United States can celebrate democracy within its own borders and lay waste to it outside of them? How can the United States justify its economical, logistical, and military support of undemocratic regimes—some of which are involved in acts of genocide? And how can the U.S. government pillory those critics who raise these questions for the public record? What kind of racist arithmetic makes U.S. casualties more important than, for instance, the dead of indigenous Guatemala? The world will judge the United States not solely in terms of its payback against the repugnant and odious actions of Osama bin Laden and his followers but in terms of the collateral damage resulting from its regular bombing campaigns against rogue nations and the political integrity of its foreign and economic policies.

The terrorist attacks—real and anticipated—have given Bush a cloak of Teflon; criticism cannot stick. His public support with white males is as steady as a power plant in the middle of a Midwestern cornfield. All Bush has to do is put on a pair of cowboy boots and make bold proclamations, bereft of complexity. The shallower the proclamations, the more profound they appear as long as they are seeped in hagiography and biblical prophecy. Well, maybe not direct biblical prophecy, but the illusion of biblical prophecy. Apocalyptic overkill is the prophylactic gel that kills criticism on contact. The point is that it is profoundly more effective to hide complex geopolitics in the simplistic, infantilizing language of religious apocalypse and millennialist logic. Here, Manichean dualisms abound uncontested: good versus evil, civilized values versus tribal barbarism, warlords versus elected officials, and so on. Within such a scenario, the act of critique itself is seen as intemperate. Critique is tolerated in the opinion pages of newspapers, but not as editorial commentary. It can appear in local television venues with relatively small viewing audiences, but it cannot be tolerated on major televised news shows. Those who would critique a president in the midst of directing a global war against terrorism could only be seen by the public at large as self-interested, as a "spoiler" at best and a traitor at worst. We saw what happened to Bill Maher, Susan Sontag, the Dixie Chicks, Linda Ronstadt, Sean Penn, and Michael Moore.

Seemingly, all that Bush has to do is to remain militantly forthright: the United States has now geographically ordained a new global partnership bent on mass destruction (and therefore in need of destruction), a new axis of evil—North Korea, Iran, and Iraq—that must be terminated. You cannot name something as evil and then work out a compromise without you, yourself, being implicated in the very evil you ostensibly oppose. You cannot say: "America will not permit the world's most dangerous regimes to threaten us with the world's most destructive weapons" (cited in Umansky 2002) without backing up the threat. Which is why the special operations AC-130 Spectre gunship, whose conventional weaponry since the time of the Vietnam War has been used to pulverize any and every opponent of civilization that has dared stand in its path, is now to be fitted with a laser that can bring down missiles, melt holes in aircraft, and eliminate ground radar stations. A key factor here is that it might take years to defeat an evil regime but decades to defeat an axis of evil—even with laser-equipped gunships.

During a meeting of the Senate Judiciary Committee on December 6, 2001, then Attorney General John Ashcroft took conservative phrasemongering to new heights. In a rabid, sermonlike tone, Ashcroft issued a warning so politically toxic it spiked the air like aerosolized anthrax: "To those who scare peace-loving people with phantoms of lost liberty, my message is this: Your tactics only aid terrorists, for they erode our national unity and diminish our resolve. They give ammunition to America's enemies, and pause to America's friends. They encourage people of goodwill to remain silent in the face of evil" (Powers 2001, p. 18). These are ringing statements for someone whose nomination as attorney general was surrounded by controversy. It wasn't that long ago that Ashcroft, a devout evangelical Pentecostal who proclaimed at Bob Jones University that the United States has "no king but Jesus," and an open admirer of the Confederacy, had to defend himself against numerous allegations of racism during his confirmation hearings in the Senate in January 2001. An avowed opponent of desegregation, abortion, contraception, and gay rights, Ashcroft is clearly relishing his new duties that include undermining the Constitution. Unmoored from reason and set adrift in the lagoon of repressed rage, Ashcroft's deft machinations of legal priestcraft employed in developing draconian antiterrorism legislation in the wake of September 11 effectively scuppers civil liberties and the constitution in one foul swoop. Ashcroft's comments echo those made by former FBI Director William Webster, in 1982, when he argued that groups that "produce propaganda, disinformation, and 'legal assistance' may even be more dangerous than those who actually throw the bombs" (*New York Times*, June 24, 1982, as cited in *Workers Vanguard* 2001). The admonitions of both Webster and Ashcroft are underwritten by the logic of what Alexander Cockburn (2001a) calls "comic-book advisories" reflected in Bush hijo's statements such as "You're for us or against us" (p. 10). Clearly the stakes are too high to leave civil liberties in the hands of characters out of *Batman.*

Bush hijo believes that by challenging the interminable evil engulfing the globe, he can transform the maleficent violence of the terrorists into the sacred beneficence of America the Beautiful, promoting unanimity and the redemption of secular culture and its vile moral incohesion. Bush's behavior can be seen in the light of mimetic desire, as a reaffirmation of the spirit of the traditional values of civilization that emerges from the faultline separating the barbarians from the saved during moments of volcanic political upheaval. Bush's bombastic odes dedicated to the military machine, defining war as a way of cleansing the world of evil—an evil projected onto others so we can have our own sins expiated—are helping to prepare the cultural cornerstone for our new surrogate victim: the Muslim. Muslims have become ritual vehicles for catharsis, purification, purgation, and exorcism. Rene Girard (1977) notes that "the working basis of human thought, the process of 'symbolization,' is rooted in the surrogate victim" (p. 306). And while the act of generative unanimity vomited up immediately after September 11—symbolized in the phrase "United We Stand"—does not appear to be backed with the same resolve now that we have had time to engage with more digested reactions to the horror and bring to it a more critical stance (i.e., what did Bush know and when did he know it?), Bush is still crafty enough (with Karl Rove ideologically grafted to his brainstem) to serve his potential voters what they want so much to hear: We are the world's only superpower and that gives us the right to rewrite the rules of the game.

Christian fundamentalists see nuclear annihilation as a sign that Jesus Christ is about to return to Earth to prevent humankind from destroying itself. Only those who heed God's Word are to be protected from this nuclear holocaust. On February 27, 2002, the Doomsday Clock—on which midnight marks the onset of widespread nuclear destruction—was adjusted by physicist Leon Lederman to seven minutes to midnight, as a result of a higher perceived risk of international terrorism and tension between India and Pakistan. Bush, as well as his father and Reagan before him, appear to uphold this belief in the imminence of Armageddon. Once Jesus returns to earth after a hard-fought battle against the Axis of Evil, and sets up headquarters in Disneyland, He promises to all the faithful a holographic version of the Elysium Fields, accompanied by muzak versions of John Ashcroft's favorite Pentecostal hymns (courtesy of John Tesh on leave from some other galaxy).

Clearly, interpretation of religious texts can be used to justify the most heinous policies, and we needn't point all fingers at Muslims in this regard. When Nathan Lewin, a prominent DC attorney, writes that the families of Palestinian suicide bombers should be executed as a deterrent against such attacks, and he cites biblical destruction of the tribe of Amalek—where under God's orders, King Saul hacked to pieces King Agag and all of his Amalekite subjects—as a precedent for his proposal (Cockburn 2002b), many Christian fundamentalists would nod their head in agreement.

At the helm of just states must be leaders who exemplify a religiously motivated patriotism that positions income redistribution, multilateralism, and any restraint on individual liberty as mortal enemies of the development of democracy. They must defend global capitalism as the source of freedom, even to the extent of justifying bankruptcies of corporations such as Enron as part of the survival of the fittest (even religious pundits will draw upon Darwin-inspired theories if it suits their purposes). The terrorist attacks of September 11—that infamous saber slash across the cheekbones of world history—were truly acts against humanity. But Bush and his administration are defeating democracy in their vainglorious attempt to defend it.

At this point some might prefer to follow the advice of a novelist, and not an academic. John Le Carre (2001) admonishes the Manichean rivals that God is better left out of this debate:

> To imagine that God fights wars is to credit Him with the worst follies of mankind. God, if we know anything about Him, which I don't profess to, prefers effective food drops, dedicated medical teams, comfort and good tents for the homelessness and bereaved, and, without strings, a decent acceptance of our past sins and a readiness to put them right. He prefers us less greedy, less arrogant, less evangelical and less dismissive of life's losers. It's not a new world order, not yet, and it's not God's war. (p. 17)

President Bush has given himself over of late to comparing his policy in Iraq with the legacy of Harry Truman. Perhaps Bush needs a history lesson. "You don't 'prevent' anything by war except peace" (cited in Dickey 2004), President Harry S. Truman wrote in his memoirs. If President Bush is so fond of reaching into the rucksack of history only to distort the facts to suit his ideological predilictions, he would do well to take to heart some advice by the nineteenth-century satirical character Mr. Dooley, who defined a fanatic as someone who "does what he thinks th'Lord wud do if He only knew th'facts in th'case" (cited in Dickey 2004). Or he could follow some advice provided by John Quincy Adams when he was secretary of state—in 1821—that the United States "goes not abroad in search of monsters to destroy" lest the centerpiece of American policy change "from liberty to force" and thus America "might become the dictatress of the world: she would no longer be the ruler of her own spirit" (cited in Dickey 2004).

U.S. foreign policy pundits believe that it is possible to bomb a country into oblivion, install ex-CIA employees (in the case of Iraq's Allawi) or oil consultants (in the case of Afghanistan's Hamid Karzai), build up the infrastructure (using the same companies once commandeered by high-ranking members of White House administration), and leave liberation to take its course. Those whose country is being occupied, whose children are being killed in "surgical strikes" and whose homes are being demolished likely will never be convinced in the efficacy of trickle-down liberation. As Naomi Klein (2004) writes in the case of Iraq:

> Liberation will never be a trickle-down effect of this invasion because domination, not liberation, was always its goal. Even under the best scenario, the current choice in Iraq is not between Sadr's dangerous fundamentalism and a secular democratic government made up of trade unionists and feminists. It's between open elections—which risk handing power to fundamentalists but would also allow secular and moderate religious forces to organize—and rigged elections designed to leave the country in the hands of Iyad Allawi and the rest of his CIA/Mukhabarat-trained thugs, fully dependent on Washington for both money and might. (p. 12)

The U.S. occupiers see themselves as harbingers of democracy up against stubbornly fierce enemies of freedom. Frustration builds among troops who just don't understand why they are not greeted as liberators; after all, the U.S. military claims to be making attempts at respecting Islamic culture, holy sites, and local customs. Klein (2004) notes:

> This is the same culturally sensitive military whose first act as occupier was to hang a U.S. flag over the statue of Saddam Hussein in Firdos Square, sending the unmistakable message that Iraq had just been conquered, not liberated. This military is part of the same culturally sensitive occupation that thought it would be a good idea to get an NYU professor who had never been to Iraq to write the first draft of Iraq's Constitution, then unveiled a new blue-and-white Iraqi flag that looked remarkably like the Israeli flag (both schemes were scrapped due to public outrage). It's the same military that, in April, bombed Falluja's Abdel-Aziz al-Samarrai mosque and in August provoked the siege that damaged mosaics on the outer walls of Najaf's sacred Imam Ali Shrine. (p. 30)

One can only wonder what the great architect of the American Revolution and nonpareil revolutionary figure Thomas Paine, who fought against class privilege and the entitled aristocracy, would make of today's Republican administration. The propertied class who decried Paine for penning *The Rights of Man*, the British government who charged him with treason, the preachers throughout the country who, during the entire nineteenth century, made his name synonymous with the Devil would, no doubt, feel comfortable in the current White House. Without question, Paine would be in trouble. Lapham (2002) remarks: "Were Paine still within reach of the federal authorities, Attorney General John Ashcroft undoubtedly would prosecute him for blasphemy under a technologically enhanced version of the Alien and Sedition Acts" (p. 7). Lapham elaborates:

Paine would have recognized the government now situated in Washington as
royalist in sentiment, "monarchical" and "aristocratical" in its actions, Federal-
ist in its mistrust of freedom, imperialist in the bluster of its military pretensions,
evangelical in its worship of property. In the White House we have a president
appointed by the Supreme Court; at the Justice Department, an attorney general
believing that in America "we have no kind but Jesus"; in both houses of Congress, a corpulent majority that on matters of tax and regulatory policy votes its
allegiance to the principles of hereditary succession and class privilege.
(p. 9)

By all reckoning, George Bush and his administration have enjoyed a very
successful war. Bush has impressively adhered to the "three grand imperatives of geostrategy" as put forward by Zbigniew Brzezinski, former national
security advisor to Jimmy Carter and the infamous architect of Washington's
policy of creating ultrareactionary, anticommunist Islamic terrorists (such as
the Jamiat-ul-Ulema-e-Islam and its many breakaway factions) to defeat the
People's Democratic Party of Afghanistan and Soviet troops. These imperatives are "to prevent collusion and maintain security among the vassals, to
keep tributaries pliant and protected, and to keep the barbarians from coming
together" (cited in Lorimer 2002). The engineering of the globe is proceeding
apace and the sustained conquest of other parts of the globe are (at the very
least) in their planning stages. But Bush and his hawk-headed advisors are really part of the larger political will of global market agents and the logic of
transnational capital. It is not surprising to read in a 1995 Harper's Round-
table discussion titled "A Revolution, or Business as Usual?" Wall Street ed-
itorialist David Frum arguing that the government should "get rid of"
Medicare, Medicaid, and all other social programs for children, the poor, the
elderly, and the racially or otherwise disadvantaged "overnight" if possible,
and conservative pundit William Kristol is railing against the Roosevelt New
Deal and proclaiming that "you cannot have a federal guarantee that people
won't starve" (*Harper's Magazine*, March 1995, p. 42, as cited in McMurtry
in press). It is as if the transnationalization of the productive forces and the
emergence of the transnational capitalist class carries an ethnocidal *logos*
within its structural unconscious.

As Bush moves toward the creation of a permanent war, the Left is faced
with powerful challenges. One of these is to move beyond a narrow anti-U.S.
imperialism and to get on with the crucial business of class struggle against
monopoly capitalism. As Peter Hudis (2002) importantly remarks, we need to
move beyond the limitations of an anti-U.S. imperialism and get back to the
principled anti-imperialism displayed by Lenin during World War I. In this
sense, we need to move away from an anti-Westernism and get on with the
task of supporting class struggle in the interests of creating a new human

society. Remaining critical of U.S. foreign and economic policies is important but in our practice of criticism we need to avoid falling into a reactionary anti-Americanism. Instead, it is important to set our sights on the struggle against monopoly capitalism, which is, after all, at the root of imperialism. As Hudis (2002) notes, imperialism is an outgrowth, a state monopoly capitalism writ large on the world stage.

Facing up to acts of U.S. imperialism provides the crucial context for discussing world history in light of the globalization of capitalism and contemporary imbroglios that flare up the night skies of international geopolitics. We in the United States must share the burden of history. We cannot exempt our history from discussion and debate simply because it is *our* history. Our frangible history. We are not morally or politically above the fray. To share the burden of history we need to become critically self-reflexive about our political system, its economic, domestic, and foreign policies in the context of the globalization of capitalism or what I have called the new imperialism.

Part of the challenge that faces the educational left is in redefining the role of the intellectual. In a review of *Where Have All the Intellectuals Gone?* by Frank Furedi, Terry Eagleton (2004) joins Furedi in decrying the current demise of the critical intellectual and the rise of the cultural intellectual as social therapist:

> With the decline of the critical intellectual, the thinker gives way to the expert, politics yields to technocracy, and culture and education lapse into forms of social therapy. The promotion of ideas plays second fiddle to the provision of services. Art and culture become substitute forms of cohesion, participation and self-esteem in a deeply divided society. Culture is deployed to make us feel good about ourselves, rather than to tackle the causes of those divisions, implying that social exclusion is simply a psychological affair. That to feel bad about ourselves is the first step towards transforming our situation is thus neatly side-stepped. What matters is not the quality of the activity, but whether it gets people off the streets. Extravagant justifications for culture are piously touted: it can cure crime, promote social bonding, pump up self-assurance, even tackle Aids. It helps to heal conflict and create community—a case, ironically, dear to the heart of that bogeyman of the anti-elitists, Matthew Arnold.

Eagleton also joins Furedi in condemning the uncritical affirmation of student experience in university settings and the phony populism that is little more than a reheated paternalism:

> The feel-good factor flourishes in education as well. University academics are discouraged from fostering adversarial debate, in case it should hurt someone's feelings. Why indulge in it anyway, if what matters is not truth but self-expression? "Student-centered learning" assumes that the student's "personal experience" is to

be revered rather than challenged. People are to be comforted rather than confronted. In what one American sociologist has termed the McDonaldisation of the universities, students are redefined as consumers of services rather than junior partners in a public service. This phony populism, as Furedi points out, is in fact a thinly veiled paternalism, assuming as it does that ordinary men and women aren't up to having their experience questioned. Rigorous discriminations are branded as "elitist"—an elitist attitude in itself, given that ordinary people have always fiercely argued the toss over the relative merits of everything from films to football clubs. Meanwhile, libraries try frantically not to look like libraries, or to let slip intimidatingly elitist words such as "book."

And while Eagleton (despite the fact that I find Furedi's work woefully problematic in other contexts) is on the mark in his descriptions of what happens when culture is substituted for analysis and when the search for harmony and cohesion replaces critique, it is James Petras who offers the most illuminating discussion on what is at stake in the formation of the critical intellectual within the academy.

In discussing responses to the imperial barbarism and corruption of the empire, Petras (2001) distinguishes stoics, cynics, pessimists, and critical intellectuals (categories that encompass those who serve the hegemony of empire, from the prostrated academics who bend their knees in the face of capitalism while at the same time denouncing its excesses to the coffee-sipping intellectuals of Soho) from what he refers to as irreverent intellectuals (who serve the cause of developing revolutionary socialist consciousness and a new internationalism). The stoics are repulsed by the "predatory pillage of the empire" but because they are paralyzed by feelings of political impotence, choose to form small cadres of academics in order to debate theory in as much isolation as possible from both the imperial powers and the oppressed and degraded masses. The cynics condemn both the victims of predatory capitalism and their victimizers as equally afflicted with consumerism; they believe that the oppressed masses seek advantage only to reverse the roles of oppressor and oppressed. The cynics are obsessed with the history of failed revolutions where the exploited eventually become the exploiters. They usually work in universities and specialize in providing testimonials to the perversions of liberation movements. The pessimists are usually leftists or ex-leftists who are also obsessed with the historical defeats of revolutionary social movements, which they have come to see as inevitable and irreversible, but who use these defeats as a pretext for adopting a pragmatic accommodation with the status quo. The have a motivated amnesia for new revolutionary movements now struggling to oppose the empire (i.e., movements by militant farmers and transport workers) and use their pessimism as an alibi for inaction and disengagement. The pessimists are reduced to a liberal politics who can often be co-opted by the ideologists of empire. Critical intellectuals frequently gain notoriety among the educated classes. Professing indignation at the ravages of empire and neoliberalism and attempting to expose their lies, critical intellectuals appeal to the elite to reform the power structures so that the poor will no longer suffer. This collaborationist approach of critical intellectuals "vents indignation that resonates with the educated classes without asking them to sacrifice anything" (Petras 2001, p. 15). In contrast to all of the aforementioned, the irreverent intellectual respects the militants on the frontlines of the anticapitalist and anti-imperialist struggles. Petras (2001) describes them as "self-ironic anti-heroes whose work is respected by the people who are actively working for basic transformation" (p. 15). He notes that they are "objectively partisan and partisanly objective" and work together with intellectuals and activists involved in popular struggles:

> They conduct research looking for original sources of data. They create their own indicators and concepts, for example, to identify the real depths of poverty, exploitation and exclusion. They recognise that there are a few intellectuals in prestigious institutions and award recipients who are clearly committed to popular struggles, and they acknowledge that these exceptions should be noted, while recognizing the many others who in climbing the academic ladder succumb to the blandishments of bourgeois certification. The irreverent intellectuals admire a Jean-Paul Sartre, who rejected a Nobel Prize in the midst of the Vietnam War. Most of all, the irreverent intellectuals fight against bourgeois hegemony within the left by integrating their writing and teaching with practice, avoiding divided loyalties. (Petras 2001, p. 15)

Working as irreverent intellectuals means shifting from what Zygmunt Bauman (2002, p. 14) calls a "solidarity of fate" (we are all interdependent creatures sharing the planet) to a "solidarity of purpose and action" (to live in dignity, to be free from fear, and to be allowed to pursue happiness). While it is true that Marx described human beings as ensembles of social relations, Marx's value system was based on an inherent or internal criterion and not on imposed, external criteria. In his *Theses on Feuerbach* (see *The German Ideology*), Marx affirmed certain common attributes shared by all human beings and the existence of a common human nature in the sense that human beings are all social, economic, political, and moral beings. It is here that we can begin anew. Where we can be joined by that which we all share, our common humanity, and our quest for freedom and liberty. We need to draw upon such a common humanity to deepen our scientific and philosophical understanding of the world, not in order to interpret the world, but as Marx argued, in order to change it. To change the world is to humanize the world in such a fashion that terrorism recedes into the bad infinity of the past and comradeship and creativity lock arms in a commitment to bring about a global society of peace and justice. The revolutionary multicultural unity sought by irreverent intellectuals is unflaggingly opposed to its class collaborationist counterpart represented by Bush, Powell, and Rice. We must work toward a reappropriation of our confiscated rights in the larger struggle for economic justice.

In order to be effective in the fight against terrorism, teachers also need to move beyond solutions that legitimize or naturalize capitalist-driven globalization as the only viable option available for humanity, and instead focus on the needs of the world's population. Feldman and Lotz (in press) have put forward a number of important socialist principles that are designed to extend the gains and advances that capitalism has given the few, to people in all countries, through the struggle toward and development of a global, socialist society. Teachers would do well to incorporate these principles in their struggle for a critical pedagogy. The most important of these principles include the social ownership of land, banking and finance, transport and communications infrastructure; the social ownership of production facilities of the major corporations through a variety of forms of co-ownership; democratic control and self-management of economic and financial resources that include public services; steering the development of productive capacity toward satisfying need; ecologically sustainable production and distribution; encouraging and supporting small-scale enterprises, creative workers and farmers; favoring local production for local needs; and facilitating the development of the "conscious market." The central aims for the classless society for which these principles are put into practice encompass the following: ensuring that the majority have access to the benefits currently only available to the few; ensuring survival of the planet, ecosystems, and humanity; the creation of a society based on cooperation, satisfying need and not profit; releasing the potential of automation, substantially reducing working hours; overcoming alienation of people from their work, what is produced, and society as a whole; employing an abundance of products to alleviate poverty and need worldwide; allowing and enabling people to fulfill their potential and aspirations; and making health and well-being the single dominant social objective for the global population.

Feldman and Lotz (in press) have used these principles and aims in their development of specific strategies for addressing issues of the state, including communications and the media, the legal system, state administration, the political system, criminal law, and the police as well as cultural strategies aimed at the visual arts, the music industry, the Internet, and the educational system. They have also worked out broad strategies for transforming the global financial system and addressing the ecological crisis. Visiting such alternatives is not enough; teachers need to be actively engaged in creating their own strategies and programs for transcending the alienating imperatives of capital as a structure and bringing us closer to the goal of creating a socialist future.

As critical social agents, whether we are working inside or outside the academy, we are faced with a new sense of urgency in our fight to create social justice on a global scale, establishing what Karl Marx called a "positive humanism" to replace what Arendt (1955) called the "negative solidarity" of atomized and displaced individuals. At a time when Marxist social theory seems destined for the political dustbin, it is needed more than ever to help us understand the forces and relations that now shape our national and international destinies. As Ollman (2001) opines:

> Marxism encourages us to contextualize what happened and who is involved; of how this happened in our world today and how it fits into history, into time. When you do that you can't avoid dealing with and trying to make sense of the role that the U.S. has played in its foreign policy and also in global capitalism. One must look at that and figure out ways of dealing with it so that we can handle not only September 11th but all of the September 11ths which are coming up ahead. (p. 7)

ACKNOWLEDGMENT

The author wishes to thank Carl Boggs for suggestions on an earlier draft of this chapter. This chapter was previously published in Carl Boggs, ed., *Empire, War, and Terrorism: U.S. Militarism and the New World Order* (New York: Routledge, 2004), pp. 149–90. Reprinted with permission.

REFERENCES

Afzal-Khan, F. 2002. "Here Are the Muslim Feminist Voices, Mr. Rushdie!" *Television & New Media*, 3(2, May), 139–142.

Ahmad, A. 2000. *A Task That Never Ends*. Unpublished manuscript, at www.peoplesgeography.org/ahmed.html.

Ahmad, E. 1998. *Terrorism: Theirs and Ours*. A presentation at the University of Boulder, Colorado, October 12, 1998. Association of Tamils of Eelam & Sri Lanka in the US. At www.sangam.org/ANALYSIS/Ahmad.htm.

Amin, S. 2001. "Political Islam." *Covert Action Quarterly*, 71 (Winter), 3–6.

Anderson, K. 2001. "Immigrant Victims of the WTC Attack." *NACLA Report on the Americas*, XXXV(3), 1–2, 4.

Arendt, H. 1955. *The Origins of Totalitarianism*. London: George Allen and Unwin.

Baker, D. 2001. "From New Economy to War Economy." *Dollars & Sense*, 238, (November–December), 39.

Bamford, J. 2001. *Body of Secrets: Anatomy of the Ultra-Secret National Security Agency. From the Cold War through the Dawn of a New Century*. New York: Doubleday.

Barber, B. 2002. "Beyond Jihad vs. McWorld: On Terrorism and the New Democratic Realism." *The Nation*, 274(2, January 21), 11–18.

Barry, T. 2002. "Frontier Justice: A Weekly Chronicle." *The Progressive Response*, 6(22, July 25), 1–12, at www.fpif.org/progresp/volume6/v6n22.html.

Barsamian, D. 2001a. Arundhati Roy Interview, at file:///Hard%20Drive/The%20Progressive%20Interview%20%7C%20Dav.

Barsamian, D. 2001b. Edward Said Interview. *The Progressive*. November, at www.progressive.org.

Barsamian, D. 2001c. "What They Want is My Silence: Edward Said Interview." *International Socialist Review*, 18 (June–July), at www.isreview.org/issues/18/Said_part1.shtml.

Bauman, Z. 2002. "Global Solidarity." *Tikkun*, 17(1, January–February), 12–14, 62.

Beccaria, C. 1963 [1764]. *On Crimes and Punishment*. Translated and with an introduction by Henry Paolucci. New York: Macmillan.

Bennett, W. 2002. *Why We Fight: Moral Clarity and the War on Terrorism*. New York: Doubleday.

Bortfeld, J., and Naureckas, J. 2001. Extra! 14(3, June), 14.

Boyle, F. 2001. Speech at Illinois Disciples. October 18, 2001, at msanews.mynet?Scholars/Boyle/nowar.html

Brown, M. H. 2001. "Bioterrorism: Nothing New To Native Americans." *Hartford Courant*. November 1, at www.ctnow.com/news/local/hc-smallpox1031.artnov01.story.

Callinicos, A. 2001. *Against the Third Way*. Cambridge: Polity Press.

Castro, F. 2001. Televised Presentation by Commander in Chief Fidel Castro Ruz, President of the Republic of Cuba, on the Present International Situation, the Economic and World Crisis and its Impact on Cuba. Havana, November 2, 2001.

Chomsky, N. 2001a. *9-11*. New York: Seven Stories Press, at www.guardian.co.uk/Archive/Article/0,4273,4266289,00.html.

Chomsky, N. 2001b. "The New War against Terror." *Counterpunch*. October 24, at www.counterpunch.org/chomskyterror.html.

Cockburn, A. 2001a. "Sharon or Arafat: Which is the Sponsor of Terror?" *The Nation*, 273(21, December 24), 10.

Cockburn, A. 2001b. "The Wide World of Torture." *The Nation*, 273(17, November 26), 10.

Cockburn, A. 2002a. "Forbidden Truth?" *The Nation*, 274(3, January 28), 9.

Cockburn, A. 2002b. "Terrorism as Normalcy." *The Nation*, 275(1, July), 9.

Coen, R. 2002. "*New York Times* Buries Stories of Airstrikes on Civilians." *Extra! Update*. February, 3.

Congressional Statement. Federal Bureau of Investigation. May 10, 2001, at www.fbi.gov/congress/congress01/freeh051001.htm.

Corson, T. 2001. "The Race to Bomb." *The Nation*, 273(13, October 29), 25–30.

Cypher, J. M. 2002. "Return of the Iron Triangle: The New Military Buildup." *Dollars & Sense* 239, January–February, 16–19, 37–38.

Dickey, C. 2004. *Newsweek National News*, at www.msnbc.msn.com/id/5935541/site/newsweek/.

Dorfman, A. 2001. "Unique No More." *Counterpunch*. October 3, at www
.counterpunch.org/dorman.html.

Eagelton, T. 2004. "Too Clever by Half." *New Statesman*. September 13, at www.new
statesman.com/site.php3?newTemplate=NSArticle_NS&newDisplay
URN=200409130043.

Eco, U. 2001. "The Roots of Conflict." *The Guardian*. October 13, at www
.guardian.co.uk/Archive/Article/0,4273,4275868,00.html.

El-Sayed Sae'ed, Mohammad. 2001. "Osama bin Laden: A Primitive Rebel." *Islam On-line*. October 23, at www.islam-online.net/english/Views/2001/10/
article11.shtml.

Feldman, P., and Lotz, C. In press. *A World to Win! Ideas for a Future without Global
Capitalism*. London: Movement for a Socialist Future.

Fishman, T. 2002. "Making A Killing: The Myth of Capital's Good Intentions."
Harper's Magazine, 1850(1827, August), 33–41.

Fuentes, C. 2001. "New Reality, New Legality." *El Andar*, 12(3, Fall–Winter),
33–34.

Furedi, F. 2004. *Where Have All the Intellectuals Gone?* London: Continuum.

Galeano, E. 2000. *Upside Down: A Primer for the Looking-Glass World*. New York:
Metropolitan Books.

Galeano, E. 2001. "The Theatre of Good and Evil." *La Jornada*. September 21, translated by Justin Podur at progressiveaustin.org/galeano.htm.

Girard, R. 1977. *Violence and the Sacred*. Translated by Patrick Gregory. Baltimore,
Md.: Johns Hopkins University Press.

Glendinning, C. 2002. "Remembering Decolonization." *Tikkun*, 17(1, January–
February) 41–43.

Goering, H. Cited in Fogel, C. 2001. Globalization: The Destruction of the Rule of
Law. Defence of Canadian Liberty Committee. November 21, 2001, at www
.canadianliberty.bc.ca/liberty-vs-security/no-21-2-1.html.

Goldstein, R. 2002. "Foundations Are in Place for Martial Law in the US." *The Sydney Morning Herald*. July 27, at smh.com.au/articles/2002/07/27/1027497418339
.html.

Grosso, M. 1995. *The Millennium Myth: Love and Death at the End of Time*.
Wheaton, Ill.: Quest Books.

Hart, P. 2001. "No Spin Zone?" *Extra!* 14(6, December), 8.

Hart, P., and Ackerman, S. 2001. "Patriotism & Censorship." *Extra!* 14(6, December),
6–9.

Hess, J. L. 2002. "Indirect from the Battlefield." *Extra! Update*, (February), 4.

Hill, D. 2001. "State Theory and the Neo-Liberal Reconstruction of Schooling and
Teacher Education: A Structuralist Neo-Marxist Critique of Postmodernist, Quasi-
Postmodernist, and Culturalist Neo-Marxist Theory." *British Journal of Sociology
of Education*, 22(1), 137–157.

Hill, D., and Cole, M. 2001. "Social Class." In *Schooling and Equality: Fact, Concept
and Policy*, edited by D. Hill and M. Cole, 137–159. London: Kogan Page.

Hudis, P. 2001. "Terrorism, Bush's Retaliation Show Inhumanity of Class Society."
News & Letters, 46(8, October), 1, 10–11.

Hudis, P. 2002. The Power of Negativity *in Today's Search for a Way to Transform Reality.* Presentation to Expanded Resident Editorial Board on January 20, 2002. Chicago: News & Letters.

Huntington, S. 1996. *The Clash of Civilizations and the Remaking of World Order.* New York: Touchstone Books.

Johnson, C. 2000. *Blowback: The Costs and Consequences of American Empire.* New York: Owl Books.

Johnson, C. 2001. "Blowback." *The Nation,* 273(11, October 15), 13–15.

Kawell, J. 2001. "Terror's Latin American Profile." *NACLA Report on the Americas,* XXXV(3), 50–53.

Keever, B. 2004. *News Zero: The New York Times and the Bomb.* Monroe, Maine: Common Courage Press.

Kellner, D. 2001. *September 11, Terror War, and Blowback.* Unpublished manuscript.

Klare, M. T. 2001a. "Asking 'Why.'" *Foreign Policy in Focus.* September, at fpif.org/commentary/0109why.html.

Klare, M. T. 2001b. "The Geopolitics of War." *The Nation,* 273(14, November 5), 11–15.

Klare, M. T. 2001c. *Resource Wars: The New Landscape of Global Conflict.* New York: Metropolitan Books.

Klare, M. 2002. "Endless Military Superiority." *The Nation,* 275(3, June 15), 12–16.

Klein, N. 2004. "You Can't Bomb Beliefs." *The Nation,* 279(12, October 18), 12, 30.

Kovel, J. 2002. "Ground Work." *Tikkun,* 17(1, January–February), 17, 20.

Lapham, L. 2001. "Drums along the Potomac." *Harper's Magazine.* 303(1818, November), 35–41.

Lapham, L. H. 2002a. "Notebook: Deus Lo Volt." *Harper's Magazine,* 304(1824, May), 7-9.

Lapham, L. 2002b. "Uncommon Sense." *Harper's Magazine,* 305(1826, July), 7–9.

Le Carre, J. 2001. "A War We Cannot Win." *The Nation,* 273(16, November 19), 15–17.

Lorimer, D. 2002. "Imperialism in the 21st Century." *Links,* 21, (May–August), at www.dsp.org.au/links/back/issue21/Lorimer/htm.

Los Angeles Times. 2001. "Response to Terror: In Brief." *Los Angeles Times,* Tuesday, November 16, A10.

Luxemburg, R. 1919. *The Crisis in German Social Democracy: The Junius Pamphlet.* New York: The Socialist Publication Society.

Macdonald, L. 2002. "The Nature of Islamic Fundamentalism." *Links,* no. 21. (May–August), at www.dsp.org.au/links/back/issue21/Macdonald/htm.

Marable, M. 2001a. "The Failure of U.S. Foreign Policies. Along the Color Line. November, at www.manningmarable.net.

Marable, M. 2001b. "Terrorism and the Struggle for Peace." *Along the Color Line,* at www.manningmarable.net.

Maresca, J. 1998. Testimony by John J. Maresca, Vice President, International Relations, Unocal Corporation to House Committee on International Relations, Subcommittee on Asia and the Pacific, February 12, 1998, Washington, D.C., at file:///Hard%20Drive/Statement%20by%20John%20J.%20Maresca%2C%20V.

Marlowe, L. 2001. "US Efforts to Make Peace Summed up by 'Oil.'" *The Irish Times.* Monday, November 19, at www.ireland.com/newspaper/world/2001/1119/wor8 .htm.

Marx, K. 1973. *Grundrisse: Foundations of the Critique of Political Economy.* Translated by M. Nicolaus. London: Penguin Books.

Marx, K. 1845 [1998]. *The German Ideology.* Amherst, NY: Prometheus Books.

McLaren, P., and Pinkney-Pastrana, J. 2001. "Cuba, Yanquizacion, and the Cult of Elian Gonzales: A View from the 'Enlightened' States." *International Journal of Qualitative Studies in Education,* edited by D. Blum and P. McLaren, vol. 14, no. 2, 201–219.

McMurtry, J. 2001. "Why Is There a War in Afghanistan?" Opening address, Science for Peace Forum and Teach-in, University of Toronto, Canada, December 9, 1-13, at scienceforpeace.sa.utoronto.ca/special_activities/mcmurtry_page.html.

McMurtry, J. In press. *Value Wars: Moral Philosophy and Humanity.* London: Pluto Press.

"Media Advisory: Pentagon Plan Is Undemocratic, Possibly Illegal. FAIR-L (Fairness and Accuracy in Reporting, Media Analysis, Critiques, and Activism)." 2002, February 19, at fair@fair.org .

Mészáros, I. 1999. "Marxism, the Capital System, and Social Revolution: An Interview with István Mészáros." *Science and Society,* 63(3), 338–361.

Mikulan, S. 2001. "A Small Universe of People." *LA Weekly,* 24(2, November 30–December 6), 22–23.

Monbiot, G. 2001a. "Backyard Terrorism." *The Guardian.* October 30, at www.guardian.co.uk/Archive/Article/0,4273,4287795,00.html.

Monbiot, G. 2001b. "The Taliban of the West." *The Guardian.* Tuesday, December 18, at www.guardian.co.uk/Archive/Article/0,4273,4321856,00.html.

Monchinski, T. 2001. "Capitalist Schooling: An Interview with Bertell Ollman," at es-erver.org/clogic/4-1/monchinski.html.

Niva, S. 2001a. "Addressing the Sources of Middle Eastern Violence against the United States." Common Dreams News Center. Friday, September 14, 2001, at www.commondreams.org/views01/0914-04.htm.

Niva, S. 2001b. "Fight the Roots of Terrorism." Common Dreams News Center. Friday, September 21, at commondreams.org/views01/0921-06.htm.

O'Brien, B. 2001. "Say Anything." *Slate Magazine.* Saturday, December 15, at slate@slate.com.

Ollman, B. 2001. *How to Take an Exam and Remake the World.* Montreal: Black Rose Books.

Pasco, J. O. 2002."Cheney Hits Right Notes for Nixon Library Audience." *Los Angeles Times,* Wednesday, February 20, B6.

Petras, J. 2001. "Notes Toward an Understanding of Revolutionary Politics Today." *Links,* no. 19 (September–December), at www.dsp.org.au/links/back/issue19/ petras.htm.

Petras, J. 2002a. "Empire without Imperialists?" *Links,* 20 (January–April), at www.dsp.org.au/links/back/issue20/Petras.htm.

Petras, J. 2002b. "Signs of a Police State are Everywhere." *Z Magazine*, 15(1, January), 10–12.

Petras, J, and Veltmeyer, H. 2001. *Globalization Unmasked: Imperialism in the 21ˢᵗ Century*. London: ZedBooks.

Pilger, J. 1999. *Hidden Agendas*. London: Vintage.

Pilger, J. 2001a. "There Is No War on Terrorism. If There Was, the SAS Would Be Storming the Beaches of Florida." *New Statesman*, 14(680, October 29), 16–18.

Pilger, J. (2001b, October 29). "This War Is a Farce." *The Mirror*, at mirror. icnetwork.co.uk/printable_version.cfm?objectid=11392430.

Powers, J. 2001. "Wyatt Earp and the Witchfinder General." *LA Weekly*, 24(4, December 14–20), 18.

Powers, J. 2002. "Rank and Yank at Enron, or, the Fine Art of Bankruptcy." *LA Weekly*, 24(3, January), 11–17.

Press, E. 2002. "Rebel With a Cause: The Re-Education of Joseph Stiglitz." *The Nation*, 274(22, June 10), 11–16.

Rendall, S., and Kosseff, A. 2004. "I'm Not a Leftist, But I Play One on TV." *Extra!*, 17(5, October), 17–23.

Rikowski, G. 2000. *Messing with the Explosive Commodity: School Improvement, Educational Research and Labor-Power in the Era of Global Capitalism*. A paper prepared for the Symposium on "If We Aren't Pursuing Improvement, What Are We Doing?" British Educational Research Association Conference 2000, Cardiff University, Wales. September 7, Session 3.4.

Rikowski, G. 2001a. *The Battle in Seattle: Its Significance for Education*. London: Tufnell Press.

Rikowski, G. 2001b. *After the Manuscript Broke off: Thoughts on Marx, Social Class and Education*. A paper prepared for the British Sociological Association, Education Study Group Meeting, King's College London, June 23.

Robinson, W. 2001a. "Social Theory and Globalization: The Rise of a Transnational State." *Theory and Society*, 30, 157–200.

Robinson, W. 2001b. "Response to McMichael, Block, and Goldfrank." *Theory and Society*, 30, 223–236.

Robinson, W. 2001c. *The Debate on Globalization, The Transnational Capitalist Class, and the Rise of a Transnational State*. Paper delivered at the 2001 meeting of the American Sociological Association, Anaheim Hilton, Los Angeles, August 18–21.

Robinson, W. 2001–2002. "Global Capitalism and Nation-State-Centric Thinking— What We Don't See When We Do See Nation-States: Response to Critics." *Science & Society*, 65(1, Winter), 500–508.

Robinson, W., and Harris, J. 2000. "Towards a Global Ruling Class? Globalization and the Transnational Capitalist Class." *Science & Society*, 64(1, Spring), 11–54.

Roy, A. 2001a. "The Algebra of Infinite Justice." *The Guardian*. Sunday, September 29.

Roy, A. 2001b. "Brutality Smeared in Peanut Butter." *The Guardian*, October 23, at www.guardian.co.uk/.

Roy, A. 2001c. "War Is Peace." *Z Magazine, a*t www.zmag.org.

Said, E. 2001. "Islam and the West Are Inadequate Banners." *The Observer.* September 16, at www.observer.co.uk/comment/story/0,6903,552764,00.html.

Schell, J. 2001. "A Chain Reaction." *The Nation,* 273(21), 9.

Scigliano, E. 2001. "Naming—and Un-naming—Names." *The Nation,* 273(22, December 31), 16.

Shami, S. 2001. "A Review of *Walimath li-A'shab al-Bahr (Banquet for Seaweed)* by Haydar Haydar." *Workers Vanguard,* no. 770 (December 7), 6–7, 11.

Statement of the Emergency Committee against U.S. Intervention I Afghanistan. 2001. *Fight Back!* 4(4, Fall), 11–12.

Sudetic, C. 2001. "The Betrayal of Basra." *Mother Jones,* December, 46–51, 90–92.

Tobin, E. 2002. "Dubyaspeak." *The Nation,* 275(5, August 5–12), 40–42.

Tryferis, A. 2001. "Bill's Blather." *New Times,* December 6–12, 7.

Turner, D. 1983. *Marxism and Christianity.* Oxford: Basil Blackwell.

Umansky, E. 2002. "Eyeing the Axis." *Slate Magazine.* February 20, at slate@slate.com.

Vidal, G. 2004. "State of the Union, 2004." *The Nation,* 279(7, September), 23–29.

Weiner, B. 2002. "The War on Terrorism for Dummies." *Counterpunch.* March 3, 3t www.counterpunch.org/weinerdummies.html (accessed March 3, 2002).

Weinstein, H., Briscoe, D., and Landberg, M. 2002. "Civil Liberties Take a Back Seat to Safety." *Los Angeles Times,* March, 20, A1.

Woolcott, J. 2001. "Terror on the Dotted Line." *Vanity Fair,* January, 50–55.

Woolcott, J. 2004. *Attack Poodles and Other Media Mutants: The Looting of the News in a Time of Terror.* New York: Miramax Books.

Workers Vanguard. 2001. "Anti-Terror" Law: Shredding Your Rights." *Workers Vanguard,* no. 770, December 7, 1, 8–10.

Zinn, H. 2001. "Beyond the Fame." Media Education Foundation, at mediaed.sitepassport.net/btf/Zinn/index_html.

8

God's Cowboy Warrior: Christianity, Globalization, and the False Prophets of Imperialism

Peter McLaren and Nathalia E. Jaramillo

Whose God decides which is a "just war" and which isn't? George Bush senior once said: "I will never apologize for the United States. I don't care what the facts are." When the president of the most powerful country in the world doesn't need to care what the facts are, then we can at least be sure we have entered the Age of Empire.

—Arundhati Roy

Q: You recently created a stir when you defended the interrogation techniques at Abu Ghraib.
A: Most of the people in Mississippi came up to me and said: "Thank Goodness. America comes first." Interrogation is not a Sunday-school class. You don't get information that will save American lives by withholding pancakes.
[Trent Lott]

—Solomon (2004)

Under the sign of the Stars and Stripes, the war against terrorism unchains the attack dogs of the New World Order in defense of civilization. In the process, the United States has crossed the threshold of militant authoritarianism and goose-stepped onto the global balcony of neofascism, befouling the Constitution along the way. As long as the nation keeps cheering, and Bush's impish jaw juts ever forward, the stench goes unnoticed.

Among the Bush administration, there is a concerted effort to meld political rhetoric and apocalyptic discourse as part of a larger politics of fear and paranoia. Like a priest of the black arts, Bush has successfully disinterred the remnants of Ronald Reagan's rhetoric from the graveyard of chiliastic fantasies, appropriated it for his own interests, and played it in public like a charm. Self-fashioning one's image through the use of messianic and millenarian tropes works best on the intended audience (in this case, the American public) when the performance is disabused of shrillness, and remains unrestrained, confident, anagogic, and sometimes allegorical. Fascist plainspeak is a discursive rendering that is straightforward and unapologetic, and, like an iceberg, does most of the damage beneath the surface. Bush's handlers are masters of the fascist spin, and Bush is a perfect candidate since he hardly needs any ideological persuasion to get on board the imperial bandwagon. He is the perfect host for collapsing the distinction between religious authoritarianism and politics. Bush's defense of the war on terrorism works largely through archetypal association, and operates in the crucible of the structural unconscious. Bush may believe that Providence has assigned him the arduous yet glorious task of rescuing America from the Satanic forces of evil, as if he, himself, were the embodiment of the generalized will and the unalloyed spirit of the American people. Evoking the role of the divine prophet who identifies with the sword arm of retribution, Bush reveals the eschatological undertow to the war on terrorism, perhaps most evident in his totalizing and Manichean pronouncements where he likens bin Laden and his chthonic warriors to absolute evil, and the United States to the apogee of freedom and goodness.

Employing war as an instrument of its foreign policy, the Bush administration attacked Iraq to control two-thirds of the known reserves of the world's oil, to strengthen conditions for Israel in the region, to set the stage for a possible attack on Iran, and to build a political beachhead for creating more "democratic" client regimes in the Middle East. In addition, we believe that Bush wants to be seen as offering some kind of metaphysical hope for the rebirth of the American spirit that had wasted away in a morally comatose state within what is perceived by many conservatives as the debauched interregnum of the Clinton years. Ever since the myth of America as God's chosen nation ingressed into the collective unconscious of the American people, U.S. politics has been primed for the appearance of national saviors and sinners. Without skipping an opportunistic beat, Bush has assumed the mantle of *jefe* global warlord, taken up the Hammer of Thor, and is continuing to wield it recklessly, in blatant disregard for the court of world opinion. Bush appears to believe that God's elect—the American *ubermenschen*—in their potent attempt to realize Bush padre's vision of making America the iron-fisted steward of a New World Order—must not be compromised by the liberal ideas of militarily (and by association, morally) weaker allied nations. It is not as though Bush hijo is trying to remake the United States into a New Jerusalem. It is more likely that Bush believes unabashedly that the United States is already the New Jerusalem and must be protected by leaders ordained by the Almighty. Of course, the civilization versus chaos myth is a rewrite of the myth of white racial superiority over people of color. Instead of the echoes of Wagner, we have the music of Rocky, instead of Wotan serving as our favorite media action hero, we have Conan the American chasing Marxists through the jungles of Colombia, instead of Triumph of the Will, we have Fox News shots of Geraldo in Afghanistan fudging locations where certain events were supposed to have occurred (Hess 2002, p. 4).

The hawks around Bush genuflect at the intellectual altar of the late philosopher-king and University of Chicago classicist Leo Strauss, who imperturbably assumed the conviction that only an elite few in the government warrant the sacred custodianship of the truth, and are thereby charged with using "noble lies" to keep the truth from the unwashed masses by preoccupying everyday citizens not only with real or perceived external threats to the nation but also with the task of developing nationalist or militantly religious sentiments fanatical enough to ensure their willingness to die for the nation. An enemy of reading the meaning of history in context and a champion of using the principle of natural law as the rule of the wise master over the unwise slave, Strauss considered democracy "an act against nature [that] must be prevented at all costs" (Shorris 2004). Earl Shorris (2004) writes: "Seen in this light, the Bush Administration's public claim to be bringing 'democracy' to Iraq, all the while working to ensure that elections do not take place, takes on new meaning" (p. 69). Strauss was a harsh critic of liberalism, and his authoritarian and imperial principles of the right guided this thoroughly reactionary thinker whose antipathy to democracy and justice were well known. His pedagogy demanded that readers of the classics suspend their own judgment and demanded that they read the classical authors (i.e., Plato, Aristotle, Maimonides) in the same way that those authors understood themselves (Burnyeat 1985.) This meant avoiding contemporary ideas as a critical lens through which to establish a perspective for interpretation. It was the the perfect kind of pedagogy for living in a fascist state and for being ruled by a dictator and/or philosopher king and fawning aristocratic punditry. As a philosopher who asserted that wisdom was a greater good than justice, who evaluated modernity from the standpoint of a univocal and monolithic antiquity, who distained the canons of critical thought, who arrogantly defended the classical doctrine of natural right, who rejected democratic claims to popular sovereignty as the rule of the unwise over the wise, who doggedly opposed multiculturalism and who was a fierce opponent of universal education, Strauss believed that all and sundry works of modern criticism were so much rot in the support beams of the history of ideas. Strauss believed in the necessity of making absolute judgements but only in so far as a philosopher is able to conceal from the masses what he or she is actually saying (Xenos 2004). Rejecting contracts between men as violations of natural law, Strauss elevates writing between the lines to a sacerdotal status, to a necessary means of esoterically speaking wisdom to the cognoscenti and exoterically teaching the masses so as to prevent the mob from seeking the foolishness of justice. Coded language and frequent archaisms were the rule of thumb for Strauss. F. M. Burnyeat notes, for instance, that Strauss, an antiegalitarian conservative, does not believe that Plato is the radical utopian that mainstream scholarship believes him to be. Rather, Strauss believes that in his *Republic*, Plato means the very opposite of what Socrates says in his speeches. Strauss does this, according to Burnyeat, in order to persuade readers to subscribe to the opposite view of what Plato is thought to have held, according to most literary interpretations. And he accomplishes this through a mode of commentary that enables Strauss (through a "vicious circularity") to presuppose what he seeks to prove, so that Plato effectively becomes someone who does not believe that justice is essential for the happiness of both city and humankind.

Burnyeat reveals the errors of Strauss's reading of Plato, claiming that Strauss, in substituting exegesis for argument, turns the meaning of the *Republic* upside down. Strauss's concluding insinuation is that "the just city is not possible because of the philosopher's unwillingness to rule," but Burnyeat is able to demonstrate that it is precisely because philosophers are unwilling to rule that a just city is possible because philosophers as devotees of pure reason are not self-interested, and will therefore adhere to the principles of impartial justice. In his book, *City and Man*, Strauss writes that Plato teaches that "the just city is against nature because the equality of the sexes and absolute communism are against nature" (cited in Burnyeat 1985). Burnyeat sees this as a perverse misreading—both literary and philosophical—of the *Republic*. Strauss also holds an "eccentric view that Plato's Socrates agrees with Xenophon's in teaching that the just citizen is one who helps his friends and harms his enemies" (Burnyeat 1985; see also Xenos 2004), which pushes Strauss's belief that "civil society must, of necessity, foster warlike habits and make its citizens apply different rules of conduct to one another and to foreigners" (Burnyeat 1985). Of course, a market economy and representative democracy guided by politicians who possessed prebourgeois aristocratic characteristics such as wisdom, honor, and courage and who worked within an optic hospitable to the Machiavellian friends/enemy distinction are essential to the preferred forms of regimes that Straussians wish to see populate the planet. Natural law trumps convention each and every time according to Straussians, as does foreign policy rewritten in the stark moral terms of good versus evil, which is why, according to Shorris (2004):

The Bush regime violated the contract that was agreed to when the United States joined the United Nations; it flouted the U.S. Constitution, which is also a contract, by attacking without the required declaration of war by the Congress; and it disregarded the Geneva Conventions in its treatment of prisoners at Guantanamo Bay, Cuba, and in other secret detention camps around the world. (p. 69)

Bush's galaxy of Straussian advisors who are linked to the American Enterprise Institute and the Project for the New American Century adhere to a concept of natural law that permits them the brutal arrogance to dismiss the laws of mere mortals and to appeal to a higher power. Shorris (2004) notes that:

The administration's wise men held up Strauss's version of natural law as the model, dismissing contracts as mere laws of men. Natural law, interpreted by Bush's "wise counsels," gave the president permission to launch a preemptive war through an appeal to the higher power. Natural-law theory assumes that men seek the good and that by asking perennial questions—What is virtue? What is justice?—they will come to wisdom. Straussians, like Kristol, hold that the Founding Fathers espoused natural-law theory, saying that natural law was both divine and self-evident. But the Founders were concerned with inalienable natural rights. After much debate in their convention, they wrote a contract. (p. 70)

Straussians are first and foremost pragmatists who will resort to whatever works best to secure control. Preparing for a television interview, Deputy Defense Secretary Paul Wolfowitz, one of the primary architects of the Iraq war, transformed himself into a visual metaphor for his political philosophy when, in the words of Roger Ebert (2004), "he [put] a pocket comb in his mouth to wet it and [combed] down his hair. Still not satisfied, he [spit] on his hand and [wiped] the hair into place." Michael Moore's film *Farenheit 9/11* captured the moment.

Another philosopher that presumably has some clout with the Bush administration is Machiavelli. As Robert Scheer (2004) writes in connection to Dick Cheney:

It was a forewarning of the Machiavellian arrogance that has made him the leading individual in an administration that has consistently believed that self-serving ends—such as helping Enron at the expense of California's energy needs or boosting Halliburton's profits at the expense of American troops—justify lying, secrecy, and preemptive war.

Interestingly, Neil Gabler (2004) uses Machiavelli when describing Karl Rove, whom he refers to as "the White House Ayatollah":

Rovism begins, as one might suspect, from the most merciless of political consiglieres, with Machiavelli's rule of force: "A prince is respected when he is either a true friend or a downright enemy." No administration since Warren Harding has rewarded its friends so lavishly, and none has been as willing to bully anyone who strays from its message.

Whether devotees of the works of Machiavelli, Strauss, or Ayn Rand, the hawks all agree that fighting "preventative wars" requires a flexible fighting force that can establish U.S. military hegemony throughout the world. Chalmers Johnson (2004) writes: "According to the American Enterprise Institute, the idea is to create 'a global cavalry' that can ride in from 'frontier stockades' and shoot up the 'bad guys' as soon as we get some intelligence on them" (p. M6). Johnson (2004) also notes that most of these bases "will be what the military, in a switch of metaphors, calls 'lily pads,' to and from which our troops could jump, like well-armed frogs, depending on where they were needed" (p. M6). The Pentagon has bases in every continent except Antarctica, and occupies 702 overseas bases in approximately 130 countries (although the Defense Department does not count huge military installations such as Camp Bondsteel in Kosovo or sizeable outposts in Afghanistan, Iraq, Israel, Kuwait, Kyrgyzstan, Qatar, and Uzbekistan because it classifies these as only temporary bases). And while the U.S. military employs 71 learjets and other luxury planes to fly generals and admirals to the armed forces' ski and vacation centers at Germisch in the Bavarian Alps or to the 234 golf courses worldwide operated by the Pentagon, life is much harder for the grunts now occupying Iraq, although they are a bit happier now that the first Burger King has just gone up inside the military base at Baghdad's international airport (Johnson 2004, p. M6).

We need to ask ourselves how, exactly, the rhetoric of fascism works, assuming that the infrastructure for a transition to a fascist state is already in place—we have the USA Patriot Act, we have the military tribunals, we have the Office of Homeland Security, we have the necessary scapegoats, we have the Office of Strategic Influence working hand in hand with the U.S. Army's Psychological Operations Command (PSYOPS) operating domestically (actually, its operating domestically is against the law, but we know that during the Reagan administration that PSYOPS staffed the Office of Public Diplomacy and planted stories in the media supporting the Contras, a move made possible by Otto Reich, now the assistant secretary of state for Western Hemisphere Affairs; and we know that a few years ago PSYOPS operatives were discovered working as interns in the news division of CNN's Atlanta headquarters), we have the strongest military in the world, we have the military hawks in control of the Pentagon, we have pummeled an evil nation into prehistory, we have turned Central Asia into a zone of containment, and we have shown that we can kill mercilessly and control the media reporting in the theater of operations, as major newspapers regularly buried stories of U.S. airstrikes on civilians, such as in the case of Niazi Kala (sometimes called Qalaye Niaze), where the United Nations reported that fifty-two civilians were killed by the U.S. attack, including twenty-five children. According to the UN report, unarmed women and children were pursued and killed by American helicopters, even as they fled to shelter or tried to rescue survivors (Coen 2002, p. 3). And we have a leader who is little more than a glorified servant of the military industrial complex. And one who is able to admit this publicly and arouse little opposition. In fact, such an admission wins him the glowing admiration of the American people. The Bush administration's scheduled release of documents under the Presidential Records Act of 1978, which includes Ronald Reagan's papers, has successfully been placed on lockdown. So far Cheney's much publicized legal stonewalling has prevented full disclosure of the extent of Enron–National Energy Policy Development Group contacts. Government secrecy and the withholding of information available to the public by law have become a guiding axiom of government practice.

What a culture this administration has spawned. What in 1995 I labeled as "predatory culture" has transmogrified into a lurid culture of malice that James Wolcott has captured so vividly in the following description:

> It's the phrase "malicious indignities" that arrows to the heart of our heartless time, flash-forwards to the string of shabby degradations that affront us daily, when Vietnam War veteran Max Cleland can be mocked for the loss of his limbs, Christopher Reeve disparaged in death for championing stem-cell research, hostage Kenneth Bigley criticized by conservatives for the "ignoble and unmanly" pleas that his life be spared, 9/11 widows maligned as publicity junkies, George Soros slandered by the editorial-page editor of the *Washington Times* as "a Jew who figured out a way to survive the Holocaust" and Michelle Malkin given generous airtime to defend the internment of Japanese-Americans during World War II and propose new camps for suspicious Muslims—it just never stops. (2004, p. 26)

What is driving an administration when a Justice Department lawyer writes a secret memo to the White House in 2001 concluding that President George W. Bush has the authority to wage preemptive war against terrorists even if they were not linked to the September 11 attacks? What does it mean when there are effectively "no limits" on the president's authority to wage war, even without congressional approval? What does this say about American exceptionalism, about American triumphalism, about the return to frontier-style imperialism?

The culture of malice spawned in the putrid swamplands of Bush-era morality is not unlike the culture of the battlefield in occupied Iraq. It is a culture of the strong against the weak, of an unrelenting pursuit of the power to dominate others, of contempt for the vulnerable by those with the will, the overwhelming means, and the unrestricted opportunity to obliterate them.

Those who carry out the crimes of the state pay a high price. Their acts alone manage to lift the veil of common sense from their eyes and force them to see their deeds in a new, more critical light. Chris Hedges writes:

> These Marines have learned the awful truth about our civil religion. They have learned that our nation is not righteous. They have understood that there are no transcendent goals at the heart of our political process. The Sunday School God that blesses our nation above all others vanishes in war zones like Iraq. These young troops disdain the teachers, religious authorities, and government officials, who feed them these lies. (2004, p. 12)

In the words of one Marine, who was invited to be a guest of honor in a gated community in Malibu, where the tanned and relaxed residents anxiously needed a hero to toast: "I'm not a hero. . . . Guys like me are just a necessary part of things. To maintain this way of life in a fine community like this, you need psychos like us to go out and drop a bomb on somebody else's house" (cited in Hedges, 2004, p. 12). How appropriate, especially now, is the phrase from the thirteenth scene of Bertolt Brecht's play, *Life of Galileo*: "Unhappy is the land that is in need of heroes."

The fascism that is slowly settling into place is generously assisted by former Attorney General John Ashcroft. Consider his recent remarks on the struggle against terrorism: "Civilized people—Muslims, Christians and Jews—all understand that the source of freedom and human dignity is the Creator" (Umansky 2000). Ashcroft made these remarks in front of a group of Christian broadcasters. At the same event he proclaimed: "Civilized people of all religious faiths are called to the defense of His creation. We are a nation called to defend freedom—a freedom that is not the grant of any government or document, but is our endowment from God" (Umansky 2000). And while our attorney general exiles Orpheus into the political hinterland by covering up the breasts of the statues located in the lobby of his workplace, he offers the wrath of Jehovah as a libidinal replacement to Christian fundamentalists embarking on their torchlit rallies and declaring that "united we stand." Recently Vice President Dick Cheney told Orange County Republicans gathered at the Richard Nixon Library and Birthplace in Yorba Linda, California, that "the United States must accept the place of leadership given to us by history" (Pasco 2002, p. B6). Clearly, his peace-through-strength message was a secular rewrite of a divine mandate to destroy the infidel. Reverend Jerry Falwell, who in the 1980s was told by President Ronald Reagan that Armageddon was fast approaching, invoked a God of vengeance and destruction when he blamed feminists, civil libertarians, abortion rights advocates, and gays and lesbians for the terrorist attacks of September 11. He echoed a belief shared by other evangelicals that divine protection is summarily withdrawn from nations who have followed in the footsteps of the inhabitants of Sodom and Gomorrah and have irredeemably become steeped in sin.

Essentially George Bush, Cheney, Ashcroft, and Falwell express similar sentiments, but Falwell has failed where the others have succeeded because their attack demonizes "them" rather than splitting "us" into an "us and them" (good Americans versus bad Americans). Lynne Cheney can spearhead a report designed to demonize professors who speak out against civilization (read as speak out against Bush's war on terrorism), but it is unlikely that there will be serious repercussions for professors unless further terrorist attacks within the United States provoke the general population to feel more comfortable with the idea of eating their own children. If attacks recur, then clearly the stage is set to go after with more vigilance dissenters in the universities. Unless there is an academic version of the Swift Boat Veterans, most Americans won't be interested in rooting out internal enemies (unless, of course, they fit the right ethnic profile). At the present time, the American public is not seeking internal scapegoats, even if some of the candidates are what the "moral majority" would regard as enemies of civilization. For the time being, the public wants an enemy that remains "out there," one that is easily outsourced, like sweatshop labor by transnational corporations, conveniently externalized and seen as wholly Other to the values of mainstream U.S. society. We want to fight the detritus of global humanity. And anyone not willing to submit to the law of the marketplace, and the desires of its global curate in the White House, is an automatic contender for the label of dregs of the New World Order.

At this particular historical moment, democracy seems acutely perishable. Its contradictions have become as difficult to ignore as sand rubbed in the eyes. While dressed up as a promise, democracy has functioned more as a threat. Spurred on by feelings of "righteous victimhood" and by a "wounded and vengeful nationalism" (Lieven 2003) that has arisen in the wake of the attacks of September 11, and pushing its war on terrorism to the far reaches of the globe (with what Terry Eagleton [2003] calls a "world-hating hubris" [p. 227]), the United States is shamelessly defining its global empire as an extension of its democratic project. The U.S. National Security Strategy of 2002 states quite clearly that the United States will not hesitate to act alone and will "preemptively" attack against "terrorists" that threaten its national interests at home or abroad. And one of its national interests is to bring free-market democracy to the rest of the world. What used to be called gunboat diplomacy is being rewritten as a diplomatic and literal gunning down of any and all opposition to the unfettered movement of finance capital in and out of new markets. Sidestepping the inconvenient possibility that Iraq had no connection to al Qaeda, the Pentagon hawks swept through the streets of Baghdad like whirling dervishes on steroids and arrived at the near culmination of their civilizing mission by marching into the very den of the barbarians, enacting a negation as one-sided as the positivity they oppose.

Despite the fact that tens of millions of people—many of whom were presumably within a hair's breadth of Saddam's weapons of mass destruction—marched in the streets of cities on every continent to denounce the U.S. decision to launch an unprovoked invasion of Iraq, the United States pressed ahead with its plan to seize its oil fields, privatize its industries, demonstrate to would-be "evil doers" what was in store for them and secure a strategic geopolitical stranglehold on the Middle East. Those nations that supported its imperial design on behalf of fighting terrorism are now being rewarded with some of the spoils of victory (i.e., subcontracts to rebuild the infrastructure of Afghanistan or Iraq) or at least assurance they will not to be invaded. Nearly $5 billion in military aid and training will be distributed to countries that have contributed to the so-called global war on terrorism or to the war in Iraq (a war whose definition remains a known unknown) in the coming months. Human Rights Watch International warns that these same nations have a recent history of committing human rights violations. The Philippines is primed to receive $19 million worth of sniper rifles, mortars, grenade launchers, and helicopters. A broadened U.S. role in Colombia has extended from counternarcotics to a unified campaign against insurgents. In the case of Colombia, this signals the connivance of U.S. special operations protecting oil pipelines working side by side with right-wing paramilitaries. Indonesia, Uzbekistan, Tajikistan, the Republic of Georgia, and Kyrgyzstan, will soon profit from the global market for terror—they too will receive millions in military aid from the United States

But perhaps the most alarming case is that of India and Pakistan. Two nations that have taunted each other with nuclear warfare and have had little success in achieving a modest political rapprochement have had their sanctions lifted and are being provided with millions of dollars worth of artillery for their support to the United States. Rather than trying to quell the possibility of nuclear warfare over Kashmir, the United States has equipped India with $78 million worth of artillery, while Pakistan, a much more visible force post–9/11, stands to gain fighter jets and armored personnel carriers with a price tag of over $1 billion.

In a fit of familiar paradoxical behavior that is consistent with symptoms of clinical paranoia, the United States is seeking help from countries to contribute troops to Iraq while at the same time threatening countries, including members of the "coalition of the willing"—Bulgaria, Latvia, Lithuania, Estonia, Slovakia, and Slovenia—who have not signed bilateral agreements exempting U.S. citizens from prosecution by the International Criminal Court. The United States has threatened to cut $150 million of the Pentagon's annual aid to Bogota unless it signs the exemption. Not surprisingly, John Bolton, undersecretary of state for arms control and international security explains: "We have not been pressuring countries" (Richter 2003).

With promiscuous persistence, the United States distributes itself around the world in gleeful anticipation of being welcomed with open arms as long-awaited liberators. The problem is that those welcoming arms have been, more often than not of late, severed at the joint by U.S. imperialism's signature cluster bombs, shells of depleted uranium, and cruise missiles. When democracy does announce itself, it arrives under the sign of its own negation. Claiming to bring freedom and liberation to the Iraqi people, the U.S. invasion, according to some estimates, has been responsible for the death of approximately ten thousand innocent civilians. The occupying force has prohibited the Iraqi people from forming their own government, preferring to select its leaders for them from a group of perfumed and pampered exiles, already thoroughly Westernized and plumping for the creation of an Iraqi neoliberal state. U.S. officials have begun to stage manage the country for democracy's free-market drama: privatization of its oil, agriculture, and just about everything that will put U.S. dollars in investors' pockets. Like drooling hyenas descending on a carcass, the trade lawyers, consultants, bankers, and CEOs of transnational corporations are licking their chops in anticipation of the United States fulfilling its mission of opening up Iraq to foreign (mainly U.S. and British) investment, and bringing Washington's neoliberal imperative to the uncivilized territories of the Middle East.

When the Ministry of Oil claimed the dubious status of the only Ministry the U.S. troops deemed worthy of protection after the fall of Baghdad, the Iraqi people should have known at that very moment that America's self-designation as a bastion of freedom was vacuous. By now they should realize that the United States is also a major oil-producing nation since so much snake oil drips persistently from the lips of its politicians and policy makers. It is now as clear as the business suit on Paul Bremer's back that Iraq is up for sale to the highest foreign bidder, with the United States serving as the Divine Broker.

A sandstorm has erupted in the hourglass of history where the liberators from Fort Hood or Fort Benning squint through steel burkas affixed with turrets and cannons and treads while dreaming they are back home rollerblading down Venice Boulevard, eating Krispy Kremes at the Valley drive-thru, renting the latest Arnold video at Blockbusters and watching The Terminator dunk a woman's head in a toilet bowl; maybe these young recruits are thinking life might be better in the golden state under the terminator's red robotic eye in Sacramento. Maybe they are thinking they can caress a woman's breast whenever and wherever they please and do all the things their fraternity brothers bragged about doing. Now they can publicly apologize for all their sins and at the same time claim that they didn't commit them. When the soldiers return to the Homeland after their "tour" of duty in Iraq, they might notice a long list of everyday consumer items that bear the term "Shock and Awe." The U.S. Patent and Trademark Office in Washington has recently been hit by an onslaught of trademark applications using "Shock and Awe" in their names for items as various as condoms, coffees, golf clubs, pesticides, dietary supplements, salsa, energy drinks, yo-yos, lingerie, Bloody Mary mix, and "infant action crib toys." This is the commodification of militarism run amok, exactly what will keep adults primed for future offensives and young people socialized to killing as a solution to foreign and domestic "problems."

The accelerating bellicosity of the liberating army can be put in its proper perspective when you recognize that its overall goal is to open up Iraq to the free market. But the end results will not be what the many Iraqis believe them to be. Once the transition to the neoliberal marketplace has been accomplished, the Iraqi business elite will be able to purchase for themselves the best democracy money can buy, and the bogus freedom that goes with it (i.e., the freedom to be rich or poor, to own a palace or to lack shelter, to shop at an upscale supermarket or to starve in the streets).

In light of present historical circumstances, it was a bad idea for Iraquis to think that Washington's vision of a post-Saddam Iraq resembled anything like Baywatch reruns. Now that the country lies in tatters, its infrastructure in ruins, its water and electricity supplies failing to meet even the most basic needs of the people, its museums and hospitals looted and destroyed beyond redemption, and its protesters shot like animals, is it any wonder the U.S. occupation has produced such an incandescent anger among the Iraqi populace? Any occupying power that decides in advance who will rule their conquered territories cannot lay claim to being liberators. U.S. forces are currently engaged in Vietnam-style operations eerily similar to the "search-and-destroy" tactics of forty years ago with predictable responses from an increasingly tense civilian population whose anger against the U.S. troops is growing steadily to a fever pitch.

The United States is following a "carrot-and-stick" approach to occupational warfare. The military raids civilian homes and "enemy outposts" at night, before the scorching 120-degree heat begins to set in. Targeted missions are patterned after an occupation of Palestine and are designed to intimidate and frighten an already humiliated and degraded population into acquiescence. However, this is sure to increase resentment and armed reprisals. An Iraqi truck driver captured this resentment following the armed search of his truckload of potatoes. Stoically facing the lens of an American photographer, he asked, "Do they think we are monkeys?"

Some may argue that the Iraqi postwar state is better off than before and that nation building takes time, perhaps decades. But from where will democracy arise? It failed to take hold with Paul Bremer, the former Iraqi governor who is better known among the ruling elite as a terror expert entrepreneur. Following 9/11 and the subsequent attacks on Afghanistan and Iraq, Bremer helped to form Crisis Consulting Practice, a business designed to assist U.S. multinationals in taking advantage of nations newly destroyed on behalf of democracy. Meanwhile, millions of Iraqis remain jobless, without electricity and wondering—when will the occupation end?

The ongoing war in Iraq has signaled to the world that the United States is willing to use any means necessary in its fanatical plight for world dominance. A recent survey by the Pew Research Center unveils the stark reality that a majority of civilians in the predominantly Muslim nations of Indonesia, Nigeria, Pakistan, Turkey, Kuwait, Lebanon, and Jordan fear a military strike from the United States. About the only place where people of color do not appear threatened by patterns of merciless war and imperialism is on the moon or other uninhabited celestial bodies, which cautions us about the prospect of interplanetary travel (see Views of a Changing World 2003).

Citizens of the world have placed their hope in the hands of international organizations such as the United Nations, designated to halt unilateral massacres. However, the UN has proven to be more like a vaudeville stage for the political charades of Powell and Blair than a viable organ for peace. While the Security Council staged a temporary revolt, it has now obediently fallen back into line. No longer content to play Edgar Bergen to the UN's Charlie McCarthy or Mortimer Snerd,[1] the United States recognizes that in a world with only one superpower, it's no longer in need of ventriloquism. If you are in control of the most powerful military force in world history, you can speak directly without a mediator, even if your words fall from both sides of your mouth.

Having used the Reagan-Shultz doctrine to interpret Article 51 of the UN Charter as giving license to the United States to resort to force in "self-defense against future attack" (Chomsky 2003), the U.S. administration is now transforming itself into the same *junta* it once supported in the person of Saddam (recall the 1983 photo of Rumsfeld and Saddam shaking hands) but later turned against when it was in their best interest to do so. The U.S. administration looks at the Iraqis like Custer's cavalry looked at the Indians: They couldn't possibly be ready for democracy yet. They inhabit a culture so incommensurable with our own that they are not yet able to grasp fully enough the fiscal advantages and moral superiority of global capitalism and free market democracy. It's a democracy that will enable the United States to raid their raw materials and exploit their labor-power (with all those bid-free contracts awarded to Republican-friendly U.S. corporations). It's a democracy that is designed not for the Iraqi people but so that the United States can ensure its own economy will reap enough oil profits to be able to keep any upstart country from challenging its sole military superpower status for another century and beyond (Bush's inner circle of neocon zealots don't belong to a think-tank called the Project for the New American Century without taking the name seriously). Of course, the United States will make sure that a new class of Iraqi businessmen will become rich beyond their wildest dreams, maybe even as rich as Saddam used to be.

The key point to be made is recognizing that the Untied States is out to weaken and cheapen labor in order to compensate for a major loss of profits and dramatic increase in debts over the last several years. As further evidence one need only witness Bush invoking the Taft-Hartley Act against the West Coast dockworkers' union or his granting of federal aid to failing airlines on condition that management purges the airline unions. How many social services will need to be cut in order to finance Homeland security? How much rebuilding can occur in Iraq in the face of U.S. budget deficits as a result of the current recession? How will tax cuts for corporations and the wealthy help to pay for the war and occupation? Is reducing domestic budget deficits by exclusive U.S. control of Iraqi oil production worth the price of further enraging France, Germany, Russia, and China and making Trotsky's concept of interimperialist rivalry seen tame by comparison? Is it worth increasing the number of terrorist recruits who will dedicate themselves to eliminating the U.S. military presence in the Middle East? Here it is easy to recognize how capitalism has been turned into a quasi-natural force by the corporatized lawmaking of the International Monetary Fund and World Bank of which workers are the passive, unnamed victims. The United States has successfully alienated much of both the developed and Third World, and has sent an unmistakable message to both Russia and China that Washington's newfound military brinkmanship and aggression are a profound threat to their strategic interests and geopolitical influence. As if the lessons of Afghanistan and Iraq were not enough, Washington is now clearly preparing the ground for a possible attack on Iran.

Here at home the pusillanimity and fecklessness of the Democrats has been as difficult to stomach as Bush hijo's bumptious belligerence toward the nation's poor and his failure to recognize how he is in ironic violation of democracy's own fundamentals. Their integrity addled, the Democrats for the most part remain unwilling to name Bush the liar and deceiver that he is.

What worries them is the spin that the media are likely to give their criticisms of Bush; they fear that going too far in attacking a wartime president will condemn them irrevocably in the public eye as unpatriotic.

The relatively compliant U.S. citizenry should have known they were orbiting disaster when, as early as July 2001, Attorney General John Ashcroft was warned not to fly commercial airlines due to a CIA threat assessment but did not share with the public what that assessment was, when Bush delayed to release the Reagan presidential papers, violating a post-Watergate law and protecting those in his administration who were involved in the Iran-Contra crimes when they worked for Reagan and Bush padre, when the House of Representatives passed the USA Patriot Act without reading it or holding a hearing or public debate about it, when Bush and Cheney urged Tom Daschle not to make an inquiry related to 9/11 (when the inquiry finally did take place it was a tragic piece of political obfuscation), when thousands of librarians started destroying records so federal agents would have nothing to seize under the Patriot Act, when convicted felon Vice Admiral John Poindexter began to run a clandestine new government agency known as the Information Awareness Office, when the government created a no-fly list in order to prevent certain political dissidents (like some members of the Green Party) from using commercial airplanes, when CIA director Tenet told the country there was no 9/11 intelligence failure, when the U.S. military unveiled the Total Information Awareness System, when FBI director Mueller denied that information related to any aspect of the September 11 plot crossed his desk before that fateful day when the Twin Towers collapsed, when the Pentagon started to consider the creation of execution chambers for Camp Delta in Guantanamo Bay, when Bush hijo opposed establishing a special independent commission to probe how the government dealt with terror warnings before 9/11 (he finally consented to a "token" commission after public pressure), when Ashcroft permitted government agents to monitor domestic religious and political groups without advanced approval from superiors, and when Bush unveiled Operation Tips, a program encouraging Americans to spy on each other, and when the U.S. death toll kept mounting in Iraq long after Bush hijo appeared (in a flight suit) on the deck of an aircraft carrier, revealing his trademark smirk and a proud set of ungainly gonads, bragging: Mission accomplished! But these incidents don't seem to phase the American public, partly because they are played down in the news shows and partly because many citizens have become exceptionally adept at hearing only what they want to hear (McLaren 2003). And that's really not such a difficult task when the official media are there to help you along.

The sheer duplicity and hypocrisy of the Bush administration was in glaring evidence recently, when it allowed three known international terrorists into

Florida, to the thronging crowds of a fanatical Miami anti-Castro community. Members of the infamous Posada gang arrived in Miami after being released by Panamanian authorities after serving a short sentence for attempting to assassinate Fidel Castro during a 2000 international summit in Panama. While the most notorious member of this anti-Castro cell, Luis Posada Carriles, who participated in numerous acts of terrorism—among them blowing up an Air Cubana passenger plane in 1976, killing seventy-three civilians—is still in hiding, his confederates, Guillermo Novo, Gaspar Jimenez, and Pedro Remon, are in the safe hands of Miami millionaires. Novo once fired a bazooka at the UN building in 1979 and is said to have assassinated former Chilean diplomat Orlando Letelier and his American colleague, Ronni Moffitt, in Washington. Jimenez was once imprisoned in Mexico for murdering a Cuban consulate official and Remon was imprisoned for conspiring to kill Cuba's ambassador to the United Nations. The Bush administration has not indicated any intention of detaining or deporting Novo, Jimenez, and Remon, even though they have deported hundreds of foreigners on the mere suspicion of having links to terrorists (see Sweig and Kornbluh 2004). God's Holy Warrior, after all, has a brother who is the governor of Florida, and the Posada gang arrived during election year.

Rarely has any country been in such total control by the media. A recent opinion poll, conducted by the Program on International Policy Attitudes at the University of Maryland, found that one third of the American public believed that American military forces had found weapons of mass destruction in Iraq. Approximately 22 percent said that Iraq had actually used chemical or biological weapons in the war. Other polls have reported that some 50 percent of those questioned believed Iraqi citizens participated in the September 11 attacks, while 40 percent believed that Saddam Hussein directly assisted the hijack-bombers (see Program on International Policy Attitudes, www .americans-world.org/digest/regional_issues/Conflict_Iraq/linkstoTerr.cfm). This reflects the staggering power of the U.S. corporate media as a whole—and not just Fox TV—to distort dramatically the facts in favor of the Bush administration and the business elite.

The captains of U.S. media have realized (perhaps more fully than anyone else) that the more pervasive the lie, the more it will be harmonized with everyday common sense. One glaringly inconspicuous manifestation of this ideological process is the way in which the term "democracy" is constantly conflated with the "free market." These two terms are yolked together as frequently as the term weapons of mass destruction is spoken in the same breath as terrorists or the foreign leader of any county whose resources we have decided to acquire and whose markets we seek to control. The "free market" is collapsed into exchangeable referents: "jobs," "wealth," "political stability," and "security." Capitalism has always been the "religion" of individualism, of individual rights, of constitutional freedom, and of private property. Given this reading, a successful socialist economy would obviously appear threatening to democracy. Democracy and the free market have struck a deal. The capitalist values that adhere to the concept of "democracy" like flies to a sticky tongue of flypaper preclude any real challenge to its sacred resting place in the structural unconscious of the U.S. public.

Personally, we believe that the Bush *junta* is so self-discrediting that it doesn't need a commentary such as ours to make a case against it. Yet we offer our perspective nevertheless, if only because of the shameful lack of venues available these days for an analysis of the Bush administration. For all his self-inflating rhetoric about cleaning up the Middle East of its freedom-hating terrorists, his stagey relish for challenging evil-doers, and his dyspeptic remarks about his antiwar critics being nothing more than punk ass revisionists, we believe there is a strong case for impeaching our commander-in-chief for using misleading evidence to bring the country into war. The Bush administration's arguments about Iraq's so-called imminent danger to the safety of the United States and world-at-large constituted a flagrant lie to the American people and a shameful abuse of power that would increase terrorist threats. The deployment of America's vast military machine was undertaken for reasons Bush and his entire foreign-policy apparatus knew to be based on false and falsified information. No government in Europe or the Middle East regarded Iraq as a serious threat to their safety. The UN weapons inspectors had for months been unable to locate any weapons of mass destruction, despite meticulous searching.

While the White House hawks presented the attack on Iraq as an extension of the "war on terrorism," it was revealed that the Bush administration had drawn up plans to use military force to overthrow the regime of Saddam Hussein well in advance of the attacks on the World Trade Center and the Pentagon. September 11 was seized upon as a pretext to shape pubic opinion in favor of the war and now the White House lies about the extent of Saddam's weapons of mass destruction have come to light. Consider the June 15 edition of NBC's *Meet the Press*. During the show, former General Wesley Clark—himself the ruthless military architect of the destruction of Yugoslavia—told anchor Tim Russert that Bush administration officials had engaged in a campaign to implicate Saddam Hussein in the September 11 attacks on the very day of the attacks. Clark said that he'd been called on by Bush administration officials on September 11 and urged to link the regime of Saddam Hussein to the terror attacks. Clark declined to do so because of a lack of evidence (not surprisingly, there was little media coverage of Clark's remarks during the presidential primaries). Even Deputy Defense Secretary Paul Wolfowitz later admitted that the charge that Iraq possessed weapons of mass destruction was selected for "bureaucratic reasons"—that is, it was the one allegation that the State Department, the Pentagon, and the CIA all agreed could provide a workable excuse for a U.S. invasion. The editors of the

World Socialist Web site (Editorial Board 2003) captured the essence of this situation with the following remark: "Not since Hitler and the Nazis dressed up storm troopers as Polish soldiers and staged 'attacks' on German positions in 1939 has there been such a flagrant and cynical effort to manufacture a casus belli."

The Bush family ties to the Nazi Party are well known among historians but not the general public. The 1994 book written by Mark Aarons and John Loftus, *The Secret War against the Jews*, uses official U.S. documents to establish that George Herbert Walker, George W. Bush's maternal great-grandfather, was one of Hitler's most important early backers who "funneled money to the rising young fascist through the Union Banking Corporation" Walker arranged to have his new son-in-law, Prescott Bush—father of President George Bush I, grandfather of George Bush II—hired as vice president at W. A. Harriman and Company in 1926. Prescott became a senior partner when Harriman merged with a British-American investment company to become Brown Brothers Harriman. In 1934 Prescott Bush joined the board of directors of Union Banking and assisted in the efforts to put Hitler and the Nazis into power and also to carry out their murderous war campaign. It has also been documented that Prescott Bush knowingly served as a money launderer for the Nazis (Fitrakis and Wasserman 2003).

According to Fitrakis and Wasserman (2003), Karl Rove has parallel ties. They write:

> The shadowy Rove serves as "Bush's Brain" in the current White House. He is the political mastermind behind the California coup, and is now in the headlines for outing Valerie Plame, the CIA wife of Ambassador Joseph Wilson. A consummate strategist, Rove may have outed Plame in retaliation for Wilson's failure to back up the Bush claim that Saddam Hussein was buying nuclear weapons materials in Africa. According to some published reports, as many as seventy CIA operatives have been put at risk by Rove's retaliatory strike. . . . Rove, who has been based in Utah and associated with the Mormon Church, is widely viewed as the chief engineer of the current Bush administration. He and Tom De-Lay are attempting to force the Texas legislature to redistrict its Congressional delegations, adding seven sure seats to the Republican column. By controlling the state houses in New York, Florida, Texas, and California, the GOP would have a lock on the four largest states in the union, and thus the ability to manipulate vote counts and strip voter registration rolls in the run-up to the 2004 election. Rove is a prime behind-the-scenes mover in the Schwarzenegger campaign.

Fitrakis and Wasserman (2003) further note:

> According to Bob Woodward's *Bush at War*, Bush attended a New York Yankees game soon after the September 11 World Trade Center disaster. He wore a fire-

man's jacket. As he threw out the first pitch, the crowd roared. Thousands of fans stuck out their arms with thumbs up. Karl Rove, sitting in the box of Yankee owner George Steinbrenner, likened the roar of the crowd to "a Nazi rally."

THE QUESTION OF EMPIRE

Peter Hudis (2003) has underscored that which distinguishes today's imperialism from that of previous periods. One factor is that the United States no longer seeks direct territorial control of the rest of the world, in contrast to its behavior during the classic stage of imperialist-colonialism of the late nineteenth and early twentieth century. After World War II, the United States shifted toward more indirect methods of domination through the creation of local surrogates and by relying on economic compulsion. Whereas imperialism once tried to disguise the tendency in the decline of the rate of profits through the extraction of super-profits from exploited lands overseas, the tendency of the rate of profit to decline is now what openly drives capital's quest for imperialist expansion. Hudis further notes that the export of capital was once the prime motive for imperialist expansion whereas now capitalist production compels dominant capitals to incorporate and submit to the domination of foreign national capital. The United States, for instance, was once the world's biggest exporter of capital but ever since the Vietnam War it has shifted from a creditor nation to a debtor nation whose importation of surplus capital (mostly from Europe and Asia) has become a defining feature of the world economy. Foreign companies continue to invest in the United States because here wages are low and health benefits are shrinking, and workers are being laid off, which has created a phenomena of rising productivity (production increases while employment decreases—a jobless economic recovery). The militarization of the U.S. economy in its drive for permanent war has also helped to attract foreign capital to the United States since the country that rules the world allegedly provides the most stability for investment.

The vicissitudes and contingencies of imperialism have brought into question the expansion—or fall—of what is commonly referred to as the American empire. While Peter Hudis expands on Lenin's view of imperialism as rooted in the notion of state capital, and not only private capital, he argues that the new age of imperialism is at a point of rupture. Hudis remarks:

Just as the emergence of "classical" imperialism blinded many of its most astute critiques (like Hilferding and Bukharin) into emphasizing its role as "stabilizer" of capitalism rather than that which portends endless, even permanent crises of

DISequilibrium, so today, the U.S.'s unmatched global dominance has many thinking the same, when in fact the whole edifice is shaky and prone to severe crisis, if not "transformation into opposite." (Author's personal communication with Peter Hudis 2003)

In direct contrast to Hudis, James Petras believes that U.S. imperial dominance is in no danger of immediate or near future collapse. For Petras, two simultaneously existing U.S.-based economies suggest that in fact, the gluttonous feast is far from over. Rooted in both a domestic and international economy, the U.S. empire (while on a domestic economic downturn) has demonstrated resilience internationally. In fact, both economies mutually inform one another since "the high profits earned by the MNC's [multinational corporations] relocated throughout the new colonial and semicolonial economies of Asia and Latin America strengthen imperial institutions while weakening the domestic economy, its budget financing and its external accounts" (Petras 2003, p. 10). According to Petras, U.S.-based multinational corporations (MNCs) represent the impetus of economic empire building. Saturating a handful of economic sectors that include among others, oil and gas, U.S.-owned and -operated MNCs currently represent nearly half of the top 500 companies of the world while its subservient counterpart, Europe, and eager rival, Japan, lag far behind (Petras 2003, pp. 3–4). Key to this view is the assertion that "no state can aspire to global dominance if its principle economic institutions do not exercise a paramount role in the world economy" (Petras 2003, p. 4). In pursuit of increased profit making and control over competitors such as Europe and Japan, U.S. MNCs currently exist in an ascending phase in the global world order. Petras concludes that an increasing share of profits and the exercise of military force places the United States as the dominant empire provocateur.

With a significant portion of the world's wealth tucked neatly under its bedside pillow, the United States shamelessly decides how many lives will be relinquished as "collateral damage," marking it the "most powerful and aggressive superpower" in history (Petras 2003). But the relationship between the military and economic empire builders is far from fluid. Under the current Bush regime, Secretary of Defense Donald Rumsfeld has exacerbated tensions between those who are in sole pursuit of economic conquest by military means and those who consider themselves military professionals by design. Petras (2003) describes this phenomenon thusly:

There is no doubt that Rumsfeld has been the controlling figure in the formulation and execution of the strategy of world military conquest—an imperial strategy which closely resembles that of Nazi Germany. Rumsfeld's concentration of power within the imperial elite and the hostility toward the professionals was dramatically expressed by his nomination of retired General Schoomaker, former commander of the Special Forces "Delta," which was described to me by senior military officers at the Delta headquarters at Fort Bragg as a collection of "psychopaths trained to murder." Clearly the ex-Delta general was selected precisely because his ideological and behavioral profile fits in with Rumsfeld's own Nazi propensities. (p. 15)

And while the military professional "intelligentsia" may covertly object to ideological demagoguery lacking sufficient military expertise, it hasn't slowed down the momentum of the empire builders. The fact that economic empire builders are able to secure and expand their economic interests at the expense of an overzealous militant cabal is a small price to pay for the inordinate superprofits that will result from obtaining the obvious: control over untapped markets. Key to the expansion of empire is a sophisticated military apparatus that on the surface is seemingly able to "disarm" its host and force it to submit to "economic empire-building" (Petras 2003, p. 6). All of this leads Petras to the affirmation that "the notion of an 'overextended' empire is a piece of ahistorical speculation . . . the benefits of empire building go to the overseas and domestic corporate elite, the costs are paid by U.S. tax payers and the low income families which provide the combat and occupation soldiers" (2003, p. 7). And while the U.S. domestic economy is in decline, the general populace up to the moment has showed no signs of mounting an uprising against a bludgeoning domestic deficit, against the hundreds of corpses returning from Iraq, or against the eviscerated state capacity to offer social services such as health and education. Rather, as stated by Scheer (2003), "too many Americans betray the proud tradition of an independent citizenry by buying into the 'aw shucks' irresponsibility of a president who daily does a grave injustice to the awesome obligations of the office that he has sworn—in the name of God, no less—to uphold" (p. B11).

Currently the majority of U.S. citizens are enjoying the "empire chic" status of the victor and comforting themselves with the notion that, although no weapons of mass destruction were found, mass graves of Saddam's enemies were. This ignores the whole question of organized deception on the part of the Bush administration and his cabal of hawks and conforms to the fascist vocabulary of the newly minted Bush doctrine of preventative war. Those justifying the war on the basis of Saddam's mass graveyards are all too willing to discount the reason that Bush claims to have gone to war and therefore support the notion that the ends justify the means. Are those people who support the war for humanitarian reasons aware that many of Saddam's victims were the result of his reprisals after 1991, when Bush padre exhorted the Iraqis to rise up against Saddam, only to abandon them later on to the ensuing slaughter? It may seem quixotic for us to remark that we believe another world outside of capitalism's military industrial precincts is possible. We believe that calling for a socialist future is more than a hollow paean to the revolution by cross-grained polemicists but a creditable—and necessary—stance given the crisis of overaccumulation and overcapacity that drives capital's endless wars and environmental destruction. Marxists have unpacked the whole discreditable logic upon which capitalism rests, and we would do well to take stock of those arguments today in our struggle to lay the groundwork for a future of peace and prosperity. George Katsiaficas (2003) is correct when he identifies the true "axis of evil" as composed of the World Trade Organization, the World Bank, and the International Monetary Fund. Their policies and practices clearly means more poverty for nations on the periphery of the world system, and have led to a dynamic "of increasing political democracy in the North coinciding with intensified exploitation in the South" (Katsiaficas 2003, p. 348).

TOWARD AN ALTERNATIVE FUTURE

Borrowing from Callinicos (2003), we reject the bourgeois anticapitalism that critiques civil society but ultimately endorses the proposition that market capitalism is the best solution for meeting the overall needs of humankind. We reject, as well, localist anticapitalism that endorses economic self-sufficiency by means of microrelationships among producers and consumers because this simply paves the way for market efficiency. Reformist anticapitalism shares a similar problematic solution, the least of which is an endorsement of a more regulated capitalism at the level of the nation-state. The most egregious effects of the capitalist system cannot be eliminated by taming the global corporation or by trying to make their CEOs more socially conscious. Decentralized networks characteristic of autonomist anticapitalism advocates a concept of radical democracy in which decentralization and the deterritorialized multitude replaces the antistate approach of the proletariat of classical Marxism. We prefer a socialist anticapitalist approach that is nonsectarian and promotes a conception of the world in which the working class is still the most important agent of social transformation (Callinicos 2003). We adopt a multiracial, gender-balanced, anti-imperialist approach that struggles to bring about a world in which everyone has equal access to the resources that they need in order to live a valuable and worthwhile life. Such an assertion is based on need and not productive contribution (Callinicos 2003). We do not focus here on the immediate needs of the workers that can be met in a "social partnership" with capital, but on the needs of the global community of immiserated and disenfranchised workers.

The search for social transformation in the form of redistributive justice—that is, striving to equalize material resources under existing conditions of global capitalism —often works to console those who are oppressed rather than to provoke them to rise up against the world of capitalism. It is a way of temporarily seeking relief from capitalism by ultimately adapting to its inevitability through a struggle to create more humane forms of its instantiation. It helps to soothe or console their alienation by finding temporary relief from their enslavement to capitalism and its attendant suffering. Especially among the privileged strata, the struggle for social justice ultimately rationalizes and thus further integrates their parasitic relationship to the oppressed since they can unknot the tightening noose of capitalism without having to cut the rope that is strangling the disenfranchised. It enables them to cling to power and economic security while having the appearance of being progressive. It affords them the opportunity to advertise their discontent with capitalism without having to root out and transform the social relations of exploitation and property relations in which their parasitism is uncomfortably nested and upon which the scaffold is built to render a final judgement against the propertyless. Often social justice agendas do more for the privileged strata than they do for the oppressed classes because they address the myriad contradictions that surround the lives of the oppressed and alleviate some of the pain and confusion associated with it. In other words, social justice agendas ease the psychological suffering of the privileged strata while at the same time camouflage their complicity in a system that is inextricably bound up with the suffering of the masses, a suffering that can only be alleviated by slicing through the Gordian knot of capital and moving toward a socialist alternative.

For many of us who were part of the burgeoning U.S. antiwar movement, protesting at every turn the Bush administration prior to its invasion of Iraq, hope seemed to be within grasp as momentum against the Bush *junta* was building worldwide. But shortly after the ground invasion began, the antiwar movement began to stagger, as many of the protestors were not prepared to continue their activism once U.S. troops were in the war theater itself. What seemed like a light at the end of the tunnel for the U.S. Left was really Bush hijo igniting a flame-thrower, incinerating the dream of a new revolutionary dawn. With the mighty chains of his Christian faith, Bush has hoisted his conscience onto the biblical back of God, to whose wrath he has faithfully committed himself and his armies of invasion. Bush wraps his depleted uranium shells in the "divine right of kings" and the doctrine of U.S. Manifest Destiny before hurling them into the theater of war with the deftness of a Super Bowl quarterback. As U.S. weapons of mass destruction effortlessly saw through tendon and bone, blast apart organs and incinerate flesh with a vengeful fury, Bush sleeps as soundly as the 10,000 innocent Iraqi civilians that he has recently killed, but remains oblivious to the wails and shrieks of the countless numbers that he has left orphaned and crippled.

After his routine three-mile jog and bedtime prayers, the former Governor of Texas who set the record for most executions by any governor in American history has learned to unburden his heart by invoking the Lord for foreign policy direction. His mind unburdened by the power of analysis, Bush unhesitatingly made his decision to invade and occupy Iraq "because be believes, he truly believes, that God squats in his brainpan and tells him what to do" (Floyd 2003, p. 4). The Israeli newspaper *Haaretz* was given transcripts of a negotiating session between Palestinian Prime Minister Mahmoud Abbas and faction leaders from Hamas and other militant groups. In these transcripts, Abbas described his recent summit with Ariel Sharon and Bush hijo. During the summit, Bush told Abbas: "God told me to strike at al Qaeda and I struck them, and then He instructed me to strike at Saddam, which I did, and now I am determined to solve the problem in the Middle East. If you help me I will act, and if not, the elections will come and I will have to focus on them" (Regular 2003, p. 1). Bush should consult any standard copy of proverbs, maxims, and phrases where he would likely encounter the following saying: He that preaches a war when it might well be avoided is the devil's chaplain. But perhaps such a maxim doesn't apply to a sitting U.S. president who speaks directly to God.

Meeting privately with a group of Old Order Amish during a visit to Lancaster County, Pennsylvania, President Bush asked them to vote for him in November. When told by the Amish that not all members of the church vote but they would pray for him, Bush's eyes reportedly moistened. Brubaker (2004) describes Bush's response as follows: "Bush had tears in his eyes when he replied. He said the president needs their prayers. He also said that having a strong belief in God is the only way he can do his job. . . . At the end of the session, Bush reportedly told the group, 'I trust God speaks through me. Without that, I couldn't do my job.'"

Like 55 percent of his fellow Americans, Bush hijo has been born again. His evangelical Christian perspective converges on the absolute authority and literal truth of the Bible and the redemptive power of Jesus. When asked by journalist Bob Woodward if he had ever doubted his invasion of

Iraq, no wonder Bush retorted: "I haven't suffered any doubt" (cited in Steinberg 2004). According to Jonathan Steinberg (2004), "In the president's view, to doubt his policy would be to doubt his God-given calling." Approximately 55 percent of those who voted for Bush in 2000 had placed moral reform as their highest political priority. The vast majority of evangelicals who make up 30 percent of the U.S. population voted for Bush in 2004 since this election represented for them "the ultimate struggle between good and evil in American life" (Steinberg 2004). The view of Republican Rep. Tom Cole of Oklahoma—who told supporters that a vote against George Bush was a vote for Osama bin Laden and Adolf Hitler—may seem ludicrous to nonevangelicals, but is not particularly disturbing in light of Bush hijo's State of the Union message of 2002 in which he called Iran, Iraq, and North Korea "the axis of evil" and threw down the gauntlet of the holy warrior. After his address, Bush proclaimed to an audience in Daytona Beach: "We've got a great opportunity. . . . As a result of evil, there's some amazing things that are taking place in America. People have begun to challenge the culture of the past that said, 'If it feels good, do it.' This great nation has a chance to change the culture" (cited in Steinberg 2004). But what kind of culture is Bush advancing? A culture in which people have no hesitation in invading other sovereign countries who are clearly no immediate threat, and a culture in which violence against "evil-doers" should never be second-guessed.

The jackhammer spiritual logic that is pervasive among the numerous evangelical troops that make up the U.S. occupation force in Iraq equates their mission as a battle waged on behalf of God. Sage Stossel (2004) writes that on Palm Sunday, before a scheduled attack by the United States on an Iraqi target, "a military chaplain issued a blessing in which he reminded them that it was Palm Sunday and referred to the task at hand as 'a spiritual battle' and to the Marines themselves as 'tools of mercy.'" Of course, there are some servicemen who are confused about their role as mercy relief and about killing those branded by Bush hijo as "evil-doers." Patrolling Najaf, Iraq, Spc. Joshua Dubois of the 2nd Armored Cavalry Regiment recently confessed: "I'm confused about how I should feel about killing. . . . The first time I shot someone, it was the most exhilarating thing I'd ever felt. . . . We talk about killing all the time. . . . I never used to talk this way. I'm not proud of it, but it's like I can't stop. I'm worried what I will be like when I get home" (Duhigg 2004, p. A1). Capt. Brandon Payne is similarly worried about killing: "I'm a Christian. I feel I'm saving my soldiers' lives by destroying as many enemy as I can. But at the end of the day, I pray to God. I worry about my soul" (Duhigg 2004, p. A11). If we are to believe President Bush, he shares no such doubt; however, he has never had to kill anyone in cold blood,

Peter McLaren and Nathalia E. Jaramillo

having successfully avoided being drafted to Vietnam. Or perhaps Bush just has more Christian faith. No doubt Bush would be proudest of the soldiers who reveal absolutely no ambivalence about exterminating "evil-doers." Duhigg (2004) reports:

> "I enjoy killing Iraqis," says Staff Sgt. William Deaton, 30, who killed a hostile fighter the night before. Deaton has lost a good friend in Iraq. "I just feel rage, hate when I'm out there. I feel like I carry it all the time. We talk about it. We all feel the same way."
>
> Sgt. Cleveland T. Rogers, 25, avoids dwelling on his actions. "The other day an Iraqi guy was hit real bad, he was gonna die within an hour, but he was still alive and he started saying, 'Baby, baby,' telling me he has a kid," Rogers says. "I mentioned it to my guys after the mission. It doesn't bother me. It can't bother me. If it was the other way around, I'm sure it wouldn't bother him." (p. A11)

Often critics of the Bush administration will make the point that criticizing Bush Junior is too easy, that the serious problems that need to be addressed are part of wider decisions by his administration and tied to policies, ideologies, and social relations of the U.S. ruling class, whether Republican or Democrat. Of course, this observation is true. But it is also true that Bush, with his "taunting jack-o'-lantern grin" (Wolcott 2004, 23), reflects the spirit of the country, his persona embodies what the country would like to project as its national character, a window into the soul of the country. In short, the president is what E. L. Doctorow (2004) calls the "artificer of our malleable national soul." He writes:

> The president we get is the country we get. With each president the nation is conformed spiritually. He is the artificer of our malleable national soul. He proposes not only the laws but the kinds of lawlessness that govern our lives and invoke our responses. The people he appoints are cast in his image. The trouble they get into and get us into, is his characteristic trouble. Finally, the media amplify his character into our moral weather report. He becomes the face of our sky, the conditions that prevail.

What does this say about the country when we have elected somebody of the character and mettle of President Bush, besides an annoying admission that the country has put itself and its national credibility at risk with the rest of the world? It says that, to a large extent, Americans are an insular lot, who are still easy prey for the populist rhetoric (however phony) of someone with whom they can identify as "just folks." They love the I-don't-care-about-what-any-foreigner-thinks-of-this-country temper and rhetoric displayed by its conservative politicians and for the most part are not adverse to a go-it-alone philosophy when it comes to foreign policy. But what is it about this

president that especially irks so many of us? Is it that he is so good at playing a Texan that the self-parody is lost on most people, that he manages the
art of deception with such characteristic ease that we are willing to enjoy his
uncomfortableness with the English language and his petulant smirk? Perhaps. But we believe it has more to do with his hollow sincerity and incapac-
ity to feel empathy and compassion, despite his claims to the contrary.
Doctorow (2004) captures this dimension of Bush when he writes:

> He is the president who does not feel. He does not feel for the families of the
> dead, he does not feel for the 35 million of us who live in poverty, he does not
> feel for the 40 percent who cannot afford health insurance, he does not feel for
> the miners whose lungs are turning black or for the working people he has de-
> prived of the chance to work overtime at time-and-a-half to pay their bills—it is
> amazing for how many people in this country this president does not feel. But
> he will dissemble feeling. He will say in all sincerity he is relieving the wealth-
> iest 1 percent of the population of their tax burden for the sake of the rest of us,
> and that he is polluting the air we breathe for the sake of our economy, and that
> he is decreasing the quality of air in coal mines to save the coal miners' jobs,
> and that he is depriving workers of their time-and-a-half benefits for overtime
> because this is actually a way to honor them by raising them into the profes-
> sional class. And this litany of lies he will versify with reverences for God and
> the flag and democracy, when just what he and his party are doing to our de-
> mocracy is choking the life out of it.

The sight of the Highway of Death (the destruction that took place on the
road from Mutlaa, Kuwait, to Basra, Iraq) after the Persian Gulf War, where
U.S. forces slaughtered tens of thousands of retreating Iraqi soldiers (and
most likely fleeing civilians) in an infamous strike that was described as
"shooting sheep in a pen," apparently was not enough for the likes of the
hard-line neocon movement around Bush Jr. Nor apparently was the
American-led embargo of Iraq that in over ten years killed half a million
Iraqi children (an action of violence that rivaled any committed by the
homicidal maniac Saddam). But now that Iraq is in U.S. hands, some of
the most fervent warmongers among the Bush advisors—Bush, Perle, and
Rumsfeld—for whom brokering a political compromise is tantamount to
anti-Americanism worry that opportunities to use the terror of al-Qaeda
to launch a holy war against more evil Islamic nations are perilously wan-
ing, and further opportunities to redraw the map of the Middle East through
naked military power might be lost (at least until the next major terrorist
strike on U.S. soil). When, in 1973, Henry Kissinger (then Nixon's national
security advisor) referred to military men as "dumb, stupid animals to be
used" as pawns for foreign policy, he was reflecting what is still the prevailing attitude within the U.S. military industrial complex. One of the most

alarming aspects of life in the United States after the terrorist attacks of September 11, 2001, has been the religious punditry that characterizes Bush's claim to be a special Viceroy of God.

In the eyes of many U.S. citizens, this claim has provided Bush hijo with the moral authority not only to order the nation's "dumb, stupid animals" into war, but also to turn the carnage inflicted by the world's most fearsome military machine into a mass graveyard for evil-doers who have been designated by his administration hawks and Likudites as enemies of civilization. Unerring on punctilio when it comes to internalizing the monstrous banality of a Manichean universe of demons and deliverers, Bush has been alarmingly effective in putting God's imprimatur on capitalism as the structure preferred by goodness.

When a war can be prosecuted against sovereign nations "by the working class against the working class, for the rich" (Wypijewski 2004, p. 291), then it is a win-win situation for God's capitalist militia. After all, trusting in God is the most assured way to become rich, as the evangelical mega-churches so vociferously proclaim in their "prosperity preaching" throughout the country. A recent comment by Jonathan Steinberg (2004) is apposite: "Poverty still exists in America, as Bush argued in the State of the Union address of 2003, because the poor fail to find true Christian charity among their neighbors. Hence, his 'compassionate conservatism' requires 'faith-based initiatives' by local churches and not progressive taxation." And this view pervades the ranks of the U.S. public at a time when the poor are becoming more like contemporary analogates of the Dickensian outcast, the forgotten and the excluded, social excrement that fills the sewers where Marx's reserve army of labor are barracked.

Joe Conason (2003) has compared Bush hijo's compassionate conservatism—which rages against the sins of a welfare state—to Puritanism and feudalism, contrasting it to modern American values as developed over the last hundred years. Conason notes that public support for the poor and powerless represents for Bush and his evangelical fundamentalist ilk an "affront to God" (although they will tolerate it for temporary partisan expedience). Conason argues further that Bush's evangelical perspective constitutes "an unwholesome stew of libertarian economics and religious orthodoxy" that "exalts church and corporation over the modern democratic state," "condemns democratic initiatives to constrain corporate power or regulate economic activity," and "defines the wealthy as God's elect, even if, like George W. Bush, they have inherited wealth and power that made their lives easy from the beginning" (2003, p. 183). In fact, a case can easily be made that Muslims as a whole have much more favorable opinions about the ideals of democracy than Bush and his cabal of ultraconservative religious sages. Conason writes that Bush's spiritual guru, Marvin Olasky, is financially connected and ideologically aligned to Christian Reconstructionism, which Conason describes as follows:

> The Reconstructionists despise American democracy, the First Amendment, and the separation of church and state. Their ideal society would be ruled by Christians like themselves, according to a literal interpretation of Old Testament biblical law, which prescribes the death penalty for such offenses as homosexuality, abortion, atheism, juvenile delinquency, adultery, and blasphemy. They openly advocate the suppression of other religions, including that of Christians who don't share their interpretation of God's will. (2003, p. 181)

Of course, this version of Christianity benefits the Republican Party as a whole. As Jonathan Steinberg (2004) notes:

> Large corporations are delighted to accept the evangelical attack on the state. They like to see the Federal Communications Commission relax regulations on media mergers; the Federal Power Commission ease strictures on energy companies; the Environmental Protection Agency modify air pollution regulations; and the Interior Department condone logging in the national parks. Bush easily raises record-breaking sums for his presidential campaigns from all the biggest corporations, even though only a few have evangelical chief executive officers.

JESUS'S GENERAL

While Bush hijo has gone out of his way to praise Islam as "a religion of peace" and has invited Muslim clerics to the White House for Ramadan dinners and has publicly opposed labeling Islam a dangerous faith, as is the wont of some evangelical Christian leaders, it is interesting to note that the Pentagon has assigned the task of tracking down and eliminating Osama bin Laden and other high-profile targets to an army general who characterizes the war on terrorism "as a clash between Judeo-Christian values and Satan" (Cooper 2003). According to Richard T. Cooper of the *Los Angeles Times*, Lt. Gen. William G. "Jerry" Boykin, the new deputy undersecretary of defense for intelligence (whose new high-level policy position at the Pentagon was confirmed by the Senate in June) is a celebrated veteran of covert military operations, from the storied 1993 clash with Muslim warlords in Somalia chronicled in "Black Hawk Down" and the hunt for Colombian drug czar Pablo Escobar to the 1980 failed rescue attempt of American hostages in Iran. He also was an advisor to Attorney General Janet Reno during Waco. What is being studiously avoided in the press is the fact that Boykin, as head of "Delta

Force," is presumably implicated in torture at a top-secret prison known as "BIF" (Battlefield Interrogation Prison) at Baghdad airport. The army's elite Delta Force is now the subject of a Pentagon inspector general investigation into abuse against detainees. According to several top U.S. government sources, it is the scene of the most vicious and brutal violations of the Geneva Conventions in all of Iraq's prisons. At this facility the prisoners are allegedly hooded from the moment they are captured, warehoused in tiny dark cells, routinely drugged, and often are held under water or smothered to the point of suffocation. Top Pentagon officials will neither confirm nor deny the existence of Battlefield Interrogation Prison.

Cooper (2003) describes Boykin's new duties as "speeding up the flow of intelligence on terrorist leaders to combat teams in the field so that they can attack top-ranking terrorist leaders." According to Cooper, this former commander and thirteen-year veteran of the army's top-secret Delta Force "is also an outspoken evangelical Christian who appeared in dress uniform and polished jump boots before a religious group in Oregon one mild June day to declare that radical Islamists hated the United States 'because we're a Christian nation, because our foundation and our roots are Judeo-Christian . . . and the enemy is a guy named Satan.'" Last year Boykin is reported to have said: "We in the army of God, in the house of God, kingdom of God have been raised for such a time as this" (Cooper 2003). Boykin has admitted that radical Muslims who resort to terrorism are not representative of the Islamic faith. Cooper reports that Boykin "has compared Islamic extremists to 'hooded Christians' who terrorized blacks, Catholics, Jews and others from beneath the robes of the Ku Klux Klan."

According to military affairs analyst William M. Arkin (2003), Boykin described his battle in Mogadishu, Somalia, as one that pitted the U.S. forces against a Satanic presence, whose hovering image Boykin claims to have captured in a photograph of the sky over the city:

In June 2002, Jerry Boykin stepped to the pulpit at the First Baptist Church of Broken Arrow, Oklahoma, and described a set of photographs he had taken of Mogadishu, Somalia, from an army helicopter in 1993. The photographs were taken shortly after the disastrous "Blackhawk Down" mission had resulted in the death of eighteen Americans. When Boykin came home and had them developed, he said, he noticed a strange dark mark over the city. He had an imagery interpreter trained by the military look at the mark. "This is not a blemish on your photograph," the interpreter told him, "This is real." "Ladies and gentleman, this is your enemy," Boykin said to the congregation as he flashed his pictures on a screen. "It is the principalities of darkness. It is a demonic presence in that city that God revealed to me as the enemy." (Arkin, 2003)

At the pulpit of the Good Shepherd Community Church in Sandy, Oregon, Boykin displayed slides of Osama bin Laden, Saddam Hussein, and North Korea's Kim Jung II. After posing the question as to why these individuals hate America, he answered his own question: "The answer to that is because we're a Christian nation. We are hated because we are a nation of believers" (Arkin 2003). Boykin also claimed from the pulpit that America's "spiritual enemy will only be defeated if we come against them in the name of Jesus" (Arkin 2003). He also proclaimed to the congregation that the faith that the U.S. special operations forces had in God was what gave them victory: "Ladies and gentlemen I want to impress upon you that the battle that we're in is a spiritual battle. Satan wants to destroy this nation, he wants to destroy us as a nation, and he wants to destroy us as a Christian army" (Arkin 2003).

Boykin also sees the actions of providence in the fact that George Bush is now in charge of the White House. While he admits that in the 2000 presidential election "George Bush was not elected by a majority of the voters in the United States," he nevertheless was "appointed by God" (Arkin, 2003). Arkin (2003) recounts a story Boykin told a church congregation in Daytona, Florida. With the fervor of a football player bragging in the locker room that his penis is larger than that of his opponent, Boykin claims that his Christian God is far bigger than that of his Muslim warlord rival:

> "There was a man in Mogadishu named Osman Atto," whom Boykin described as a top lieutenant of Mohammed Farah Aidid. When Boykin's Delta Force commandos went after Atto, they missed him by seconds, he said. "He went on CNN and he laughed at us, and he said, 'They'll never get me because Allah will protect me. Allah will protect me.' Well, you know what?" Boykin continued. "I knew that my God was bigger than his. I knew that my God was a real God and his was an idol." Atto later was captured. Other countries, Boykin said last year, "have lost their morals, lost their values. But America is still a Christian nation." (Arkin 2003)

Unsurprisingly, Boykin apologized for these comments when they became widely publicized:

> "I am not anti-Islam or any other religion." "I support the free exercise of all religions." "For those who have been offended by my statements, I offer a sincere apology." (Jensen, 2003)

Of course, the statement that he is not anti-Islam is quite absurd. Robert Jensen's (2003) comments are apposite here:

> It seems pretty clear that Boykin is anti-Islam and anti-any-religion-other-than-Christianity, just as are many evangelical Christians who claim a "literalist" view of the Bible. Such folks agree that everyone should be free to practice any religion, but they also believe those religions are nothing more than cults. That's what Boykin meant when he said of the Muslim warlord in Somalia he was fighting, "I knew that my God was a real God, and his was an idol."

Jensen goes on to note the following:

> Idols are false gods, not real ones. To such Christians, who sometimes refer to themselves as "biblical Christians," there is only one religion—Christianity, which is truth. All others are cults. The general can believe in freedom of religion and feel bad when he offends a person with another religion, yet still be convinced that all those other religions are, in fact, false.

Boykin's comments reflect a broadly held Christian theological perspective whose implications at this present moment have world-historical impact in the context of Bush's so-called permanent war on terror. According to James Carroll (2003):

> The general's offense was to speak aloud the implication of a still broadly held theology. But that theology is dangerous now. A respectful religious pluralism is no longer just a liberal hope but an urgent precondition of justice and peace. In the 21st century, exclusivist religion, no matter how "mainstream" and no matter how muted the anathemas that follow from its absolutes, is a sure way to religious war.

According to Stephen Zunes (2004), right-wing Christian Zionists who have long supported George W. Bush (and who follow a Messianic theology that holds a Manichean belief that reality is divided between absolute good and absolute evil and believe that a hegemonic Israel is a necessary precursor to the second coming of Jesus) feel that an expansionist and militaristic Jewish state is indispensable to bring about Armageddon (the final battle between Christ and Satan) and are, at this point in time, more significant in the formulation of U.S. policy toward Israel than even Jewish Zionists. He illustrates this with three recent incidents in a passage that is worth quoting *in extenso*:

- After the Bush administration's initial condemnation of the attempted assassination of militant Palestinian Islamist Abdel Aziz Rantisi in June 2003, the Christian Right mobilized its constituents to send thousands of e-mails to the White House protesting the criticism. A key element in these e-mails was the threat that if such pressure continued to be placed upon Israel, the Christian Right would stay home on election day. Within 24 hours, there was a notable change in tone by the president. Indeed, when Rantisi fell victim to a successful Israeli assassination in April 2004, the administration—as it did with the assassination of Hamas leader Sheik Ahmed Yassin the previous month—largely defended the Israeli action.

- When the Bush administration insisted that Israel stop its April 2002 military offensive in the West Bank, the White House received over 100,000 e-mails from Christian conservatives in protest of its criticism. Almost immediately, President Bush came to Israel's defense. Over the objections of the State Department, the Republican-led Congress adopted resolutions supporting Israel's actions and blaming the violence exclusively on the Palestinians.
- When President Bush announced his support for the Road Map for Middle East peace, the White House received more than 50,000 postcards over the next two weeks from Christian conservatives opposing any plan that called for the establishment of a Palestinian state. The administration quickly backpedaled, and the once-highly touted Road Map essentially died.

Any dismissal of the millenarian aspects of Christian Zionism on the impact of White House foreign policy may be much too precipitate in light of events of the Bush hijo administration. Those who might think that the Democratic Party would be a good counterpoint to the Christian Zionists of the Bush administration would not necessarily be on solid ground to make their case. Zunes (2004) points out a disturbing feature of the Democratic Party by demonstrating that their position on the Israeli-Palestinian conflict is closer to that of the Christian Zionists than to more liberal church-based organizations:

The Christian Right has long been a favorite target for the Democratic Party, particularly its liberal wing, since most Americans are profoundly disturbed by fundamentalists of any kind influencing policies of a government with a centuries-old tradition of separating church and state. Yet the positions of most liberal Democrats in Congress regarding the Israeli-Palestinian conflict are far closer to those of the reactionary Christian Coalition than to those of the moderate National Council of Churches, far closer to the rightist Rev. Pat Robertson than to the leftist Rev. William Sloan Coffin, far closer to the ultraconservative Moral Majority than to the liberal Churches for Middle East Peace, and far closer to the fundamentalist Southern Baptist Convention than to any of the mainline Protestant churches.

When President Bush told Texas evangelist James Robinson that "I feel like God wants me to run for President. I can't explain it, but I sense my country is going to need me. Something is going to happen. . . . I know it won't be easy on me or my family, but God wants me to do it" (Fitrakis 2004), few Americas realized at the time that Bush would become a raving right-wing evangelical prophet who would carefully craft theocratic nationalist rhetoric to advance his standing among the most exploited and powerless in the United States: the working and unemployed poor who have little to share other than their fervent Christian faith. A more tempered view of Bush's Christianity is that Bush is not doctrinally dogmatic and is theologically moderate. He did, after all, say to Laurie Goodstein (2004): "From Scripture you can gain a lot of strength and solace and learn life's lessons. That's what I believe, and I don't necessarily believe every single word is literally true." Bush worships in an Episcopal church in Washington that welcomes gay couples and a Methodist church in Texas where some congregants support abortion rights. Yet, even so, as Goodstein (2004) notes, "When it comes to policy . . . his opponents and supporters agree that he has done more than any president in recent history to advance the agenda of Christian social conservatives." And, clearly, Bush has repeatedly justified the war in theological terms, often drawing upon a favorite axiom: "Freedom is not America's gift to the world; freedom is the Almighty God's gift to each man and woman in this world" (cited in Goodstein, 2004).

Bob Fitrakis (2004) cogently notes that "Bush's assertion that 'I trust God speaks through me. Without that, I couldn't do my job' brings to mind God as a dull-witted, cognitively-impaired nationalist unable to utter a simple declarative sentence who spends his time preaching 'blessed are the warmongers and profit-makers.'" Even more chilling, as Fitrakis argues, is that the last time a Western nation had a leader so obsessed with the conviction that he was directed by God's leadership, it was Adolf Hitler and Nazi Germany. Far from being "a barbaric pagan or Godless totalitarian," Hitler believed he was chosen by God to lead Germany to victory. Before launching his preemptive strikes throughout Europe, Hitler remarked: "I would like to thank Providence and the Almighty for choosing me of all people to be allowed to wage this battle for Germany" (cited in Fitrakis 2004). He further remarked, "I follow the path assigned to me by Providence with the instinctive sureness of a sleepwalker" (cited in Fitrakis 2004). Fitrakis notes some spine-tingling comparisons between Bush and Hitler on this issue:

> Hitler stated in February 1940, "But there is something else I believe, and that is that there is a God. . . . And this God again has blessed our efforts during the past 13 years." After the Iraqi invasion, Bush announced, "God told me to strike at al Qaeda and I struck them, and then he instructed me to strike at Saddam, which I did." Neither the similarity between Hitler and Bush's religious rhetoric nor the fact that the current president's grandfather was called "Hitler's Angel" by the *New York Tribune* for his financing of the Fuher's rise to power is lost on Europeans. Pat Robertson called Bush "a prophet" and Ralph Reed claimed, after the 9/11 attack, God picked the president because "he knew George Bush had the abil-

ity to lead in this compelling way." Hitler told the German people in March 1936, "Providence withdrew its protection and our people fell, fell as scarcely any other people heretofore. In this deep misery we again learn to pray. . . . The mercy of the Lord slowly returns to us again. And in this hour we sink to our knees and beseech our almighty God that he may bless us, that He may give us the strength to carry on the struggle for the freedom, the future, the honor, and the peace of our people. So help us God." At the beginning of Hitler's crusade on April 12, 1922, he spelled out his version of the warmongering Jesus: "My feeling as a Christian points me to my Lord and Savior as a fighter." Randall Balmer in *The Nation*, noted that "Bush's God is the eye-for-an-eye God of the Hebrew prophets and the Book of Revelation, the God of vengeance and retribution."

Are those of us living in the United States, to borrow a phrase from Dale Maharidge (2004), "heading toward the end stage of a Weimaresque journey" (pp. 13–14)? Clearly, Bush is no Adolf Hitler when you look at the current historical record, but the "anticipative" and "preventative" wars of the current U.S. regime reflect the ambition and quest for global dominance that finds its most recent precedent in the history of the Third Reich. At the same time, it is important not to underestimate the means by which Christian fundamentalism (or Islamic fundamentalism, for that matter) can become employed—wittingly or unwittingly—by a national leader as an ideological cover and alibi for laying waste to vast numbers of enemies, often depicted as barbaric or evil (although it must be said that Hitler's religious rhetoric was not strictly Christian, as old heathen Germanic beliefs in the chosen warrior king set the tone, nor were the Germans of his time taken by American-style evangelism or by Christian fundamentalism).

With support for Bush's infinite war against the infidels now the default position of so many white males, and with Bush in the clammy hands of a fiendishly cunning Karl Rove and under the manic thrall of the Pentagon superhawks, there is reason to be concerned about the comparisons. Fitrakis's comments, while surely seen by many as overdrawn and a manipulative "stretch" of the imagination, deserve to be taken seriously:

> As Bush has invoked the cross of Jesus to simultaneously attack the Islamic and Arab world, Hitler also saw the value of exalting the cross while waging endless war: "To be sure, our Christian Cross should be the most exalted symbol of the struggle against the Jewish-Marxist-Bolshevik spirit." Like Bush-ites, Hitler was fond of invoking the Ten Commandments as the foundation of Nazi Germany: "The Ten Commandments are a code of living to which there's no refutation. These precepts correspond to irrefragable needs of the human soul."

Fitrakis points out that, like Bush, Hitler was a strong proponent of faith-based initiatives, as evidenced by Hitler's January 30, 1939, speech to the Reichstag when he proclaimed: "Amongst the accusations which are directed against Germany in the so-called democracy is the charge that the National Socialist State is hostile to religion" (cited in Fitrakis 2004). Hitler then expanded upon how much "public monies derived from taxation through the organs of the State have been placed at the disposal of both churches [Protestant and Catholic]" (cited in Fitrakis 2004). If giving nearly 1.8 billion Reichsmarks between 1933 and 1938 directly to the Christian churches was not a faith-based initiative, we don't know what is. Hitler spelled out the intent of his faith-based initiative with the comment "With a tenth of our budget for religion, we would thus have a Church devoted to the State and of unshakable loyalty . . . the little sects, which receive only a few hundred thousand marks, are devoted to us body and soul" (cited in Fitrakis 2004). Back in the days of the war in Vietnam, Bob Dylan's song "With God on Our Side" struck a chord with Americans who decried the influence of the Christian right in conscripting God into America's war against the godless communist Viet Cong. It is time we took that concern to heart.

George W. Bush is clearly out to defeat the Biblical Beast of the Apocalypse. But unbeknownst to Bush, the Beast that so terrifies him and other evangelicals of his ilk does not slither through smoking corridors of fire and brimstone dragging behind it naked virgins in leather hip boots and wrapped in chains; rather, it gleefully straddles the behemoth of neoliberal capitalism, sporting a Ronald Reagan mask and leather chaps, and digging its spurs into the flesh of the poor as it garrisons capitalism for the benefit of the transnational ruling elite. It leaves in its wake worldwide empowerment of the rich and devastation for the ranks of the poor as oligopolistic corporations swallow the globe and industry becomes dominated by new technologies. It is the very behemoth that was created and is currently supported by those politicians who rule the world from positions of personal delusion, private fear, arrogance, and stupidity. Bush may choose to ride the demiurge like a deputy sherriff trying to round up a posse to go after a group of evil rustlers, but he must one day wake up to his role in the Manichean battle he so forcefully advocates. While he may feel that his special charismata has given him access to the pleroma, and secured the loyalty of the ecclesia of his base (the haves and have-mores), Bush is content to play imperialism's New Adam, spreading his own hayseed Philipics through the oracle of Fox News, while unbenowst to him he has become the Supreme Commodity enfleshed and made human by capital's law of value.

When, on the freshly mopped deck of the carrier *USS Abraham Lincoln*, the U.S. warrior president emerged in a snug-fitting flight suit from an S-3B Viking aircraft, tautened groin-accentuating straps strung salaciously between his legs, and glistening helmet clasped snugly against a proud chest (a brazenly hypocritical move considering his military records reveal that he stopped flying during his final eighteen months of National Guard duty in 1972 and 1973 and was not observed by his commanders at his Texas unit for a year), his trademark swagger and petulant grin were greeted by patriotic cheers from throngs of wild-eyed officers and sailors. The image of our little Odin's bulging male appurtenances (surely there is no undescended Hitleresque testicle here) impudently—and we dare say unpresidentially—well disciplined by diagonal straps, surely serves as a stage-managed challenge to Clinton's reputation as alpha male stud and is about as close to a presidential "money shot" as can be had in the public arena without being perceived as indecent (which is not to say it cannot serve as someone's private pornography with the comforting knowledge that it is not a crime to download images of the testicles of U.S. presidents).

Appearing topside before a bold banner that announced "Mission Accomplished" he declared the "battle of Iraq" a "victory" in the ongoing "war on terror."[2] This event was carefully choreographed by Bush's team of seasoned image makers that included a former ABC producer, a former Fox TV producer, and a former NBC cameraman paid for out of an annual budget of $3.7 million that Bush allots for his media coordinators. (No doubt the same image makers that organized Bush's visit to the NASCAR Daytona 500 on February 15, 2004, where, in the words of Marc Cooper [2004, p. 18], "he buzzed the gathered 180,000 stock-car-racing fans with Air Force One and two streaking F-15s," then "tickled the crowd by running a lap around the legendary 2.5 mile track in his blacked-out motorcade fleet of spiffy SUVs," extending the spectacle with a rendition of "God Bless the USA" from country singer Lee Greenwood, followed by another overflight from a wedge-shaped B-2 bomber flanked by fighter escorts. When Bush emerged on the speedway stage in a dark NASCAR windbreaker, he announced: "We ask God's blessing," paused, then commanded: "Gentlemen, start your engines!") We do not believe that it's coincidental that a comparison clearly can be drawn between this example of right-wing showmanship on the *USS Abraham Lincoln* and Leni Riefenstahl's infamous propaganda film about the 1934 Nazi *Parteitag* in Nuremberg, *Triumph des Willens* (*Triumph of the Will*) that displayed Adolf Hitler as the world savior. In the German version, Hitler emerges from a Junker 52 aircraft that had been filmed landing at Nuremberg airport to the lofty strains of a Wagner composition. Thousands of Nazi onlookers chant, *Sieg hiel*! as the musical score builds to a thunderous crescendo. And while the scene was carefully crafted to suggest that Hitler was a modern manifestation of the ancient Aryan deity Odin (see *The Internationalist* May 2003), the event on the *USS Abraham Lincoln* was pitching our tumescent boy emperor as a major player in the decidedly Christian drama known as the Second Coming.

Bush's speech on the carrier paraphrased Chapter 61 of Isaiah, the very book that Jesus used when proclaiming that Isaiah's prophecies of the Messiah had come true, suggesting perhaps that Bush believes the Second Coming has begun (Pitt 2003) and that his war on terror is playing an important role in this biblical prophecy. (Interestingly, Eagleton [2003] notes that the book of Isaiah is a revolutionary document in which Yahweh tells his people to seek justice and correct oppression and "is only left in hotel rooms because nobody bothers to read it. If those who deposit it there had any idea what it contained, they would be well advised to treat it like pornography and burn it on the spot" [p. 178]). Leftist commentators have noted that the Pentagon's "Shock and Awe" bombing strategy was copied form the Nazi strategy of *Blitzkrieg* (lightning war) and the Luftwaffe's doctrine of *Schrecklichkeit* aimed at terrorizing a population into surrender and that the Bush doctrine of preventative war mirrors the rationale behind Hitler's march into Poland (Hitler had claimed Poland was an immediate threat to the safety of the Reich). And while Bush padre's vow to establish a New World Order and Hitler's vow to create a *Neue Ordung* have to be seen in their historical and contextual specificity, the comparison of the Bush dynasty to the Third Reich does extend beyond fascist aesthetics, media spectacle, and the police state tactics of the Office of Homeland Security. It can be seen in the machinations of capital and the role of the military-industrial complex in imperialist acts of aggression disguised as "freedom."

With Hitler, it was the Jews who were subhuman—the *untermensch*—and with Bush the vermin of choice are the unholy Muslims. Hitler fancied himself as God's chosen leader of the Aryan Race and was in the thrall of a Volkism that prophesized a mighty God-chosen Aryan leader who would lead the people to their rightful destiny through a bloody conquest of the lebensraum (Paul 2003) while Bush thinks God wears a Stetson hat and speaks in a drawl and is content in his role as God's own Texas Ranger.

In his unconscious attempt to achieve aplótès (simplicity of the soul) over dipsukia (duplicity of the soul), has Bush forsaken human reason? Has his unwrinkled faith that he is an emissary of God's will placed the world in grave danger of nuclear destruction? These are not unreasonable questions.

Opportunism and hypocrisy are the operative words when it comes to assessing Bush's professed religious beliefs. According to a recent report by John Gorenfeld (2003), Bush hijo's Faith Based Initiative has given plenty of financial support to disciples of the Rev. Sun Myung Moon. We know that when John Ashcroft was the incoming attorney general, he attended Moon's Inaugural Prayer Luncheon for Unity and Renewal just before Bush took office. We know, too, that Moon's *Washington Times* foundation gave a million dollars to the George H. W. Bush presidential library and has paid the former president large sums as speaking honoraria. We question the so-called "family values" that, according to Bush padre, Moon's organization is supposed to support, especially in light of a number of uncomfortable facts, such as Moon's own criminal conviction for tax fraud and conspiracy to obstruct justice; his stipulation that his photograph must be placed nearby when spouses have sex; his instructions that spouses wipe their genitalia with the Holy Handkerchief (which is never supposed to be laundered) supplied by Moon's organization; his labeling of gays as "dung eating dogs" and of American women as "a line of prostitutes"; his claim that the Holocaust was payback for the Jews for the crucifixion of Christ; his claim that he will succeed where Christ had failed in attaining worldly power; his illegal funding of the murderous Nicaraguan Contras during the Iran-Contra affair; his claim that spiritual messages from Confucius and former U.S. President James Buchanan have verified that he is the savior of the world; his attack on the crucifix as the final obstacle in keeping Moon from being accepted by the American public as the Messiah; and his instructions to cherish and punish one's sexual organs with pliers, if necessary (Gorenfeld, 2003).

Lacking the enameled self-importance that often accompanies an aristocratic intellect, Bush hijo betrays the spittoon arrogance of the tough-talking, God-fearing Texas oil baron, a ghostly veneer of saloon sawdust coating his forked tongue. Bush himself has remarked: "Some folks look at me and see a certain swagger, which in Texas is called walking" (cited in Gourevitch 2004). His cowboy hauteur affords him a hayseed endearedness among paleocons, radiocons, and loyal viewers of Fox TV news. But he positively repulses sober thinkers averse to displays of unvarnished contempt for the world community. Philip Gourevitch (2004) writes:

> He [Bush] has a repertoire of stock poses and expressions, as does any professional performer, but the freedom of his movements is striking. Flip through snapshots of him, and you'll find any number that catch him in a bizarre or comical position. The mobility of his face leaves him open to lampooning, not least because of its simian modeling, which is underscored by his affectation of an equally simian gait—the dangle-armed swagger, like a knuckle-walker startled to find himself suddenly upright. But even when he looks foolish, or simply coarse, Bush is never less than an expressive presence.

But how is it that Bush can command such respect among everyday, working-class Americans? How is it that the policies that he initiates can destroy their jobs, destroy environmental resources, and yet blue-collar workers still vote for him? How is it that the very sector of American society now poised to keep him in the White House—working-class males or what Arlie Hochschild (2003) describes the prototypical "Nascar Dad" who watches car races on television, who listens to Rush Limbaugh on the drive home from work, who turns on Fox TV at dinner, and who is too tired after working overtime to catch more than the headlines—is the one that stands to lose the most from his antiworker, antilabor policies? How is it that, as some polls reveal, blue-collar males support massive tax cuts for the rich? Hochschild (2003) put the issue thusly:

> Let's consider the situation. Since Bush took office in 2000, the U.S. has lost 4.9 million jobs, (2.5 million net), the vast majority of them in manufacturing. While this cannot be blamed entirely on Bush, his bleed-'em-dry approach to the non-Pentagon parts of the government has led him to do nothing to help blue-collar workers learn new trades, find affordable housing, or help their children go to college. The loosening of Occupational Health and Safety Administration regulations has made plants less safe. Bush's agricultural policies favor agribusiness and have put many small and medium-sized farms into bankruptcy. His tax cuts are creating state budget shortfalls, which will hit the public schools blue-collar children go to, and erode what services they now get. He has put industrialists in his environmental posts, so that the air and water will grow dirtier. His administration's disregard for the severe understaffing of America's nursing homes means worse care for the elderly parents of the Nascar Dad as they live out their last days. His invasion of Iraq has sent blue-collar children and relatives to the front. Indeed, his entire tap-the-hornets'-nest foreign policy has made the U.S. arguably less secure than it was before he took office. Indeed, a recent series of polls revealed that most people around the world believe him to be a greater danger than Osama Bin Laden. Many blue-collar voters know at least some of this already. So why are so many of them pro-Bush anyway? (pp. 1–2)

Part of the answer is that a large percentage of blue-collar workers are evangelical Christians who regard Bush as possessing a direct line of communication to the Man sitting on the pearly throne. And certainly a large majority of working-class Americans are working far too hard for them to have the time to be as politically informed as they could be. They are also in the thrall of right-wing radio and television talk shows that permeate U.S. airwaves. Many are receptive to the messages of the corporate media that refuse to challenge the Bush administration except in mild-mannered ways. Part of the answer is, of course, that Bush reflects the core values of the blue-collar family and his authoritarian father figure image resonates well with male members, especially after 9/ll. Another part of the answer is that Bush has been successful for some time in concealing massive unemployment figures while he has been in office. The Bureau of Labor Statistics ended its Mass Layoff Tracking Study on Christmas Eve of 2002, thanks to the Bush administration. Congressional Democrats successfully raised funding so that the study could be restored in February 2003 but the loss of 614,167 jobs in those two months went unannounced to the public (Hochschild 2003). Another explanation is captured by Nelson Peery (2002), who notes:

> The stability of America has always rested upon that huge section of the population that had just enough to give them the hope that they were going to get some more. So long as they had that hope, they wouldn't change the system for love nor money no matter how hard they were hurting. They weren't going to change the system because they believed there was a golden egg up there somewhere. They were the ones who stabilized America. (p. 104)

Equally as relevant is the argument that Bush is following a highly successful Republican strategy that began with Nixon and was followed by Ford, which included a deliberate attempt to avoid focusing on the material grievances of the working class, but rather on the "feeling of being forgotten" among white male workers (Hochschild 2003). Hochschild notes that "Nixon appealed not to a desire for real economic change but to the distress caused by the absence of it." Citing Norman Mailer, who recently claimed that the war in Iraq rejuvenated white males by returning to them a lost sense of mastery over the world and offered them a feeling of revenge for their perceived loss of power, Hochschild (2003) provides the following statistics:

> In the last thirty years, white men have taken a drubbing, he notes, especially the three-quarters of them who lack college degrees. Between 1979 and 1999, for example, real wages for male high-school graduates dropped 24 percent. In addition, Mailer notes, white working-class men have lost white champs in football, basketball and boxing. (p. 4)

Bush has clearly filled the void of the great white hero for the angry white working-class American male. Arnold Schwarzenegger is doing the same for the white males of California, who are witnessing large numbers of immigrants from Latin America and feeling overwhelmed by the collapsing economy. But Bush is taking Nixon's blueprint for winning over the white working-class male one step further. According to Hochschild, "instead of appealing, as Nixon did, to anger at economic decline, Bush is appealing to fear of economic displacement." He is also "offering the Nascar Dad a set of villains to blame, and a hero to thank." In effect, Bush has been "strip-mining the emotional responses of blue-collar men to the problems his own administration is so intent on causing." Hochschild (2003) elaborates:

> Unhinging the personal from the political, playing on identity politics, Republican strategists have offered the blue-collar voter a Faustian bargain: We'll lift your self-respect by putting down women, minorities, immigrants,

even those spotted owls. We'll honor the manly fortitude you've shown in taking bad news. But (and this is implicit) don't ask us to do anything to change
that bad news. . . . Paired with this is an aggressive right-wing attempt to mo-
bilize blue-collar fear, resentment and a sense of being lost—and attach it to
the fear of American vulnerability, American loss. By doing so, Bush aims
to win the blue-collar man's identification with big business, empire, and himself. The resentment anyone might feel at the personnel officer who didn't
have the courtesy to call him back and tell him he didn't have the job, Bush
now redirects toward the target of Osama bin Laden, and when we can't find
him, Saddam Hussein and when we can't find him. . . . And these enemies are
now so intimate that we see them close up on the small screen in our bedrooms
and call them by their first names. (p. 6)

Of course, blame also needs to be placed on the policies of the Democrats,
who over the years have abandoned blue-collar workers by "dropping the
class language that once distinguished them sharply from Republicans" and
by ignoring the advances made by working-class struggles that "were the result of decades of movement-building, of bloody fights between strikers and
state militias, of agitating, educating and thankless organizing" (Frank 2004,
p. M6). As a result, Democrats have stood idle while the right has "embraced
the task of building a movement that speaks to those at society's bottom"
(Frank 2004, p. A6) through messages spiked with Christian triumphalism
and acrimony against liberals. What makes Bush so frightening is that both
the Christian Right and the Pentagon hawks have Bush by his Ponderosa belt
buckle and are in no danger of losing their central role in leading the march
toward empire. Even as the economy takes major hits, Bush still is able to
rewrite the losses as a plus for his administration by regulating and channel-
ing the emotions of an angry white male population. Hochschild (2003)
writes:

> George W. Bush is deregulating American global capitalism with one hand
> while regulating the feelings it produces with the other. Or, to put it another way,
> he is doing nothing to change the causes of fear and everything to channel the
> feeling and expression of it. He speaks to a working man's lost pride and his fear
> of the future by offering an image of fearlessness. He poses here in his union
> jacket, there in his pilot's jumpsuit, taunting the Iraqis to "bring 'em on"—all of
> it meant to feed something in the heart of a frightened man. (p. 6)

At this point in time, even after the disclosures of torture at Abu Ghraib
prison and the practice of "secret detentions," and in the wake of stinging criticism of the Bush administration by the congressional commission on 9/11,
and with the knowledge provided by Human Rights First (the new name of
the Lawyers Committee for Human Rights) that there exists a vast global

network of U.S. detention facilities holding suspects in the "war on terror" (the report lists more than two dozen facilities, half of which operate in total secrecy), polls still reveal that the majority of Americans continue to believe that the war in Iraq has been worth the effort. By scapegoating individuals or individual departments as opposed to condemning systematic abuse that would implicate high-ranking officials in the Bush administration, the congressional hearings on Abu Ghraib and the 9/11 commission serve as a system-stabilizing function and provide apertures through which the populace can focus its collective anxiety. This, combined with the fact that a recent Gallup poll reveals that Americans most trust the military, religious organizations, the police, and the presidency (in that order) over any other organizations, and that, according to a recent poll by the Scripps Networks (Mann 2004), to win a sweepstakes or to obtain the ultimate dream home, or to take a dream vacation in an exotic place rank much higher on Americans' wish lists than to achieve world peace, makes it not very difficult to acknowledge the vast and holy power of the ideological state apparatuses in the United States.

This propaganda approach is decidedly costly, not only in terms of human life, but also in terms of U.S. dollars. Because the only way Bush can pull off his image as the great American protector of the white male is if military spending becomes his major priority. Katsiaficas (2003) reveals that:

> [s]ince 1948, the United States has spent more than $15 trillion on the military—more than the cumulative monetary value of all human-made wealth in the United States—more than the value of all airports, factories, highways, bridges, buildings, shopping centers, hotels, houses, and automobiles. If we add the current Pentagon budget (over $346 billion in fiscal 2002) to foreign military aid, veterans' pensions, the military portion of NASA, the nuclear weapons budget of the Energy Department, and the interest payments on debt from past military spending, the U.S. spends $670 billion every year on the military—more than a million dollars a minute. The U.S. military budget is larger than those of the world's next 15 biggest spenders combined, accounting for 36 percent of global military expenditures. (p. 344)

The U.S. military currently is building its tenth supercarrier battle group (no other country possesses even one supercarrier), brags the most advanced fighters and bombers than all the other countries of the world combined and possesses the world's only Stealth aircraft, the world's largest aerial tanker fleet, the heaviest bombers, the most advanced tanks, the most deadly air-to-air and air-to-ground missiles, and the most sophisticated military electronics, including space satellites and drone airplanes (Baker 2003). And while the United States has no storied class of generals who routinely become the country's

304 Peter McLaren and Nathalia E. Jaramillo

president, the military rules by proxy. The United States has now been transformed into a national-security state, where the military has become the most revered institution in a country now overpopulated by right-ideologues, overburdened with military solutions, unengaged by democratic dialogue, and in the primal thrall of the military industrial complex's inexorable logic of empire. James Baker (2003) describes in chilling prose a recent visit by Bush hijo to Fort Hood in central Texas on January 3, where the supreme commander addressed the troops:

> "The Iraqi regime is a grave threat to the United States," he told them—and the rest of us. "Our country is in a great contest of will and purpose. We're being tested. . . . We must, and we will, protect the American people and our friends and allies from catastrophic violence wherever the source, whatever the threat." (pp. 35–36)

What was more frightening than Bush's own words was the response of the troops who were listening. Baker continues:

> The soldiers answered their commander in chief not with cheers or claps, or any sort of ordinary, civilian applause, but with a sudden, violent roar of "Hu-AH! Hu-AH!" Shouted simultaneously from 4,500 throats, it came across on the evening news as a primal, lusting sound; unexpected and voracious and thoroughly martial, like something one might have expected to hear from the Spartans or a Falangist street demonstration in the 1930s. It was not anything like I had ever heard at a rally convened by an American president. The chant continued throughout the speech, turning Bush's address into a churchy call-and-response. Individual cries of "Yeah!" and "Let's go!" rose from the crowd when he explained why we would invade Iraq though not North Korea, but again and again there was that same swift chant, sweeping all before it—"Hu-AH! Hu-AH! Hu-AH!"—reverberating around the gym until Bush, who just before the rally had exchanged his dark suit coat for a green waist-length army jacket, held up his left hand, palm out, in grand, imperious acknowledgement. (2003, p. 36)

When, as leader of the most powerful nation that has ever existed, you declare war not only on terrorists but also on those who *might* one day become terrorists, you are, in effect, declaring war on the structural unconscious of the nation that you are supposed to be serving, nourishing the psychic roots of national paranoia. It is a war of both direction and indirection, a war without limits and without end, a war that can never be won except on the Manichean battleground that exists not in "the desert of the real" but in the maniacal flights of fancy of religious fundamentalism. The powers and principalities that duke it out with flaming swords beyond the pale of our cynical reason can only be glimpsed in the reverse mirror image of our particular liberties and values that we attribute to the resilience and successes of free-market capitalism. But the issue exceeds that of the role of the United States. The detritus of capitalist security states is growing more and more visible throughout the world, as the poor in numerous developed and developing countries continue to be exterminated by war, genocide, starvation, military and police repression, slavery, and suicide. In a very real sense, capital performs itself through our laboring and toiling bodies. And in the process we become "capitalized," that is, we are transformed into commodities, into human capital. As actors in the labor process, we become machines for capital accumulation, we become the jaws of the hyenas whose driving compulsion is to devour surplus value; we are transformed into the living dead, a personification of dead labor in the theater of the damned. We are being integrated into the system because the social character of our performances appears to be the objective character of the performances themselves. This misrecognition becomes the necessary condition for our subjection to our own past performances and to the service to capital provided by such performances. The ideological character of our performances can only be understood when we consider our performances to be social relations, alienated expressions of our enslavement to the commodification process that produce our performances. Capital offers hope to humankind but as it fails to deliver on its promise, the search for alternatives to its social universe continues.

While the steely-eyed generals salivate over the next installment of the military budget, the Bush administration continues to build new military bases throughout the world (the United States has over 250,000 troops in 141 countries), works behind the scenes to support a coup against (and likely an assassination of) President Hugo Chavez of Venezuela, stampedes its neoliberal policies throughout Latin America, and provides funds to so-called "dissidents" in Cuba in an attempt to undermine the Cuban government. In response to a recent criticism by Colin Powell that Cuba sponsors child prostitution as part of its tourism industry, Cuban author and journalist, Rosa Miriam Elizalde, captured the current spirit of U.S. diplomacy when she called the secretary of state "ese comprador de almas que va como Mefistófeles con una mancha de sangre en la solapa del traje, y que quiere hacernos creer a la fuerza que es apenas un clavelito iraquí (a merchant of souls who goes about like Mephistopheles, bearing a blood stain on his attire, but wanting us to believe that it is merely a little Iraqi carnation)" (Rebelde 2003).

How quickly the organized fight against terrorism launched by the United States the day after September 11, 2001, has turned into its opposite: the regime of terror. This is not so difficult to fathom when we consider the history of the U.S. empire. The United States was founded upon the systematic slaughter of its Indigenous peoples. As Katsiaficas (2003) notes, "The dialectical irony of history means that [the U.S.] is simultaneously a white European settler colony founded on genocide and slavery as well as on freedom and democracy" (p. 348). Tens of millions of Native Americans were massacred and between 15 to 50 million Africans were killed in the slave trade (with tens of millions more enslaved).

Perhaps not many people realize that when they dine out at the fancy restaurant, the "Lord Jeff" near Amherst College, that the restaurant's name-sake, Lord Jeffery Amherst (of whom entire towns have been named after in Massachusetts, New York, and New Hampshire), was celebrated because he devised a method of exterminating Indigenous people without risking white lives: delivering to Native Americans blankets carrying the smallpox virus (Katsiaficas 2003). Of course, even if the patrons of the Lord Jeff are con-scious of this part of U.S. history, it is doubtful that it would ruin the taste of their filet mignon. Nineteenth-century U.S. imperialism involved the slaugh-ter of 600,000 Filipinos on the island of Luzon alone, and this effort was praised not only by the director of Presbyterian ministries (who noted that the murders were "a great step in the civilization of the world") but also by both William McKinley and Theodore Roosevelt (Katsiaficas 2003, p. 344). The latter wrote that the slaughter in the Philippines was "for civilization over the black chaos of savagery and barbarism" (cited in Katsiaficas 2003, p. 344). Between 1898 and 1934, the U.S. Marines invaded Cuba four times, Honduras seven times, Nicaragua five times, the Dominican Republic four times, and Haiti and Panama twice each. But we shouldn't overlook U.S. slaughter in Indochina, where between three and five million people were killed in Korea, and two million were killed—many by chemical weapons— in Vietnam. Katsiaficas writes:

> For every man, woman, and child in South Vietnam, the U.S. dropped more than 1,000 pounds of bombs (the equivalent of 700 Hiroshima bombs), sprayed a gal-lon of Agent Orange, and used 40 pounds of napalm and half a ton of CS gas on people whose only wrong doing was to struggle for national independence. The kill ratio in these two Asian wars [Korea and Vietnam] was about 1,000 times that of wars in Central America and perhaps just as high for the more than 200 other U.S. military interventions during the "Cold War." (p. 346)

While there has been a great deal of discussion linking U.S. imperialism and the bloody path of military intervention, too little has been said about the intentional targeting of civilians by the U.S. military. As Tariq Ali has argued: "The massacre of civilian populations was always an integral part of U.S. war strategy" (cited in Boggs 2003, p. 207). Boggs describes the matrix of capi-talism, imperialism, and racism that led to the systematic extermination of Native Americans and asserts that the American tradition of war was given ideological meaning through Manifest Destiny and the Monroe Doctrine. He also points out that the United States has consistently rejected international treaties and protocols for protecting civilians from the carnage of war. Boggs writes:

> Americans have pursued their global ambitions through every conceivable bar-
> baric method: wars of attrition, carpet bombing, free-fire zones, massacres of
> unarmed civilians, support for death squads, forced relocations, destruction
> of public infrastructures, the burning down of cities, use of weapons of mass de-
> struction including atomic bombs. Filled with an imperial contempt for others
> and a sense of moral supremacy, U.S. leaders have predictably established them-
> selves as beyond the reach of international law, immune to any moral or legal
> rules of engagement. (2003, p. 208)

The Korean War is just one example. In this war, the infamous "search and destroy" missions meant attacking not only combatants but also civilians, animals, and the whole ecology as part of effective counterinsurgency operations. When troops came upon any village, they usually came in opening fire, often with support of helicopter gunships. U.S. troops were rewarded according to the well-known "body count," never limited simply to identifiable combatants. (Boggs 2003, p. 210)

Of course, the United States has pursued this logic in most of its wars since that time, up to and including the Gulf War and the bombing of Iraq's civilian infrastructure that lasted for years up to the recent invasion. In a capitalist society—especially in the world's most dominant capitalist society and military superpower—this bloody reality cannot be otherwise. This is because those who are invested in protecting capitalist society and who possess the necessary power (including firepower) not only to defend it but expand its global sweep, are those who have benefited most by it and whose stature has been the most elevated because of it. The guardians of capital represent those whose character has been most fully formed by the ruthless imperatives and unquenchable desires of capital. They have embodied those ensembles of social relations that most estrange them from love and distance them from compassion. Joel Kovel (2002) remarks that capitalism cannot be relegated only to the social relations of economic production but also represents a "regime of the ego." He reminds us that:

> Each society selects for the psychological types that serve its needs. It is quite
> possible in this way to mold a great range of characters toward a unified, class
> purpose. To succeed in the capitalist marketplace and rise to the top, one needs
> a hard, cold, calculating mentality, the ability to sell oneself, and a hefty dose of
> the will to power. (p. 78)

There is little doubt that President Bush believes that he is an avenging instrument of God, perhaps even the sword arm of the most high and holy. Richard Land, a leader of the Southern Baptist Convention, recalls hearing Mr. Bush say in a meeting with close associates on the day of his second inaugural as governor of Texas: "I believe that God wants me to be president" (Stanley 2004). The Bush administration is filled with God-fearing holy warriors who seek to make the presence of God felt in all aspects of public life. When he became president, Bush proclaimed: "We need common-sense judges who understand our rights were derived from God. . . . And those are the kind of judges I intend to put on the bench" (Stanley 2004). Keeping the country's secular barbarians at bay and preventing American interests from being savaged by foreign infidels who are, after all, an obstacle to the Lord's mission to save souls, Bush holds the scales of justice in one hand and a crusader's broadsword in the other. According to a 1993 interview with a reporter for *The Houston Post*, Ken Herman, on the day he announced his intention to run for governor, Mr. Bush asserted that only believers in Christ could go to heaven (Stanley 2004). Furthermore, during the 2000 campaign our "Is Our Children Learning?" education president who reads children's books upside down said that he thought schools should teach both creationism and evolution. Alessandra Stanley (2004) writes:

> The imprint of Mr. Bush's faith can be seen on his appointments to the bench and on his decisions on embryonic stem-cell research and so-called partial-birth abortion. And religion also veins Mr. Bush's discussion of war. Mr. Land describes him as a believer in "American exceptionalism." Jim Wallis, editor in chief of *Sojourners* magazine, a liberal evangelical publication, refers to his talk of a divine mission as the "language of righteous empire."

Referring to President Bush as a "fundagelical," John Sutherland (2004) places Bush among the growing extremists within the evangelical movement. Not without sarcasm, he depicts fundagelicals as follows:

> What do fundagelicals instinctively oppose? Gay marriage, abortion, gun control, taxes, the UN (and the currently top-rated candidate for Antichrist, Kofi Annan), withdrawal from Iraq, Michael Moore, Janet Jackson's left breast. What do they believe in? Christian values and the future as foretold in the Book of Revelation. According to a *Time Magazine* poll (which strains credulity but seems to be valid) 59 percent of Americans trust that St John's prophecies will be fulfilled—probably during their lifetime. November could be a last opportunity to vote for God's preferred candidate. Iraq (ancient Babylon) figures centrally in the fundagelist vision of things, as does the Rapture, and the imminent mass conversion of the Jews (hence fundagelist-Zionism). . . . The White House has recently been accused of inveighing (via NASA) against the movie *The Day*

After Tomorrow (out on May 28) because it narrates the wrong apocalypse. One caused by man-made global warming, that is, rather than God's white-hot rage against sinners. The apocalypse depicted in Tim LaHaye's Left Behind books is, we assume, the U.S. government-approved version.

If you have watched the 700 Club hosted by Pat Robertson or have heard Jerry Falwell (who blamed 9/11 on a select group of sinners: feminists, gays, lesbians, and members of the ACLU), or are familiar with programming from the Christian Broadcasting Network, or subscribe to the Elijah List where you can get daily messages from Christian prophets, you know a bit about the mind-set of President Bush. The Elijah List is based on a literal reading of the scriptures and a logic that would reject as the Word of God alternative gospels (such as the gnostic gospels of Thomas or Mary Magdalene) through the circular logic of the retrospective illusion whereby nothing other than what is could ever have been—a self-referential loop if there ever was one. Consider the following prophecy by Kim Clement on October 4, 2001, published on The Elijah List: "I am going to change everything for you. It's not going to be a long drawn out war. It's going to be a swift war that I am going to win for you. This is not going to be a drawn out thing, even though it's been prognosticated to be a drawn out thing. You will take a while to find those that are hidden in their holes." Apparently, this "prophecy" supports the claim that God is on the side of the United States, because it predicted the capture of Saddam in his hole in the ground.

The Elijah List provides a template for its readers to ponder apocrophyl history that ignores economics, political science, sociology, and historical analysis and provides only a retrospective reading of mainstream historical events through a skewed circular logic aimed at hatred of the other. This logic represents the repressed supplement of the teachings of Jesus. A recent posting by the Elijah List (U.S. War on Terrorism Goes Back to Founding Fathers) claims that the war on terrorism declared by George W. Bush goes back to the eighteenth century when Thomas Jefferson and the United States fought the "Barbary pirates" who, like the "terrorists" today saw themselves engaged in jihad and called themselves "mujahiddin" (Elijah List 2004). Apparently, after three months researching the history of militant Islam, Jefferson urged the building of a navy to rescue American hostages held in North Africa and to deter future attacks on U.S. ships. In 1792, John Paul Jones was directed by Jefferson to go to Algiers under the guise of diplomatic negotiations, but with the real intent of sizing up a future target of a naval attack. The Elijah List writes that, in the fall 1793, the Algerians seized 11 U.S. merchant ships and enslaved more than 100 Americans—which the Elijah List describes as "America's first September 11." It was only when the United States engaged in what became a four-year war against Tripoli in 1801, followed by the

French occupation of Algiers, Tunisia, and Morocco, that the terrorism on the high seas finally ended. However, when France left North Africa in 1962—it quickly became a major base of terrorism once again. The moral of the story, according to the Elijah List prophets, is that appeasement never works, we must fight the ongoing war against the unholy barbarians until the very moment that the "Rapture" takes us into the lap of Jesus or leaves us to fight another day against the forces of the Antichrist.

George Monbiot (2004) helps set the stage for helping us understand what is at stake in Bush's embrace of Christian fundamentalism, especially as it pertains to his foreign policy initiatives and his support among the American people. Monbiot notes:

> In the United States, several million people have succumbed to an extraordinary delusion. In the nineteenth century, two immigrant preachers cobbled together a series of unrelated passages from the Bible to create what appears to be a consistent narrative: Jesus will return to Earth when certain preconditions have been met. The first of these was the establishment of a state of Israel. The next involves Israel's occupation of the rest of its "biblical lands" (most of the Middle East), and the rebuilding of the Third Temple on the site now occupied by the Dome of the Rock and al-Aqsa mosques. The legions of the Antichrist will then be deployed against Israel, and their war will lead to a final showdown in the valley of Armageddon. The Jews will either burn or convert to Christianity, and the Messiah will return to Earth.

According to this scenario, all "true believers" (i.e., those who believe what the evangelicals believe) will be "lifted out of their clothes and wafted up to heaven during an event called the Rapture." Those who miss out on the Rapture (who would want to miss out on being among all those naked bodies rising to the heavens in ecstasy?) will be plagued by boils, sores, locusts, and frogs during the seven years that follow, a time known as the Tribulation. True believers who hope to bring about Armageddon and the defeat of the Antichrist (some evangelicals think it's Kofi Annan but our bet is on Dick Cheney) are now taking action. Monbiot explains that, among other things, such action mandates "staging confrontations at the old temple site (in 2000, three U.S. Christians were deported for trying to blow up the mosques there), sponsoring Jewish settlements in the occupied territories, demanding ever more U.S. support for Israel, and seeking to provoke a final battle with the Muslim world/Axis of Evil/United Nations/ European Union/France or whoever the legions of the Antichrist turn out to be." What this also means is that there exists enormous pressure on the Bush administration to support Israel at any cost, despite Israel's brutal state terrorist campaign against the Palestinians. True to Christian evangelical form, Bush has supported Israeli Prime

Minister Ariel Sharon and has given this war criminal a free hand in punishing the Palestinians. Monbiot elaborates:

> For 15 percent of the electorate, the Middle East is not just a domestic matter, it's a personal one: if the president fails to start a conflagration there, his core voters don't get to sit at the right hand of God. Bush, in other words, stands to lose fewer votes by encouraging Israeli aggression than he stands to lose by restraining it. He would be mad to listen to these people. He would also be mad not to.

It is important to remember that President Bush is an aristocratic evangelical. It is likely that his faith helps to rationalize his wealth and power, and justifies the consequences of his domestic and foreign decisions. In this sense he is little different from generations of evangelical imperialists that went before him. John Blunt (2004) reminds us that:

> George Bush is not just an evangelical, born again Christian, and a reformed 12-step alcoholic; he's also a Yale and a Harvard business graduate, a prodigy of an elite and protected childhood, the inheritor of a family history steeped in war profiteering, banking scandals, Texas Oil Wildcatting and awesome political power. The norm in that culture is to leverage all the wealth and might at your disposal, crush your adversaries, take deep profits, then smile and go to church on Sunday. It is, in part, the American way. Unfortunately, peoples of the Arab world, the Asian world, the African world, and the Latin American world have seen these men march in and out of their countries, waving the flag, thumping the good book, filling their pockets and leaving a trail of disease, slaughter and ruin behind them for centuries. Many of them preached a better world, and a divine inspiration, but betrayed them nonetheless. Most of them turned out not to be accountable to their various gospels, and created the cruel, hypocritical reputation of the West—which is how we grew to be so envied, mistrusted, and despised.

Appealing to evangelical Christians during a National Day of Prayer ceremony broadcast coast to coast by religious networks on Thursday, May 6, 2004, President Bush brought his electioneering to a shameful new low point when he recognized Oliver North, the Iran-Contra figure turned radio talkshow host who was serving as the honorary chairman of the National Day of Prayer. Bush left little doubt that he considered God to be backing his foreign policy when he remarked:

> We cannot be neutral in the face of injustice or cruelty or evil . . . God is not on the side of any nation, yet we know that he is on the side of justice. And it is the deepest strength of America that from the hour of our founding, we have chosen justice as our goal. . . . Our greatest failures as a nation have come when we lost

sight of that goal: in slavery, in segregation, and in every wrong that has denied
the value and dignity of life. Our finest moments have come when we have
faithfully served the cause of justice for our own citizens and for the people of
other lands. (cited in Riechmann 2004, p. A6)

In this national broadcast our Holy Ghost Warrior President, to his credit,
left room for some reflective criticism of the United States, with the understanding that admitting some faults actually strengthens his hand at convincing the public that America has stayed the course for God. Yet Bush glaringly
failed to recognize in his address that the very founding moment of the United
States as one indivisible nation under God was the unimpeachably loathsome
practice of settlerism and the unconscionable acts of genocide against Indigenous peoples. And given that the National Day of Prayer broadcast per-
colated with references to the U.S. troops in Iraq and Afghanistan, there was
little doubt that Bush made a convincing case that his war on terrorism was a
signal moment in the campaign to carry out God's holy plan of world salvation through war.

Lewis Lapham (2004) has observed that "Bush prefers the secular forms of
escape to unreality, and so instead of appealing to the spherical predomi-
nances found in the realm of policy, he transfer[s] the reason for the American presence in Iraq to a heavenly compulsion" (p. 13). At a March 2004
news conference, Bush remarked: "Liberty is not America's gift to the world:
it is God's gift to each and every person. . . . I believe that when we see totalitarianism, that we must deal with it" (cited in Weiss 2004, p. H1). At his
press conference in April of the same year, Bush exclaimed: "Freedom is the
Almighty's gift to every man and woman in this world. And as the greatest
power on the face of the earth, we have an obligation to help the spread of
freedom" (cited in Lapham 2004, p. 13). These remarks prompted Lapham
(2004) to respond: "Also the obligation to remember that what is real is the
theory of war that appears on the maps and the computer screen, not the experience of war that blots the flow charts with the smudges of human suffering, mutilation, and death" (p. 13).

Robert Scheer (2004) criticizes Bush for shredding the U.S. Constitution
when describing himself as a "messenger of God" who was "praying for
strength to do the Lord's will" (p. B15) by waging war on Iraq. Contrasting
Bush with his "more worldly and cautious father," Scheer writes:

Asked by Woodward, an assistant managing editor at the Washington Post, if he
had ever consulted the former president before ordering the invasion of Iraq,
Bush replied that "he is the wrong father to appeal to in terms of strength; there
is a higher father that I appeal to." Reading the elder Bush's books and even his
speeches before the latest Iraq war, one finds that the former president at least

seems to understand that diplomacy, international cooperation and patience are not just the tools of naïve do-gooders but in fact are far more effective as advancing global stability and American aims than reckless adventures like the current quagmire in Mesopotamia. Religious crusades are often counterproductive; they tend to end up in unsustainable occupations of people who—surprise!—believe they have their own pipeline to the Almighty.

Jonathan Steinberg (2004) minces no words in evaluating the dire impact of Bush hijo's evangelical Christianity on the U.S. electorate. His comments are worth repeating in full:

> Just as the president sees nothing wrong with his Iraq policy, he can't accept the view that his tax cuts are immoral. Bush is not disturbed by the huge transfer of wealth from poor to rich. He believes that returning moral choice and economic liberty to individuals matters more than any obligation of the rich to help the poor. He was entirely consistent when he urged his fellow citizens to react to the 9/11 attacks by going shopping. When the president repeats the mantra, "It's your money," he reiterates that very American, individualistic morality that makes each of us the architect of our own salvation. The state stands for alien power and, in the black-and-white morality of conservative Christians, it—together with the United Nations—shows the power of the Antichrist.

How was Bush able to subordinate the national trauma over 9/11 to his religious triumphalism and, with the help of his policy makers, reignite the mythological mission of the United States as securing the world order for Christ by waging war against the infidels? In other words, how did the Bush administration so effectively manage to rewrite the securing of U.S. strategic interests such as oil and natural gas reserves in Afghanistan and Iraq as the battle of Christian civilization over the barbarism of the infidel? The answer, according to Donald Pease (2004), can be found in recognizing that, on September 11, 2001, the trauma of America's founding moment—the genocide of Native Americans—returned with a vengeance after centuries of repression. Furthermore, this birth-of-a-nation trauma—repressed by the myth of the United States as an unsullied land whose redemptive role is to prepare the nations of the world for democracy and reactivated by the terrorist attacks of 9/11—has been cathected to the image of a wounded nation, one in which the narrative of America as an unsullied Virgin Land could no longer be sustained once the airplanes crashed into the Twin Towers and the Pentagon. The reaction of the Bush gang to the terrorist attacks against the United States—attacks that exiled the American people from their dream of being part of an innocent redeemer nation and that needed to be punished by preventative strikes—recalled at the same time the repressed historical memory of genocide against native peoples.

Pease compellingly argues that the reaction of the Bush administration to the attacks of September 11, 2001—the bombing of Afghanistan, the invasion of Iraq, the Patriot Act, and the creation of the Department of Homeland Security—makes visible the very violence that characterized the founding moments of U.S. history with the genocide of its native peoples. Such violence had been repressed, according to Pease, in part through the creation of master narratives of America as the Virgin Land, Redeemer Nation, American Adam, Nature's Nation, and Errand into the Wilderness that, "freighted with metaphorical significance and possessed of performative force," have been sedimented into the structural unconscious of the nation. The claim that the master narrative of the United States as the world's peacekeeper and ambassador of democracy has overdetermined the American public's view of themselves as a national people cannot be easily dismissed. This master narrative has been secured for centuries through the ideological state apparatuses, most particularly through public education, the media and the culture industries. Slavoj Žižek (2004a) contends that "Americans have historically seen their role in the world in altruistic terms" and maintains that movies such as John Ford's *The Searchers* and Martin Scorsese's *Taxi Driver* or books like Graham Greene's *The Quiet American* help shed important light on what he calls "the naive benevolence of Americans. Žižek (2004a) has elaborated on what he calls the good intentions underlying the ideological dream of America:

> The supposition underlying these good intentions is that underneath our skins, we are all Americans. If that is humanity's true desire, then all that Americans need to do is to give people a chance, liberate them from their imposed constraints, and they will embrace America's ideological dream.

The mythological themes that help to construct the ideological dream known as America provide, in Pease's (2004) terms, "the transformational grammar through which the state attempts to shape the public's understanding of contemporary political and historical events" (p. 1). Bush's policy makers have reinscribed such themes through a relay of signifiers between 9/11 and the security state that Pease refers to as a "regulatory intertext that transmits a normative system of values and beliefs from generation to generation" (p. 1), subordinating the terrorist attacks of 9/11 to these mythological themes and then fashioning imaginary resolutions to them. In his addresses to the nation, Bush and his administration have been able to use phrases and discursive strategies that, in the words of Pease, "inaugurated a symbolic drama that would subsequently transform the primary integers in the narrative the nation has formerly told itself with the aid of a new lexicon—with terms such as Ground Zero, Homeland, Operation Enduring Justice, Operation Iraqi

Freedom—that authorized the Bush administration's state of emergency" (p. 2). In the end, the Bush administration was able to effect "a shift in the nation's governing self-presentations—from secured innocent nation to a wounded, insecure emergency state" (Pease 2004, p. 3) and established a "newly formed structure of governmentality." Playing on the fact that America was a Virgin Land that had never before been subjected to foreign violation, the Bush administration supplied this myth with a moral rationale. It utilized both historical as well as mythological registers, by describing, as Bush did, the attacks on 9/11 as a "wound to our country" (Pease 2004, p. 3). Pease is worth quoting at length:

> The wound was directed against the Virgin Land as well as the U.S. people's myth of themselves as radically innocent. The state of emergency Bush erected at Ground Zero was thereafter endowed with the responsibility to defend the Homeland because the foreign violation of Virgin Land had alienated the national people from their imaginary way of inhabiting the nation. This substitution anchored the people to a very different state formation. It also drastically altered the national people's foundational fantasy about their relationship to the national territory, redefining it in terms of the longing of a dislocated population for their lost homeland. (p. 3)

Not only did the state of emergency erected by Bush trouble the fantasy of the United States as a nation unstained by the violence of the Other, but recalled from the pit of the structural unconscious the horror that had been disavowed and suppressed when the myth of the Virgin Land was first constructed over the killing fields of native peoples.

As Roxanne Dunbar-Ortiz (2003) notes, "the very origin of the United States is fundamentally imperialist" as the quest for empire driven by white supremacist thinking has been a fundamental way of rationalizing American "civilization" since its beginnings. She elaborates as follows:

> "American" supremacy and populist imperialism are inseparable from the content of the U.S. origin story and the definition of patriotism in the United States today. And it began at the beginning, even before the founding of the United States, not as an accident or aberration in the progression of democracy. The founding of the United States marked a split in the British Empire, not an anti-colonial liberation movement. The very term "frontier," used to define the border between independent Native American nations and the United States, implies a foreign country on the other side of a demarcation line—a country to be invaded, its inhabitants controlled and then expelled, while settlers move in protected by the army. Everything accounted for in the first hundred years plus as "movement of the frontier" was plain and simple imperialism, fitting all the definitions thereof. (p. 90)

In Pease's (2004) terms, the myth of the Virgin Land after 9/11 was "demetaphorized into the actuality of the states's violence" (p. 9). Pease (2004) writes that the "violation of the land's inviolability not only disinhibited the state of its need to mask its history of violence but also required the state to bring the event which the public had formerly disavowed—the forcible dispossession of national peoples from their homelands—into spectacular visibility" (p. 7). Pease elaborates:

> After they were figured in relation to the Homeland Security Act, the unprecedented events that took place on 9/11 seemed familiar because they recalled the suppressed historical knowledge of the United States' origins in the devastation of Native peoples' homelands. The sites of residence of the Paiute and the Shoshone had more recently been destroyed as a result of the state's decision to turn their tribal lands into toxic dumps for the disposal of nuclear waste. The events also appeared familiar, as the signifier *Ground Zero* attests, because the unimaginable sight of the crumbling Twin Towers recovered memories of the fire bombings of civilian populations over Dresden and Tokyo as well as the unspeakable aftereffects of the atomic fallout on the inhabitants of Hiroshima and Nagasaki . . . Ground Zero evoked the specter of the nation-founding violence out of whose exclusion the fantasy of radical innocence on which the nation was founded encountered the violence it had formerly concealed. (p. 5)

The term "Homeland"—the name of a prior state of unity achieved through decades of overt and subliminal indoctrination by the ideological state apparatuses and overdetermined by the imperatives of the military industrial complex and what Pease terms the "global biopolitical settlement"—is now one of forced unity under conditions of exile where all of us have been turned into insecure and displaced "minorities" in need of protection by the security state. At the same time, we are all potential terrorist surrogates who recklessly place the Homeland in danger by speaking out, by organizing dissent, by encouraging civil disobedience against the government's foreign and domestic policies, and the pressure to join the legions of Homeland tipsters and civilian snitches and government informants is irresistible (Valentine 2003). Valentine writes that "[a]s in Vietnam, only five percent of the people need to be organized in this fashion in order to wield control over the indifferent ninety percent, and defeat the five percent that form the resistance" (2003, p. 11). What we are left with is a spectacular space where citizens are more easily refigured as patriots willing to defend the security state as they become more and more enraged at being exiled from their erstwhile providential image of the United States as a Virgin Land, an image that Pease claims is dependent upon the dismembering of homelands elsewhere, homelands that are least like ours. In other words, we are in the process of being reterritorialized by the lexicon and figurative meanings of freedom and democracy adopted by the Bush gang who equate democracy and freedom with the "free market" and who demonize as barbaric, any feudal state or country that refuses to allow takeovers of its natural resources by more developed (and hence more civilized) nations—the United States in particular. The Bush *junta* infantilizes the collective political unconscious of the United States (what Bush refers to as "Joe public") by resignifying its space of violent contradictions with tropes, motifs and conceits of danger that "correlate[s] this repression in political standing with the reenactment of a formerly suppressed prehistoric event" (Pease 2004, pp. 8–9). The Homeland is redescribed as a space to which the U.S. citizenry could one day return, once the war on terror abated and the "thugs" and "enemies of freedom" have been exterminated. According to Pease (2004), "The Homeland Security State constructed the preemptive strikes against others' homelands as a spectacular form of domestic defense against foreign aggression" (p. 10). The spectacles of the invasions of Afghanistan and Iraq, freighted with historically venerated significations of the United States as the world's liberator:

> invited their audiences to take scopic pleasure in the return of the traumatic memory of the unprovoked aggression that the colonial settlers had previously exerted against Native populations. These massacres, which could not be authorized or legitimated by the Virgin Land narrative, became the foundational acts that inaugurated the Global Homeland as a realm outside the law. (Pease 2004, p. 10)

In effect, forms of civil and political life through which the majority of the American populace recognized themselves as redemptive descendents of the Founding Fathers were replaced by a biologically vulnerable body politic. The loss of the Virgin Land myth has to be compensated for by the pleasures of shock-and-awe—in legal, military, and political registers.

Žižek (2004a) points to another layer of this mythology of vengeful benevolence that became unchained from the caverns of the structural unconcious of the United States when Bush made the following remark in his January 2003 State of the Union message: "The liberty we prize is not America's gift to the world, it is God's gift to humanity." For Žižek (2004a), "this apparent burst of humility, in fact, concealed its totalitarian opposite." Žižek explains:

> Every totalitarian leader claims that, in himself, he is nothing at all: His strength is only the strength of the people who stand behind him, whose deepest strivings only he expresses. The catch is, those who oppose the leader by definition not only oppose him, but they also oppose the deepest and noblest strivings of the people. And does the same not hold for Bush's claim? It would have been easier

if freedom effectively were to be just the United States' gift to other nations; that way, those who oppose U.S. policies would merely be against the policies of a single nation-state. But if freedom is God's gift to humanity, and the U.S. government sees itself as the chosen instrument for showering this gift on all the nations of the world, then those who oppose U.S. policies are rejecting the noblest gift of God to humanity.

Of course, further giving lie to the notion that the United States is saving the world from evil-doers (especially by citizens of other countries who know more about the history of U.S. war crimes than most of the U.S. public) are the recent revelations about the treatment of Iraqi detainees by the U.S. military in the prisons of Iraq and Guantanamo Bay, Cuba. We are all too familiar with the images of leering U.S. soldiers torturing naked Iraqi prisoners in Abu Ghraib prison. William Rivers Pitt (2004) captures the situation as well as any other reporter when he writes:

> We are awash in photographs of Iraqi men—not terrorists, just people—lying in heaps on cold floors with leashes around their necks. We are awash in photographs of men chained so remorselessly that their backs are arched in agony, men forced to masturbate for cameras, men forced to pretend to have sex with one another for cameras, men forced to endure attacks from dogs, men with electrodes attached to them as they stand, hooded, in fear of their lives. The worst, amazingly, is yet to come. A new battery of photographs and videotapes, as yet unreleased, awaits over the horizon of our abused understanding. These photos and videos, also from the Abu Ghraib prison, are reported to show U.S. soldiers gang raping an Iraqi woman, U.S. soldiers beating an Iraqi man nearly to death, U.S. troops posing, smirks affixed, with decomposing Iraqi bodies, and Iraqi troops under U.S. command raping young boys. George W. Bush would have us believe these horrors were restricted to a sadistic few, and would have us believe these horrors happened only in Abu Ghraib. Yet reports are surfacing now of similar treatment at another U.S. detention center in Iraq called Camp Bucca. According to these reports, Iraqi prisoners in Camp Bucca were beaten, humiliated, hogtied, and had scorpions placed on their naked bodies. In the eyes of the world, this is America today.

The torture at Abu Ghraib prison was not an aberration but rather a continuation of the legacy of the treatment of prisoners throughout the United States, the most brutal of which occurred under Bush hijo's watch in Texas when he served as governor. It is extremely unlikely that Governor Bush was unaware that female prisoners were regularly kept in portable detention cells in the summer heat for hours with no water so that they would more easily submit sexually to their oppressors; there is little reason to believe that Governor Bush did not see the tape of prison guards in the Brazoria County Detention Center in Angleton, Texas, forcing inmates to crawl while kicking them and poking them with electric prods. Surely he heard the remarks of attorney Donna Brorby, who described the super-max prisons as "the worst in the country, where guards reportedly gas prisoners and thrown them down on concrete floors while handcuffed" (Office of the Americas 2004). But many teachers and students remain unaware that the type of torture that occurred in Abu Ghraib, is similar to the type of torture inflicted upon Indigenous and Third World peoples by the U.S. military and the CIA. Such torture, like forced masturbation, was copied from the Nazis. The 1983 Honduran Interrogation Manual and the 1984 Contra Manual remain as powerful evidence of a long-standing practice of torture by the U.S. military. More recently, a CIA torture manual used to instruct five Latin American nations' security forces was revealed to the public in January 1997 by a *Baltimore Sun* report (Matthews 1997). A year earlier, a U.S. government investigation into the U.S. Army School of the Americas (renamed in 2001 as the Western Hemisphere Institute for The School of the Americas [SOA]) in Ft. Benning, Georgia, led to "the release of no less than seven training manuals used at the school which taught murder, torture, and extortion as a means of repressing so-called subversives, according to a Congressional report" (Office of the Americas 2004, p. 2). That the U.S. military and its "independent contractors" teach and participate in torture and offer advice on how to circumvent laws on due press, arrest, and detention should come as no surprise to observers of the current conflict in Iraq. Critical educators have condemned not only the 100,000 innocent civilians killed to date in this war, but also the hypocrisy that underlies the claims by the United States that Iraq is on its way to becoming a sovereign democracy.

Yoshie Furuhashi remarks that the American men and women who had themselves photographed while torturing Iraqis presented themselves in a "mythical All-American sort of way, with big grins and thumbs up." Further, he asks: "Where does their apparent enjoyment come from?" To answer this, he draws on a quotation by Žižek, in his explanation of the dominant ideology of "totalitarian democracy" in a seemingly "permissive" society such as the United States:

> The superficial opposition between pleasure and duty is overcome in two different ways. Totalitarian power goes even further than traditional authoritarian power. What it says, in effect, is not, "Do your duty, I don't care whether you like it or not," but: "You must do your duty, and you must enjoy doing it." (This is how totalitarian democracy works: it is not enough for the people to follow their leader, they must love him.) Duty becomes pleasure. Second, there is the obverse paradox of pleasure becoming duty in a "permissive" society. Subjects

experience the need to "have a good time," to enjoy themselves, as a kind of duty, and, consequently, feel guilty for failing to be happy. The superego controls the zone in which these two opposites overlap—in which the command to enjoy doing your duty coincides with the duty to enjoy yourself. (Žižek 1999, cited in Furuhashi 2004)

Furuhashi notes that the territory in which "the command to enjoy doing your duty coincides with the duty to enjoy yourself" is as "potentially all-encompassing as global capitalism itself" and is the prevailing social drama that underlies U.S. consumer-driven, self-help capitalism. He writes:

Americans, trapped in the land of vanguard capitalists (who ceaselessly command them to enjoy doing their duty) and self-help handbooks (which endlessly teach them the duty to enjoy themselves), appear to obey both the command to enjoy doing their duty and the duty to enjoy themselves more readily than any other people. The grins and thumbs up in the photographs of torture are not so much evidence of character flaws of particular individuals as social tableaux of the American tragedy, i.e. the tragedy of "totalitarian democracy" in a seemingly "permissive" society. (Furuhashi 2004)

For Furuhashi, these photos represent "the social laws" under which the soldiers are acting—and in Furuhashi's mind they are ominously reminiscent of Brecht's concept of "social guests" or "scenes where people adopt attitudes of such a sort that the social laws under which they are acting spring into sight" (Brecht 1964, p. 86).

Žižek (2004b) reflects a similar sentiment himself when he observes that what we see when we examine the photos of humiliated Iraqi prisoners is not, as Bush proclaims, the isolated acts of a few, but rather "a direct insight into 'American values,' into the core of an obscene enjoyment that sustains the American way of life" (p. 31). As Žižek (2004b) reports:

To anyone acquainted with the reality of the American way of life, the photos brought to mind the obscene underside of U.S. popular culture—say, the initiatory rituals of torture and humiliation one has to undergo to be accepted into a closed community. Similar photos appear at regular intervals in the U.S. press after some scandal explodes at an Army base or high school campus, when such rituals went overboard. Far too often we are treated to images of soldiers and students forced to assume humiliating poses, perform debasing gestures and suffer sadistic punishments. The torture at Abu Ghraib was thus not simply a case of American arrogance toward a Third World people. In being submitted to the humiliating tortures, the Iraqi prisoners were effectively *initiated into American culture*: They got a taste of the culture's obscene underside that forms the necessary supplement to the public values of personal dignity, democracy and freedom. (p. 31)

CONCLUSION: PARADISE REGAINED

We have to come to terms with the politics around the issue of strategies of resistance if we are to stop today's corporate, military, religious, and individual terrorists. Arundhati Roy (2004) writes that, "There is no discussion taking place in the world today that is more crucial than the debate about strategies of resistance. And the choice of strategy is not entirely in the hands of the public." Attempting to understand terrorism's root causes—religious, cultural, and economic—is not the same thing as condoning terrorism. We ask the American public to take the first step toward such an understanding not by listening to the White House administration (Republican or Democrat) who are in bed with the fundamental economic interests of the corporate media, but by engaging in a public debate in the churches, the schools, the factories, and the public arenas of struggle. If governments want oppressed and aggrieved communities to exercise nonviolent as opposed to violent resistance, then they will need to honor and respect such resistance. Roy makes our argument with devastating effectiveness and it is worth repeating in full:

> [W]hen the U.S. invades and occupies Iraq in the way it has done, with such overwhelming military force, can the resistance be expected to be a conventional military one? (Of course, even if it were conventional, it would still be called terrorist.) In a strange sense, the U.S. government's arsenal of weapons and unrivalled air and fire power makes terrorism an all-but-inescapable response. What people lack in wealth and power, they will make up with stealth and strategy. In this restive, despairing time, if governments do not do all they can to honor nonviolent resistance, then by default they privilege those who turn to violence. No government's condemnation of terrorism is credible if it cannot show itself to be open to change by . . . nonviolent dissent. But instead nonviolent resistance movements are being crushed. Any kind of mass political mobilization or organization is being bought off, or broken, or simply ignored. Meanwhile, governments and the corporate media, and let's not forget the film industry, lavish their time, attention, technology, research, and admiration on war and terrorism. Violence has been deified. The message this sends is disturbing and dangerous: If you seek to air a public grievance, violence is more effective than nonviolence.

Roy understands that terrorism is exacerbated by the global needs of capital and the blood of the poor that is spilled in order to feed its unquenchable thirst. As economic globalization increases, we will see the battle lines being even more firmly drawn. The difference is that the weapons of mass destruction that the transnational ruling class is willing to unleash are more terrifying than at any time in the history of class struggle. Roy writes:

> As the rift between the rich and poor grows, as the need to appropriate and control the world's resources to feed the great capitalist machine becomes more urgent, the

unrest will only escalate. For those of us who are on the wrong side of Empire, the humiliation is becoming unbearable. Each of the Iraqi children killed by the United States was our child. Each of the prisoners tortured in Abu Ghraib was our comrade. Each of their screams was ours. When they were humiliated, we were humiliated. The U.S. soldiers fighting in Iraq—mostly volunteers in a poverty draft from small towns and poor urban neighborhoods—are victims just as much as the Iraqis of the same horrendous process, which asks them to die for a victory that will never be theirs. The mandarins of the corporate world, the CEOs, the bankers, the politicians, the judges, and generals look down on us from on high and shake their heads sternly. "There's no alternative," they say. And let slip the dogs of war. Then, from the ruins of Afghanistan, from the rubble of Iraq and Chechnya, from the streets of occupied Palestine and the mountains of Kashmir, from the hills and plains of Colombia and the forests of Andhra Pradesh and Assam comes the chilling reply: "There's no alternative but terrorism." Terrorism. Armed struggle. Insurgency. Call it what you want. Terrorism is vicious, ugly, and dehumanizing for its perpetrators, as well as its victims. But so is war. You could say that terrorism is the privatization of war. Terrorists are the free marketers of war. They are people who don't believe that the state has a monopoly on the legitimate use of violence. Human society is journeying to a terrible place. . . . The urge for hegemony and preponderance by some will be matched with greater intensity by the longing for dignity and justice by others.

The longing for dignity and justice for others, as well as for ourselves, has been a primary motivation for critical educators worldwide to engage in the politics and practice of critical pedagogy. Critical educators have not inherited a certain gene for making revolution; they do not bless us with their presence every hundred years or so, like a Che Guevara or an Emiliano Zapata; rather, they are forged in the crucible of class struggle and critical consciousness. They live every day with a mindful eye to history, to past and present and future.

Die-hard exponents of revolutionary critical pedagogy do not seek capital's self-expansion at the expense of ecologies but rather the emancipation of labor and the creation of a social universe "in which humanity is restored to ecosystemic differentiation with nature" (Kovel 2002, p. 210). This does not imply the transfer of ownership from the expropriators of surplus value to the expropriated, but the rejection of the very idea of ownership. Kovel uses the term "usufructuary" to describe this relationship, a term used by Marx in *Capital, Volume 3*, which referred to the gratification expressed in freely associated labor beginning with the free association of producers. Kovel (2002) importantly notes that "the whole making of the human world is to be taken into account rather than just that which contributes or controls exchange-value" (p. 241). This will require a total break with capitalism's law of value. As McLaren and Farahmandpur (forthcoming) have written:

We do not look to the Heavenly Kingdom of Great Peace, the Paris Commune, or the Russian Revolution for blueprints for our efforts, but the examples of the Taipings, the Communards, and the Bolsheviks—and numerous others—can certainly provide us with inspiration. While socialist struggle must necessarily be international in scope it must not disregard the contextual specificity of regional and local dynamics. We need to remember, too, that we become disinherited from democracy precisely at the moment we believe we have attained it. The struggle never ceases. There are always new unanticipated challenges ahead.

The greatest challenge to the United States is itself. The United States is advertised as a secular democracy, which it is, but in name only. While its leaders claim to be inspired by providence or guided by the Almighty, the U.S. culture industry continues to profit mightily from the sexualization and sacralization of violence. Thousands of young Americans, thrilled despite newspaper accounts of Arnold Schwarzenegger's alleged "gang bang" of an African American woman during his "pumping iron" days, were only too eager to cast their votes for "The Terminator" for governor of California. When Schwarzenegger told assembled U.S. troops that they are "the real terminators," thousands of young people couldn't wait to sign up for the next war. Imperialism has been made sexy by the editors of *People Magazine* who voted Defense Secretary Donald Rumsfeld as one of the sexiest men in the United States. Apparently, many Americans are libidinally aroused by the ruthless way he wields war and slaughters the innocent.

There is little evidence to indicate that the United States is prepared to consider a socialist alternative to its imperialist democracy anytime soon. Freely associated labor can't compete in a capitalist society with the promise of endless shopping adventures in Planet Mall or with being free to conquer and plunder on a scale never imagined by the rulers of ancient Rome. As long as exploitation remains gratifying and continues to accumulate value, there is little motivation for U.S. citizens to create a world outside of capital's value form.

We clearly live in a divided nation, a divided world. If we are to make inroads that will transcend this divide, our discourse of critical pedagogy must shift into another register, forming itself around new axes of commitment and solidarity and understanding. If it is to open up possibilities in the world beyond the scope of preexisting conditions and commonsense assumptions, it needs to confront the issue not of how to address the exploited but how they can address us; not how to create a discourse of desire to grant the Other recognition, but rather of how to respond to challenges that the Other has posed to the politics of what we regard as recognition. We need to be oriented to the world of the Other not in order that the Other recognize us in terms that we provide, but in order to express and disclose what is at stake in the terms that we use in the dialogue between us, and what is at risk in signifying across a class divide, across a chasm of silence that is produced by the discourse and practice of class exploitation. The discourse of critical pedagogy must not take an enigmatically risky path, relentlessly pursuing the intangible, a path lit with intricate theoretical coruscations but bereft of praxis. We are not seeking a new critical pedagogy salon in pursuit of some celestial, light-filled critics' utopia, rather we wish to travel down the more well-trodden path of what Gramsci called the pessimism of the intellect and optimism of the will. Here, critical discourse is not a medium for universal harmony but cuts like a sword into the entrails of the social rendering an interpretation of the real in such a way as to invite rejoinder and dialogue. The discourse of critical pedagogy needs to make clear what it means to interrogate meanings signified in the gap between class relations that has become the prime intermediary in how we understand and participate in our struggle for justice and freedom. If we shift our discourse of critical pedagogy into a new signifying space, into a new nexus of social relations, that speaks to the encroachment of silence upon the current shape of our daily life, that more clearly and powerfully discloses the political order within the capitalist law of value, then our challenge to transform the social fate of the victims of capital must be presented in a language with a corporeal surface. It should be a surface that has receptors for generating intentionality, that makes a provision for a radical intercorporeity, for speaking to other bodies rather than presenting abstractions devoid of feelings, thoughts, and histories. We need to be able to speak our struggle not just in abstract terms, but in ways that touch hearts and minds. Thus, we must move outside the legacy of colonialism, of embarking upon the salvation of Others, and engage in finding ways of recognizing points of commonality, of mutual interest, where our own struggle for liberation intersects with the struggles of others, where we can begin to transcend the limitations of what is, in the struggle for what could be.

That is why any revolutionary struggle must be dedicated to educating the emotions as much as the intellect and why anti-imperialist struggle must be waged on the triple continents of reason, passion, and revolution. It must take place not only on the picket line or protest march, but also in the schools, places of worship, libraries, shop floors, and corporate offices—in every venue where people come together to learn, to labor, and to love.

In order to shift critical pedagogy into a new register, we need to rethink the very premises of critical pedagogy, not as some grand contemplative act, but as part of a philosophy of everyday life. This challenge has to do with creating a living Marxism, a way of negotiating the reality of a racist and class society on a daily basis so as to transform such a society. Here we turn to the work of philosopher Raya Dunayevskaya, the founder of Marxist-Humanism

in the United States, and her Marxist-Hegelian approach to developing a philosophy of praxis. Dunayevskaya (1973, 1978, 2000, 2002) rethought Marx's
relations to Hegelian dialectics in a profound way, in particular, Hegel's concept of the self-movement of the Idea from which Marx argued the need to
transcend objective reality rather than thought. Dunayevskaya notes how
Marx was able to put a living, breathing, and thinking subject of history at the
center of the Hegelian dialectic. She also pointed out that what for Hegel is
Absolute knowledge (the realm of realized transcendence), Marx referred to
as the new society. While Hegel's self-referential, all-embracing, totalizing
Absolute is greatly admired by Marx, it is, nevertheless, greatly modified by
him. For Marx, Absolute knowledge (or the self-movement of pure thought)
did not absorb objective reality or objects of thought but provided a ground
from which objective reality could be transcended.

By reinserting the human subject into the dialectic, and by defining the subject as corporal being (rather than pure thought or abstract self-consciousness),
Marx appropriates Hegel's self-movement of subjectivity as an act of transcendence and transforms it into a critical humanism. In her rethinking of
Marx's relationship to the Hegelian dialectic, Dunayevskaya parts company
with Derrida, Adorno, Marcuse, Habermas, Negri, Deleuze, Mészáros, and
others. She has given absolute negativity a new urgency, linking it not only to
the negation of today's economic and political realities but also to developing
new human relations (Hudis, 2004). The second negation (or negation of the
negation) constitutes drawing out the positive within the negative and ex-
pressing the desire of the oppressed for freedom. Second negativity is intrinsic to the human subject as an agent; it is what gives direction and coherence
to revolutionary action as praxis. Abstract, alienated labor can be challenged
by freely associated labor and concrete, human sensuousness. The answer is
in envisioning a noncapitalist future. Such a future can be achieved, as Hudis
(2000b) notes, after Dunayevskaya, by means of subjective self-movement
through absolute negativity so that a new relation between theory and practice can connect us to the realization of human freedom.

Of course, Marx rejects Hegel's idealization and dehumanization of self-
movement through double negation because this leaves untouched alienation
in the world of labor–capital relations. Marx sees this absolute negativity as
objective movement and the creative force of history. Absolute negativity in
this instance becomes a constitutive feature of a self-critical social revolution
that, in turn, forms the basis of permanent revolution. Hudis (2000b) raises a
number of difficult questions with respect to developing a project that moves
beyond controlling the labor process. It is a project that is directed at abol-
ishing capital itself through the creation of freely associated labor: The creation of a social universe not parallel to the social universe of capital (whose

substance is value) is the challenge here. The form that this society will take is that which has been suppressed within the social universe of capital: socialism, a society based not on value but on the fulfillment of human need. For Dunayevskaya (2002), absolute negativity entails more than economic struggle but the liberation of humanity from class society. This is necessarily a political and a revolutionary struggle and not only an economic one. This particular insight is what, for us, signals the fecundating power of Dunayevskaya's Marxist-Humanism—the recognition that Marx isn't talking about class relations only but human relations.

But how do we unchain Dunayevskaya's work for the development of a new approach to critical pedagogy? We take our cue here from Hudis, one of the leading exponents of Dunayevskaya's work. Hudis (1983, 2000a, 2000b, 2003a, 2003b, 2004, forthcoming) advocates for the capacity in all human beings to become philosophers. As a philosopher, Marx was able to transcend the separation between the subjective and the objective and to concretize its dialectical relationship. A philosophy of praxis approaches dialectical cognition as a means of engaging life in all of its hydra-headed manifestations, in short, as a way of life. We do not distance ourselves from everyday life by living a philosophy of praxis, rather, we are able to concretely grasp how human sociality needs to change in order to free us from capitalism's law of value. Hudis describes philosophy as something that can actually free thought from a formalist or contemplative relation to reality by posing, as Marx did, the reunification of mental and manual abilities in the individual, that is, by living a philosophy of praxis that permeates all dimensions of social life and all facets of existence. We need to grasp not only the constitution of the subject using sociologically established fixed premises or truths (a mainly theoretical endeavor) but also the relationship between the subject and the social context and totality in which the subject is embedded while at the same time seeking to move beyond appearances to grasp the "thing" in itself (a mainly philosophical enterprise). This does not mean becoming inkhorns armed with philosophical formulae, but being able to penetrate beneath the façade of appearances that constitute everyday life in order to grasp the interwoven structures beyond the surface. Part of the problem, notes Hudis, is the confusion between theory and philosophy. Hudis (2004) remarks that:

> [t]he thing itself refers not only to external objects but also to the categories which underlay human cognition. Philosophy is different from theory as it is traditionally understood in that it does not take its premises for granted. Philosophy is not about "accepting" certain fixed truths which one then simply projects without further self-examination. Philosophy subjects everything to self-examination, including its own premises—not for the sake of just tearing these things down (that would be sophistry) but as part of creating something

new. As Raya [Dunayevskaya] said, theory is about tearing down the old, philosophy is about creating the new.

But because, as Marx maintained, the practice of philosophy is itself theoretical (Hudis 2004), we can't dispense with theory since philosophy necessarily includes theoretical discussion. However, Hudis (2004) argues that philosophy engages in discussion and debate in a fundamentally new way:

> The new way is that when theory becomes infused with philosophy, thought ceases to take its premises for granted. Theory is urgently needed because it's only through theoretic work that philosophic conclusions can be justified. But while theory is necessary, it is not sufficient. It is not sufficient because cognition isn't only about justifying certain assumptions and claims; our assumptions and claims also have to be critically examined. In a word, when theoretic work becomes infused with philosophy, "projection" no longer gets reduced to propagating fixed conclusions; it becomes a process of creating something *new* by developing ideas to their logical conclusion.

In effect, philosophy changes the way that we think. According to Hudis (2004), it renews the "image of thought." Marxist-Humanism, in particular, "has freed thought from a contemplative or formalist relation to reality by posing the reunification of mental and manual abilities in the individual." When theory is left out of philosophy, philosophy often becomes reduced to a contemplative act that "fails to connect with your inner life," which is why Marxist-Humanism unites philosophic discussions and voices from below in a way that does not cleave theory from practice, but unifies them "in living individuals so that we can concretize the dialectic of second negativity in both theoretical and practical realms" (Hudis 2004). Which is why the negation of the negation as a function of philosophy is always the seedbed of the new. In this way Marxist dialectics is always in tune with the historical moment, always shifting in concert with living human beings struggling to reshape social existence. Where we go, and how we get there will depend not upon the automatic self-activity of the oppressed. It will demand that we all become dialecticians, philosophers of praxis armed not with formulaic answers but with an openness of mind and spirit and a creative vision of what we can—and must—achieve.

Rethinking theory and practice in the context of becoming philosophers of our daily lives is one of the challenges of critical educators today. But such a challenge only becomes salient for a politics of liberation when our pedagogical possibilities are directed toward the creation of another world outside the precincts of imperialist war, ecological violence, and the capitalist law of value.

The guiding maxim of the past 3,400 years of recorded human history appears to have been *pax paritur bello* (peace is produced by war) since there have been approximately 3,170 years of war and those years absent of war were spent preparing for war. Those of us who seek a new dialectic of freedom refuse to be obedient to this history. Our struggle is for a social universe of peace and prosperity that will allow us one day to name our three millennia of blood as the prehistory of the new universal citizen.

NOTES

To Rachel Corrie and Imam al-Hams. This is a greatly expanded version of Peter McLaren and Nathalia E. Jaramillo, "A Moveable Fascism: Fear and Loathing in the Empire of Sand," *Cultural Studies/Critical Methodologies*, in press. It was originally expanded for the collection, "Rethinking Imperialism in the 21st Century," to be published by the Indian Institute of Marxist Studies (Delhi Chapter). Nathalia E. Jaramillo is a doctoral candidate at the Graduate School of Education and Information Studies, University of California, Los Angeles.

1. The names of famous puppets that were made popular on U.S. television in the 1950's.
2. From the deck of the *Abraham Lincoln*, Bush triumphantly declared the war over; the fall of Baghdad had culminated the one-month-long military coup. And yet, when confronted by the media with reports of regular assaults on American troops, Bush had the bombastic arrogance to assert on July 2: "bring them on."

REFERENCES

Arkin, W. M. 2003. "The Pentagon Unleashes a Holy Warrior." *Los Angeles Times.* Thursday, October 16, at www.latimes.com/news/opinion/la-oe-arkin16oct16,1, 6651326.story?coll=la-headlines-oped-manual (accessed October 16, 2003).
Baker, K. 2003. "We're in the Army Now: The G.O.P.'s Plan to Militarize Our Culture." *Harper's Magazine*, 307, (1841, October), 35–46.
Boggs, C. 2003. "Outlaw Nation: The Legacy of U.S. War Crimes." In *Masters of War: Empire and Blowback in the Age of American Empire*, edited by Carl Boggs, 191–226. New York: Routledge.
Brecht, B. 1964. *Brecht on Theatre*. Translated and edited by John Willett. New York: Hill and Wong.
Brecht, B. 2001. *Life of Galileo*. Edited by John Willet and Ralph Manhelm. Translated by John Willet. London: Methuen.
Brown, C. 2004. "New Front in Iraqi Detainee Abuse Scandal?" MSNBC News (updated from May 20), at www.msnbc.msn.com/id/5024068/ (accessed October 10, 2004).
Brubaker, J. 2004. "Bush Quietly Meets with Amish Here; They Offer Their Prayers." *Lancaster New Era*. July 16, at lancasteronline.com/pages/news/local/4/7564 (accessed July 16, 2004).

Burnyeat, M. F. 1985. "Sphinx without a Secret." *The New York Review of Books*, 32(9). May 30 , at www.nybooks.com/articles/5444 (accessed October 10, 2004).

Callinicos, A. 2003. *An Anti-Capitalist Manifesto*. Cambridge: Polity Press.

Carroll, J. 2003. "Warring with God." *The Boston Globe*. October 21, at www .boston.com/news/globe/editorial_opinion/oped/articles/2003/10/21/warring_with _god/ (accessed October 10, 2004).

Chomsky, N. 2003. "Wars of Terror." In *Masters of War: Empire and Blowback in the Age of American Empire*, edited by Carl Boggs, 131—147. New York: Routledge.

Clement, K. 2001. "Prophesies on Finding Saddam (and Others) in a HOLE." Posted October 1, 2001, at www.elijahlist.com/subscription/storesubs.htm (accessed October 10, 2004).

Coen, R. 2002. *"New York Times* Buries Stories of Airstrikes on Civilians." *Extra! Update*, (February), 3.

Conason, J. 2003. *Big Lies: The Right-Wing Propaganda Machine and How It Distorts the Truth*. New York: St. Martin's Press.

Cooper, M. 2004. "Among the NASCAR Dads." *The Nation*, 278(11, March 22), 18.

Cooper, R. T. 2003. "General Casts War in Religious Terms." *Los Angeles Times*, October 16, A1.

Doctorow, E. L. 2004. "The Unfeeling President." *East Hampton Star*. September 9, at www.commondreams.org/views04/0920-13.htm.

Duhigg, C. 2004. "Enemy Contact. Kill 'em, Kill 'em." *Los Angeles Times*, Sunday, July 18, A1, A10–11.

Dunayevskaya, R. 1973. *Philosophy and Revolution*. New York: Columbia University Press.

Dunayevskaya, R. 1978. *Marx's "Capital" and Today's Global Crisis*. Detroit, Mich.: News & Letters.

Dunayevskaya, R. 2000. *Marxism & Freedom: From 1776 Until Today*. Amherst, New York: Humanity Books.

Dunayevskaya, R. 2002. *The Power of Negativity*. Lanham, Md.: Lexington Books.

Dunbar-Ortiz, R. 2003. "The Grid of History: Cowboys and Indians." *Monthly Review*, 55(3), 83–92.

Eagleton, T. 2003. *After Theory*. New York: Basic Books.

Ebert, R. 2004. "Less is Moore in Subdued, Effective '9/11.'" *Chicago Sun-Times*, May 18, 43.

The Editorial Board. 2003. "Weapons of Mass Destruction in Iraq: Bush's 'Big Lie' and the Crisis of American Imperialism." World Socialist Web Site. June 21, at wsws.org/articles/2003/jun2003/wmd-j21.shtml (accessed October 10, 2004).

Elijah List. 2004. "US War ON Terrorism Goes Back to Founding Fathers," at www.elijahlist.com/words/display_word.html?ID=2240 (accessed October 10, 2004).

Fitrakis, B. 2004. "Gott mit uns: On Bush and Hitler's Rhetoric," at www .informationclearinghouse.info/article6838.htm.

Fitrakis, B., and Wasserman, H. 2003. "Fourth Reich? The Bush-Rove-Schwarzenegger Nazi Nexus," at www.counterpunch.org/wasserman10062003.html (accessed October 10, 2004).

Floyd, C. 2003. "The Revelation of St. George." *Counterpunch.* June 30, at www.counterpunch.org/floyd06302003.html (accessed October 10, 2004).

Foster, J. B. 2003. "The New Age of Imperialism." *Monthly Review* 55 (3, July–August).

Frank, T. 2004. "How the Left Lost Its Heart." *Los Angeles Times*, Sunday, July 16, M1, M6.

Furuhashi, Y. 2004. "Grins and Thumbs Up: Social Gests of the American Tragedy." *Critical Montages.* May 2, at montages.blogspot.com/2004_05_01_montages_ archive.html#108351723206766410 (accessed October 10, 2004).

Gabler, Neal. 2004. "Karl Rove: America's Mull'ah." *Los Angeles Times*, October 24, M1-2.

Goodstein, Laurie. 2004. "Personal and Political, Bush's Faith Blurs Lines." *The New York Times*, October 26, at www.nytimes.com/2004/10/26/politics/campaign/ 26religion.html.

Gorenfeld, J. 2003. "Bad Moon on the Rise." *Salon* September 24, at www.salon.com/ news/feaure/2003/09/24/moon/print.html (accessed October 10, 2004).

Gourevitch, P. 2004. "Bushspeak: The President's Vernacular Style." *The New Yorker.* September 13, at www.newyorker.com/fact/content/?040913fa_fact1.

Grosso, M. 1995. *The Millennium Myth: Love and Death at the End of Time.* Wheaton, Ill.: Quest Books.

Hedges, Chris. 2004. "On War." *New York Review of Books*, December 16, 8–14.

Hess, J. L. 2002. "Indirect from the Battlefield." *Extra! Update* (February), 4.

Hochschild, A. 2003. "Let Them Eat War." *ZNet.* October 2, at www.zmag.org/ content/showarticle.cfm?SectionID=12&ItemID=4294_(accessed October 10, 2004).

Hudis, P. 1983. *Marx and the Third World: New Perspectives on Writing from His Last Decade.* Chicago: News & Letters.

Hudis, P. 2000a. "Can Capital Be Controlled?" *News & Letters Online*, at www .newsandletters.org/4.00_essay.htm.

Hudis, P. 2000b. "The Dialectical Structure of Marx's Concept of 'Revolution in Permanence.'" *Capital & Class,* 70 (Spring), 127–142.

Hudis, Peter. 2003a. *The Future of Dialectical Marxism: Towards a New Relation of Theory and Practice.* A paper presented at Rethinking Marxism Conference, November 2003.

Hudis, P. 2003b. *Report to National Plenum of News and Letters Committees*, August 30, 2003. Organizational Responsibility for Marxist-Humanism in Light of War, Resistance, and the Need for a New Alternative.

Hudis, P. 2004. *Working out a Philosophically Grounded Vision of the Future.* Report to 2004 Convention of News & Letters Committees.

Hudis, P. Forthcoming. "Marx among the Muslims." *Capitalism, Nature, Socialism.* Human Rights First, at www.humanrightsfirst.org/media/2004_alerts/0617.htm (accessed October 10, 2004).

Jensen, R. 2003. "Anti-Islam?" *ZNet.* October 29, at www.zmag.org/sustainers/ content/2003-10/23jensen.cfm (accessed October 10, 2004).

Johnson, C. 2004. "Bases for an Empire." *Los Angeles Times*, Sunday, January 18, pp. M4, M6.

Katsiaficas, G. 2003. "Conclusion: the Real Axis of Evil." In *Masters of War: Militarism and Blowback in the Era of American Empire,* edited by Carl Boggs, 343—355. New York: Routledge.

Kovel, J. 2002. *The Enemy of Nature: The End of Capitalism or the End of the World?* Nova Scotia: Fernwood Publishing Ltd.

Lapham, L. 2004. "That's Why the Lady is a Champ." *Harper's Magazine,* 308(1849, June), 1–13.

Lenin, V. I. 1913. "Marxism and Reformism." In *V.I. Lenin, Collected Works,* 4th English ed., 372–375. Moscow: Foreign Languages Publishing House, at www.marx2mao.org/Lenin/MR13.html (accessed October 10, 2004).

Lieven, A. 2003. "The Empire Strikes Back." *The Nation.* June 19, at www.thenation.com/doc.mhtml?i=20030707&s=lieven (accessed October 10, 2004).

Rebelde, Juventud. 2003. "¿Los Niños Tambien?" *Cuba Vision.* June 23, at http://www.cubavision.cubaweb.cu/prensa_detalles.asp?ID=71.

Loftus, J., and Aarons, M. 1994. *The Secret War against the Jews: How Western Espionage Betrayed the Jewish People.* New York: St. Martin's Press.

Maharidge, D. 2004. "Rust & Rage in the Heartland." *The Nation,* 278(8), 11–14.

Mann, L. 2004. "Perfect Home Ranks Higher with Many Than World Peace." *Chicago Tribune,* June 19, at www.chicagotribune.com/classified/realestate/newhomes/chi-0406190279jun19,1,6169645.story.

Matthews, Mark. 1997. "Probe Demanded into Use of CIA Torture Manuals." *Baltimore Sun.* January 29, 9A.

McLaren, P. 1995. *Critical Pedogogy and Predatory Culture: Oppositional Politics in a Postmodern Era.* New York: Routledge.

McLaren, P. 2003. "The Dialectics of Terrorism." In *Masters of War: Empire and Blowback in the Age of American Empire,* edited by Carl Boggs, 149–189. New York: Routledge.

McLaren, P., and Farahmandpur, R. Forthcoming. In Conference proceedings, edited by Arif Dirlik.

"Media Advisory: Pentagon Plan Is Undemocratic, Possibly Illegal." FAIR-L (Fairness and Accuracy in Reporting, Media Analysis, Critiques, and Activism), at www.fair.org/activism/osi-propaganda.html (accessed October 10, 2004).

Mészáros, I. 2003. "Militarism and the Coming Wars." *Monthly Review,* 55(2), 17–24.

Monbiot, G. 2004. "Their Beliefs are Bonkers." *The Guardian.* Reprinted from Truthout. April 20, at www.truthout.org/docs_04/042504J.shtml (accessed October 10, 2004).

"Nevada Brothel Offers Free Sex to Returning Troops." Tuesday, June 3, 2003. Posted 5:02 PM EDT (2102 GMT) CNN.com./U.S., at www.cnn.com/2003/US/West/06/03/offbeat.brothel.reut/index.html (accessed October 10, 2004).

Office of the Americas. 2004. "Tactics of U.S. Prisons and the School of the Americas Exported to Iraq." *Focus: Peace Now!* (August, pamphlet).

"Ok, But Should You Even Trust This?" Gallup Poll results. *Chicago Tribune,* Sunday, June 20, p. 6.

Pasco, J. O. 2002."Cheney Hits Right Notes for Nixon Library Audience." *Los Angeles Times,* Wednesday, February 20, B6.

Paul, G. 2003. "The Great Scandal: Christianity's Role in the Rise of the Nazis." *Free Inquiry*, 23(4, October–November), 20–29.

Pease, D. E. 2003. "The Global Homeland State: Bush's Biopolitical Settlement." *Boundary*, 2(30), 1–18.

Peery, N. 2002. *The Future is up to US. A Revolutionary Talking Politics with the American People.* Chicago: Speakers for a New America Books.

Petras, J. 2003. "Empire Building and Rule: U.S. and Latin America." June 25, at Found at www.rebelion.org (accessed October 10, 2004).

The Pew Research Center Survey Report. Public Support for War Resilient. Released June 17, 2004, at people-press.org/reports/display.php3?ReportID=216 (accessed October 10, 2004).

Pitt, W. 2003. "George W. Christ?" *Truthout.* May 5, at www.truthout.org/docs_03/050503A.shtml (accessed October 10, 2004).

Program on International Policy Attitudes. 2004. "Many Americans Unaware WMD Have Not Been Found," at www.pipa.org/whatsnew/html/new_6_04_03.html (accessed October 10, 2004).

Regular, A. 2003. "'Road Map Is a Life Saver for Us.' PM Abbas Tells Hamas, Haaron." Monday, August 11, at www.haaretz.com/hasen/pages/ShArt.jhtml?itemNo=310788&contrassID=2&subContrassID=1&sbSubContrassID=0&listSrc=Y (accessed October 10, 2004).

Richter, P. 2003. "No Give for US on Tribunal." Los Angeles Times. September 28, at www.globalpolicy.org/intljustice/icc/2003/0928iccball.htm (accessed October 11, 2003).

Riechmann, D. 2004. "Bush Joins Evangelical Broadcast." *The Seattle Times*, Friday, May 7, A6.

Rikowski, G. 2003. "Marx and the Future of the Human." *Historical Materialism*, 11(2), 121–164.

Robinson, W. 2003. *Social Activism and Democracy in South Africa: A Globalization Perspective.* Remarks for the Institute for Democracy in South Africa conference "Social Activism and Socio-Economic Rights: Deepening Democracy in South Africa," Cape Town, August 11–13.

Roy, A. 2004. "Tide? Or Ivory Snow? Public Power in the Age of Empire," at www.democracynow.org/static/Arundhati_Trans.shtml

Scheer, R. 2003. "Bush Was All Too Willing to Use Emigres' Lies; American Experts Urged the White House to be Skeptical, But They Hit a Stone Wall. *Los Angeles Times,* September 2, B11.

Scheer, Robert. 2004. "The Man Behind the Oval Office Curtain." *Los Angeles Times*, October 26, at www.latimes.com/news/printedition/opinion/la-oe-scheer26oct26,1,3875008.column.

Shorris, E. 2004. "Ignoble Liars: Leo Strauss, George Bush, and the Philosophy of Mass Deception." *Harper's Magazine*, 308(1849, June), 65–71.

"Sleaze in the Capitol." 2005. *New York Times*, January 2, at www.nytimes.com/2005/01/02/opinion/02sun2.html?hp.

Solomon, D. 2004. "'All's Fair': Questions for Trent Lott," interview. *New York Times Magazine*, June 20.

Stanley, A. 2004. "Understanding the President and His God." *The New York Times*, April 29, at www.nytimes.com/2004/04/29/arts/television/29STAN.html (accessed October 10, 2004).

Steinberg, J. 2004. "A Mighty Fortress is His God." *The Miami Herald*, July 18, at www.miami.com/mld/miamiherald/news/9172536.htm?1c.

Stossel, S. 2004. "In the Line of Fire: An Interview with Robert D. Kaplan." *Atlantic Unbound.* June 15, At www.theatlantic.com/unbound/interviews/int2004-06-15.htm (accessed October 10, 2004).

Sutherland, J. 2004. "America's Fundagelicals." Guardian Newspapers, at www.buzzle.com/editorials/text5-2-2004-53667.asp (accessed October 10, 2004).

Sweig, J. E., and Kornbluh, P. 2004. "Amid Cheers, Terrorists Have Landed in the U.S." *Los Angeles Times*, September 12, M2.

Umansky, E. 2002. "Eyeing the Axis." *Slate Magazine*, Wednesday, February 20, at www.slate.com (accessed October 10, 2004).

Valentine, D. 2003. "Homeland Security: Where the Phoenix Came Home to Roost." *CovertAction Quarterly*, 75(Fall), 5–13.

Views of a Changing World. 2003. "War with Iraq Further Divides Global Publics." June 3, at people-press.org/reports/display.php3?ReportID=185 (accessed October 10, 2004).

Weiss, J. 2004. "Prison Scandal Shows How Moral Compasses Can Go Astray." *Fresno Bee*, Saturday May 15, H1.

Wolcott, James. 2004. "The Counter-Life." *The Nation* 279, 17(November 22), 23–28.

Wypijewski, J. 2004. "Labor in the Dawn of Empire." In *Imperial Crusades: Iraq, Afghanistan and Yugoslavia*, edited by A. Cockburn and J. St. Clair, 289–298. London: Verso.

Xenos, N. 2004. "Leo Strauss and the Rhetoric of the War on Terror." *Logos*, 3(2, Spring), at www.logosjournal.com/xenos.htm (accessed October 10, 2004).

Žižek, S. 1999. "'You May!'" *London Review of Books,* 21(6, March 18), at www.lrb.co.uk/v21/n06/zize01_.html.

Žižek, S. 2004a. "Iraq's False Promises." *Foreign Policy.* January–February, at www.lacan.com/zizek-iraq2.htm.

Žižek, S. 2004b. "What Rumsfeld Doesn't Know That He Knows about Abu Ghraib." *In These Times* 28(15), 31–32.

Zunes, S. 2004. "The Influence of the Christian Right on U.S. Middle East Policy." *Foreign Policy in Focus.* June 20, at www.fpif.org/papers/0406christian.html (accessed October 10, 2004).

Postscript

Peter McLaren

George Bush Jr. might have been a gadabout waiting tables in a louche café on the Venice boardwalk and maundering in dank alleys during the night were it not for his being born into the political clerisy with a silver spoon in his mouth. Yet Bush will never recognize his good fortune (and the world's misfortune) as a matter of chance.

Long before Dubya sinks into senescence and death, he will be called upon to account for his political malversation and the enormity of his sins. He will be forced to look beyond fawning and hackneyed Grover Norquist screeds and take firm stock of his legacy as a so-called "wartime president." Even then he will no doubt conscript the logic of preemptive and preventative strikes to his aid and convince himself that had he not slaughtered so many infidels in their own homelands far far away, many more would have died in *our* Homeland. And that wouldn't be good for the business of running a country on the protection, security, and morals ticket.

Exercising this kind of logic can always let your conscience off the hook. This is the same kind of retrofitted rationality that has served dictators well in the past.

Bush Jr. has impaled himself on the pike of absolute certainty about the relationship between faith and politics, rather than allow even a sliver of doubt to penetrate the permanent slumber of his waking consciousness. To doubt that providence has bequeathed the universal norms of civilization to America—norms to be imposed on the rest of humanity through the use of brute force, if necessary—would betray for Bush the ultimate sacrifice of the Lamb of God. It would also embolden those radical critics who hold that the fundamentalism that most threatens world peace is U.S. imperialism.

If God would permit Bush Jr. to speak to the dead, to the souls of hundreds of thousands of Filipinos, Iraqis, Salvadorians, Panamanians, Guatemalans, Haitians, Cubans, and Mexicans killed by U.S. troops or U.S.-backed death squads over the last century, his faith might harvest compassion and wisdom—and a change of direction in foreign policy.

Sitting on a rock beside the San Francisco Bay, I had a sudden moment of inspiration. Bush Jr. will be visited on Christmas Eve by the Three Ghosts of South American Past, Present, and Future: Che Guevara of Argentina and Cuba (and in a larger sense, of all of Latin America), Paulo Freire of Brazil, and Archbishop Romero of El Salvador. Che—with eyes the smoldering fierceness of a volcano about to erupt—would transport Bush to the blood-soaked slaughterhouses of Argentina during the U.S.-backed military dictatorship where he would witness women giving birth while they are chained to beds, then being butchered and their infants given to families from the ruling elite. Paulo Freire, very much resembling Gandhi with a Papa Noel beard, would transport Bush to the streets and homes in the *favelas* of Rio, where every day children die of treatable diseases. Here Bush could witness first-hand the results of his free trade policies. Archbishop Romero, in blood-soaked vestments (the result of his assassination by a U.S.-backed death squad), would take him from the future slums of El Salvador to those of North America, where children are facing an epidemic of asthma, where military service becomes mandatory, where political dissenters are held in unnamed military camps run by Halliburton, and where national paranoia sends gays and lesbians and atheists into hiding.

The moment of inspiration slowly fades as I realize that the root of the problem is not the religious fanaticism of one man—be that Bush or bin Laden—but in the system of exploitation wedded to capital's law of value.

I watch my granddaughter playing on the rocky shore, her blonde hair kissed by dancing sunlight. News quickly reaches our innocent moment that the death toll in Iraq is growing as its cities are convulsed by relentless military assaults that have left the bodies of women and children lying nameless and etiolated on the streets. Acute "wasting" among Iraqi children my granddaughter's age has become epidemic, as dirty water, lack of electricity, and a crippled economy wreaks havoc. Under the banner of democracy, the U.S. military has not become the harbinger of freedom, but the midwife of a new generation of jihadists. They are preparing the ground not for peace, but for a piece of capital, and the ultimate price will be paid for in blood.

A rustle of wind stirs up memories of antiwar demonstrations on the streets of Los Angeles where workers, students, socialists, anarchists, priests, ministers, and antiglobalization activists found common ground in the struggle against U.S. imperialism. It is this spirit of communitas at work in the picket lines, in the demonstrations for peace, and in our social justice classrooms that will continue to provide the spiritual fuel for the challenge ahead. It is this surfeit of liminality, this excess of life that cannot be commodified or codified, controlled or captured that connects us to our collective struggle. Echoing Raymond Williams, it will be a long revolution.

Index

About the Author

Photo by Laura McLaren-Layera.

Peter McLaren is known worldwide as one of the primary architects of critical pedagogy in North America and a leading exponent of social justice education. Considered one of the world's leading critical theorists in the field of education, Professor McLaren has authored and edited over forty books, a number of which have received awards. His writings have been translated into fifteen languages. He lectures worldwide. La Fundación Peter McLaren de Pedagogía Crítica was recently established by a group of Mexican educators as a forum to engage with Professor McLaren's work as well as coordinate scholarly and grassroots interventions in Latin America.